U0909485

新课标双语文库

培根随笔全集

The Essays of Francis Bacon

弗兰西斯·培根 著

曹明伦 译

凤凰出版传媒集团 译林出版社

图书在版编目(CIP)数据

培根随笔全集:英汉对照/(英)培根(Bacon, F.)著;曹明伦译.
—南京:译林出版社,2010.6
(新课标双语文库)
书名原文:The Essays of Francis Bacon
ISBN 978-7-5447-1221-7

Ⅰ.①培… Ⅱ.①培… ②曹… Ⅲ.①英语-汉语-对照读物 ②随笔-作品集-英国-中世纪 Ⅳ.①H319.4:I

中国版本图书馆CIP数据核字(2010)第055030号

书　　名	培根随笔全集
作　　者	[英国]弗兰西斯·培根
译　　者	曹明伦
插　　图	阮　健
责任编辑	田　智
出版发行	凤凰出版传媒集团 译林出版社(南京市湖南路1号　210009)
电子信箱	yilin@yilin.com
网　　址	http://www.yilin.com
集团网址	凤凰出版传媒网 http://www.ppm.cn
印　　刷	江苏凤凰通达印刷有限公司
开　　本	652×960 毫米　1/16
印　　张	21
插　　页	2
版　　次	2010年6月第1版　2010年6月第1次印刷
书　　号	ISBN　978-7-5447-1221-7
定　　价	24.80元(附赠光盘一张)

译林版图书若有印装错误可向出版社调换
(电话:025-83658316)

目 次
Contents

译序

一

弗兰西斯·培根是英国杰出的哲学家和文学家。他于1561年1月出生在伦敦一个官僚家庭，12岁时入剑桥大学三一学院，15岁时作为英国驻法大使的随员到巴黎供职，1579年因父亲病故而辞职回国，同年入格雷律师学院攻读法学，1582年获得律师资格，从此步入浩瀚的学海和坎坷的仕途。培根在伊丽莎白一世时代仕途屡屡受挫，直到詹姆斯一世继位(1603)后他才开始走运，1603年受封为爵士，1604年被任命为皇家法律顾问。1607年出任首席检察官助理，1613年升为首席检察官，1617年入内阁成为掌玺大臣，1618年当上大法官并被封为男爵，1620年又被封为子爵。1621年，身为大法官的培根被控受贿，他认罪下野，从此脱离官场，家居著述，1626年在一次冷冻防腐的科学实验中受寒罹病，于同年4月去世。

二

虽说培根大半生都在官场沉浮，但他从青年时代起就开始了他终生未辍的哲学思考和文学写作。他才华出众且雄心勃勃，立志要对人类知识全部加以重构，为此他计划写一套巨著，总书名为《大复兴》。培根只完成了这一计划的两个部分。第一部分是两卷本的《学术之进步》(1605)，书中抨击了中世纪的经院哲学，论证了知识的巨大作用，揭示了人类知识不如人意的现状以及补救的方法。该书的拉丁文版扩大成九卷，书名为《论知识的价值和发展》(1623)。《大复兴》之第二部分是单卷本的《新工具》(1620)，这是培根最重要的哲学著作，在近代哲学史上具有重大的意义和广泛的影响。培根于1622年出版的《自然及实验史》可被视为《大复兴》第三部分的序章。除此之外,培根的主要著作还有《论古人的智慧》(1609)和《新大西岛》(1627)等等。

三

培根在文学方面的代表作就是他的《随笔集》。这本书 1597 年初版时只收有 10 篇文章,1612 年版增至 38 篇,1625 年版(即末版)增至 58 篇。在培根逝世 31 年后的 1657 年,有一个 Rawley 版将培根的未完稿《论谣言》("Of Fame")作为第 59 篇收入其《随笔集》,但由于该篇只有"启承"尚无"转合",故后来的通行本仍多以 58 篇为标准。《随笔集》的内容涉及到政治、经济、宗教、爱情、婚姻、友谊、艺术、教育和伦理等等,几乎触及了人类生活的方方面面。作为一名学识渊博且通晓人情世故的哲学家和思想家,培根对他谈及的问题均有发人深省的独到之见。《随笔集》语言简洁,文笔优美,说理透彻,警句迭出,几百年来深受各国读者欢迎,据说有不少人的性格曾受到这本书的熏陶。于今天的青年读者,读《随笔集》就像听一位睿智的老人侃侃而谈,因为《随笔集》里包含着这位先哲的思想精髓。

四

笔者认为译散文作品的原则也应和译诗一样,即在神似的基础上追求最大限度的形似。对译文的语言表达,笔者每每有这样一种考虑:若令原作者用中文表达其原意,他(她)当作何语?正是这种考虑使笔者将"It is a prince's part to pardon"译成"高抬贵手乃贵人之举"(见《论复仇》),或将"Seek not proud riches, but such as thou mayest get justly, use soberly, distribute cheerfully, and leave contentedly"译成"千万别为摆阔炫耀而追求财富,只挣你取之有道、用之有度、施之有乐且遗之有慰的钱财"(见《论财富》)。这个译本可谓笔者对 Bacon's Essays 之解读,将其公之于众是因为笔者相信自己读有所悟,并相信在此基础上形成的译本对一般读者了解培根的随笔不无裨益。

1.论真理

何为真理?彼拉多曾戏问,[①]且问后不等回答。世上的确有人好见异思迁,视固守信仰为枷锁缠身,故而在思想行为上都追求自由意志。虽说该类学派的哲学家均已作古[②],然天下仍有些爱夸夸其谈的才子,他们与那些先贤一脉相承,只是与古人相比少些血性。但假象之所以受宠,其因不止于世人寻求真理之艰辛,亦非觅得之真理会对人类思维施加影响,而是缘于一种虽说缺德但却系世人与生俱有的对假象本身的喜好。希腊晚期学派中有位哲人[③]对此进行过研究,而思索世人为何好假令他感到困惑,因其既非像诗人好诗一般可从中获取乐趣,亦不像商人好商那样可从中捞得利润,爱假者之爱假仅仅是为了假象本身的缘故。但我不能妄下结论,因上述真理是种未加遮掩的日光,若要使这世间的种种假面舞会、化装演出和胜利庆典显得优雅高贵,此光远不及灯烛之光。在世人眼里,真理或许可贵如在光天化日下最显璀璨的珍珠,但绝不可能贵如在五彩灯火中最显辉煌的钻石或红玉。错觉假象之混合物总是能为世人添乐。假如从世人头脑中除去虚幻的印象、悦人的憧憬、错误的估价、随意的空想以及诸如此类的东西,那恐怕许多人都只会剩下个贫乏而干瘪的头脑,充于其间的只有忧郁不安和自厌自烦,对此假设有谁会质疑呢?

一位先人曾因诗能满足想象力而将其称为“魔鬼的酒浆”[④],其实诗不过是带有假象的影子罢了。大概有害的并非脑子里一闪即逝的错觉,而是

---

①见《新约·约翰福音》第18章37—38节,耶稣受审时声称他来世间之目的是为了证明真理,于是彼拉多(罗马驻犹大和撒玛利亚地区的总督)问“何为真理”。

②指源于皮浪(Pyrrhon,约前360—前272)的古希腊怀疑论诸学派。

③希腊讽刺作家卢奇安(Lucian,120—180)曾在其《爱假论》中抨击怀疑论者。

④圣哲罗姆(St Jerome,347—420)曾曰“诗乃魔鬼之佳肴”,圣奥古斯丁(St Augustine,354—430)则言“诗乃谬误之琼浆”。培根合二为一自有其道理。

上文所说的那种沉入心底并盘踞心中的假象。但纵有这些假象如此根植于世人堕落的观念与情感之中，只受自身评判的真理依然教导吾辈探究真理，认识真理并相信真理。探究真理即要对其求爱求婚，认识真理即要与之相依相随，而相信真理则要享受真理的乐趣，此乃人类天性之至善。在创天地万物的那几日中，上帝的第一创造是感觉之光，最后创造是理智之光；[①]从那时暨今，他安息日的工作便一直是以其圣灵启迪众生。起初他呈现光明于万物或混沌之表面，继而他呈现光明于世人之面庞，如今他依然为其选民[②]的面庞注入灵光。那个曾为伊壁鸠鲁学派增光，从而使其不逊于别派的诗人[③]说得极好："登高岸而濒水伫观舟楫颠簸于海上，不亦快哉；踞城堡而倚窗凭眺两军酣战于脚下，不亦快哉；然断无任何快事堪比凌真理之绝顶（一巍然高耸且风清气朗的峰顶），一览深谷间的谬误与彷徨、迷雾与风暴。"如此常凌常览，这番景象也许会诱发恻隐之心，而非引出自命不凡或目无下尘。毋庸置疑，若人心能随仁爱而行，依天意而定，且绕真理之轴而转，尘世当为人间乐园。

从神学和哲学上的真理说到世俗交往中的诚实，连那些不信奉真理者也得承认，行为光明磊落乃人性之保证，而弄虚作假则犹如往金银币里掺合金，此举或更利于钱币流通，但却降低了钱币的成色。盖此类三弯九转的做法乃蛇行之法，蛇行无足可用，只能卑贱地用其肚腹。最令人无地自容的恶行莫过于被人发现其阳奉阴违，背信弃义；因此蒙田的说法可谓恰如其分，他探究谎言为何这般可耻这般可恨时说："细细想来，说人撒谎就等于说他不畏上帝而惧世人。因谎言直面上帝而躲避世人。"[④]想必撒谎背信之恶不可能被揭示得比这更淋漓尽致了，依照此说，撒谎背信将是唤上帝来审判世人的最后钟声；盖预言曾云：基督重临之日，他在这世间将难觅忠信。[⑤]

---

①见《旧约·创世记》第1章3节及第2章7节。

②上帝的选民原指以色列人，后指信奉上帝的芸芸众生。

③古罗马诗人及哲学家卢克莱修在长诗《物性论》中以形象的语言阐述伊壁鸠鲁学说中抽象的哲学概念。

④见《蒙田随笔》第2卷18篇《论说谎》。

⑤见《新约·路加福音》第18章8节。

解析

一、有些人不喜欢真理：

1. 古代的哲学家；

2. 当今"爱夸夸其谈的才子"。

二、其原因：

1. 世人寻求真理之艰辛。

2. 觅得之真理会对人类思维施加影响。

3. 人与生俱有的对假象本身的喜好，因为——

(1) 真理会暴露过多的虚假；

(2) 错觉假象总是能为世人添乐。

三、然而真理乃人类天性之至善——

1. 是上帝永恒的造物与恩赐；

2. 如卢克莱修所言，是人类唯一的永久的着身处。

四、"世俗交往中的诚实"（道德上的诚实）：

1. 公认为是可敬的；

2. 谎言可耻可恨（蒙田）；

3. 是唤上帝来审判世人的最后钟声。

Of Truth

WHAT is truth? said jesting Pilate, and would not stay for an answer. Certainly there be, that delight in giddiness, and count it a bondage to fix a belief; affecting free-will in thinking, as well as in acting. And though the sects of philosophers of that kind be gone, yet there remain certain discoursing wits, which are of the same veins, though there be not so much blood in them, as was in those of the ancients. But it is not only the difficulty and labor, which men take in finding out of truth, nor again, that when it is found, it imposeth upon men's thoughts, that doth bring lies in favor; but a natural, though corrupt love, of the lie itself. One of the later school of the Grecians, examineth the matter, and is at a stand, to think what should be in it, that men should love lies; where neither they make it for pleasure, as with poets, nor for advantage, as with the merchant; but for the lie's sake. But I cannot tell; this same truth, is a naked, and open day-light, that doth not show the masks, and mummeries, and triumphs, of the world, half so stately and daintily as candle-lights. Truth may perhaps come to the price of a pearl, that showeth best by day; but it will not rise to the price of a diamond, or carbuncle, that showeth best in varied lights. A mixture of a lie doth ever add pleasure. Doth any man doubt, that if there were taken out of men's minds, vain opinions, flattering hopes, false valuations, imaginations as one would, and the like, but it would leave the minds, of a number of men, poor shrunken things, full of melancholy and indisposition, and unpleasing to themselves?

One of the fathers, in great severity, called poesy vinum daemonum[①], because it fireth the imagination; and yet, it is but the shadow of a lie. But it is not the lie that passeth through the mind, but the lie that sinketh in, and settleth in it, that doth the hurt; such as we spake of before. But howsoever these things are thus in men's depraved judgments, and affections, yet truth, which only doth judge itself, teacheth that the inquiry of truth, which is the love-making, or wooing of it, the knowledge of truth, which is the presence of it, and the belief of truth, which is the enjoying of it, is the sovereign good of human nature. The first creature of God, in the works of the days, was the light of the sense; the last, was the light of reason; and his Sabbath work ever since, is the illumination of his Spirit. First he breathed light, upon the face of the matter or chaos; then he breathed light, into the face of man; and still he breatheth and inspireth light, into the face of his chosen. The poet, that beautified the sect, that was otherwise inferior to the rest, saith yet excellently well: It is a pleasure, to stand upon the shore, and to see ships tossed upon the sea; a pleasure, to stand in the window of a castle, and to see a battle, and the adventures thereof below; but no pleasure is comparable to the standing upon the vantage ground of a hill (a hill not to be commanded, and where the air is always clear and serene), and to see the errors, and wanderings, and mists, and tempests, in the vale below; so always that this prospect be with pity, and not with swelling, or pride. Certainly, it is heaven upon earth, to have a man's mind move in charity, rest in providence, and turn upon the poles of truth.

To pass from theological, and philosophical truth, to the truth of civil business; it will be acknowledged, even by those that practise it not, that clear, and round dealing, is the honor of man's nature; and that mixture of falsehoods, is like alloy in coin of gold and silver, which may make the metal

---

①the wine of devils

work the better, but it embaseth it. For these winding, and crooked courses, are the goings of the serpent; which goeth basely upon the belly, and not upon the feet. There is no vice, that doth so cover a man with shame, as to be found false and perfidious. And therefore Montaigne saith prettily, when he inquired the reason, why the word of the lie should be such a disgrace, and such an odious charge. Saith he, If it be well weighed, to say that a man lieth, is as much to say, as that he is brave towards God, and a coward towards men. For a lie faces God, and shrinks from man. Surely the wickedness of falsehood, and breach of faith, cannot possibly be so highly expressed, as in that it shall be the last peal, to call the judgments of God upon the generations of men; it being foretold, that when Christ cometh, he shall not find faith upon the earth.

2. 论死亡

成人畏惧死亡犹如儿童怕进黑暗。儿童对黑暗之天然惧怕因妄言传闻而增长，成人对死亡之畏怯恐惧亦复如此。无可否认，对死亡凝神沉思，视其为罪孽之报应或天国之通途，实乃圣洁虔诚之举；而对死亡心生畏怯，视其为应向自然交纳的贡物，则属懦弱愚陋之态。不过在虔诚的沉思中偶尔亦有虚妄和迷信混杂。在某些天主教修士的禁欲书中可读到这样的文字：人当自忖，思一指被压或被拶痛当如何，进而想死亡将使全身腐烂分解，此痛又当如何。其实死上千遭也不及一肢受刑之痛，盖维系生命之最重要器官并非人体最敏感的部位。故那位仅以哲学家和正常人身份立言的先哲所言极是："伴随死亡而来的比死亡本身更可怕。"[①]呻吟与痉挛、面目之变色、亲友之哀悼、丧服与葬礼，诸如此类的场面都显出死亡之可怖。但应注意的是，人类的种种激情并非脆弱得不足以克服并压倒对死亡的恐惧；而既然人有这么多可战胜死亡的随从，那死亡就并非如此可怕的敌人。复仇之心可征服死亡，爱恋之心会蔑视死亡，荣誉之心会渴求死亡，悲痛之心会扑向死亡，连恐惧之心亦会预期死亡。而且我们还读到，在罗马皇帝奥托伏剑之后，哀怜之心(这种最脆弱的感情)使许多士兵也自戕而毙，[②]他们的死纯然是出于对其君王的同情和耿耿忠心。此外塞内加还补充了苛求之心和厌倦之心，他说："思及长年累月劳于一事之单调，欲撒手弃世的不啻勇者和悲者，尚有厌腻了无聊的人。"[③]即使一个人并不勇敢亦非不幸，可他仅为厌倦没完没了地做同一事情也会轻生。同样值得注意的是，罗马帝国那些恺撒们面对死亡是如何面不改色，因为他们在生命的最后一瞬仍显得依然故

①语出塞内加所著《道德书简》第 24 篇。

②事见塔西佗所著《历史》第 2 卷 49 章。

③见塞内加《道德书简》第 77 篇。

我。奥古斯都弥留时还在赞美其皇后,“永别了,莉维亚,勿忘我俩婚后共度的时光。”提比略危笃之际仍掩饰其病情,如塔西佗所言:“他体力已耗尽,但奸诈犹存。” 韦斯帕芗大限临头时兀自坐在凳子上戏言:“看来我正在变成神祇。”伽尔巴的临终遗言是“你们砍吧,倘若这有益于罗马人民”,一边喊一边引颈就戮。塞维鲁行将自篑时照旧发号施令:“若还有什么我该做之事,速速取来。”此类视死如归之例,不一而足。毫无疑问,斯多葛学派那些哲学家为死亡的开价太高,而由于他们对死亡筹备过甚,遂使其显得更为可怕。尤维纳利斯[1]说得较好,他认为生命之终结乃自然的一种恩惠。死之寻常犹如生之天然,不过在幼童眼里,出生与死亡也许都同样会引起痛苦。在执着追求中牺牲者之不觉死亡[2]就如同在浴血鏖战中受创者之暂时不觉伤痛。由此可见,于坚定执着且一心向善的有才有智之士,死亡之痛苦的确可以避免;但尤其是要相信,最美的圣歌乃一个人实现其高尚目标和期望之后所唱的那首:“主啊,现在请让你的仆人安然离世。”死亡尚可开启名望之门并消除妒忌之心,因“生前遭人妒忌者死后会受人爱戴”[3]。

解析

一、对死亡愚蠢的畏惧——

1. 甚至与宗教相混杂;

2. 因死亡的伴随物而加大。

二、帮助克服对死亡的恐惧:

1. 激情——复仇、悲痛、恐惧等等;

2. 死亡的临近也不能改变的高尚人生;

3. 斯多葛派的筹备过甚,反而更显死亡之可怕;

4. 对高尚目标的执着追求;

①古罗马讽刺诗人,著有《讽刺诗》五卷。

②对死而不觉之描述见于中世纪意大利诗人阿里奥斯托的长篇传奇诗《疯狂的罗兰》。

③语出贺拉斯《书札》第2卷1首14行。

5. 对声名的渴望。

Of Death

MEN fear death, as children fear to go in the dark; and as that natural fear in children, is increased with tales, so is the other. Certainly, the contemplation of death, as the wages of sin, and passage to another world, is holy and religious; but the fear of it, as a tribute due unto nature, is weak. Yet in religious meditations, there is sometimes mixture of vanity, and of superstition. You shall read, in some of the friars' books of mortification, that a man should think with himself, what the pain is, if he have but his finger's end pressed, or tortured, and thereby imagine, what the pains of death are, when the whole body is corrupted, and dissolved; when many times death passeth, with less pain than the torture of a limb; for the most vital parts, are not the quickest of sense. And by him that spake only as a philosopher, and natural man, it is well said, Pompa mortis magis terret, quam mors ipsa.① Groans, and convulsions, and a discolored face, and friends weeping, and blacks, and obsequies, and the like, show death terrible. It is worthy the observing, that there is no passion in the mind of man, so weak, but it mates, and masters, the fear of death; and therefore, death is no such terrible enemy, when a man hath so many attendants about him, that can win the combat of him. Revenge triumphs over death; love slights it; honor aspireth to it; grief flieth to it; fear preoccupateth it; nay, we read, after Otho the emperor had slain himself, pity (which is the tenderest of affections) provoked many to die, out of mere compassion to their sovereign, and as the truest sort of followers. Nay, Seneca adds niceness and satiety: Cogita quamdiu eadem feceris; mori velle, non tantum fortis aut miser, sed etiam fastidiosus potest.② A man would die, though he were neither valiant, nor miserable, only upon a weariness to do the same thing so oft, over and over. It is no less worthy, to observe, how little alteration in good spirits, the approaches of death make; for they appear to be the same men, till the last instant. Augustus Caesar died in a compliment; Livia, conjugii nostri memor, vive et vale. ③ Tiberius in dissimulation; as

①The solemn accomplishments of death are more fearful than death itself.

②Consider how long you have done the same things; a man may be willing to die not only because he is brave or unhappy, but just because he is wearied of life.

③Goodbye; never forget what a true wife you were to me.

Tacitus saith of him, Jam Tiberium vires et corpus, non dissimulatio, deserebant.[①] Vespasian in a jest, sitting up on the stool; Ut puto deus fio. [②] Galba with a sentence; Feri, si ex re sit populi Romani; [③] holding forth his neck. Septimius Severus in despatch; Adeste si quid mihi restat agendum. [④] And the like. Certainly the Stoics bestowed too much cost upon death, and by their great preparations, made it appear more fearful. Better saith he, qui finem vitae extremum inter munera ponat naturae. [⑤] It is as natural to die, as to be born; and to a little infant, perhaps, the one is as painful, as the other. He that dies in an earnest pursuit, is like one that is wounded in hot blood; who, for the time, scarce feels the hurt; and therefore a mind fixed, and bent upon somewhat that is good, doth avert the dolors of death. But, above all, believe it, the sweetest canticle is, Nunc dimittis; when a man hath obtained worthy ends, and expectations. Death hath this also; that it openeth the gate to good fame, and extinguisheth envy. —Extinctus amabitur idem.[⑥]

---

①His body strength was leaving Tiberius, but not his habit of dissimulation.

②Methinks I am becoming a god.

③Strike, if it is to benefit the Roman people.

④Be ready, if anything remains for me to do.

⑤Who can rank the last end of life among the blessings of nature.

⑥The same man who in life is hated, will be loved when he is dead.

3.谈宗教之统一

宗教是维系人类社会的主要纽带，故保持其自身的真正统一是件幸事。对异教徒而言,关于宗教的争论和分歧乃闻所未闻之恶行。其原因是异教徒的宗教更在于仪式典礼,而非在于某种永恒不变的信仰。因为他们的神学宗师都是些诗人[①],所以不难想象他们崇奉的是何等宗教。但那位真正的上帝自有其特性,即他是一个"好忌妒的上帝"[②];因此对他的崇拜和信仰既容不得龙蛇混杂亦容不得分一杯羹。鉴于此,笔者得简单谈谈教会的统一,谈谈何为统一之好处,何为统一之限界,以及何为统一之手段。

(除取悦上帝这首要的一点之外)统一的好处尚有两点:一是就教门外的俗人而论,一是对教门内的会众而言。对于前者,教门内的异端邪说和宗派分裂无疑比任何丑行都更为丑恶,甚至比仪典不纯还更有辱宗教;盖如在正常人体内,关节之受创或脱臼比血脉违和更糟,教会的宗教事务亦复如此。故而统一之破裂最能阻俗人并驱会众于教门之外。所以当听见有人说"看啊,基督在野外",而有人则说"看啊,基督在屋内",即每逢有人在异端集会处寻找基督,而有人则在教堂外面寻找耶稣的时候,那个声音须不断响在世人耳旁,"勿要出去"[③]。那位(其特殊使命使他对未皈依基督者特别在意的)异邦人的导师[④]曾说:"若有外乡人进来,闻尔等言杂语异,人家岂不说尔等癫狂耶?"而要是那些无神论者和世俗之徒闻知教会里有这么多冲突矛盾,其结果肯定也不会更佳,那无疑会使他们远避教门而"坐上嘲

---

①指古代希腊罗马之宗教多以诗人笔下的诸神为崇拜对象。

②语出《旧约·出埃及记》第20章2—5节中上帝对以色列人的训示:"吾乃耶和华汝等之上帝……尔辈除我之外不可再奉他神……吾乃好忌妒的上帝。"

③以上引言可参见《新约·马太福音》第24章25—26节。

④指圣保罗,以下引言见《新约·哥林多前书》第14章23节。

讽者的席位”[①]。这不过是从如此严重的问题中引证一区区小事,但它也充分暴露了异端之丑陋。有位讽刺大师在其虚构的一份书目中列出了《异端教徒的舞蹈》[②]这个书名;因每个异端教派都自有其独特的舞姿或媚态,而这些姿态只会引起世俗之徒和腐败政客的嘲笑,那类人天生就爱鄙视宗教事务。

至于统一对教内会众的好处,那就是包含无限神恩的和平。和平可树立信仰,和平可唤起爱心,教会表面的和平可升华成人们内心深处的和平,从而使人把炮制和翻阅争辩之作的工夫用来撰写和披览修行积善的华章。

说到统一的限界,这种限界之真正确定至关重要。眼下似乎有两个极端,在某些狂热派眼中,一切和平言谈都可厌可憎。“和平与否,耶户?”——“和平与你何干?站到我身后去罢。”[③]狂热派所关心的不是和平,而是拉帮结派。与之相反,某些老底嘉派信徒[④]和态度冷漠者则以为他们可以不偏不倚,可以巧妙地用中庸之法来调和教派纷争,仿佛他们可以在上帝与世人之间作出公断似的。这两个极端都必须避免,而若能用以下两句说法相反的箴言来正确而清晰地解释救世主亲自订下的基督教盟约,上述两个极端就可以避免。这两句箴言分别是“不与我们为伍者即我们的反对者”和“不反对我们者即与我们为伍者”,[⑤]这就是说,要辨别区分何为信仰中有关宏旨的实质问题,何为不纯然属于信仰而仅仅属于见解、礼仪或概念分歧的枝节问题。这事在许多人看来也许微不足道并且已经解决,但倘若此事之解决少些私心偏见,那它就会受到更普遍的欢迎。

限于本文篇幅,笔者就此仅提供一点忠告。世人得当心勿以两种争论分裂上帝的教会。一种争论之要点无足轻重,不值得唇枪舌剑,大动肝火;因为正如一位先哲所说:“基督的衣袍的确无缝, 但教会的衣袍却五颜六

①语出《旧约·诗篇》第1章1节。

②见拉伯雷《巨人传》第2部7章中庞大固埃在巴黎圣维克多藏书楼看到的那份书目。书名中的“异端教徒”原指16世纪被迫改信天主教的摩尔人。

③见《旧约·列王纪下》第9章18—19节。耶户乃以色列第十代王。

④见《新约·启示录》第3章14—16节。

⑤分别见《新约·马太福音》第12章30节和《新约·马可福音》第9章40节。

色。”他随即又讲:“就让这衣袍多色吧,但不要将其撕裂。”[①]由此可见,统一和划一是两个概念。另一种争论是所争之要点事关重大,但争到头来却趋于过分玄妙,以致争论变得技巧有余而内容不足。善断是非并善解人意者有时会听到一群愚氓争长论短,并深知那些人的不同说法实则言殊意合,然而他们却永远不可能达成共识。既然人与人之间因判断力不同会造成上述情况,那我们难道不可以认为:洞悉吾辈心思的上帝完全能看出世人的某些言人人殊实则异曲同工,从而对双方的意见都予以认可?关于这类争论的性质,圣保罗在对提摩太的告诫中已有精辟的阐述:“别卷入世俗的空谈和被人误以为是学问的荒谬争论。”[②]世人爱炮制子虚乌有的奇谈怪说,并为其贴上新鲜的术语,而且贴得那样紧,以致本应支配术语的内容反被术语支配。和平或统一亦有两种赝品:一种是基于愚昧无知的和平,因为在蒙昧之中,形形色色的宗派均可和平共处;另一种是靠调和根本矛盾而拼凑的和平,因为在这样的和平中,真理与谬误就像尼布甲尼撒王梦中那尊偶像脚里的金和土一样[③],二者可互相粘附,但绝不会融为一体。

说到实现统一的手段,人们务须当心,切莫在实现或加强宗教统一的同时废除并损害了仁慈博爱之大义和人类社会的律法。基督徒有两柄利剑[④],即精神之剑和世俗之剑,在维护宗教信仰的事业中,二者各有其相应的功能和职权。但我们不可拿起第三柄利剑,即不可凭金戈铁马传播宗教,或凭血腥迫害强迫人心,除非目睹有人公然诽谤教会,亵渎上帝,或把宗教活动混于反对国家的阴谋。我们更不可鼓励煽动性言论,姑息阴谋和叛乱,把利剑授予各类想颠覆顺应天意之政府的民众;因这样做无异于用第一块法版去砸第二块法版[⑤],从而以为世人皆基督教徒,好像我们已忘了他们是人。

①基督衣袍无缝说见《新约·约翰福音》第19章23节;圣奥古斯丁化用过此典。

②见《新约·提摩太前书》第6章20节。

③希伯来先知但以理在为巴比伦王尼布甲尼撒解梦时说:“既然你梦见偶像之脚乃半铁半土,那你的王国就终将分裂。”见《旧约·但以理书》第2章41节。

④见《新约·路加福音》第22章38节。

⑤第一块法版记载有人对上帝承担的五项义务,第二块则记载有人对同类的五项义务,二者相加即为“摩西十诫”。见《旧约·出埃及记》第20—34章有关章节。

在看到剧中阿伽门农忍心用亲生女儿献祭那一幕时[①]，诗人卢克莱修曾惊叹:“宗教居然能诱人如此行恶!”[②]

若这位诗人能知晓法兰西那场大屠杀[③]或英格兰的火药阴谋[④],那他又当作何语?恐怕他会变得更加安于享乐,更加不敬神明。惟其缘宗教之故拔世俗之剑须慎之又慎,所以将此剑授予平民之手乃荒唐之举,这等荒唐事就留给再洗礼派[⑤]和其他狂热派去做吧。当撒旦说“我要上升至云端,与全能的至尊媲美”[⑥],那是对上帝十足的亵渎;但若把上帝人格化,让他说“我要下降到地狱,与那黑暗之王颉颃”,这就是更名副其实的亵渎了。而若使宗教大业堕落成谋杀君主、屠戮百姓和颠覆社稷等凶残而可鄙的行当,那比之上述亵渎之言又有何较胜之处呢?毫无疑问,此等行为就是要把象征圣灵的鸽子[⑦]变成兀鹰或渡鸦，就是要在基督教会的大船上扯起海盗和凶徒的旗幡。故眼下的当务之急是:教会须凭借其教义和教令,君王们则须凭借其君权和一切表现基督精神及道德力量的学识，像凭借墨丘利的魔杖[⑧]一般，把那些有助于上述恶行的行径和邪说统统送下地狱并使之万劫不复,就像在很大程度上已经做到的那样。在有关宗教信仰的劝喻中,当首先铭记者无疑就是圣徒雅各的那句箴言:“世人的愤怒并不能实现上帝的正义。”[⑨]还有位先哲的坦诚之言也值得注意,他说:“凡怀有并劝人相信良心压力者,通常都出于个人动机才对那种压力感兴趣。”[⑩]

①希腊统帅阿伽门农曾射杀一女神之爱鹿，愤怒的女神刮逆风将欲远征特洛伊的希腊舰队阻在奥利斯港。为息女神之怒,阿伽门农用女儿伊菲格涅娅献祭。欧里庇得斯曾用此题材写成悲剧《伊菲格涅娅在奥利斯》。

②引自《物性论》第 1 卷。

③指圣巴托罗缪惨案,即 1572 年 8 月 24 日法国天主教徒屠杀胡格诺派教徒的宗教血案。

④指 1605 年 11 月 5 日福克斯 (Guy Fawkes) 等罗马天主教信徒密谋炸毁英国国会大厦并炸死英王詹姆斯一世的事件。

⑤16 世纪初在德国、瑞士和奥地利的下层民众中形成的一新教教派。

⑥见《旧约·以赛亚书》第 14 章 14 节。

⑦《新约·路加福音》第 3 章 22 节有言:“圣灵犹如鸽子降到他(耶稣)身上。”

⑧罗马神话中手持魔杖的墨丘利司职颇多。除担任诸神的信使外,他还送亡灵前往冥国。

⑨见《新约·雅各书》第 1 章 20 节。

⑩此语出处不详,有学者 (如牛津大学的 John Pitcher) 猜测说这话的先哲可能是迦太基主教圣西普里安 (St Cyprian, 200?—258) 。

解析

一、宗教纷争存在于那些崇拜一位“好忌妒的上帝”的人。

二、统一之好处：

1. 避免丑闻(教外)；

2. 保证和平(教内)。

三、统一之限界——

1. 不是由极端的狂热(耶户)所界定。

2. 也不是由极端的冷漠(老底嘉派)所界定。

3. 要仔细公正地辨别区分实质问题与枝节问题，因为——

(1) 微不足道的枝节问题会引起不必要的讨论；

(2) 要防止用不屑一顾的姿态处理重要的实质问题。

四、统一是假象，当——

1. 建立在愚昧无知的基础上；

2. 建立在忽视真正分歧的基础上。

五、统一之手段——

1. 精神之剑，合法；

2. 世俗之剑，合法；

3. 宗教迫害，非法。

Of Unity in Religion

RELIGION being the chief band of human society, it is a happy thing, when itself is well contained within the true band of unity. The quarrels, and divisions about religion, were evils unknown to the heathen. The reason was, because the religion of the heathen, consisted rather in rites and ceremonies, than in any constant belief. For you may imagine, what kind of faith theirs was, when the chief doctors, and fathers of their church, were the poets. But the true God hath this attribute, that he is a jealous God; and therefore, his worship and religion, will endure no mixture, nor partner. We shall therefore speak a few words, concerning the unity of the church; what are the fruits thereof; what the bounds; and what the means.

The fruits of unity (next unto the well pleasing of God, which is all in all) are two: the one, towards those that are without the church, the other, towards those that are within. For the former; it is certain, that heresies, and schisms, are of all others the greatest scandals; yea, more than corruption of manners. For as in the natural body, a wound, or solution of continuity, is worse than a corrupt humor; so in the spiritual. So that nothing, doth so much keep men out of the church, and drive men out of the church, as a breach of unity. And therefore, whensoever it cometh to that pass, that one saith, Ecce in deserto,① another saith, Ecce in penetralibus;② that is, when some men seek Christ, in the conventicles of heretics, and others, in an outward face of a church, that voice had need continually to sound in men's ears, Nolite exire, —Go not out. The doctor of the Gentiles (the propriety of whose vocation, drew him to have a special care of those without) saith, if an heathen come in, and hear you speak with several tongues, will he not say that you are mad? And certainly it is little better, when atheists, and profane persons, do hear of so many discordant, and contrary opinions in religion; it doth avert them from the church, and maketh them, to sit down in the chair of the scorners. It is but a light thing, to be vouched in so serious a matter, but yet it expresseth well the deformity. There is a master of scoffing, that in his catalogue of books of a feigned library, sets down this title of a book, The Morris-Dance of Heretics. For indeed, every sect of them, hath a diverse posture, or cringe by themselves, which cannot but move derision in worldlings, and depraved politics, who are apt to contemn holy things.

As for the fruit towards those that are within; it is peace; which containeth infinite blessings. It establisheth faith; it kindleth charity; the outward peace of the church, distilleth into peace of conscience; and it turneth the labors of writing, and reading of controversies, into treaties of mortification and devotion.

Concerning the bounds of unity; the true placing of them, importeth exceedingly. There appear to be two extremes. For to certain zealants, all speech of pacification is odious. Is it peace, Jehu? —What hast thou to do with peace? turn thee behind me. Peace is not the matter, but following, and party. Contrariwise, certain Laodiceans, and lukewarm persons, think they may accommodate points of religion, by middle way, and taking part of both, and witty reconcilements; as if they would make an arbitrament between God and

---

①Behold he is in the wilderness.

②Behold he is in the inner chambers.

man. Both these extremes are to be avoided; which will be done, if the league of Christians, penned by our Savior himself, were in two clauses thereof, soundly and plainly expounded: He that is not with us, is against us; and again, He that is not against us, is with us; that is, if the points fundamental and of substance in religion, were truly discerned and distinguished, from points not merely of faith, but of opinion, order, or good intention. This is a thing may seem to many a matter trivial, and done already. But if it were done less partially, it would be embraced more generally.

Of this I may give only this advice, according to my small model. Men ought to take heed, of rending God's church, by two kinds of controversies. The one is, when the matter of the point controverted, is too small and light, not worth the heat and strife about it, kindled only by contradiction. For, as it is noted, by one of the fathers, Christ's coat indeed had no seam, but the church's vesture was of divers colors; whereupon he saith, In veste varietas sit, scissura non sit; ① they be two things, unity and uniformity. The other is, when the matter of the point controverted, is great, but it is driven to an over-great subtilty, and obscurity; so that it becometh a thing rather ingenious, than substantial. A man that is of judgment and understanding, shall sometimes hear ignorant men differ, and know well within himself, that those which so differ, mean one thing, and yet they themselves would never agree. And if it come so to pass, in that distance of judgment, which is between man and man, shall we not think that God above, that knows the heart, doth not discern that frail men, in some of their contradictions, intend the same thing; and accepteth of both? The nature of such controversies is excellently expressed, by St. Paul, in the warning and precept, that he giveth concerning the same, Devita profanas vocum novitates, et oppositiones falsi nominis scientiae. ② Men create oppositions, which are not; and put them into new terms, so fixed, as whereas the meaning ought to govern the term, the term in effect governeth the meaning. There be also two false peaces, or unities: the one, when the peace is grounded, but upon an implicit ignorance; for all colors will agree in the dark: the other, when it is pieced up, upon a direct admission of contraries, in fundamental points. For truth and falsehood, in such things, are like the iron and clay, in the toes of Nebuchadnezzar's image; they may cleave, but they will not incorporate.

Concerning the means of procuring unity; men must beware, that in the procuring, or reuniting, of religious unity, they do not dissolve and deface the

①Let there be variety of colour in the vesture, but not a division.

②Avoid profane new terms and opposition based on science falsely so called.

laws of charity, and of human society. There be two swords amongst Christians, the spiritual and temporal; and both have their due office and place, in the maintenance of religion. But we may not take up the third sword, that is to propagate religion by wars, or by sanguinary persecutions to force consciences; except it be in cases of overt scandal, blasphemy, or intermixture of practice against the state; much less to nourish seditions; to authorize conspiracies and rebellions; to put the sword into the people's hands; and the like; tending to the subversion of all government, which is the ordinance of God. For this is but to dash the first table against the second; and so to consider men as Christians, as we forget that they are men. Lucretius the poet, when he beheld the act of Agamemnon, that could endure the sacrificing of his own daughter, exclaimed: Tantum Religio potuit suadere malorum.①

What would he have said, if he had known of the massacre in France, or the powder treason of England? He would have been seven times more epicure, and atheist, than he was. For as the temporal sword is to be drawn with great circumspection in cases of religion; so it is a thing monstrous to put it into the hands of the common people. Let that be left unto the Anabaptists, and other furies. It was great blasphemy, when the devil said, I will ascend, and be like the highest; but it is greater blasphemy, to personate God, and bring him in saying, I will descend, and be like the prince of darkness; and what is it better, to make the cause of religion to descend, to the cruel and execrable actions of murthering princes, butchery of people, and subversion of states and governments? Surely this is to bring down the Holy Ghost, instead of the likeness of a dove, in the shape of a vulture or raven; and set, out of the bark of a Christian church, a flag of a bark of pirates, and assassins. Therefore it is most necessary, that the church, by doctrine and decree, princes by their sword, and all learnings, both Christian and moral, as by their Mercury rod, do damn and send to hell for ever, those facts and opinions tending to the support of the same; as hath been already in good part done. Surely in counsels concerning religion, that counsel of the apostle would be prefixed, Ira hominis non implet justitiam Dei.② And it was a notable observation of a wise father, and no less ingenuously confessed; that those which held and persuaded pressure of consciences, were commonly interested therein, themselves, for their own ends.

①To such great wrongs could religion prompt.

②The wrath of man does not fulfill the justice of God.

4.论复仇

复仇乃一种原始的公道,人之天性越是爱讨这种公道,法律就越是应该将其铲除。因为首先犯罪者只是触犯了法律,而对该罪犯以牙还牙则使法律失去了效用。无可否认,若一个人对其仇敌施加报复,那他与被报复者不过半斤八两;而若是他不念旧恶,宽大为怀,那他就比对手高出一等,因高抬贵手乃贵人之举。笔者确信,所罗门曾言:“宽恕他人之过失乃宽恕者之荣耀。”[①]过去的已过去,且一去不返,而聪明人总是努力着眼于现在和将来的事情,所以对过去耿耿于怀者无非是在捉弄自己罢了。世间并无为作恶而作恶的人,作恶者之所以作恶皆为要获得名利享乐或诸如此类的东西。既然如此,我为何要因人爱己胜过爱我而对其发怒呢?而且即便有人纯然是出于恶性而作恶,那也不过像荆棘藜楛一般,刺扎戳钩皆因其没别的本事。最可原谅的一类报复是针对那些没有法律惩治的罪行而施行的报复,但此时报复者须当心,得让自己的报复行为也因没法惩治而逍遥法外,不然报复者的仇敌依然占便宜,因为受伤害的比例是二比一。有人复仇时想要仇敌知晓这复仇来自何方。这样复仇更为雍容大度,因为更痛快的报仇似乎不在于使仇敌皮肉受到伤害,而是要让其悔不当初;不过卑怯而狡猾的懦夫则往往喜欢暗中施放的冷箭。佛罗伦萨大公科西莫[②]曾用极其强烈的言辞谴责朋友的背信弃义或忘恩负义,他似乎认为这类恶行不可饶恕。他说,你可以在《圣经》里读到基督要我们宽恕仇敌的教诲[③],但你绝不会读到要我们宽恕朋友的训喻。但迄今为止还是约伯的精神高一格调,他

---

①见《旧约·箴言》第19章11节。

②科西莫(1519—1574),梅迪契家族成员,老洛伦佐后代,第二任佛罗伦萨公爵,第一任托斯卡纳大公,后当选为共和国的首脑。

③参见《新约·马太福音》第5章38—48节和《路加福音》第6章27—36节。

说："我们怎能只喜欢上帝赐福而抱怨上帝降祸呢?"[①]将此例推及朋友，亦有此问。毋庸置疑，念念不忘复仇者只会使自己的创伤新鲜如初，而那创伤本来是可以愈合的。报公仇多半会为复仇者带来幸运，如为恺撒大帝之死而复仇，为佩尔蒂纳之死而复仇，以及为法王亨利三世之死而复仇等等[②]。但报私仇却不会有这般幸运；与此相反，欲报私仇者过的是巫师一般的生活，他们活着时于人有害，死去则可叹可悲。

解析

一、复仇不可原谅，因为它——

1. 使法律失去效用；
2. 不光彩；
3. 无法消除旧恶；
4. 看不到人类的软弱与自私。

二、在下列情况中复仇最可原谅——

1. 法律没法惩治之时；
2. 雍容大度地实施之时。

三、在朋友之间，复仇应为饶恕所取代。

四、报公仇多半会成功，报私仇多半失败。

Of Revenge

REVENGE is a kind of wild justice; which the more man's nature runs to, the more ought law to weed it out. For as for the first wrong, it doth but offend the law; but the revenge of that wrong, putteth the law out of office. Certainly, in taking revenge, a man is but even with his enemy; but in

①语出《旧约·约伯记》第2章10节。

②替恺撒复仇者为屋大维，替佩尔蒂纳（罗马皇帝，在位期公元193年1—3月）复仇者为塞维鲁，替亨利三世复仇者为法王亨利四世（亨利三世之妹夫）。

passing it over, he is superior; for it is a prince's part to pardon. And Solomon, I am sure, saith, It is the glory of a man, to pass by an offence. That which is past is gone, and irrevocable; and wise men have enough to do, with things present and to come; therefore they do but trifle with themselves, that labor in past matters. There is no man doth a wrong, for the wrong's sake; but thereby to purchase himself profit, or pleasure, or honor, or the like. Therefore why should I be angry with a man, for loving himself better than me? And if any man should do wrong, merely out of ill-nature, why, yet it is but like the thorn or briar, which prick and scratch, because they can do no other. The most tolerable sort of revenge, is for those wrongs which there is no law to remedy; but then let a man take heed, the revenge be such as there is no law to punish; else a man's enemy is still before hand, and it is two for one. Some, when they take revenge, are desirous, the party should know, whence it cometh. This is the more generous. For the delight seemeth to be, not so much in doing the hurt, as in making the party repent. But base and crafty cowards, are like the arrow that flieth in the dark. Cosmus, duke of Florence, had a desperate saying against perfidious or neglecting friends, as if those wrongs were unpardonable; You shall read (saith he) that we are commanded to forgive our enemies; but you never read, that we are commanded to forgive our friends. But yet the spirit of Job was in a better tune: Shall we (saith he) take good at God's hands, and not be content to take evil also? And so of friends in a proportion. This is certain, that a man that studieth revenge, keeps his own wounds green, which otherwise would heal, and do well. Public revenges are for the most part fortunate; as that for the death of Caesar; for the death of Pertinax; for the death of Henry the Third of France; and many more. But in private revenges, it is not so. Nay rather, vindictive persons live the life of witches; who, as they are mischievous, so end they unfortunate.

5. 论厄运

“幸运的好处固然该令人向往，但厄运的好处则会令人惊叹。”这是塞内加仿斯多葛派风格发表的一则高论。毋庸置疑，如果奇迹就是超乎寻常，那它们多半都是在厄运中产生。塞内加还有句更高明的至理名言(此言出自一名异教徒之口实在是高明)，曰：“同时具有人之脆弱和神之超凡，那才算是真正的伟大。”这话要是写成诗或许更妙，惟其诗中可允许更多的神之超凡，而且诗人们也的确始终忙于对其进行描写；因为这种超凡实则古代诗人在那部奇妙的传奇[1]中所想象的东西，古人的想象似乎并不乏深邃，而且与当今基督徒的情况颇有几分相似，如当赫拉克勒斯去解救(象征人性的)普罗米修斯之时，他曾凭借一个陶瓮渡过大海，[2]而这不啻是对基督徒坚韧不拔的精神之生动描绘，因基督徒是驾脆弱的血肉之舟去横渡尘世之汪洋。一般说来，出自幸运之德行乃节制，出自厄运之德行乃坚韧，依道德标准而论，后者是更为高尚的美德。幸运乃《旧约》所言之神恩，厄运则是《新约》所言之福分[3]，后者带来上帝更浩荡的恩泽并传递上帝更昭然的启示。但甚至在你聆听《旧约》中大卫王那柄竖琴的时候[4]，你也会听到与欢歌一样多的哀乐。而且那支圣灵之笔[5]对约伯之苦难比对所罗门之幸福有更多的描述。幸运中并非没有诸多的忧虑与灾祸，而厄运中也不乏种种慰藉和希望。我们可从刺绣织锦中看出，将明丽的图案绣在暗郁的背景上比在

---

①指希腊神话。

②希腊神话中并无赫拉克勒斯凭借陶瓮渡海的情节，不过该英雄在建立另一项功绩时曾用金杯渡海。

③《新约》屡言受苦即福，尤其是《马太福音》第5章和《路加福音》第6章把贫穷、饥饿、悲伤以及受侮辱受迫害均视为福。

④意即当你读《旧约·诗篇》的时候。相传《诗篇》为以色列王大卫所作。

⑤《圣经》作者皆受圣灵启示，故有圣灵之笔一说。

明丽的背景上绣暗郁的图案更为悦目，那就从这目之愉悦去推想心之愉悦吧。德行无疑就像名贵香料，经燔焚或碾磨其香愈浓；盖幸运使恶愈昭，而厄运使善愈著。

解析

一、异教徒高度评价厄运：

1. 塞内加；
2. 普罗米修斯的神话。

二、厄运的好处：

1. 形成坚韧之德行；
2. 乃《新约》所强调之福分，在《旧约》中也有提及；
3. 其慰藉更显明丽；
4. 使善愈著。

Of Adversity

IT WAS an high speech of Seneca (after the manner of the Stoics), that the good things, which belong to prosperity, are to be wished; but the good things, that belong to adversity, are to be admired. Bona rerum secundarum optabilia; adversarum mirabilia. Certainly if miracles be the command over nature, they appear most in adversity. It is yet a higher speech of his, than the other (much too high for a heathen), It is true greatness, to have in one the frailty of a man, and the security of a God. Vere magnum habere fragilitatem hominis, securitatem Dei. This would have done better in poesy, where transcendences are more allowed. And the poets indeed have been busy with it; for it is in effect the thing, which figured in that strange fiction of the ancient poets, which seemeth not to be without mystery; nay, and to have some approach to the state of a Christian; that Hercules, when he went to unbind Prometheus (by whom human nature is represented), sailed the length of the great ocean, in an earthen pot or pitcher; lively describing Christian resolution, that saileth in the frail bark of the flesh, through the waves of the world. But to speak in a mean. The virtue of prosperity, is temperance; the virtue of adversity, is fortitude; which in morals is the more heroical virtue. Prosperity is the blessing of the Old Testament; adversity is the blessing of the New; which carrieth the greater benediction, and the clearer revelation of God's favor. Yet even in the Old Testament, if you listen to David's harp, you shall hear as many hearse-like airs as carols; and the pencil of the Holy Ghost hath labored more in describing the afflictions of Job, than the felicities of Solomon. Prosperity is not without many fears and distastes; and adversity is not without comforts and hopes. We see in needle-works and embroideries, it is more pleasing to have a lively work, upon a sad and solemn ground, than to have a dark and melancholy work, upon a lightsome ground: judge therefore of the pleasure of the heart, by the pleasure of the eye. Certainly virtue is like precious odors, most fragrant when they are incensed, or crushed: for prosperity doth best discover vice, but adversity doth best discover virtue.

6.论伪装与掩饰

掩饰仅为一种权宜之策或变通之智。因欲知何时当吐真言或何时当动真格需要敏锐的头脑和坚毅的个性,故较懦弱的一类政治家往往都善于掩饰伪装。

塔西佗曰:“莉维亚兼有其夫的雄才大略和其子的讳莫如深,即她的才略智谋来自奥古斯都,掩人耳目的本事则来自提比略。”塔氏还记述道,穆奇阿努斯劝韦斯帕芗起兵反维特里乌斯时曾说:“我们所要面对的既非奥古斯都那种明察秋毫的慧眼,亦非提比略那种藏而不露的谨慎。”[①]此类智谋韬略和谨饬审慎的确是不同的习性和才能,应当加以辨别区分;因为一个人若是有洞察力,能判明何事当扬,何事当匿,何事当半张半掩,且能看清这扬匿张掩该对何人并该在何时 (这实乃塔西佗所谓的安身治国之要术),那掩饰伪装之习性于他就是一种不利的妨碍。但一个人若是做不到明察秋毫,他通常就只能故作姿态,讳莫如深;因在遇事不能守经达权或随机应变的情况下,最好是采取这种往往都万无一失的策略,这就好比目力不济者须缓缓而行。无可否认,古往今来的豪杰行事都光明磊落,都有诚实守信的名声。然而他们就像训练有素的骏马,前进时能判断何时该停步,何时该迂回;而在这种时候,即当他们认为某事非隐瞒不可并真将其隐瞒之时,他们一般都能瞒过世人,因他们坦荡诚实的名声早已远扬,这往往使他们的欺瞒几乎不为人知。

自我掩饰有上中下三策:上策为不露声色,守口如瓶,用此策者可使自己不显破绽,不被看穿;中策为施放烟幕,欲盖故张,用此策者可故意露一些迹象以隐其真;下策则为弄虚作假,乔装打扮,用此策者常煞费苦心地把自己伪装成另一类人。

---

①以上引言分别出自塔西佗《编年史》第5卷1章和《历史》第2卷76章。

说到上策，守口如瓶实乃听忏悔的神父之美德。嘴紧的神父无疑会听到许多忏悔，因为谁肯向多嘴的人敞开心扉呢?但某人若被认为嘴严，他就会吸引人来向他倾诉，正如室内的热空气会吸引屋外的冷空气一样；而这种倾诉就像忏悔，只会使倾诉者心灵释然，不会被世人加以利用，所以嘴严者常能以这种方式探悉到诸多情况，尽管世人多乐于宣泄积愫而不是吐露隐私。简而言之，能守口如瓶方有权知道他人的秘密。另外(实话实说)，袒露总是举措失当，无论是敞露心胸还是赤裸身子；而行为举止若不肆意张扬，人便可平添几分尊严。至于那些爱高谈阔论的饶舌之徒，他们大凡都既好虚荣又好轻信，因凡爱谈己之所知者往往也会谈论其所不知。故此请记住这句话:守口如瓶既是策略又是品行。而且在这一点上，人的面容最好别越俎代庖司舌头之职，盖面部表情泄心中秘密乃一可出卖其主人的致命弱点，它在极大程度上比语言更引人注意并更使人深信不疑。

说到中策，也就是施放烟幕，此策常不可避免地用在有秘密要保守的时候；所以在某种程度上，欲不泄密者必须是个善施放烟幕者。因世人太狡诈，不容你无偏无党，不容你心藏秘密而不向任何一方透露。他们会向你提出一大堆问题，会设法引诱你开口说话，会千方百计地挖出你心底的秘密，结果你若想避免一种违情悖理的沉默，那总会在某句话中露出破绽。即或你坚持杜口不言，他们也可能从你的沉默中品出味道，就如同从你的话语中探出口风一样。至于支吾搪塞，闪烁其词，那只能暂时掩人耳目。所以若不稍稍发挥一下施烟幕的才能，任何人都难以保守秘密；也可以说烟幕好歹是秘密的一层外衣。

但说到下策，也就是弄虚作假，乔装打扮，余以为除某些重大且罕遇的情况之外，此策与其说是计谋，不如说是犯罪。故弄虚作假(即用此下策)成性乃一种恶习。此恶习之养成或是因天生虚伪，或起因于生性怯懦，要不就是因为心中有鬼，而由于不得不掩饰这些弱点，掩饰者便会在其他事情上也弄虚作假，唯恐其作假技艺日渐荒疏。

伪装掩饰有三利:利之一是可麻痹对手，然后出其不意而胜之，盖人之意图一旦暴露就等于向所有对手发出了警报；利之二是可为掩饰者留下条通畅的后路，因一个人若是明确宣布要行何事，他就必须履行诺言，不然就会被对手推翻；利之三是可更好地洞察他人意图，因一个人若是暴露无遗，其对手就不会再向他表示相反意见，他们会干脆让他继续暴露，而把他们的语言自由变成心里的放肆。因此西班牙人有句精辟的格言：谎话可换取实情。仿佛掩饰伪装是发现实情的唯一手段似的。与利均衡，伪装掩饰亦有三弊：弊之一是掩饰真相者往往显得心里发虚，而这种发虚在任何时候都有碍于他射出的箭直中目标；弊之二是假象会迷惑许多也许本可以与之合作的朋友，结果会使作假者几乎是孤家寡人地去实现自己的目的；弊之三亦是最大的弊端，因为以假掩真会使人丧失最重要的行为工具，即失去信任。故最完善的人品素质须兼有坦荡诚实的名声、守口如瓶的习惯、适当的掩饰技巧，以及在迫不得已时才使用的伪装能力。

解析

一、掩饰是懦弱的标志。

二、不露声色——

1. 吸引倾诉者；
2. 大方、得体（像衣着）；
3. 扼制虚荣；
4. 防止暴露。

三、掩饰往往是不露声色的必然结果。

四、弄虚作假——

1. 更加罪过；
2. 弄虚作假成性会成为真正的恶习。

五、伪装掩饰之利：

1. 麻痹对手；
2. 为掩饰者留下通畅的后路；
3. 帮助洞察他人意图。

六、伪装掩饰之弊：

1. 有碍于办事快捷；

2. 使作假者没有合作者；

3. 使作假者失去信任。

Of Simulation and Dissimulation

DISSIMULATION is but a faint kind of policy, or wisdom; for it asketh a strong wit, and a strong heart, to know when to tell the truth, and to do it. Therefore it is the weaker sort of politics, that are the great dissemblers.

Tacitus saith, Livia sorted well with the arts of her husband, and dissimulation of her son; attributing arts or policy to Augustus, and dissimulation to Tiberius. And again, when Mucianus encourageth Vespasian, to take arms against Vitellius, he saith, We rise not against the piercing judgment of Augustus, nor the extreme caution or closeness of Tiberius. These properties, of arts or policy, and dissimulation or closeness, are indeed habits and faculties several, and to be distinguished. For if a man have that penetration of judgment, as he can discern what things are to be laid open, and what to be secreted, and what to be showed at half lights, and to whom and when (which indeed are arts of state, and arts of life, as Tacitus well calleth them), to him, a habit of dissimulation is a hinderance and a poorness. But if a man cannot obtain to that judgment, then it is left to him generally, to be close, and a dissembler. For where a man cannot choose, or vary in particulars, there it is good to take the safest, and wariest way, in general; like the going softly, by one that cannot well see. Certainly the ablest men that ever were, have had all an openness, and frankness, of dealing; and a name of certainty and veracity; but then they were like horses well managed; for they could tell passing well, when to stop or turn; and at such times, when they thought the case indeed required dissimulation, if then they used it, it came to pass that the former opinion, spread abroad, of their good faith and clearness of dealing, made them almost invisible.

There be three degrees of this hiding and veiling of a man's self. The first, closeness, reservation, and secrecy; when a man leaveth himself without observation, or without hold to be taken, what he is. The second, dissimulation, in the negative; when a man lets fall signs and arguments, that he is not, that he is. And the third, simulation, in the affirmative; when a man industriously and expressly feigns and pretends to be, that he is not.

For the first of these, secrecy; it is indeed the virtue of a confessor. And assuredly, the secret man heareth many confessions. For who will open himself, to a blab or a babbler? But if a man be thought secret, it inviteth discovery; as the more close air sucketh in the more open; and as in confession, the revealing is not for worldly use, but for the ease of a man's heart, so secret men come to the knowledge of many things in that kind; while men rather discharge their minds, than impart their minds. In a few words, mysteries are due to secrecy. Besides (to say truth) nakedness is uncomely, as well in mind as body; and it addeth no small reverence, to men's manners and actions, if they be not altogether open. As for talkers and futile persons, they are commonly vain and credulous withal. For he that talketh what he knoweth, will also talk what he knoweth not. Therefore set it down, that an habit of secrecy, is both politic and moral. And in this part, it is good that a man's face give his tongue leave to speak. For the discovery of a man's self, by the tracts of his countenance, is a great weakness and betraying; by how much it is many times more marked, and believed, than a man's words.

For the second, which is dissimulation; it followeth many times upon secrecy, by a necessity; so that he that will be secret, must be a dissembler in some degree. For men are too cunning, to suffer a man to keep an indifferent carriage between both, and to be secret, without swaying the balance on either side. They will so beset a man with questions, and draw him on, and pick it out of him, that, without an absurd silence, he must show an inclination one way; or if he do not, they will gather as much by his silence, as by his speech. As for equivocations, or oraculous speeches, they cannot hold out long. So that no man can be secret, except he give himself a little scope of dissimulation; which is, as it were, but the skirts or train of secrecy.

But for the third degree, which is simulation, and false profession; that I hold more culpable, and less politic; except it be in great and rare matters. And therefore a general custom of simulation (which is this last degree) is a vice, using either of a natural falseness or fearfulness, or of a mind that hath some main faults, which because a man must needs disguise, it maketh him practise simulation in other things, lest his hand should be out of use.

The great advantages of simulation and dissimulation are three. First, to lay asleep opposition, and to surprise. For where a man's intentions are published, it is an alarum, to call up all that are against them. The second is, to reserve to a man's self a fair retreat. For if a man engage himself by a manifest declaration, he must go through or take a fall. The third is, the better to discover the mind of another. For to him that opens himself, men will hardly show themselves adverse; but will fair let him go on, and turn their freedom of speech, to freedom of thought. And therefore it is a good shrewd proverb of the Spaniard, Tell a lie and find a troth. As if there were no way of discovery, but by simulation. There be also three disadvantages, to set it even. The first, that simulation and dissimulation commonly carry with them a show of fearfulness, which in any business, doth spoil the feathers, of round flying up to the mark. The second, that it puzzleth and perplexeth the conceits of many, that perhaps would otherwise co-operate with him; and makes a man walk almost alone, to his own ends. The third and greatest is, that it depriveth a man of one of the most principal instruments for action; which is trust and belief. The best composition and temperature, is to have openness in fame and opinion; secrecy in habit; dissimulation in seasonable use; and a power to feign, if there be no remedy.

7.谈父母与子女

为人父母者爱把喜乐忧惧都藏在心头，因为有些感受不能说，有些则不愿说。子女可使父母的辛劳苦中有乐，但也可使父母的不幸加深；子女会增加父母对生活的忧虑，但也会减轻他们对死亡的担忧。动物皆能生殖繁衍，代代不绝，但在身后留下声名、功德和伟业则为人之独有。世人的确可见，最伟大的功业历来都由一些无后嗣者所始创，这些人因没有后嗣再现他们的肉体，便努力实现其精神之再现，所以无后嗣者往往最关心后世。未立业而先成家者大都溺爱孩子，他们不仅把孩子视为种族的延续，而且视为他们事业的继续，因此孩子于他们就如同创造的产物。

父母对子女的疼爱往往不甚均匀，而且有时还不甚恰当，尤其是母亲。正如所罗门曰："儿子聪明其父开颜，儿子愚笨其母赧颜。"[①]世人可见，若一户人家有众多子女，那他们当中每每是最长者受到重视，最幼者受到纵容，居中者则在某种程度上受到忽略，然而屡屡都是这些居中者最有出息。父母在孩子的零花钱上吝啬有害无益，那会使孩子变得卑劣，学会欺诈哄瞒，甚至结交不三不四的朋友，而且待将来有钱时会挥霍无度。所以最好的经验是：父母应保持其权威无损，但莫保持其钱包不瘪。(无论是父母、教师还是家仆)成年人都爱在孩子们小时候鼓励兄弟之间竞争，这种做法往往会造成他们成年之后失和，从而破坏家庭和睦。意大利人对儿子、侄甥或其他近亲晚辈几乎不分亲疏，只要他们是本族晚辈，纵非自己亲生也一视同仁。而毋庸讳言，实际上这些晚生也差不多是一回事，因为我们常见某个当侄甥的有时更像其叔叔、舅舅或另一位近亲长辈，而不像他自己的父亲，此乃血气使然也。当父母的应及早选定他们想让孩子从事的职业和相关学业，因孩子越小可塑性越大；同时父母不可过分注重孩子的意向，别以为孩子

---

①见《旧约·箴言》第10章1节。

想做的事他们将来也会喜欢。毫无疑问，若孩子的爱好或才能超凡出众，那当然是不加阻碍为妙；不过对一般人来说，这句格言倒很恰当：选最佳的生活道路，习惯会使那条路走起来轻松愉快。兄弟中为次幼者通常都很幸运，可一旦长兄被剥夺继承权，这种幸运则难以保全甚至不复存在。[①]

解析

一、为人父母的坏处：

1. 子女增加不幸与忧虑；
2. 有碍于建功立业。

二、父母对待子女方法的不当之处：

1. 疼爱不均匀；
2. 吝啬；
3. 鼓励兄弟间的竞争；
4. 对未来职业选择不明智。

三、“兄弟中为次幼者通常都很幸运。”

Of Parents and Children

THE joys of parents are secret; and so are their griefs and fears. They cannot utter the one; nor they will not utter the other. Children sweeten labors; but they make misfortunes more bitter. They increase the cares of life; but they mitigate the remembrance of death. The perpetuity by generation is common to beasts; but memory, merit, and noble works, are proper to men. And surely a man shall see the noblest works and foundations have proceeded from childless men; which have sought to express the images of their minds, where those of their bodies have failed. So the care of posterity is

---

①为弟者自幼便知将来得自食其力，一般都学有所成并具勤俭之风，故曰“幸运”；可他们一旦因继承遗产而富贵，则很容易弃俭从奢。

most in them, that have no posterity. They that are the first raisers of their houses, are most indulgent towards their children; beholding them as the continuance, not only of their kind, but of their work; and so both children and creatures.

The difference in affection, of parents towards their several children, is many times unequal; and sometimes unworthy; especially in the mothers; as Solomon saith, A wise son rejoiceth the father, but an ungracious son shames the mother. A man shall see, where there is a house full of children, one or two of the eldest respected, and the youngest made wantons; but in the midst, some that are as it were forgotten, who many times, nevertheless, prove the best. The illiberality of parents, in allowance towards their children, is an harmful error; makes them base; acquaints them with shifts; makes them sort with mean company; and makes them surfeit more when they come to plenty. And therefore the proof is best, when men keep their authority towards the children, but not their purse. Men have a foolish manner (both parents and schoolmasters and servants) in creating and breeding an emulation between brothers, during childhood, which many times sorteth to discord when they are men, and disturbeth families. The Italians make little difference between children, and nephews or near kinsfolks; but so they be of the lump, they care not though they pass not through their own body. And, to say truth, in nature it is much a like matter; insomuch that we see a nephew sometimes resembleth an uncle, or a kinsman, more than his own parent; as the blood happens. Let parents choose betimes, the vocations and courses they mean their children should take; for then they are most flexible; and let them not too much apply themselves to the disposition of their children, as thinking they will take best to that, which they have most mind to. It is true, that if the affection or aptness of the children be extraordinary, then it is good not to cross it; but generally the precept is good, optimum elige, suave et facile illud faciet consuetudo.① Younger brothers are commonly fortunate, but seldom or never where the elder are disinherited.

①Choose the best; practise will make it pleasant and easy.

8.谈结婚与独身

有妻室儿女者对未来已只能听天由命，因妻室儿女乃成就大业之妨碍，不管要成就的大业是善是恶。无可否认，最有益于公众的丰功伟业历来皆由无妻室或无子女的人始创，这些人在感情上已娶了公众，并用他们的钱财替公众置了嫁妆。但按理说有子女的人对将来应最为关心，因为他们知道得把自己最心爱的孩子留给将来。世上有这样一种人，他们虽然过独身生活，但却一心只想自己，认为将来与己无关；世上还有一种人，他们认为妻子儿女不过是应付的账单；更有甚者，有些愚蠢而贪婪的富翁竟为没有子女而扬扬得意，他们可能以为这样一来他们就更为富有，也许他们听过这样一段对话，有人说“某某是个大富翁”，另有一人则不以为然，“是呀，可他有一大堆孩子要养”，仿佛子女会减少那人的财富似的。不过选择独身的原因多半都是为了自由，对某些自悦而任性的人来说尤其如此，因为这种人对任何约束都极为敏感，以致他们或许会把腰带和吊袜带也视为羁绊。独身者往往意味着挚友、恩主或义仆，但并不尽然都是忠顺的臣民，因他们无牵无挂，可远走高飞，而且浪迹他乡者差不多都是独身。僧侣修士很需要过独身生活，因为须先施于家人的博爱很难普度众生。各级法官独身与否则无关紧要，因如若他们易被人左右并贪赃枉法，始作俑者多半是幕僚而不是妻子。至于士卒兵丁，笔者发现将帅激励部下时总爱让他们想到家小；同时笔者亦认为，土耳其人对婚姻之不尊重使他们的士兵变得更为卑劣。毋庸置疑，妻室儿女意味着一种人性的磨练。独身者虽因花销较少而常常慷慨施舍，但在另一方面他们却更为残忍冷酷(宜作审讯官吏)，因为他们的柔情不常被唤醒。性情庄重者因奉习俗为圭臬而能忠贞不渝，故通常皆为情深意笃的丈夫，就像传说中的尤利西斯，他宁要年迈的妻子而不愿获得永生。[①]贞洁的女人往往骄矜自负，桀骜不驯，仿佛她们因其贞洁之德而有恃无恐。让妻子觉得丈夫明智是使其既贞洁又顺从的最有力保证，但若是妻子发现丈夫忌妒多疑，她就绝不会认为丈夫明智。妻乃青年者的情人、中年者的伴侣、暮年者的护士；所以只要一个人喜欢，他任何时候娶妻都有道理。但有位被称作智者的人[②]却另有高见，他在被问及当何时娶妻时说："年少时尚不宜，年长时则不必。"世人常见劣夫偏娶上贤妻，这个中缘由或许是劣夫们偶尔一露的好心更显珍贵，或许是那些贤妻爱为自己的忍性而感到自豪；但只要那些劣夫是贤妻们未经亲友同意而自行作出的选择，这种婚姻就绝不会失败，因为要是失败的话，贤妻们就将不可避免地证明自己愚蠢。

解析

一、反对结婚：

1. 妨碍建立"丰功伟业"；
2. 有些人"认为妻子儿女不过是应付的账单"；
3. 独身生活更加自由；
4. 挚友、恩主、义仆与僧侣修士最好为独身者，士卒兵丁不尽如此。

二、赞成结婚，因为它是"人性的磨练"。

三、婚姻可能出现的问题(假如婚姻总有借口)：

1. 性情庄重者会成为情深意笃的丈夫；
2. 贞洁的女子往往骄矜自负；
3. 忌妒多疑的丈夫会丧失妻子的尊重；
4. 劣夫往往会娶到贤妻。

---

①据荷马史诗记载，尤利西斯(希腊名为奥德修斯)在从特洛伊返乡途中曾被困在一座岛上，该岛女神卡吕普索以爱相许并愿与他分享永生，但尤利西斯拒绝了女神的求爱与给予，终于回到故国与妻子团聚。

②指古希腊哲学家泰勒斯(Thales，约前624—前547)，相传他母亲曾多次敦促他结婚，但他屡屡找借口回拒，年轻时说太年幼，年长时又说太老迈。

Of Marriage and Single Life

HE THAT hath wife and children hath given hostages to fortune; for they are impediments to great enterprises, either of virtue or mischief. Certainly the best works, and of greatest merit for the public, have proceeded from the unmarried or childless men; which both in affection and means, have married and endowed the public. Yet it were great reason that those that have children, should have greatest care of future times; unto which they know they must transmit their dearest pledges. Some there are, who though they lead a single life, yet their thoughts do end with themselves, and account future times impertinences. Nay, there are some other, that account wife and children, but as bills of charges. Nay more, there are some foolish rich covetous men, that take a pride, in having no children, because they may be thought so much the richer. For perhaps they have heard some talk, Such an one is a great rich man, and another except to it, Yea, but he hath a great charge of children; as if it were an abatement to his riches. But the most ordinary cause of a single life, is liberty, especially in certain self-pleasing and humorous minds, which are so sensible of every restraint, as they will go near to think their girdles and garters, to be bonds and shackles. Unmarried men are best friends, best masters, best servants; but not always best subjects; for they are light to run away; and almost all fugitives, are of that condition. A single life doth well with churchmen; for charity will hardly water the ground, where it must first fill a pool. It is indifferent for judges and magistrates; for if they be facile and corrupt, you shall have a servant, five times worse than a wife. For soldiers, I find the generals commonly in their hortatives, put men in mind of their wives and children; and I think the despising of marriage amongst the Turks, maketh the vulgar soldier more base. Certainly wife and children are a kind of discipline of humanity; and single men, though they may be many times more charitable, because their means are less exhaust, yet, on the other side, they are more cruel and hardhearted (good to make severe inquisitors), because their tenderness is not so oft called upon. Grave natures, led by custom, and therefore constant, are commonly loving husbands, as was said of Ulysses, vetulam suam praetulit immortalitati.① Chaste women are often proud and froward, as presuming upon the merit of their chastity. It is one of the best bonds, both of chastity and obedience, in the wife, if she think her husband wise; which she will never do, if she find him jealous. Wives are young

①He preferred his old woman to immorality.

men's mistresses; companions for middle age; and old men's nurses. So as a man may have a quarrel to marry, when he will. But yet he was reputed one of the wise men, that made answer to the question, when a man should marry, —A young man not yet, an elder man not at all. It is often seen that bad husbands, have very good wives; whether it be, that it raiseth the price of their husband's kindness, when it comes; or that the wives take a pride in their patience. But this never fails, if the bad husbands were of their own choosing, against their friends' consent; for then they will be sure to make good their own folly.

9.论嫉妒

世人历来注意到，所有情感中最令人神魂颠倒者莫过于爱情和嫉妒。这两种感情都会激起强烈的欲望，而且均可迅速转化成联想和幻觉，容易钻进世人的眼睛，尤其容易降到被爱被妒者身上。这些便是导致蛊惑的要点，如果世间真有蛊惑的话。我们同样可以见到，《圣经》中把嫉妒称为“毒眼”[①]，占星术士则把不吉之星力叫做“凶象”[②]，以致世人似乎至今还承认，当嫉妒行为发生时，嫉妒者会眼红或曰红眼。而且有人更为明察秋毫，竟注意到红眼最伤人之际莫过于被嫉妒者正踌躇满志或春风得意之时，因为那种得意劲儿会使妒火燃得更旺。另外在这种时候，被嫉妒者的情绪最溢于言表，因此最容易遭受打击。

但暂且不谈这些蹊跷之处（虽说这些蹊跷并非不值得在适当的场合思量思量），笔者在此只想探讨一下哪些人好嫉妒他人，哪些人会遭受嫉妒，以及公众的嫉妒和私人间的嫉妒有何不同。

自身无德者常嫉妒他人之德，因为人心的滋养要么是自身之善，要么是他人之恶，而缺乏自身之善者必然要摄取他人之恶，于是凡无望达到他人之德行境地者便会极力贬低他人以求得平衡。

好管闲事且好探隐私者通常都好嫉妒，因为劳神费力地去打探别人的事情绝非是由于那些事与打探者的利害有关，所以其原因必定是打探者在旁观他人祸福时能获得一种观剧般的乐趣。而一心只管自家事的人无甚嫉妒的由来，因为嫉妒是一种爱游荡的感情，它总在街头闲逛，不肯待在家

①见《新约·马太福音》第7章22节。

②凶象之“凶”和毒眼之“毒”原文均为evil，其音形均与envy（嫉妒）相近。另“星力”乃一占星学术语，古代占星学认为天体相互位置之不同会产生或吉或凶的星力，这种星力会影响人事祸福。

里，所以古人说“好管闲事者必定没安好心”。

出身贵族者在新人晋爵时常生妒意，因为两者之间的差距缩短，而且这就像是看朱成碧，明明是别人上升，他们却看成是自己下降。

宦官、老人、残疾者和私生子都好嫉妒，因没法弥补自身缺陷的人总要千方百计给别人也造成缺陷，除非有上述缺陷者具有勇敢无畏的英雄气概，有志把自身的固有缺陷变成其荣誉之一部分。这样人们就会说，某宦官或瘸子竟创下如此殊勋伟业，正如宦官纳西斯以及瘸子阿偈西劳和帖木儿曾努力求得奇迹般的荣誉一样。[①]

在大苦大难后升迁的人也好嫉妒，因为他们就像时代的落伍者似的，以为别人受到伤害就可补偿自己曾经历的苦难。

那些因其轻薄和自负而想在各方面都胜过他人者亦常嫉妒，因为他们绝不会缺少嫉妒的对象，在他们想争胜的诸多方面之某一方面，不可能没有许多人会胜过他们。罗马皇帝哈德良就是这种嫉妒者，他善诗画和工艺，因此他非常嫉妒真正的诗人、画家和技师。

最后还有同族亲友、官场同僚和少时伙伴，这些人在平辈人升迁时更容易产生嫉妒，因为对他们来说，平辈的升迁不啻是在批评自己的身份，是在对自己进行指责，这种升迁会更经常地进入他们的记忆，同样也会更多地引起旁人的注意，而旁人对这种升迁的传扬往往会令嫉妒者妒意更浓。该隐对其弟亚伯的嫉妒之所以更为卑鄙邪恶，就因为亚伯的供奉被上帝悦纳时并没有旁人看见。[②]关于好嫉妒之人暂且就说到这里。

接下来笔者要谈谈那些或多或少会遭嫉妒的人的情况。首先，有大德者步入老年后较少遭人嫉妒，因为他们的幸运已显得不过是他们应得的报偿，而对应得的报偿谁也不会嫉妒，世人只嫉妒过于慷慨的奖赏和施舍。另一方面，嫉妒常产生在与人攀比之时，可以说没有攀比就没有嫉妒，故此为君者不会被其他人妒忌，除非妒忌者亦是君王。不过应该注意到，卑微之

①纳西斯（约 480—574），拜占庭帝国一宦官出身的将军，一生战功卓著；阿偈西劳（约前 444—前 360）系斯巴达国王，有“跛脚国王”之称；而堪称又“一代天骄”的帖木儿之传世之名 Timur Lang 在波斯语中本身就意为“跛子帖木儿”。

②据《旧约·创世记》第 4 章记载，亚当夏娃有二子，长子该隐种地，次子亚伯牧羊，二人均献出产物供奉上帝，上帝悦纳亚伯之供奉，该隐心生嫉妒，遂杀其弟。

人在发迹之初最遭人妒忌，其后妒忌会逐渐减弱；但与此相反，品质优秀者则是在他们的好运赓续不断时遭妒最甚，因此时他们的优点虽依然如故，但已不如当初那样耀眼，后起之秀已使其黯然失色。

出身贵族者在升迁时较少遭人嫉妒，因为那看上去无非是出身高贵的必然结果，再说这种锦上添花似乎也不会给他们带来更多的好处。且嫉妒犹如日光，它射在陡坡峭壁上比射在平地上更使人感觉其热；与此同理，逐渐高升者比骤然腾达者较少遭人嫉妒。

那些一直把自己的显赫与辛劳、焦虑或风险连在一起的人较少成为嫉妒的对象，因为世人会觉得他们的高位显职来之不易，甚至有时候还会可怜他们，而怜悯往往可以治愈嫉妒。故此世人可见，一些较老谋深算的政界人物在位高权重时常常向人家诉苦，说自己活得多苦多累，其实他们并非真那样感觉，而只是想减轻别人的嫉妒而已。不过人们能体谅的是那种依命行事的辛劳，而不是那种没事找事的忙碌，因为最让人妒上加妒的事就是那种毫无必要且野心勃勃的事必躬亲；所以对位高权重者来说，保证各级属下的充分权利和应有身份是消除嫉妒的最佳方法，因为用这种方法不啻在自己与嫉妒之间筑起了一道道屏障。

因大富大贵而趾高气扬者尤其易遭妒忌，因为这种人不炫耀其富贵就不舒服，结果他们或是在举止言谈上神气活现，或是总要压倒一切相反意见或竞争对手。可聪明人则宁愿吃点亏而给嫉妒者一点实惠，有时故意在某些与己关系不大的事情上让对手占占上风。但尽管如此，以下事实仍不谬：以直率坦荡的态度对待富贵比用虚伪狡诈的态度更少遭人妒忌，只要那直率坦荡中没有傲慢与自负的成分；因为用后一种态度者无非是否认自己的幸运，而那会让人觉得他自己都感到他不配享受福贵，因此他恰好是教别人来嫉妒自己。

最后让笔者赘言几句来结束这个部分。如本文开篇所言，嫉妒行为有几分巫术的性质，因此治嫉妒的最好方法就是治巫术的方法，也就是移开世人所谓的“符咒”，使之镇在别人头上。为达到这一目的，有些聪明的大人物总是让别人替自己抛头露面，从而使本会降到自己身上的嫉妒降到他人身上，这种他人有时候是侍从仆役，有时候是同僚伙伴或诸如此类的角色。而要找这种替身，世间还真不乏一些雄心勃勃的冒昧之徒，只要能获得权位，这种人不惜付出任何代价。

现在且来谈谈公众的嫉妒。虽说私人间的嫉妒有百害而无一利，但公众的嫉妒却还有一点好处，因为它就像陶片放逐法[①]，可除去那些位高专权者，所以它对其他大人物亦是一种制约，可使他们循规蹈矩。

这种在拉丁语中写作 invidia 的嫉妒在现代语言中又叫“不满情绪”，关于这点笔者将在谈及叛乱[②]时加以讨论。公众的嫉妒对国家来说是一种可能蔓延的疾病，正如传染病可侵入健全的肌体并使之犯疾一样，国民一旦产生这种嫉妒，他们甚至会反对最合理的国家行为，并使这些行为背上恶名。而为此采取笼络民心的举措也几乎无济于事，因为这正好表明当局害怕嫉妒，软弱可欺，结果造成的损害更大。这也像通常的传染病一样，你越怕它，它越要找上门来。

这种公众的嫉妒似乎主要是针对高官大臣，而不是针对君王和国家本身。但有一条千真万确的规律，那就是如果某位大臣并无甚过失却招来公众强烈的嫉妒，或是公众的嫉妒在某种程度上是针对一国之所有大臣，那嫉妒的矛头（虽隐而不露）实际上就是指向国家本身了。以上所言便是公众的嫉妒，或曰公众的不满，以及它与私人间的嫉妒之不同，而关于后者前文已经论及。

最后笔者再就嫉妒之情泛泛补充几句。在人类所有情感中，嫉妒是一种最纠缠不休的感情，因其他感情的生发都有特定的时间场合，只是偶尔为之。所以古人说得好：嫉妒从不休假；因为它总在某些人心中作祟。世人还注意到，爱情和嫉妒的确会使人衣带渐宽，而其他感情却不致如此，原因是其他感情都不像爱情和嫉妒那样寒暑无间。嫉妒亦是最卑劣最堕落的一种感情，因此它是魔鬼的固有属性，魔鬼就是那个趁黑夜在麦田里撒稗种的嫉妒者[③]。而就像一直所发生的那样，嫉妒也总是在暗中施展诡计，偷偷损害像麦黍之类的天下良物。

---

①又称“贝壳放逐法”，古希腊的一种政治措施，由公民将其认为危及国家民主制度的人的名字记于陶片或贝壳上进行现代意义上的公民投票，记名逾半数者被放逐国外十年。有人曾滥用此法以排除异己，一些优秀的政治家和将军亦曾被放逐。

②见本书第 15 篇。

③语出《新约·马太福音》第 13 章 25 节，但该节原文并无“嫉妒者”字样。

解析

一、嫉妒是——

1. 最令人神魂颠倒的情感,同爱情一样;

2. 在春风得意之时最为伤人。

二、易嫉妒者包括:

1. 自身无德者;

2. 好管闲事且好探隐私者;

3. 出身贵族者在新人晋爵时;

4. 有无法弥补的缺陷之人(残疾者、宦官、私生子等);

5. 在大苦大难后升迁的人;

6. 想在各方面都胜过他人者;

7. 同族亲友、官场同僚和少时伙伴。

三、易遭嫉妒者包括:

1. 品德优秀者在好运赓续不断之时(较少);

2. 出身贵族者在升迁之时(较少);

3. 逐渐高升者(较少);

4. 已功成名就者(较少);

5. 因大富大贵而趾高气扬者(较多);

备注:治嫉妒最好的办法是移开“符咒”。

四、公众的嫉妒——

1. 还有一点好处,如“陶片放逐法”;

2. 为此采取一些笼络民心的举措是愚蠢的;

3. 主要针对高官大臣,而不是针对君王与国家本身。

备注:嫉妒是无休止的,折磨人的,卑劣且堕落的。

Of Envy

THERE be none of the affections, which have been noted to fascinate or bewitch, but love and envy. They both have vehement wishes; they frame themselves readily into imaginations and suggestions; and they come easily into the eye, especially upon the present of the objects; which are the points that conduce to fascination, if any such thing there be. We see likewise, the Scripture calleth envy an evil eye; and the astrologers, call the evil influences of the stars, evil aspects; so that still there seemeth to be acknowledged, in the act of envy, an ejaculation or irradiation of the eye. Nay, some have been so curious, as to note, that the times when the stroke or percussion of an envious eye doth most hurt, are when the party envied is beheld in glory or triumph; for that sets an edge upon envy: and besides, at such times the spirits of the person envied, do come forth most into the outward parts, and so meet the blow.

But leaving these curiosities (though not unworthy to be thought on, in fit place), we will handle, what persons are apt to envy others; what persons are most subject to be envied themselves; and what is the difference between public and private envy.

A man that hath no virtue in himself, ever envieth virtue in others. For men's minds, will either feed upon their own good, or upon others' evil; and who wanteth the one, will prey upon the other; and whoso is out of hope, to attain to another's virtue, will seek to come at even hand, by depressing another's fortune.

A man that is busy, and inquisitive, is commonly envious. For to know much of other men's matters, cannot be because all that ado may concern his own estate; therefore it must needs be, that he taketh a kind of play-pleasure, in looking upon the fortunes of others. Neither can he, that mindeth but his own business, find much matter for envy. For envy is a gadding passion, and walketh the streets, and doth not keep home: Non est curiosus, quin idem sit malevolus.①

Men of noble birth, are noted to be envious towards new men, when they rise. For the distance is altered, and it is like a deceit of the eye, that when others come on, they think themselves, go back.

Deformed persons, and eunuchs, and old men, and bastards, are envious. For he that cannot possibly mend his own case, will do what he can, to impair another's; except these defects light upon a very brave, and heroical nature, which thinketh to make his natural wants part of his honor; in that it should be said, that an eunuch, or a lame man, did such great matters; affecting the honor of a miracle; as it was in Narses the eunuch, and Agesilaus and

①A man is not meddlesome without also being malicious.

Tamberlanes, that were lame men.

The same is the case of men, that rise after calamities and misfortunes. For they are as men fallen out with the times; and think other men's harms, a redemption of their own sufferings.

They that desire to excel in too many matters, out of levity and vainglory, are ever envious. For they cannot want work; it being impossible, but many, in some one of those things, should surpass them. Which was the character of Adrian the Emperor; that mortally envied poets, and painters, and artificers, in works wherein he had a vein to excel.

Lastly, near kinsfolks, and fellows in office, and those that have been bred together, are more apt to envy their equals, when they are raised. For it doth upbraid unto them their own fortunes, and pointeth at them, and cometh oftener into their remembrance, and incurreth likewise more into the note of others; and envy ever redoubleth from speech and fame. Cain's envy was the more vile and malignant, towards his brother Abel, because when his sacrifice was better accepted, there was nobody to look on. Thus much for those, that are apt to envy.

Concerning those that are more or less subject to envy: First, persons of eminent virtue, when they are advanced, are less envied. For their fortune seemeth, but due unto them; and no man envieth the payment of a debt, but rewards and liberality rather. Again, envy is ever joined with the comparing of a man's self; and where there is no comparison, no envy; and therefore kings are not envied, but by kings. Nevertheless it is to be noted, that unworthy persons are most envied, at their first coming in, and afterwards overcome it better; whereas contrariwise, persons of worth and merit are most envied, when their fortune continueth long. For by that time, though their virtue be the same, yet it hath not the same lustre; for fresh men grow up that darken it.

Persons of noble blood, are less envied in their rising. For it seemeth but right done to their birth. Besides, there seemeth not much added to their fortune; and envy is as the sunbeams, that beat hotter upon a bank, or steep rising ground, than upon a flat. And for the same reason, those that are advanced by degrees, are less envied than those that are advanced suddenly and per saltum.

Those that have joined with their honor great travels, cares, or perils, are less subject to envy. For men think that they earn their honors hardly, and pity them sometimes; and pity ever healeth envy. Wherefore you shall observe, that the more deep and sober sort of politic persons, in their greatness, are ever bemoaning themselves, what a life they lead; chanting a quanta patimur![1] Not that they feel it so, but only to abate the edge of envy. But this is to be understood, of business that is laid upon men, and not such, as they call unto themselves. For nothing increaseth envy more, than an unnecessary and ambitious engrossing of business. And nothing doth extinguish envy more, than for a great person to preserve all other inferior officers, in their full lights and pre-eminences of their places. For by that means, there be so many screens between him and envy.

Above all, those are most subject to envy, which carry the greatness of their fortunes, in an insolent and proud manner; being never well, but while they are showing how great they are, either by outward pomp, or by triumphing over all opposition or competition; whereas wise men will rather do sacrifice to envy, in suffering themselves sometimes of purpose to be crossed, and overborne in things that do not much concern them. Notwithstanding, so much is true, that the carriage of greatness, in a plain and open manner (so it be without arrogancy and vainglory) doth draw less envy, than if it be in a more crafty and cunning fashion. For in that course, a man doth but disavow fortune; and seemeth to be conscious of his own want in worth; and doth but teach others, to envy him.

Lastly, to conclude this part; as we said in the beginning, that the act of envy had somewhat in it of witchcraft, so there is no other cure of envy, but the cure of witchcraft; and that is, to remove the lot (as they call it) and to lay it upon another. For which purpose, the wiser sort of great persons, bring in ever upon the stage somebody upon whom to derive the envy, that would come upon themselves; sometimes upon ministers and servants; sometimes upon colleagues and associates; and the like; and for that turn there are never wanting, some persons of violent and undertaking natures, who, so they may have power and business, will take it at any cost.

Now, to speak of public envy. There is yet some good in public envy, whereas in private, there is none. For public envy, is as an ostracism, that eclipseth men, when they grow too great. And therefore it is a bridle also to great ones, to keep them within bounds.

This envy, being in the Latin word invidia, goeth in the modern language, by the name of discontentment; of which we shall speak, in handling sedition. It is a disease, in a state, like to infection. For as infection spreadeth upon that which is sound, and tainteth it; so when envy is gotten once into a state, it traduceth even the best actions thereof, and turneth them into an ill odor. And therefore there is little won, by intermingling of plausible actions.

---

①How much we suffer!

For that doth argue but a weakness, and fear of envy, which hurteth so much the more, as it is likewise usual in infections; which if you fear them, you call them upon you.

This public envy, seemeth to beat chiefly upon principal officers or ministers, rather than upon kings, and estates themselves. But this is a sure rule, that if the envy upon the minister be great, when the cause of it in him is small; or if the envy be general, in a manner upon all the ministers of an estate; then the envy (though hidden) is truly upon the state itself. And so much of public envy or discontentment, and the difference thereof from private envy, which was handled in the first place.

We will add this in general, touching the affection of envy; that of all other affections, it is the most importune and continual. For of other affections, there is occasion given, but now and then; and therefore it is well said, Invidia festos dies non agit[①]: for it is ever working upon some or other. And it is also noted, that love and envy do make a man pine, which other affections do not, because they are not so continual. It is also the vilest affection, and the most depraved; for which cause it is the proper attribute of the devil, who is called, the envious man, that soweth tares amongst the wheat by night; as it always cometh to pass, that envy worketh subtilly, and in the dark, and to the prejudice of good things, such as is the wheat.

①Envy keeps no holidays.

10.论爱情

舞台较之人生更受惠于爱情。因为对舞台而言，爱情有时是喜剧，有时是悲剧；但对人生来说，爱情却总是招致灾祸，它有时候像一位塞壬[①]，有时候像一个复仇女神。世人也许注意到，在我们所记得的古今伟人当中，还从不曾有谁被爱情弄到疯狂的地步，这说明高贵的心灵和伟大的事业均可抵御这种愚蠢的激情。不过有两人得除外，一是曾统治过半个罗马帝国的马尔库斯·安东尼[②]，一是曾当过罗马执政官及立法官的阿皮亚斯·克劳狄乌斯[③]；前者无疑是个耽溺女色的张狂之徒，但后者却是个老成持重的明智之人。由此可见，似乎爱情不但能钻进无遮无掩的心扉，而且（偶尔）还会闯入森严壁垒的灵台，如果守卫疏忽的话。伊壁鸠鲁有一句糟糕的格言，即"对我俩来说，彼此就是一幕看不够的剧"[④]，这话的意思像是说，天生当凝神于苍昊及崇高万物的世人竟可以无所事事，只须拜倒在一尊小小的偶像跟前，使自己成为奴仆，虽不是像禽兽之类的口喙之奴，但仍然是眼眸之奴，而上帝赋予人眼睛本是为了更崇高的目的。观察这种感情之放纵以及它如何对事物的本质和价值视而不见，那可真叫人不可思议。据此观察，无休无止的夸张言辞只适用于爱情，而不适用于其他任何方面，甚至亦不完全适用于下面这个警句，即"大大小小的恭维者相互间都明白，最讨自己喜欢的恭维者总是自己"，这说法尽管不错，但却肯定不能把热恋者也包括在内，

---

①塞壬，希腊神话中一种半人半鸟的女妖，她们用迷人的歌声引诱航海者，使之触礁毁灭。

②安东尼曾与屋大维平分权力，统治罗马帝国东方行省，后迷恋埃及女王克娄巴特拉七世，终自杀。

③阿皮亚斯·克劳狄乌斯（公元前5世纪），因企图奸污民女维尔吉尼娅而导致罗马十人委员会的颠覆。

④据塞内加《道德书简》第1卷第7篇记载，伊壁鸠鲁这句话并非对异性情人而言，而是对一位哲学家朋友而说。

因为与热恋者对所恋之人的荒唐恭维相比，再自傲的人也不曾把自己想得那般完美，所以古人说得好：爱情和智慧不可兼而得之。热恋者这一弱点也并非只是旁观者清，其实大多数被恋者也看得分明，除非被恋者与热恋者互相爱恋；因为这世上有条基本法则，那就是爱情总会得到报偿，要么得到被恋者的回恋，要么得到一种深藏于心的轻蔑。由此可见，世人应当更多地提防这种激情，因为它不仅会使人丧失其他东西，而且会使人丧失自我。至于会丧失其他什么东西，古代那位诗人在其诗中说得很明白：帕里斯更喜爱海伦，故而放弃了赫拉和雅典娜的礼物。[①]因为任何过分看重爱情的人都会放弃财富和智慧。爱情泛滥之时往往正是人们软弱之际，也就是在人鸿运高照或背运倒霉的时候，不过这后一种情况历来较少被世人注意。其实这两种时候都容易点燃爱火并使之燃得更旺，因而也可说明爱情的确是愚蠢的产物。如果有人不得不接受爱，但却能将其摆在适当的位置，使之与人生的重要使命截然分开，那这人就算把爱情处理得最为妥当。因为若让爱情干扰事业，它就会影响人的时运，使之无法忠于自己的目标。我不明白军人为什么都多情好色，想来这与他们都贪杯好酒一样，因为冒险生涯通常都需要享乐作为报偿。

人之天性中潜藏着一种欲施爱于人的倾向，如果世人不只是将爱施于某人或某几个人，那爱自然而然就会普及众生，从而使人变得高尚仁慈，像有时候见到的某些修士一样。夫妻之爱使人类繁衍，朋友之爱使人类完善，但淫荡之爱则会使人类堕落。

解析

一、爱情的荒唐：

1. 为“伟人”所抵御；

2. 是一尊可鄙的偶像；

①据希腊罗马神话传说，天后赫拉、智慧女神雅典娜和爱与美之女神维纳斯互相争美，请特洛伊王子帕里斯替她们裁决，三女神分别以财富、智慧和天下最美之女人行贿，帕里斯偏袒维纳斯而得美女海伦，遂引起特洛伊战争。奥维德、荷马和维吉尔都写过这段传说。

3. 极大地歪曲和夸张了真相；

4. 剥夺了一个人赫拉与雅典娜的礼物(财富与智慧)。

二、关于爱情的评论：

1. 在人们软弱之际(即在鸿运高照或背运倒霉的时候)最为泛滥；

2. 如果有人不得不接受爱，应该将其摆在适当的位置；

3. 士兵的多情好色是他们在享乐中寻得的对冒险生涯的报偿；

4. 个人之爱应普及众生；

5. 有朋友之爱、夫妻之爱与淫荡之爱。

Of Love

THE stage is more beholding to love, than the life of man. For as to the stage, love is ever a matter of comedies, and now and then of tragedies; but in life it doth much mischief; sometimes like a siren, sometimes like a fury. You may observe, that amongst all the great and worthy persons (whereof the memory retaineth, either ancient or recent) there is not one, that hath been transported to the mad degree of love: which shows that great spirits, and great business, do keep out this weak passion. You must except, nevertheless, Marcus Antonius, the half partner of the empire of Rome, and Appius Claudius, the decemvir and lawgiver; whereof the former was indeed a voluptuous man, and inordinate; but the latter was an austere and wise man: and therefore it seems (though rarely) that love can find entrance, not only into an open heart, but also into a heart well fortified, if watch be not well kept. It is a poor saying of Epicurus, Satis magnum alter alteri theatrum sumus;[①] as if man, made for the contemplation of heaven, and all noble objects, should do nothing but kneel before a little idol, and make himself a subject, though not of the mouth (as beasts are), yet of the eye; which was given him for higher purposes. It is a strange thing, to note the excess of this passion, and how it braves the nature, and value of things, by this; that the speaking in a perpetual hyperbole, is comely in nothing but in love. Neither is it merely in the phrase; for whereas it hath been well said, that the arch-flatterer, with whom all the petty flatterers have intelligence, is a man's self; certainly the lover is more. For there was never proud man thought so absurdly well of

①We are a sufficient theatre for one another.

himself, as the lover doth of the person loved; and therefore it is well said, That it is impossible to love, and to be wise. Neither doth this weakness appear to others only, and not to the party loved; but to the loved most of all, except the love be reciproque. For it is a true rule, that love is ever rewarded, either with the reciproque, or with an inward and secret contempt. By how much the more, men ought to beware of this passion, which loseth not only other things, but itself! As for the other losses, the poet's relation doth well figure them: that he that preferred Helena, quitted the gifts of Juno and Pallas. For whosoever esteemeth too much of amorous affection, quitteth both riches and wisdom. This passion hath his floods, in very times of weakness; which are great prosperity, and great adversity; though this latter hath been less observed: both which times kindle love, and make it more fervent, and therefore show it to be the child of folly. They do best, who if they cannot but admit love, yet make it keep quarters; and sever it wholly from their serious affairs, and actions, of life; for if it check once with business, it troubleth men's fortunes, and maketh men, that they can no ways be true to their own ends. I know not how, but martial men are given to love: I think, it is but as they are given to wine; for perils commonly ask to be paid in pleasures.

There is in man's nature, a secret inclination and motion, towards love of others, which if it be not spent upon someone or a few, doth naturally spread itself towards many, and maketh men become humane and charitable; as is seen sometime in friars. Nuptial love maketh mankind; friendly love perfecteth it; but wanton love corrupteth, and embaseth it.

11.论高位

身居高位者可谓三重之奴仆：君王或国家的奴仆、公众舆论的奴仆、职权职责的奴仆；以致他们在人身、行动和时间上均无自由。追求权力而丧失自由，或曰求治人之权而失律己之力，这种欲望真匪夷所思。欲登高位须历尽艰辛，然世人偏愿吃苦头以求更大苦头；钻营有时不免失之卑劣，然世人偏以卑劣行径求得尊贵。居高位如履薄冰，而退路若非垮台，至少也是隐退，其结果都可叹可悲。有古人曾言：既已非当年盛时，还有何理由贪生。① 但此言差矣，居高位者往往是欲退时不能退，而到该退时则不愿退，甚至到年迈多病需要静养时亦不甘寂寞，犹如城中老翁仍临街倚门而坐，徒让老迈成为他人笑柄。无可否认，居高位者须借他人感观方觉自己快活，若自行判断则无切身体会。惟当念及他人对其所思、对其所慕，他们才会在某种程度上认为自己快活，虽说此时他们内心的感受也许恰好相反；因居高位者虽对自身过失最为木讷，但对自己的烦忧却最为敏感。毋庸置疑，官运亨通者大凡都不复自如，由于事务纠缠，他们甚至连自家身心健康也无暇顾及。恰如古人之叹：悲哉，世人皆知死者何人而独死者无自知！②

居高位者有权行善，亦有权作恶，然作恶总会留下祸根；故消灾弭祸之前提一是无作恶之念，二是无作恶之力。但行善之权则是谋权位者天经地义的目标，因善心虽蒙上帝嘉许，但若不付之于行，于人也无非只是场好梦，而要让善心变善举，就非要有权位作为有利依托。谋高位之目的在于建功立业，而自知功成名就乃安度余生之慰藉。如果人能分享上帝之所为，那他同样也能分享上帝之歇息。《圣经》有言道："上帝回顾所创万物，见一切

---

①语出西塞罗《致友人书简》第7卷。在公元前48年的法萨罗战役中，西塞罗支持的庞培被恺撒击败，西塞罗在政治上失意，此言即他当时的感叹。

②语出塞内加所著悲剧《提埃斯忒斯》第2幕。

无不美好。”[1]于是便有了安息日。

为官者上任之初，须以最佳楷模为师，因仿效就等于全套准则；稍后则可以己为典范，并严审当初所为是否无可非议。前任失误之处亦不可忽略，这并非是要揭他人之短以显自家之长，而是要找出前车之鉴以免重蹈覆辙。故有改良之举不宜大肆炫耀，亦不可贬责旧时和前任；但仍须坚持己为，不仅要循合理之成规，而且要创良好之先例。凡事均应追本溯源，以观其由盛及衰之原因；但同时仍须向古今二时讨教，问古时何事最佳，问今时何事最当。行事之道须力求有规律可循，以便众人可知其所期，但此道也不宜过分死板，而遇本人违背常规时应详陈原委。本位职权须悉心维护，但职权范围则无须过问，宁可不声不响地操纵实权，不要大张旗鼓地要求名分。下属之职权亦应加以维护，切记坐镇指挥比事必躬亲更显尊贵。若有人就分内事进言或提供帮助，应欣然接受并加以鼓励，勿将报信者作为好事者拒之门外，应当乐意接待他们。

当权者有四种主要的恶习，即拖沓、受贿、粗暴和抹不开情面。若要避免拖沓，则须保证衙门畅通，严守约定时刻，尽快完成已着手之公务，非万不得已不可兼理数事。若要避免受贿，不仅须约束自己和属下使之不受，而且须约束求情者使之不送；因形成惯例的廉洁可约束一方，而公开昭示的廉洁和对贿赂的厌恶则可约束另一方，此举既能免错，亦可消疑。当权者朝令夕改，且有明显改变而无明显原因，这极易招受贿之嫌，故每逢要改变主张或办法，务必明确表示，公开宣告，并同时解释改变的原因，切莫打算悄然行事。如有属员或亲信与当权者过从甚密，但却无其他应受器重的明显理由，那世人往往会疑之为秘密行贿的后门。至于粗暴，此乃一种毫无必要的招怨之因，如果说严厉使人生畏，那粗暴则招致怨恨。即便是责备下属，当权者亦应措辞庄重，切不可恶语痛斥。说到抹不开情面，这比受贿危害更大，因受贿不过是偶尔为之；但当权者若被人情关系牵着鼻子走，那他将永远也脱不了干系。正如所罗门言：“徇私情并非好心，因徇私情者会为一块面包而枉法。”[2]

---

①见《旧约·创世记》第1章31节。

②见《旧约·箴言》第28章21节。

有句古话所言极是：当官便露真相。高位使有些人显得更好，有些人显得更糟。塔西佗谈及伽尔巴时说："倘若他从不曾统治帝国，也许人人都会认为他适于统治。"[①]但他谈及韦斯帕芗时却说："当皇帝后而变得更好，韦斯帕芗乃唯一之人。"[②]不过塔西佗前句话是就治国之才而言，后句话则是就道德情操而论。登高位而德行愈增，此乃高洁之士的明显标志，因高位显职实则(或曰应该是)德行之所在。犹如自然界中，万物疾动而奔其所，一旦各就各位则静然处之，德行亦是如此，追求显职时则动，问鼎高位后则静。一切升迁腾达均须循小梯迂回而上，上升时若遇派系纷攘则不妨加入一派，然登顶后必须保持中立，无朋无党。追忆前任时应持论公允，言辞审慎，如若反其道而行之，那就将欠下一笔自己卸任后非还不可的旧账。若有同僚，应予以尊重，宁可在他们不想求见时召见他们，也不要在他们有事求见时将其拒之门外。在与人私下会谈和答复私人请求的时候，切莫时时想到或念念不忘自己的地位，最好让别人去说：此公为官和居家真是判若两人。

解析

一、身居高位的不幸：

1. 三重之奴仆；
2. 登高位者历尽艰辛、如履薄冰——之后或是垮台，或是隐退；
3. 它的奴役是永久的，人无法摆脱；
4. 须借他人感观方觉自己快活；
5. 提供更多行善或作恶的机会。

二、身居高位的告诫：

1. 学习的榜样，好坏皆需；
2. 实施改良须谨慎；
3. 凡事均应追本溯源，以观其由盛及衰之原因；

---

①见塔西佗《历史》第1卷49章。

②见塔西佗《历史》第1卷50章。

4. 行为要前后一致；

5. 维护自己的实权(不声不响地)与下属的职权；

6. 寻求与接纳他人的意见。

三、当权者的恶习及其补救的方法：

1. 拖沓：补救的方法——

(1) 衙门畅通；

(2) 守时；

(3) 不兼理数事。

2. 受贿：补救的方法——

(1) 约束求情者使之不送；

(2) 不可无明显原因地朝令夕改；

(3) 不用亲信。

3. 粗暴——一种不必要的招怨之因。

4. 抹不开情面——一个永久性的弊病。

四、结语：

1. 当官便露真相。高位使有些人显得更好，有些人显得更糟。
伽尔巴——韦斯帕芗

2. 上升时应加入一派。

3. 在私人事务上切莫念念不忘自己的地位。

Of Great Place

MEN in great place are thrice servants: servants of the sovereign or state; servants of fame; and servants of business. So as they have no freedom; neither in their persons, nor in their actions, nor in their times. It is a strange desire, to seek power and to lose liberty: or to seek power over others, and to lose power over a man's self. The rising unto place is laborious; and by pains, men come to greater pains; and it is sometimes base; and by indignities, men come to dignities. The standing is slippery, and the regress is either a downfall, or at least an eclipse, which is a melancholy thing. Cum non sis qui fueris, non esse cur velis vivere. ① Nay, retire men cannot when they would, neither will they, when it were reason; but are impatient of privateness, even in age and sickness, which require the shadow; like old townsmen, that will be still sitting at their street door, though thereby they offer age to scorn. Certainly great persons had need to borrow other men's opinions, to think themselves happy; for if they judge by their own feeling, they cannot find it; but if they think with themselves, what other men think of them, and that other men would fain be, as they are, then they are happy, as it were, by report; when perhaps they find the contrary within. For they are the first, that find their own griefs, though they be the last, that find their own faults. Certainly men in great fortunes are strangers to themselves, and while they are in the puzzle of business, they have no time to tend their health, either of mind or body. Illi mors gravis incubat, qui notus nimis omnibus, ignotus moritur sibi.②

In place, there is license to do good, and evil; whereof the latter is a curse: for in evil, the best condition is not to win; the second, not to can. But power to do good, is the true and lawful end of aspiring. For good thoughts (though God accept them) yet, towards men, are little better than good dreams, except they be put in act; and that cannot be, without power and place, as the vantage, and commanding ground. Merit and good works, is the end of a man's motion; and conscience of the same is the accomplishment of man's rest. For if a man can be partaker of God's theatre, he shall likewise be partaker of God's rest. Et conversus Deus, ut aspiceret opera quae fecerunt manus suae, vidit quod omnia essent bona nimis;③ and then the Sabbath.

In the discharge of thy place, set before thee the best examples; for imitation is a globe of precepts. And after a time, set before thee thine own example; and examine thyself strictly, whether thou didst not best at first. Neglect not also the examples, of those that have carried themselves ill, in the same place; not to set off thyself, by taxing their memory, but to direct thyself, what to avoid. Reform therefore, without bravery, or scandal of former times and persons; but yet set it down to thyself, as well to create good precedents, as to follow them. Reduce things to the first institution, and observe wherein, and how, they have degenerate; but yet ask counsel of both times; of the ancient

---

①When you are no longer what you were, there is no reason why you should wish to live.

②Death falls heavy on him, who dies too well known to all others but unknown to himself.

③And God turned to look at the works which His hands had done, and saw that they were all very good.

time, what is best; and of the latter time, what is fittest. Seek to make thy course regular, that men may know beforehand, what they may expect; but be not too positive and peremptory; and express thyself well, when thou digressest from thy rule. Preserve the right of thy place; but stir not questions of jurisdiction; and rather assume thy right, in silence and de facto①, than voice it with claims, and challenges. Preserve likewise the rights of inferior places; and think it more honor, to direct in chief, than to be busy in all. Embrace and invite helps, and advices, touching the execution of thy place; and do not drive away such, as bring thee information, as meddlers; but accept of them in good part.

The vices of authority are chiefly four: delays, corruption, roughness, and facility. For delays: give easy access; keep times appointed; go through with that which is in hand, and interlace not business, but of necessity. For corruption: do not only bind thine own hands, or thy servants' hands, from taking, but bind the hands of suitors also, from offering. For integrity used doth the one; but integrity professed, and with a manifest detestation of bribery, doth the other. And avoid not only the fault, but the suspicion. Whosoever is found variable, and changeth manifestly without manifest cause, giveth suspicion of corruption. Therefore always, when thou changest thine opinion or course, profess it plainly, and declare it, together with the reasons that move thee to change; and do not think to steal it. A servant or a favorite, if he be inward, and no other apparent cause of esteem, is commonly thought, but a by-way to close corruption. For roughness: it is a needless cause of discontent: severity breedeth fear, but roughness breedeth hate. Even reproofs from authority, ought to be grave, and not taunting. As for facility: it is worse than bribery. For bribes come but now and then; but if importunity, or idle respects, lead a man, he shall never be without. As Solomon saith, To respect persons is not good; for such a man will transgress for a piece of bread.

It is most true, that was anciently spoken, A place showeth the man. And it showeth some to the better, and some to the worse. Omnium consensu capax imperii, nisi imperasset,② saith Tacitus of Galba; but of Vespasian he saith, Solus imperantium, Vespasianus mutatus in melius;③ though the one was meant of sufficiency, the other of manners, and affection. It is an assured sign of a worthy and generous spirit, whom honor amends. For honor is, or should be, the place of virtue; and as in nature, things move violently to their place, and

---

①in fact

②By common consent fit for empire, if he had not been emperor.

③Vespasian was the only emperor who changed for the better.

calmly in their place, so virtue in ambition is violent, in authority settled and calm. All rising to great place is by a winding star; and if there be factions, it is good to side a man's self, whilst he is in the rising, and to balance himself when he is placed. Use the memory of thy predecessor, fairly and tenderly; for if thou dost not, it is a debt will sure be paid when thou art gone. If thou have colleagues, respect them, and rather call them, when they look not for it, than exclude them, when they have reason to look to be called. Be not too sensible, or too remembering, of thy place in conversation, and private answers to suitors; but let it rather be said, When he sits in place, he is another man.

12.说胆大

下文这则故事是段浅显的小学课文，但依然值得智者深思。故事讲有人问狄摩西尼：对演说家而言什么最重要？他回答说，动作。其次呢？——动作。再其次呢？——还是动作。[①]这说话人对他所言之事最为精通，而对他所力荐的动作并无天生的优势。[②]演说家的动作不过是外在表现，确切地说那只是演员的优点，可它居然被捧得那么高，甚至超过了题目选择和论辩方式等诸多重要的技能。不啻如此，它简直被说成了演说的唯一要素，仿佛它就是一切的一切，这听来真叫人觉得奇怪。然而这个中缘由非常清楚。因人之天性中通常是愚钝多于聪明，故能让愚钝者开窍的技能才最具效力。有种情况与上文所说有惊人的相似之处，这就是国家事务中的胆大妄为。对国事而言什么最重要？——胆大。其次呢？——胆大。再其次呢？——还是胆大。可这种胆大只是无知和无赖的产物，与治国之才压根儿不能相提并论，但尽管如此，它却能蛊惑并控制那些愚钝或怯懦的民众，而这些人占国民之最大部分，更有甚者，聪明人一时糊涂亦会受它引诱。所以我们看到，在缺乏元老院和王公贵族的民主国家，胆大已经创造出惊人的奇迹。我们也看到，胆大总是在胆大者行动之初见效，不久之后便功效全无，因为胆大从来不守信用。正如替人看病者有走方郎中，想必为国献策者也有江湖术士，这些人保证其良策会见奇效，而且有两三次试验也许已侥幸成功，但这种试验缺乏科学根据，所以终归不能持久。那些江湖术士也一样，只要他们的胆已大到能包天包地的程度，那即便他们保证要做成的大事遭到极其可耻的失败，他们也只会轻描淡写地嘀咕两句，然后干干脆脆地转身溜之大吉。

---

①西塞罗在其《论演说家》、普鲁塔克在其《十大演说家生平》中都记述了这段故事。

②这位演说家口含石子练发音的传说或许人人皆知，但少有人知道他还曾悬剑坠权于身边镜子规范自己的演讲动作。

毋庸置疑，在有见识的人看来，胆大妄为者只是一种可供消遣的笑柄，甚至在一般人眼中，胆大妄为亦有几分荒唐可笑，因为如果说荒唐应是嘲笑的对象，那切莫怀疑胆大包天也包有几分荒唐。胆大者感到难堪时尤其值得一看，因为此时他们的脸会缩成一团，就像木头雕成似的；一般人感到难堪时会稍稍搓手蹭足，可胆大者在这种场合却往往呆若木鸡，这就像棋局中王棋受困，虽然没被将死，但已无子可动。不过这场面更适宜写进讽刺文章，而不适宜写进一篇严肃评论。应该充分注意到，胆大往往盲目，因为它看不见麻烦和危险。由此可见，胆大于决策有害，但对执行决策有利，故此对胆大者必须知人善用，绝不可放手让他们统领全局，只能让他们受辖于人地充当副手，因为在运筹决策时须预见种种风险，而执行决策时则须对风险视而不见，除非那些风险人命关天。

解析

一、如同动作是演讲的全部，胆大也是国事的全部。

二、为什么胆大（无知与无赖的产物）如此有力？

1. 它能蛊惑并控制那些占国民大多数的愚钝民众；
2. 它往往能取得暂时性的成功（如走方郎中）；
3. 厚颜无耻有助于胆大，然厚颜无耻之人失败时的模样最为滑稽。

三、胆大的真正用处：它于决策有害，于执行决策有利。

Of Boldness

IT IS a trivial grammar-school text, but yet worthy a wise man's consideration. Question was asked of Demosthenes, what was the chief part of an orator? he answered, action; what next? action; what next again? action. He said it, that knew it best, and had, by nature, himself no advantage in that he commended. A strange thing, that that part of an orator, which is but superficial, and rather the virtue of a player, should be placed so high, above those other noble parts, of invention, elocution, and the rest; nay, almost alone, as if it were all in all. But the reason is plain. There is in human nature generally, more of the fool than of the wise; and therefore those faculties, by which the foolish part of men's minds is taken, are most potent. Wonderful like is the case of boldness in civil business: what first? boldness; what second and third? boldness. And yet boldness is a child of ignorance and baseness, far inferior to other parts. But nevertheless it doth fascinate, and bind hand and foot, those that are either shallow in judgment, or weak in courage, which are the greatest part; yea and prevaileth with wise men at weak times. Therefore we see it hath done wonders, in popular states; but with senates, and princes less; and more ever upon the first entrance of bold persons into action, than soon after; for boldness is an ill keeper of promise. Surely, as there are mountebanks for the natural body, so are there mountebanks for the politic body; men that undertake great cures, and perhaps have been lucky, in two or three experiments, but want the grounds of science, and therefore cannot hold out. So these men, when they have promised great matters, and failed most shamefully, yet (if they have the perfection of boldness) they will but slight it over, and make a turn, and no more ado. Certainly to men of great judgment, bold persons are a sport to behold; nay, and to the vulgar also, boldness has somewhat of the ridiculous. For if absurdity be the subject of laughter, doubt you not but great boldness is seldom without some absurdity. Especially it is a sport to see, when a bold fellow is out of countenance; for that puts his face into a most shrunken, and wooden posture; as needs it must; for in bashfulness, the spirits do a little go and come; but with bold men, upon like occasion, they stand at a stay; like a stale at chess, where it is no mate, but yet the game cannot stir. But this last were fitter for a satire than for a serious observation. This is well to be weighed; that boldness is ever blind; for it seeth not danger, and inconveniences. Therefore it is ill in counsel, good in execution; so that the right use of bold persons is, that they never command in chief, but be seconds, and under the direction of others. For in counsel, it is good to see dangers; and in execution, not to see them, except they be very great.

13.论善与性善

笔者以为善之真义乃造福于人的愿望,也就是古代希腊人所谓的仁爱之心,而用时下流行的"人道"一词来表示它还稍嫌不足。我称善为人之习性,而性善则为性格之倾向。在人类高尚美好的品性中,善乃至高至美,因为善是上帝的特性。倘若无善,人类将变得庸庸碌碌,有害无益,如虫豸蠹蛆之类。善与神学三德[①]中的博爱相符,也许会被误施,但永远不会过度。权欲之过度曾导致天使们堕落,[②]求知欲过度曾导致人类堕落,[③]但博爱却无过度之虞,天使和人类均不会因之而遭受危险。善心深深地根植于人性之中,以致善若不施于人类,也会施于其他生物,如同世人在土耳其所见那样。土耳其是个残暴的民族,可他们对禽兽却很仁慈,甚至为狗和鸟发放施舍物。据比斯贝克[④]记述,一名基督教青年在君士坦丁堡开玩笑时塞住了一只长喙鸟的嘴,结果差点儿被人用石头砸死。善心或博爱有时的确会被误施。意大利人有句令人不快的谚语:对谁都行善则无善可言。而意大利学者马基雅弗利则大胆地将这种看法诉诸笔墨,他几乎直截了当地写道:"基督教信仰已把善良的人们作为牺牲献给了那些专横无道的暴君。"[⑤]他之所以这么说,是因为与基督教相比,确实从不曾有过任何律法、教派或信仰如此劝人从善。因此,要避免上述诋毁和危险,就应该懂得如何才能不误施善

①即基督教徒应具之三德:信仰、希望、博爱;或曰:有信,有望,有爱。

②指撒旦及其同伙欲篡上帝之位未遂而被罚入地狱一事。参见弥尔顿《失乐园》第 1 卷 27—81 行。

③指夏娃携亚当偷吃智慧树禁果而被逐出伊甸园一事。参见《旧约·创世记》第 3 章。

④比斯贝克 (Ghislain de Busbecq,1522—1592),佛兰芒学者,曾作为神圣罗马帝国皇帝斐迪南一世的特使驻君士坦丁堡。

⑤马基雅弗利即《君主论》(又译《霸术》)一书的作者。此处引言出自他的《论李维》,不过培根似乎是断章取义,因为马氏在这段话后接着说:"这种看法是错误的……"

心。必须追求为他人造福，但不可被他人的厚颜和妄想所支配，因为那样只会是讨好或软弱，而讨好和软弱会让诚实的人作茧自缚。也不要把宝石给伊索那只公鸡，因为它大概更高兴得到一把麦粒。上帝创下的先例便是最正确的榜样：他让阳光照好人，也照坏人；他降雨给善人，也给恶人。[①]但他从不把财富、荣耀和德行平均地施与芸芸众生，因一般的恩惠应该人人分享，但特殊的恩惠则须有所选择。而且世人须当心，别在画肖像时把原型给毁了，因为上帝要世人以爱己为原型，而爱他则只是照着这原型画像。耶稣说："卖掉你所有的财产，把钱捐给穷人，然后来跟随我。"[②]但除非你真要跟耶稣去，或者说除非你真得到神召，使你用其微薄的财产也能像用万贯家财一样行善于天下，那你最好还是别卖掉你所有的财产，不然你就是在竭泉注川。这世上不仅有受真理引导的善性，而且有些人天生就具有从善的倾向；可另一方面，人世间亦有一种天生的恶性，因为有些人生来就不具为他人造福的愿望。恶性较轻者只是性格暴躁、鲁莽、好斗和固执等等，但恶性较重者则会妒忌并伤害他人。这种人好像是专以他人的痛苦和不幸为乐，因而总爱落井下石。他们甚至不如替拉撒路舐疮的那些狗[③]，而只像那种一见伤口就围上去嗡嗡叫的苍蝇。这种"憎恨人类者"把引人上吊当成职业，可他们连泰门也不如，[④]因为他们的花园里连一棵供人上吊的树也没有。这种恶性是极大的人性之误，但却是造就高官大员的最佳材料，正如弯曲的木材适宜造须颠簸于风浪的船舶，而不适宜造须岿然不动的房屋。善具有诸多要素和特征。要是某人对外邦人谦恭有礼，那说明他是个四海为家者，他的心不是一座与世隔绝的孤岛，而是与其相连的一片大陆。如果他对别人的苦难会产生同情，那说明他的心就像那种高贵的树，宁可自己受伤也要奉出香膏。倘若他对别人的冒犯能宽容不究，那说明他的心远在伤害之上，因此他不可能受到伤害。假使他对滴水之恩能涌泉相报，那说明他看重人的精神而不看重他们的钱财。但最重要的是，如果他能像圣保罗那

①见《新约·马太福音》第5章45节。

②见《新约·马可福音》第10章21节。

③参见《新约·路加福音》第16章21节。

④因泰门公开宣称他愿提供一棵树供走投无路者上吊。参见莎士比亚戏剧《雅典的泰门》。

样完美，能为拯救自己的兄弟们而甘愿被逐离基督，[①]那就充分说明他已经具有一种神性，与基督本人已有了一种共同之处。

解析

一、善之真义：它与性善、人道、仁爱与慈善的关系。

二、善之本性：

1. 会被误施，但不会过度；
2. 根植于人性之中，若不施于人类，也会施于其他动物。

三、对行善的忠告：

1. 追求真正为他人造福——而非被他人或自己的妄想所支配；
2. 让你的善行真正有益于你想帮助的人；
3. 不要忽视优先于善行的义务。

四、善的对立面是恶：

1. 恶性较轻者（鲁莽、固执等等）；
2. 恶性较重者（嫉妒、中伤），如厌世者泰门之所为。

五、善的要素与特征：

1. 谦恭有礼表明博大的情怀；
2. 同情心表明高贵的情怀；
3. 宽容让人的性情游离于伤害；
4. 报恩表明对人的精神的看重；
5. 自我牺牲则显示一种神性。

Of Goodness & Goodness of Nature

I TAKE goodness in this sense, the affecting of the weal of men, which is

①保罗在《新约·罗马书》第 9 章3 节中说："为了我的兄弟，我的骨肉之亲，就是自己被诅咒，与基督分离，我也愿意。"

that the Grecians call philanthropia; and the word humanity (as it is used) is a little too light to express it. Goodness I call the habit, and goodness of nature, the inclination. This of all virtues, and dignities of the mind, is the greatest; being the character of the Deity: and without it, man is a busy, mischievous, wretched thing; no better than a kind of vermin. Goodness answers to the theological virtue, charity, and admits no excess, but error. The desire of power in excess, caused the angels to fall; the desire of knowledge in excess, caused man to fall: but in charity there is no excess; neither can angel, nor man, come in danger by it. The inclination to goodness, is imprinted deeply in the nature of man; insomuch, that if it issue not towards men, it will take unto other living creatures; as it is seen in the Turks, a cruel people, who nevertheless are kind to beasts, and give alms, to dogs and birds; insomuch, as Busbechius reporteth, a Christian boy, in Constantinople, had like to have been stoned, for gagging in a waggishness a long-billed fowl. Errors indeed in this virtue of goodness, or charity, may be committed. The Italians have an ungracious proverb, Tanto buon che val niente: so good, that he is good for nothing. And one of the doctors of Italy, Nicholas Machiavel, had the confidence to put in writing, almost in plain terms, That the Christian faith, had given up good men, in prey to those that are tyrannical and unjust. Which he spake, because indeed there was never law, or sect, or opinion, did so much magnify goodness, as the Christian religion doth. Therefore, to avoid the scandal and the danger both, it is good, to take knowledge of the errors of an habit so excellent. Seek the good of other men, but be not in bondage to their faces or fancies; for that is but facility, or softness; which taketh an honest mind prisoner. Neither give thou Aesop's cock a gem, who would be better pleased, and happier, if he had had a barley-corn. The example of God, teacheth the lesson truly: He sendeth his rain, and maketh his sun to shine, upon the just and unjust; but he doth not rain wealth, nor shine honor and virtues, upon men equally. Common benefits, are to be communicate with all; but peculiar benefits, with choice. And beware how in making the portraiture, thou breakest the pattern. For divinity, maketh the love of ourselves the pattern; the love of our neighbors, but the portraiture. Sell all thou hast, and give it to the poor, and follow me: but, sell not all thou hast, except thou come and follow me; that is, except thou have a vocation, wherein thou mayest do as much good, with little means as with great; for otherwise, in feeding the streams, thou driest the fountain. Neither is there only a habit of goodness, directed by right reason; but there is in some men, even in nature, a disposition towards it; as on the other side, there is a natural malignity. For there be, that in their nature do not affect the good of others. The lighter sort of malignity, turneth but to a crassness, or frowardness, or aptness to oppose, or difficulties, or the like; but the deeper sort, to envy and mere mischief. Such men, in other men's calamities, are, as it were, in season, and are ever on the loading part: not so good as the dogs, that licked Lazarus' sores; but like flies, that are still buzzing upon anything that is raw; misanthropi, that make it their practice, to bring men to the bough, and yet never a tree for the purpose in their gardens, as Timon had. Such dispositions, are the very errors of human nature; and yet they are the fittest timber, to make great politics of; like to knee timber, that is good for ships, that are ordained to be tossed; but not for building houses, that shall stand firm. The parts and signs of goodness, are many. If a man be gracious and courteous to strangers, it shows he is a citizen of the world, and that his heart is no island, cut off from other lands, but a continent, that joins to them. If he be compassionate towards the afflictions of others, it shows that his heart is like the noble tree, that is wounded itself, when it gives the balm. If he easily pardons, and remits offences, it shows that his mind is planted above injuries; so that he cannot be shot. If he be thankful for small benefits, it shows that he weighs men's minds, and not their trash. But above all, if he have St. Paul's perfection, that he would wish to be anathema from Christ, for the salvation of his brethren, it shows much of a divine nature, and a kind of conformity with Christ himself.

14.谈贵族

论及贵族，笔者将首先谈其作为国家的一个阶层，然后再谈其作为一种个人身份。就君主国家而言，若国内完全没有贵族，那它就会像土耳其一样始终是个专制国家；因为贵族可削弱君权，可在一定程度上把公众的注意力从王室引开。但以民主国家而论，它们则不需要贵族，与有贵族豪门的君主国家相比，民主国家通常更为安宁而少有叛乱；因为民主国家的人注重职责而不注重个人，或即便说他们注重个人，那也是为了职责的缘故，是要看个人是否堪当其职，而不是要看他的门第血统。我们可见瑞士国运昌盛，尽管那里有宗教歧异和州邦差别，但维系联邦的纽带是共同利益而非豪门望族。尼德兰联省共和国[①]政府治国有方，因为那里有一种平等制度，所以他们的磋商会议较不偏不倚，各省纳税付捐也较欣然。一个强有力的贵族阶层可增加君主的威严，但同时亦会削弱君主的权力；贵族可为国民注入活力与生机，但同时亦会降低国民的身份。较为理想的情况是，贵族阶层不至于强大到凌驾于君权和国法之上，但又保持一定的高位，这样下民的犯上作乱就得先与贵族碰撞，而不会过早地触及君主的权威。贵族人众会导致一国之贫困，因为贵族的花销是一笔额外的负担。此外随着时间的推移，许多贵族豪门必然家道中落，这便会造成一种尊号与财富不相称的情况。

接下来且谈作为个人身份的贵族。当看见一座尚未破败的古堡或古宅，或是看见一棵依然枝繁叶茂的参天古树，谁都免不了会肃然起敬；而当目睹一个曾历经岁月沧桑的贵族世家，这种恭敬之情当然会更深更甚！因为新封的贵族不过是权力所致，但古老的贵族却是时间造就。贵族世家的

①又称荷兰共和国，尼德兰北方七省在尼德兰资产阶级革命后脱离宗主国西班牙而建立的世界上第一个资产阶级共和国。

第一代祖先往往比他们的子孙更有才干,但却不如子孙们清白;因为少有追逐高位者不在其雄图大略中杂以阴谋诡计。不过后人只记得祖先的长处,他们的短处早已随其死亡一道消失,这也可谓天经地义。生为贵族者大凡都不勤勉,而自身不勤勉者往往会嫉妒勤勉之人;并且既生为贵族就不大可能再高升,而固守旧位者见别人腾达难免不生妒忌之情。但另一方面,世袭贵族可消除他人对其潜在的嫉妒,因为他们天生就拥有那份尊荣。毋庸置疑,拥有贵族中之能人的君王应该发现,他可以得心应手地利用这些贵族精英,而且他们也能轻松自如地各司其职,因为国民会认为这些人天生就有权发号施令,从而会自然而然地服从他们。

解析

一、贵族作为一个阶层:

1. 它的好处——

(1) 削弱君权;

(2) 让国家更安宁、更有威信。

民主国家安宁且满足的原因:

(a) 共同的利益(瑞士);

(b) 公正(荷兰)。

2. 它的坏处——

(1) 会过于强大而影响司法;

(2) 导致贫困。

二、个人身份的贵族:

1. 一个古老的贵族值得尊敬。

2. 贵族在其子孙身上形成美德,尽管早期贵族身份的获得也许是通过犯罪。

3. 促生嫉妒之情——

(1) 不勤勉;

(2) 他人的腾达。

4. 让贵族少遭嫉妒。

5. 国民自然而然服从出身高贵者。

Of Nobility

WE WILL speak of nobility, first as a portion of an estate, then as a condition of particular persons. A monarchy, where there is no nobility at all, is ever a pure and absolute tyranny; as that of the Turks. For nobility attempers sovereignty, and draws the eyes of the people, somewhat aside from the line royal. But for democracies, they need it not; and they are commonly more quiet, and less subject to sedition, than where there are stirps of nobles. For men's eyes are upon the business, and not upon the persons; or if upon the persons, it is for the business' sake, as fittest, and not for flags and pedigree. We see the Switzers last well, notwithstanding their diversity of religion, and of cantons. For utility is their bond, and not respects. The united provinces of the Low Countries, in their government, excel; for where there is an equality, the consultations are more indifferent, and the payments and tributes, more cheerful. A great and potent nobility, addeth majesty to a monarch, but diminisheth power; and putteth life and spirit into the people, but presseth their fortune. It is well, when nobles are not too great for sovereignty nor for justice; and yet maintained in that height, as the insolency of inferiors may be broken upon them, before it come on too fast upon the majesty of kings. A numerous nobility causeth poverty, and inconvenience in a state; for it is a surcharge of expense; and besides, it being of necessity, that many of the nobility fall, in time, to be weak in fortune, it maketh a kind of disproportion, between honor and means.

As for nobility in particular persons; it is a reverend thing, to see an ancient castle or building, not in decay; or to see a fair timber tree, sound and perfect. How much more, to behold an ancient noble family, which has stood against the waves and weathers of time! For new nobility is but the act of power, but ancient nobility is the act of time. Those that are first raised to nobility, are commonly more virtuous, but less innocent, than their descendants; for there is rarely any rising, but by a commixture of good and evil arts. But it is reason, the memory of their virtues remain to their posterity, and their faults die with themselves. Nobility of birth commonly abateth industry; and he that is not industrious, envieth him that is. Besides, noble persons cannot go much higher; and he that standeth at a stay, when others rise, can hardly avoid motions of envy. On the other side, nobility extinguisheth the passive envy from others, towards them; because they are in possession of honor. Certainly, kings that have able men of their nobility, shall find ease in employing them, and a better slide into their business; for people naturally bend to them, as born in some sort to command.

15.论叛乱与骚动

国民之保护者须知国内风云变幻之迹象，而这种变幻通常在各种力量形成均势时最为急剧。一如自然界之风暴在春分前后最猛烈，又如暴风雨之前谷间有阵风海里有潜潮，国家的风云气候亦有种种征兆：太阳时时告诫我们有秘密暴动的威胁，阴谋叛逆和隐藏的战争正在酝酿。[①]对政府的恶意中伤、对内阁的肆意诽谤，以及与之类似的不利于国家的谣言传闻，全都属于动乱的前兆，尤其在诽谤中伤频繁并公开之际，当谣言传闻不胫而走并被广为相信之时。维吉尔在叙述"谣言女神"的家世时说她是提坦众巨神的妹妹：大地之母在对诸神的愤怒中将她生下，她是科俄斯和恩刻拉多斯最小的妹妹。[②]

如此说来，谣言似乎是从前神祇叛乱的遗物，然而它的的确确又是未来叛乱之前奏。但不管怎么说，维吉尔正确地指出了一点，即举行叛乱和以谣言煽动叛乱的差别不过就像兄妹之间或男女之间的差别。尤其当谣言导致严重后果时，这种差别更加细微，如当政府最值得称道并最该赢得民心之最佳举措因谣言而被曲解被诽谤之时；因为它引导了极大的怨愤，而正如塔西佗所说："当对政府的厌恶之情弥散时，政府的行为无论好坏都会激怒民众。" 但别以为既然谣言是动乱的征兆，那对其严加查禁便可防止动乱，其实到处去辟谣只会引起公众久久不消的疑惑，而对其置之不理往往是制止谣言的最佳手段。除此之外，对塔西佗曾言及的那种"忠顺"也须有所察觉，他说："某些人食国家俸禄，但对上司的命令却乐于非议而不乐于执行。"可对于命令和指示，无论是争长论短、吹毛求疵还是借故推诿，都是

---

①引自维吉尔《农事诗》第1卷464—465行。

②引自维吉尔《埃涅阿斯纪》第4卷178—180行。培根引此诗似乎是以大地之母喻民众，以奥林匹斯山诸神喻统治者，以提坦（又译泰坦）神喻叛乱者。

一种不服管辖和违令抗命的尝试，若遇下述情况则更是如此，即在此类争论中，赞成服从者说话战战兢兢，反对服从者说话则肆无忌惮。

另外，正如马基雅弗利所指出的那样，本应为万民之父母的君主自成一党或偏向一方的时候，也就是他们将像载重不平衡的船舶倾覆之时。此例最早见于法兰西国王亨利三世时代，起初国王为根除新教而偏向天主教同盟，但不久之后该同盟就反过来要根除国王本人；因君王的权威若是仅仅被作为某个事业起装饰作用的纽带，那当有比君权更结实的纽带出现时，君王差不多就该被逐出该事业了。

再者，明目张胆的党同伐异和勾心斗角亦是政府失去威望的信号，因若用古典天文学理论[①]来作比喻，政府要员的行为就该像第十重天下天体之运动，即每一天体受第一运动支配的公转应迅疾，而本身的自转则应和缓；故若是大臣要员们自行其是时行动迅疾，或像塔西佗所言“其行动之自由与尊君之道不符”，那就说明这些“天体”已偏离常轨。君王的尊严乃上帝赋予，因此只有上帝可威胁要取消这种尊严，比如说“我要解开列王的腰带”[②]。

如上所言，当政府的四大支柱(宗教、法律、议会和财政)中之任何一柱遭猛烈动摇或严重削弱之时，人们亦须祈祷风平浪静。关于动乱之先兆就暂谈于此(不过读者从后文中还可对其有进一步的了解)，现在且让笔者依序来谈谈叛乱之要素、叛乱之动机，以及防止叛乱的方法。

叛乱之要素值得认真注意，因为(要是时间允许的话)防止叛乱最稳妥的措施就是消除这种要素。须知只要有备好的柴薪，就很难预测何时有火星会将其引燃。叛乱的要素有二：一是贫者甚众，一是不满甚广。毋庸置疑，破产的业主越多，赞成叛乱的人也越多。卢坎对罗马内战前的状况描写得恰如其分：“于是有了吃人的高利贷和贪婪的重利，于是将有信誉危机和对众人有利的战争。”[③]这种“对众人有利的战争”便是国家将有叛乱和暴动的

①指“地球中心说”，据古希腊天文学家托勒密的《大综合论》所述，静止不动的地球乃宇宙之中心，中心外有十重天，每重天下有若干天体围绕地球旋转，其动力来自被称为第十重天的第一运动。

②参见《旧约·以赛亚书》第 45 章 1 节。

③引自罗马诗人卢坎 (39—65) 所著史诗《内战记》第 1 卷 181—182 行。

明确无误的征兆。而若是有产可破者之贫困与贱民的缺衣少食连在一起，那么危险就已迫在眉睫并将致命，因为为填饱肚子而举行的叛乱最难戡平。至于不满，政府内部的不满情绪和人心中的抑郁不平一样，都容易积成一种异常的愤怒喷发而出。为人君者不可凭民怨是否合理来衡量其危险，因那样就把民众想得太理智了，其实他们连自己的好东西也经常摒弃。君王亦不可凭产生不满的痛苦大小来估量危险，因为在最危险的不满情绪中恐惧的成分往往大于痛苦，而“痛苦是有限的，但恐惧无限”[①]。再说迫于高压，使人产生忍耐力的痛苦也会使人丧失勇气，但对恐惧来说则不然。作为君王或政府，切不可因为屡见不鲜或由来已久的不满并未导致险情而对其掉以轻心，因为虽说并非每一团乌云都会化为暴雨，而且乌云有时候也会被风吹散，但暴雨始终有降下的可能。有句西班牙谚语说得好：绳子终究会被轻轻地一拉扯断。

叛乱的原因和动机通常有：宗教之改革、赋税之增减、法律之更新、惯例之变易、特权之废除、压迫之普遍、小人之重用、异族之入侵、供应之不足、兵士之遣散、内讧之激化，以及任何会激怒国民并使其为一共同目标而抱成团的事件。

说到防止叛乱的方法，笔者将讨论一些常规对策。至于具体措施，那得视具体事态对症下药，故应留待临时定夺而不作为通例。

第一种方法，或曰预防措施，就是尽可能消除上文谈及的第一个致乱要素，即消除国内的贫困。欲达此目的可采取以下步骤：开放并平衡贸易，保护合法厂商，消除游手好闲，禁止铺张浪费，改良并耕耘土地，控制市场物价，以及减轻捐税贡赋等等。一般说来，须注意别让一国之人口超过该国可供养他们的财富(在该国人口未因战争锐减时尤须注意)。考虑人口不可仅凭数量，因为少数消费大于其积累者比多数积累大于其消费者能更快地使国家财富消耗殆尽。由此可见，若贵族和官吏的增长超过了与平民人口的合理比例，那国家很快就会陷入贫困。神职人员的过度增长也有害无益，因为他们并不为国家创造财富。培养的学者人数超过任用他们的职位亦属此类情况。

---

①语出小普林尼《书信集》第 8 卷。

同时也须牢记，鉴于任何国家的财富增长均须依赖别国(因本国的财富总是此得彼失)，又鉴于一国可向外输出的东西只有三种，即天然物产、工业产品和商务运输，所以只有这三个轮子正常运转，财富方会像春潮般滚滚而来。[①]而且往往会出现“劳作胜于物产”[②]的情况，即劳作和运输比物产更值钱，更能为国家增加财富，如荷兰人就是明显的例证，他们拥有世界上最好的地上矿藏。

最重要之步骤是采用良策以保证国家的财富不致被聚敛到少数人手中，不然就会出现国富民穷的局面。财富犹如肥料，不广施于田就毫无效益。要使财富合理分配，就须严令禁止或至少着手整治高利盘剥、垄断商品和毁田畜牧[③]等唯利是图的交易。

至于如何消除不满情绪，或至少消除不满情绪中之危险成分，我们知道，各国都有两类臣民，即贵族和平民。当这二者之一心怀不满时其危险并不可怕，因为平民若无贵族煽动往往不会轻易作乱，而贵族若得不到平民的支持则力量不足。真正的危险在于贵族们恰好等到平民的不满情绪爆发时才表明他们自己的不满。诗人们讲过这样一段故事，说有一次众神想缚住主神朱庇特，这一密谋被朱庇特闻知，于是他听从帕拉斯的建议，召来百臂巨人布里阿柔斯相助。这段故事无疑可作为一则寓言，说明为君王者若能确得民心是何等安然无虞。

适当给予民众发泄其悲愤不满的自由，这也不失为一种防乱措施(只要这种发泄别过于肆无忌惮)；因为若让人把怨气往肚里吞，或是把脓血捂起来，那就会有积郁成疾或恶性脓肿的危险。

在消除不满的事例中，埃庇米修斯之所为很可能适合于普罗米修斯，因为再没有比那更好的方法可消除不满。当各种痛苦和邪恶飞出箱子之时，埃庇米修斯终于盖上了箱盖，从而把“希望”留在了箱底。毫无疑问，能巧妙地孕育并怀有希望，且能引导民众从一个希望到另一个希望，此乃治

①此段论述之根据乃资本主义初级阶段的重商主义(或曰重金主义)，这种学说认为只有金银货币才是一国之真正财富，而只有外贸出超和顺差方可使金银流入本国。

②语出奥维德《变形记》第2章5节。

③指英国始于15世纪的“圈地运动”。当时羊毛价格上涨，养羊有利可图，于是贵族大规模强占公地和农民的耕地以建牧场。

疗不满这种流毒的最佳良药。一个明智政府的明智之举无疑该是：当其没法用令人满意的手段赢得民心时，仍能凭各种希望使民心所向；当某种天灾人祸出现时，仍能泰然处之，仿佛灾祸并非不可避免，而是还有某种避免的希望。这后一点做起来不太难，因为不管是个人或党派都容易为还有希望而暗自庆幸，或至少容易装出不相信大祸临头的样子。

此外还有一种虽众所周知但仍不失为上策的预防措施，即预见并提防某些适合心怀不满者向其求助并在其麾下麇聚的领头人物。余以为能充当这种为首者的人大凡都拥有伟绩和声望，深受不满现政的党派之信任和尊崇，同时他们自己也被认为对现政心怀不满。对这种领头人物，政府要么用切实可行的方法对其加以争取并使之归顺，要么就使其同党中有另一领头人物与之对立以分割其声望。概而言之，对各类反政府的党派集团实行分化瓦解，调弄离间，或至少使其内部互相猜疑，这并非一种最糟的手段，因若是拥护政府者内部四分五裂，而反对政府者内部却万众一心，那将是极危险的情况。

笔者注意到有些出自帝王之口的趣言妙语曾引起叛乱。恺撒曾戏言："苏拉非才子，故不会独裁。"[①]结果为他招来杀身之祸，因为此言使那些以为他迟早会放弃独裁的贵族元老们彻底失望。伽尔巴则因其口头禅"只征募士兵但不收买士兵"而毁了自己，因为他的话使想得到赏赐的士兵们失去了希望。普罗巴斯[②]也同样因言罹祸，他说"只要我在世，罗马帝国就不再需要士兵"，这话令他的士兵们感到绝望。此类祸从口出之例，不胜枚举。因此在事态微妙或时势不稳之际，为君者务必出言谨慎，说只言片语时尤须当心，因这类短句会像箭矢一般不胫而走，且往往被视为君王吐露的心声；反之长篇大论倒会因其单调而不甚受人注意。

最后一点，为了防止不测，君王身边应有一名或若干名骁勇大将，以备把叛乱镇压于起事之初；否则骚乱一起朝中便更会惊慌失措，政府便会面

①罗马独裁者苏拉自行隐退的原因历来众说纷纭。其中一说认为那是他利用独裁手段恢复贵族共和制后还政于民的义举，故恺撒时代的共和派贵族元老也曾抱有恺撒将放弃独裁的希望。另恺撒这句戏言之妙处在于拉丁文 dictare 兼有"口授文章"和"独裁"二义，并非真说苏拉无才。

②普罗巴斯，古罗马皇帝（在位期 276—282），为叛军所杀。

临塔西佗曾说过的那种危险，即叛乱之初人们的心态是：“真敢为祸首者寡，但乐意参加者众，而所有人对叛乱都会默认。”[①]但这种猛将须是忠实可靠且名声良好之辈，而非好拉帮结派并哗众取宠之流；他们还须和政府中其他要员保持一致，不然这种治病良药将会比疾病本身更要命。

解析

一、叛乱之征兆（同暴风雨的征兆类似）：

1. 谣言与诽谤——置之不理为最佳处理方法；

2. 命令执行前的非议；

3. 君主自成一党或偏向一方；

4. 明目张胆的党同伐异与勾心斗角。

总之，一切动摇政府四大支柱（宗教、法律、议会与财政）的东西。

二、叛乱之要素：

1. 贫穷——形成对战争的渴望；

2. 不满——没有君王或国家可以对此高枕无忧。

三、叛乱之原因与动机：宗教之改革、赋税之增减、压迫之普遍、小人之重用、异族之入侵，以及供应之不足等等。

四、防止叛乱之方法：

1. 消除贫困的方法：

（1）制定律法开放贸易、保护合法厂商、禁止铺张浪费等；

（2）控制贵族人数的过分膨胀；

（3）不伤害对外贸易；

（4）保证国家财富不被聚敛在少数人手中。

2. 消除不满的方法：

（1）安抚平民；

（2）适当给予发泄悲愤不满的自由；

①此言描述的是奥托宣布要推翻伽尔巴时士兵们的心态，见塔西佗《历史》第1卷28章。

(3) 提供对未来的希望而非暂时性的满足;

(4) 让党派集团无领头人物,内部不团结;

(5) 为君者须出言谨慎;

(6) 军队领袖的帮助。

Of Seditions and Troubles

SHEPHERDS of people, had need know the calendars of tempests in state; which are commonly greatest, when things grow to equality; as natural tempests are greatest about the Equinoctia. And as there are certain hollow blasts of wind, and secret swellings of seas before a tempest, so are there in states: —Ille etiam caecos instare tumultus Saepe monet, fraudesque et operta tunescere bella.① Libels and licentious discourses against the state, when they are frequent and open; and in like sort, false news often running up and down, to the disadvantage of the state, and hastily embraced; are amongst the signs of troubles. Virgil, giving the pedigree of Fame, saith, she was sister to the Giants: Illam Terra parens, ira irritata deorum, Extremam (ut perhibent) Coeo Enceladoque sororem Progenuit.②

As if fames were the relics of seditions past; but they are no less, indeed, the preludes of seditions to come. Howsoever he noteth it right, that seditious tumults, and seditious fames, differ no more but as brother and sister, masculine and feminine; especially if it come to that, that the best actions of a state, and the most plausible, and which ought to give greatest contentment, are taken in ill sense, and traduced: for that shows the envy great, as Tacitus saith; conflata magna invidia, seu bene seu male gesta premunt.③ Neither doth it follow, that because these fames are a sign of troubles, that the suppressing of them with too much severity, should be a remedy of troubles. For the despising of them, many times checks them best; and the going about to stop them, doth but make a wonder long-lived. Also that kind of obedience, which

①He often warns men also that cloaked rebellions are at hand, and the treachery and war unseen are swelling to a head.

② Earth her mother, goaded by anger against the gods, bore her, so they tell, the youngest sister to Coeus and Enceladus.

③When great discontentment is kindled, all his actions good or bad tend to his ruin.

Tacitus speaketh of, is to be held suspected: Erant in officio, sed tamen qui mallent mandata imperantium interpretari quam exequi;① disputing, excusing, cavilling upon mandates and directions, is a kind of shaking off the yoke, and assay of disobedience; especially if in those disputings, they which are for the direction, speak fearfully and tenderly, and those that are against it, audaciously.

Also, as Machiavel noteth well, when princes, that ought to be common parents, make themselves as a party, and lean to a side, it is as a boat, that is overthrown by uneven weight on the one side; as was well seen, in the time of Henry the Third of France; for first, himself entered league for the extirpation of the Protestants; and presently after, the same league was turned upon himself. For when the authority of princes, is made but an accessory to a cause, and that there be other bands, that tie faster than the band of sovereignty, kings begin to be put almost out of possession.

Also, when discords, and quarrels, and factions are carried openly and audaciously, it is a sign the reverence of government is lost. For the motions of the greatest persons in a government, ought to be as the motions of the planets under primum mobile; according to the old opinion: which is, that every of them, is carried swiftly by the highest motion, and softly in their own motion. And therefore, when great ones in their own particular motion, move violently, and, as Tacitus expresseth it well, liberius quam ut imperantium meminissent②; it is a sign the orbs are out of frame. For reverence is that, wherewith princes are girt from God; who threateneth the dissolving thereof; Solvam cingula regum.③

So when any of the four pillars of government, are mainly shaken, or weakened (which are religion, justice, counsel, and treasure), men had need to pray for fair weather. But let us pass from this part of predictions (concerning which, nevertheless, more light may be taken from that which followeth); and let us speak first, of the materials of seditions; then of the motives of them; and thirdly of the remedies.

Concerning the materials of seditions. It is a thing well to be considered; for the surest way to prevent seditions (if the times do bear it) is to take away the matter of them. For if there be fuel prepared, it is hard to tell, whence the spark shall come, that shall set it on fire. The matter of seditions is of two

①They were alternative, but at the same time inclined rather to discuss the meaning of their officers' orders than to obey them.

②too freely to remember their rulers

③I will lose the girdles of Kings.

kinds: much poverty, and much discontentment. It is certain, so many overthrown estates, so many votes for troubles. Lucan noteth well the state of Rome before the Civil War, Hinc usura vorax, rapidumque in tempore foenus, Hinc concussa fides, et multis utile bellum.① This same multis utile bellum②, is an assured and infallible sign, of a state disposed to seditions and troubles. And if this poverty and broken estate in the better sort, be joined with a want and necessity in the mean people, the danger is imminent and great. For the rebellions of the belly are the worst. As for discontentments, they are, in the politic body, like the humors in the natural, which are apt to gather a preternatural heat, and to inflame. And let no prince measure the danger of them by this, whether they be just or unjust: for that were to imagine people, to be too reasonable; who do often spurn at their own good: nor yet by this, whether the griefs whereupon they rise, be in fact great or small: for they are the most dangerous discontentments, where the fear is greater than the feeling. Dolendi modus, timendi non item. ③ Besides, in great oppressions, the same things that provoke the patience, do withal mate the courage; but in fears it is not so. Neither let any prince, or state, be secure concerning discontentments, because they have been often, or have been long, and yet no peril hath ensued: for as it is true, that every vapor or fume doth not turn into a storm; so it is nevertheless true, that storms, though they blow over divers times, yet may fall at last; and, as the Spanish proverb noteth well, The cord breaketh at the last by the weakest pull.

The causes and motives of seditions are, innovation in religion; taxes; alteration of laws and customs; breaking of privileges; general oppression; advancement of unworthy persons; strangers; dearths; disbanded soldiers; factions grown desperate; and whatsoever, in offending people, joineth and knitteth them in a common cause.

For the remedies; there may be some general preservatives, whereof we will speak: as for the just cure, it must answer to the particular disease; and so be left to counsel, rather than rule.

The first remedy or prevention is to remove, by all means possible, that material cause of sedition whereof we spake; which is, want and poverty in the estate. To which purpose serveth the opening, and well-balancing of trade; the cherishing of manufactures; the banishing of idleness; the repressing of

①Hence came insatiate usury and interest quickly falling due, hence shaken credit, and war that benefited many.

②war that benefited many

③There is a limit to pain, but none to fear.

waste, and excess, by sumptuary laws; the improvement and husbanding of the soil; the regulating of prices of things vendible; the moderating of taxes and tributes; and the like. Generally, it is to be foreseen that the population of a kingdom (especially if it be not mown down by wars) do not exceed the stock of the kingdom, which should maintain them. Neither is the population to be reckoned only by number; for a smaller number, that spend more and earn less, do wear out an estate sooner, than a greater number that live lower, and gather more. Therefore the multiplying of nobility, and other degrees of quality, in an over proportion to the common people, doth speedily bring a state to necessity; and so doth likewise an overgrown clergy; for they bring nothing to the stock; and in like manner, when more are bred scholars, than preferments can take off.

It is likewise to be remembered, that forasmuch as the increase of any estate must be upon the foreigner (for whatsoever is somewhere gotten, is somewhere lost), there be but three things, which one nation selleth unto another; the commodity as nature yieldeth it; the manufacture; and the vecture, or carriage. So that if these three wheels go, wealth will flow as in a spring tide. And it cometh many times to pass, that materiam superabit opus; ① that the work and carriage is more worth than the material, and enricheth a state more; as is notably seen in the Low-Countrymen, who have the best mines above ground, in the world.

Above all things, good policy is to be used, that the treasure and moneys, in a state, be not gathered into few hands. For otherwise a state may have a great stock, and yet starve. And money is like muck, not good except it be spread. This is done, chiefly by suppressing, or at least keeping a strait hand, upon the devouring trades of usury, ingrossing great pasturages, and the like.

For removing discontentments, or at least the danger of them; there is in every state (as we know) two portions of subjects; the noblesse and the commonalty. When one of these is discontent, the danger is not great; for common people are of slow motion, if they be not excited by the greater sort; and the greater sort are of small strength, except the multitude be apt, and ready to move of themselves. Then is the danger, when the greater sort, do but wait for the troubling of the waters amongst the meaner, that then they may declare themselves. The poets feign, that the rest of the gods would have bound Jupiter; which he hearing of, by the counsel of Pallas, sent for Briareus, with his hundred hands, to come in to his aid. As an emblem, no doubt, to show how safe it is for monarchs, to make sure of the good will of common people.

---

①The workmanship will excel the material.

To give moderate liberty for griefs and discontentments to evaporate (so it be without too great insolency or bravery), is a safe way. For he that turneth the humors back, and maketh the wound bleed inwards, endangereth malign ulcers, and pernicious imposthumations.

The part of Epimetheus mought well become Prometheus, in the case of discontentments: for there is not a better provision against them. Epimetheus, when griefs and evils flew abroad, at last shut the lid, and kept hope in the bottom of the vessel. Certainly, the politic and artificial nourishing, and entertaining of hopes, and carrying men from hopes to hopes, is one of the best antidotes against the poison of discontentments. And it is a certain sign of a wise government and proceeding, when it can hold men's hearts by hopes, when it cannot by satisfaction; and when it can handle things, in such manner, as no evil shall appear so peremptory, but that it hath some outlet of hope; which is the less hard to do, because both particular persons and factions, are apt enough to flatter themselves, or at least to brave that, which they believe not.

Also the foresight and prevention, that there be no likely or fit head, whereunto discontented persons may resort, and under whom they may join, is a known, but an excellent point of caution. I understand a fit head, to be one that hath greatness and reputation; that hath confidence with the discontented party, and upon whom they turn their eyes; and that is thought discontented, in his own particular: which kind of persons, are either to be won, and reconciled to the state, and that in a fast and true manner; or to be fronted with some other, of the same party, that may oppose them, and so divide the reputation. Generally, the dividing and breaking, of all factions and combinations that are adverse to the state, and setting them at distance, or at least distrust, amongst themselves, is not one of the worst remedies. For it is a desperate case, if those that hold with the proceeding of the state, be full of discord and faction, and those that are against it, be entire and united.

I have noted, that some witty and sharp speeches, which have fallen from princes, have given fire to seditions. Caesar did himself infinite hurt in that speech, Sylla nescivit literas, non potuit dictare; ① for it did utterly cut off that hope, which men had entertained, that he would at one time or other give over his dictatorship. Galba undid himself by that speech, legi a se militem, non emi;② for it put the soldiers out of hope of the donative. Probus likewise, by that speech, Si vixero, non opus erit amplius Romano imperio

①Sylla didn't know his letters: he could not dictate.

②His soldiers were levied, not bought, by him.

militibus; [①] a speech of great despair for the soldiers. And many the like. Surely princes had need, in tender matters and ticklish times, to beware what they say; especially in these short speeches, which fly abroad like darts, and are thought to be shot out of their secret intentions. For as for large discourses, they are like flat things, and not so much noted.

Lastly, let princes, against all events, not be without some great person, one or rather more, of military valor, near unto them, for the repressing of seditions in their beginnings. For without that, there useth to be more trepidation in court upon the first breaking out of troubles, than were fit. And the state runneth the danger of that which Tacitus saith; Atque is habitus animorum fuit, ut pessimum facinus auderent pauci, plures vellent, omnes paterentur. [②] But let such military persons be assured, and well reputed of, rather than factious and popular; holding also good correspondence with the other great men in the state; or else the remedy, is worse than the disease.

---

①If I live, the Roman Empire will no longer need soliders.

②And such was the state of men's minds that though few dared to commit this dastardly crime, many desired it and all acquiesced in it.

16.谈无神论

笔者宁信《圣徒传记》[①]、《塔木德经》[②]和《古兰经》中的所有故事,也不信宇宙之既定秩序中没有神灵。只因上帝创造的自然万物已证明无神论之悖谬,故他无须创造奇迹来使无神论者悔悟。毋庸置疑,对哲学的一知半解会使人倾向于无神论,但对哲学的深入研究则会使人心皈依宗教。因为当人之心智专注于零散的第二动因[③]之时,有时不免会以之为源而不再穷根;但当人注意到所有第二动因都相互关联并环环相扣之时,其心就必然会飞向天道和造物主了。不啻如此,连那个最被世人斥为无神论派的哲学学派(即以留基伯、德谟克利特和伊壁鸠鲁为代表的原子说派)也几乎证明了有神存在,其原因如下:原子说派认为大量无限小的原子或不固定的粒子无需神的支配便可造就这大千世界的道与美,而亚里士多德学派则认为宇宙的道与美由四种可变元素和一种不可变的第五元素恰如其分并周而复始地配制而成,其中无需神力相助,两相比较,把后者作为无神论之说比前者可信千倍。《圣经》有言:"愚顽者心中说没有上帝。"[④]但《圣经》并不是说愚顽者心中想,所以与其说愚顽者心里那么说就可能那么想,倒不如说他完全有可能相信上帝,或者说有可能使其相信;因为除了那些可从无神论中捞取好处的人外,没人会否认世间有上帝。以下事实最能说明无神论者之

---

①由13世纪热那亚大主教雅各布斯·德沃拉日勒(Jacobus de Voragine)所著,因其广为流传故又名《黄金传记》。

②一部关于犹太人生活、宗教及道德的口传律法集,为犹太教仅次于《圣经》的主要经典。

③第二动因又称次因,此处指由于第一动因(the first cause,又译第一推动力)之推动而产生的个别事物和运动的原因。亚里士多德学派认为第一动因是一切事物的最后目的和运动的最终原因,牛顿则用它指最初推动一切行星由静止而开始运动的某种外来力量。第一动因亦是上帝的别称。

④语出《旧约·诗篇》第14篇1节和第53篇1节。

口是心非，无神论者总是不厌其烦地大谈其主张，仿佛他们因心里没底而乐意用他人的赞同来增强信心似的。更有甚者，世人可见无神论者也像各宗教教派一样拼命招收信徒。而最有意思的是，世人还可见某些无神论者宁愿备受折磨也不愿放弃其主张。可要是他们真以为根本就没有上帝之类的神灵，那他们为何要如此折磨自己呢？伊壁鸠鲁曾断言有神之存在，但认为神只顾自己逍遥快活而不问世事，此说被斥为他为其声望之故而散布的掩饰之词。于是人们说他圆滑世故，说其实他心中并不认为有神存在；但这无疑是对他的中伤，因为他的言辞既崇高又虔诚，他说："不信俗人所谓之神并非亵渎，亵渎在于把俗人之见加于神灵。"恐怕连柏拉图也难说出比这更精辟的话语，而且尽管伊壁鸠鲁有胆量否认神对世事的支配，但他却没有能力否认神之本质。西印度群岛的蛮族虽不知上帝之圣名，但他们却为自己崇拜的神取有各种名称；似乎古代欧洲的异邦人也只有朱庇特、阿波罗和玛尔斯之类的称谓，而没有天神这个字眼。这说明那些尚未开化的民族也早就有神的概念，只不过他们的概念不甚清晰。因此在反无神论这一点上，甚至连野蛮人也站在缜密的哲学家一边。好沉思的无神论者并不多见，一个迪亚哥拉斯①，一个彼翁②，或许还有个卢奇安③和其他一些人，但他们似乎显得人多势众，其原因是所有对公认的宗教或迷信表示怀疑的人都被其反对派贴上了无神论的标签。不过十足的无神论者的确都是些伪君子，他们总在谈论圣事圣物，但却没有丝毫感觉，所以他们到头来必然会变得麻木不仁。无神论之产生有若干原因，首先是宗教分裂，虽说一次大分裂可为分裂之双方增添热情，但分裂的教派太多却会导致无神论。另一个原因是神职人员有辱宗教的丑闻，尤其是出现圣贝尔纳④曾说过的那种情况："如今我们不能说神父就像俗人，因为现在的俗人并不比神父败坏。"原因之三是对圣事圣物的嘲讽和亵渎蔚然成风，这种风气一点一点地损害了宗教的尊严。最后一个原因是学术昌盛的时代，尤其是这种时代兼有太平和

①迪亚哥拉斯，公元前5世纪雅典哲学家及诗人，后因不敬神灵而被判死刑，逃往科林斯避祸。

②彼翁，公元前3世纪希腊哲学家，曾撰文嘲讽诸神，相传他病入膏肓时曾忏悔其所为。

③古希腊作家卢奇安在其《演悲剧的宙斯》一文中批驳神造世界之学说。

④圣贝尔纳(1090—1153)，法国教士。

繁荣，因为祸乱与不幸倒更能使人皈依宗教。无神论者可毁掉人之高贵，因为人类在肉体方面无疑与野兽相似，而如果在精神方面再不与神灵相近，那人类真会成为一种低级下贱的动物。无神论亦可毁掉人的高尚品质并阻碍人性之升华。若以狗为例，世人可见当狗意识到有人收养它时会显示出何等的豪情和勇气，因为人于狗就是神灵，或曰一种更高级的生命，而若无对一种比自身更高级的生命之信赖，狗无论如何也不可能拥有它显示出来的那种勇气。人也是如此，如果他信赖或使自己确信有神的庇护和恩宠，他便会获得人性本身无法获得的力量和信心。由此可见，正如其在任何方面都可厌可恨一样，无神论在这一点上也不例外，因为它会剥夺人性借以自我升华并超越脆弱的工具。此理于人如斯，于国家民族亦然。人世间再没有比罗马更高贵的国家，而关于这个国家，且听西塞罗所言："诸位元老，我们尽可以为自己感到骄傲，虽说我们论人数不如西班牙人，论体力不如高卢人，论灵巧不如迦太基人，论计谋不如希腊人，甚至论对这片土地和这个国家的眷恋之心，我们也不如土生土长的意大利人和拉丁人；但若是论虔诚和宗教信仰，论把不朽的诸神视为万物之主宰这一智慧，我们却胜过了所有的国家和所有的民族。"①

解析

一、无神论的荒谬之处体现在——

1. 上帝创造的自然万物；
2. 对哲学的深入研究，虽然对哲学的一知半解似乎证明其合理性；
3.《圣经》，仅将其作为一种表白；
4. 无神论者自己信仰的改变与受苦难上的不真诚；
5. 异邦人的神话以及野蛮人的崇拜；
6. "好沉思的无神论者"的缺乏。

①西塞罗这段话仍把传说中的故事作为罗马之起源。据希腊罗马神话传说，战败的特洛伊人在全城被毁后跟着英雄埃涅阿斯出海寻觅新的国土，最后在意大利创建了罗马。

二、无神论产生的原因：

1. 分裂的教派太多；

2. 神职人员有辱宗教的丑闻；

3. 对圣事圣物的嘲讽蔚然成风；

4. 学术昌盛的时代，兼有太平与繁荣。

三、无神论的可恨之处：

1. 它毁掉了人的高尚品质；

2. 它剥夺了人性借以自我升华并超越脆弱的工具——

（1）于人如斯，

（2）于国家民族亦然。

Of Atheism

I HAD rather believe all the fables in the Legend, and the Talmud, and the Alcoran, than that this universal frame is without a mind. And therefore, God never wrought miracle, to convince atheism, because his ordinary works convince it. It is true, that a little philosophy inclineth man's mind to atheism; but depth in philosophy bringeth men's minds about to religion. For while the mind of man looketh upon second causes scattered, it may sometimes rest in them, and go no further; but when it beholdeth the chain of them, confederate and linked together, it must needs fly to Providence and Deity. Nay, even that school which is most accused of atheism doth most demonstrate religion; that is, the school of Leucippus and Democritus and Epicurus. For it is a thousand times more credible, that four mutable elements, and one immutable fifth essence, duly and eternally placed, need no God, than that an army of infinite small portions, or seeds unplaced, should have produced this order and beauty, without a divine marshal. The Scripture saith, The fool hath said in his heart, there is no God; it is not said, The fool hath thought in his heart; so as he rather saith it, by rote to himself, as that he would have, than that he can thoroughly believe it, or be persuaded of it. For none deny, there is a God, but those, for whom it maketh that there were no God. It appeareth in nothing more, that atheism is rather in the lip, than in the heart of man, than by this; that atheists will ever be talking of that their opinion, as if they fainted in it, within themselves, and would be glad to be strengthened, by the consent of others. Nay more, you shall have atheists strive to get disciples, as it fareth with other sects. And, which is most of all, you shall have of them, that will suffer for atheism, and not recant; whereas if they did truly think, that there were no such thing as God, why should they trouble themselves? Epicurus is charged, that he did but dissemble for his credit's sake, when he affirmed there were blessed natures, but such as enjoyed themselves, without having respect to the government of the world. Wherein they say he did temporize; though in secret, he thought there was no God. But certainly he is traduced; for his words are noble and divine: Non deos vulgi negare profanum; sed vulgi opiniones diis applicare profanum. ① Plato could have said no more. And although he had the confidence, to deny the administration, he had not the power, to deny the nature. The Indians of the West, have names for their particular gods, though they have no name for God: as if the heathens should have had the names Jupiter, Apollo, Mars, etc., but not the word Deus; which shows that even those barbarous people have the notion, though they have not the latitude and extent of it. So that against atheists, the very savages take part, with the very subtlest philosophers. The contemplative atheist is rare: a Diagoras, a Bion, a Lucian perhaps, and some others; and yet they seem to be more than they are; for that all that impugn a received religion, or superstition, are by the adverse part branded with the name of atheists. But the great atheists, indeed are hypocrites; which are ever handling holy things, but without feeling; so as they must needs be cauterized in the end. The causes of atheism are: divisions in religion, if they be many; for any one main division, addeth zeal to both sides; but many divisions introduce atheism. Another is, scandal of priests; when it is come to that which St. Bernard saith, non est jam dicere, ut populus sic sacerdos; quia nec sic populus ut sacerdos.② A third is, custom of profane scoffing in holy matters; which doth, by little and little, deface the reverence of religion. And lastly, learned times, specially with peace and prosperity; for troubles and adversities do more bow men's minds to religion. They that deny a God, destroy man's nobility; for certainly man is of kin to the beasts, by his body; and, if he be not of kin to God, by his spirit, he is a base and ignoble creature. It destroys likewise magnanimity, and the raising of human nature; for take an example of a dog, and mark what a generosity and courage he will put on, when he finds

---

①It is not profane to deny that the gods in whom the people believe, exist, but it is profane to attribute to the gods the opinions of the people.

②It is no longer possible to say "as the people, so the priest"; for the people are not so bad as the priest.

himself maintained by a man; who to him is instead of a God, or melior natura[①]; which courage is manifestly such, as that creature, without that confidence of a better nature than his own, could never attain. So man, when he resteth and assureth himself, upon divine protection and favor, gathered a force and faith, which human nature in itself could not obtain. Therefore, as atheism is in all respects hateful, so in this, that it depriveth human nature of the means to exalt itself, above human frailty. As it is in particular persons, so it is in nations. Never was there such a state for magnanimity as Rome. Of this state hear what Cicero saith: Quam volumus licet, patres conscripti, nos amemus, tamen nec numero Hispanos, nec robore Gallos, nec calliditate Poenos, nec artibus Graecos, nec denique hoc ipso hujus gentis et terrae domestico nativoque sensu Italos ipsos et Latinos; sed pietate, ac religione, atque hac una sapientia, quod deorum immortalium numine omnia regi gubernarique perspeximus, omnes gentes nationesque superavimus.[②]

---

①a higher being

②Though we may admire ourselves, conscript fathers, as much as we please, yet we have not surpassed the Spaniards in number, the Gauls in strength, the Carthaginians in cleverness, the Greeks in art, or even the Italians and Latins in that inborn domestic sentiment which prevails in these people and in this country; but in piety and religion, and in the great philosophic conviction that all things are guided and controlled by the providence of immortal gods, we have surpassed all the peoples of the world.

17.说迷信

对于神灵，与其妄加评说，不如一无所知；因后者只是不信神，而前者则是渎神。无可置疑，对神的迷信实乃对神的侮辱。普鲁塔克对此早有至言，他说："我宁愿世人说天底下从没有过普鲁塔克其人，也不愿人家说曾有位其儿女一生下来就被他吃掉的普鲁塔克。"就像诗人们说萨图尔努斯[①]那样。世人须知，对神的侮辱越甚，对人的危险就越大。无神论会给人留下理智、哲学和法律，留下骨肉亲情和名誉之心，而所有这些均可把人引向一种美德，哪怕没有宗教作为路标；但迷信却会使人丧失所有这些向导，并在人心中建起一种绝对的专制统治。由此可见，无神论不曾扰乱过社稷，因为它使人谨小慎微，别无他顾，而且世人可见倾向于无神论的时代(如奥古斯都时代)都是太平盛世；然而迷信却在许多国家引起过混乱，因为它带来一个新的"第十重天"，使政府的其他九重天都脱离常轨。迷信的主人乃民众，而且在所有迷信中都有一种本末倒置，即往往是智者去追随愚者，理论去符合行为。在经院派[②]学说占上风的特兰托宗教会议[③]上，一些主教们曾严肃地指出，经院派学者就像某些天文学家，后者曾想象出偏心圆、本轮和诸如此类的轨道模具，用以解释行星运动现象，然而他们知道他们的想象纯属子虚乌有；而经院派学者也以同样的方式杜撰出无数玄妙难懂的准则和原理，用以解释教会的行为。导致迷信的原因有：悦人耳目刺激感官的宗教

①罗马古神萨图尔努斯(即希腊神话中的克洛诺斯)曾统治宇宙，有预言说他将被自己的子女推翻，于是他在子女一出生时就把他们吞掉，其妻用石块代替刚出生的朱庇特(或宙斯)让他吞下，后预言终于应验。

②指中世纪欧洲的经院神学家，他们曾试图以亚里士多德学说的原理来规范教规教义。

③天主教在意大利北部特兰托城举行的第19次宗教会议，断断续续历时18年(1545—1547，1551—1552，1562—1563)，目的是反对宗教改革，维护天主教的地位和教皇的最高权威。

仪式、华而不实拘泥形式的假装虔诚、对只能加重教会负担的传统之过于尊重、高层教士为个人野心和金钱而玩弄的诡计、对迎合别出心裁和标新立异的良好动机之过分偏爱、由只会引起胡思乱想的人主持圣事，以及各个缺乏文化教养的时期，尤其是那些兼有天灾人祸的时期。迷信一旦被揭去面纱便丑陋无比。犹如猿之像人使其更显丑陋，迷信欲乔装成宗教也使之更显畸形；又如有益于健康的鲜肉腐烂后会生出小小蛆虫，得体的教规教礼腐败后也会变成繁文缛节。但若是人们以为离先前的迷信越远越好，那又会出现一种为避免迷信而产生的迷信。所以就像用药物催泻得小心一样，纠正迷信也得当心勿矫枉过正，不过若让平民来主持改良，那他们十有八九会干出这种蠢事。

解析

一、迷信之恶劣在于——

1. 比无神论更不虔诚，因为渎神比不信神更为恶劣；
2. 比无神论更罪恶，因为它毁坏了道德与社稷；
3. 由愚者发起，却往往得到天文学家与经院学者等智者的追捧。

二、导致迷信的原因——仪式、形式、传统、追逐私利等等。

三、结语：

1. 迷信类似于宗教，所以更为可怕。
2. 纠正迷信本身也得当心勿矫枉过正，以免变成另一种迷信。

Of Superstition

IT WERE better to have no opinion of God at all, than such an opinion, as is unworthy of him. For the one is unbelief, the other is contumely; and certainly superstition is the reproach of the Deity. Plutarch saith well to that purpose: Surely (saith he) I had rather a great deal, men should say, there was no such man at all, as Plutarch, than that they should say, that there was one Plutarch, that would eat his children as soon as they were born; as the poets speak of Saturn. And as the contumely is greater towards God, so the danger is greater towards men. Atheism leaves a man to sense, to philosophy, to natural piety, to laws, to reputation; all which may be guides to an outward moral virtue, though religion were not; but superstition dismounts all these, and erecteth an absolute monarchy, in the minds of men. Therefore atheism did never perturb states; for it makes men wary of themselves, as looking no further: and we see the times inclined to atheism (as the time of Augustus Caesar) were civil times. But superstition hath been the confusion of many states, and bringeth in a new primum mobile, that ravisheth all the spheres of government. The master of superstition, is the people; and in all superstition, wise men follow fools; and arguments are fitted to practice, in a reversed order. It was gravely said by some of the prelates in the Council of Trent, where the doctrine of the Schoolmen bare great sway, that the Schoolmen were like astronomers, which did feign eccentrics and epicycles, and such engines of orbs, to save the phenomena; though they knew there were no such things; and in like manner, that the Schoolmen had framed a number of subtle and intricate axioms, and theorems, to save the practice of the church. The causes of superstition are: pleasing and sensual rites and ceremonies; excess of outward and pharisaical holiness; overgreat reverence of traditions, which cannot but load the church; the stratagems of prelates, for their own ambition and lucre; the favoring too much of good intentions, which openeth the gate to conceits and novelties; the taking an aim at divine matters, by human, which cannot but breed mixture of imaginations: and, lastly, barbarous times, especially joined with calamities and disasters. Superstition, without a veil, is a deformed thing; for, as it addeth deformity to an ape, to be so like a man, so the similitude of superstition to religion, makes it the more deformed. And as wholesome meat corrupteth to little worms, so good forms and orders corrupt, into a number of petty observances. There is a superstition in avoiding superstition, when men think to do best, if they go furthest from the superstition, formerly received; therefore care would be had that (as it fareth in ill purgings) the good be not taken away with the bad; which commonly is done, when the people is the reformer.

18.论远游

远游于年少者乃教育之一部分，于年长者则为经验之一部分。未习一国之语言而去该国，那与其说是去旅游，不如说是去求学。余赞成年少者游异邦须有一私家教师或老成持重的仆人随行，但随行者须通该邦语言并去过该邦，这样他便可告知主人在所去国度有何事当看，有何人当交，有何等运动可习，或有何等学问可得，不然年少者将犹如雾中看花，虽远游他邦但所见甚少。远游者有一怪习，当其航行于大海，除水天之外别无他景可看之时，他们往往会大写日记，但当其漫游于大陆，有诸多景象可观之时，他们却往往疏于着墨，仿佛偶然之所见比刻意之观察更适于记载似的。所以写日记得养成习惯。远游者在所游国度应观其皇家宫廷，尤其当遇到君王们接见各国使节的时候；应观其讼庭法院，尤其当遇到法官开庭审案之时；还应观各派教会举行的宗教会议；观各教堂寺院及其中的历史古迹；观各城镇之墙垣及堡垒要塞；观码头和海港、遗迹和废墟；观书楼和学校以及偶遇的答辩和演讲；观该国的航运船舶和海军舰队；观都市近郊壮美的建筑和花园；观军械库、大仓房、交易所和基金会；观马术、击剑、兵训及诸如此类的操演；观当地上流人士趋之若鹜的戏剧；观珠宝服饰和各类珍奇标本。一言以蔽之，应观看所到之处一切值得记忆的风光名胜和礼仪习俗，反正打探上述去处应是随行的那名私家教师或贴身随从的事。至于庆祝大典、化装舞会、琼筵盛宴、婚礼葬礼以及行刑等热闹场面，游者倒不必过分注意，但也不应视而不见。若要让一名年少者在短期内游一小国且要受益甚多，那就必须让他做到以下几点：首先他必须如前文所述在动身前已略知该国语言；其次他必须有一名上文所说的那种熟悉该国的私家教师或随从；其三他得带若干介绍该国的书籍地图以资随时查阅释疑；他还必须坚持天天写日记；他不可在一城一镇久居，时间长短可视地方而定，但不宜太

久；当居于某城某镇时，他须在该城不同地域变换住处，以便吸引更多人相识；他得使自己不与本国同胞交往，而且应在可结交当地朋友的地方用餐；当从一地迁往另一地时，他须设法获得写给另一地某位上流人物的推荐信，以便在他想见识或了解某些事时可得到那人的帮助。只要做到上述各点，他就能在短期游历中受益良多。至于在旅行中当与何等人相交相识，余以为最值得结识者莫过于各国使节的秘书雇员之类，这样在一国旅行者亦可获得游多国之体验。游人在所游之地亦应去拜望各类名扬天下的卓越人物，如此便有可能看出那些大活人在多大程度上与其名声相符。旅行中务必谨言慎行以免引起争吵，须知引发争吵的事由多是为情人、饮酒、座次或出言不逊。游人与易怒好争者结伴时尤须当心，因为后者可能把游人也扯进他们自己的争吵。远游者归国返乡后，不可将曾游历过的国家抛到九霄云外，而应该与那些新结识且值得结识的友人保持通信。他还须注意，与其让自己的远游经历反映在衣着或举止上，不如让其反映在言谈之中；但在谈及自己的旅行时，最好是谨慎答问，别急于津津乐道。他还须注意，勿显得因游过异国他邦就改变了自己本国的某些习惯，而应该让人觉得自己是把在国外学到的某些最好的东西融进了本国的习俗。

解析

若能使去异邦旅游得到好处，要——

1. 动身前略知该邦语言，旅行时有懂该邦语言的私家教师或仆人陪同。
2. 养成写日记的习惯。
3. 观一切值得观的东西。
4. 带若干地图与书籍——不断变换住处——避免与本国同胞交往——结识有益的朋友。
5. 避免争吵。
6. 归国返乡之后——

   (1)与结识的友人保持通信；

   (2)避免在衣着、言谈中吹嘘对国外的认知。

Of Travel

TRAVEL, in the younger sort, is a part of education, in the elder, a part of experience. He that travelleth into a country, before he hath some entrance into the language, goeth to school, and not to travel. That young men travel under some tutor, or grave servant, I allow well; so that he be such a one that hath the language, and hath been in the country before; whereby he may be able to tell them what things are worthy to be seen, in the country where they go; what acquaintances they are to seek; what exercises, or discipline, the place yieldeth. For else, young men shall go hooded, and look abroad little. It is a strange thing, that in sea voyages, where there is nothing to be seen, but sky and sea, men should make diaries; but in land-travel, wherein so much is to be observed, for the most part they omit it; as if chance were fitter to be registered, than observation. Let diaries, therefore, be brought in use. The things to be seen and observed are: the courts of princes, especially when they give audience to ambassadors; the courts of justice, while they sit and hear causes; and so of consistories ecclesiastic; the churches and monasteries, with the monuments which are therein extant; the walls and fortifications of cities, and towns, and so the heavens and harbors; antiquities and ruins; libraries; colleges, disputations, and lectures, where any are; shipping and navies; houses and gardens of state and pleasure, near great cities; armories; arsenals; magazines; exchanges; burses; warehouses; exercises of horsemanship, fencing, training of soldiers, and the like; comedies, such whereunto the better sort of persons do resort; treasuries of jewels and robes; cabinets and rarities; and, to conclude, whatsoever is memorable, in the places where they go. After all which, the tutors, or servants, ought to make diligent inquiry. As for triumphs, masks, feasts, weddings, funerals, capital executions, and such shows, men need not to be put in mind of them; yet are they not to be neglected. If you will have a young man to put his travel into a little room, and in short time to gather much, this you must do. First, as was said, he must have some entrance into the language before he goeth. Then he must have such a servant, or tutor, as knoweth the country, as was likewise said. Let him carry with him also, some card or book, describing the country where he travelleth; which will be a good key to his inquiry. Let him keep also a diary. Let him not stay long, in one city or town; more or less as the place deserveth, but not long; nay, when he stayeth in one city or town, let him change his lodging from one end and part of the town, to another; which is a great adamant of acquaintance. Let him sequester himself, from the company of his countrymen, and diet in such places, where there is good company of the nation where he travelleth. Let him, upon his removes from one place to another, procure recommendation to some person of quality, residing in the place whither he removeth; that he may use his favor, in those things he desireth to see or know. Thus he may abridge his travel, with much profit. As for the acquaintance, which is to be sought in travel; that which is most of all profitable, is acquaintance with the secretaries and employed men of ambassadors: for so in travelling in one country, he shall suck the experience of many. Let him also see, and visit, eminent persons in all kinds, which are of great name abroad; that he may be able to tell, how the life agreeth with the fame. For quarrels, they are with care and discretion to be avoided. They are commonly for mistresses, healths, place, and words. And let a man beware, how he keepeth company with choleric and quarrelsome persons; for they will engage him into their own quarrels. When a traveller returneth home, let him not leave the countries, where he hath travelled, altogether behind him; but maintain a correspondence by letters, with those of his acquaintance, which are of most worth. And let his travel appear rather in his discourse, than his apparel or gesture; and in his discourse, let him be rather advised in his answers, than forward to tell stories; and let it appear that he doth not change his country manners, for those of foreign parts; but only prick in some flowers, of that he hath learned abroad, into the customs of his own country.

19.论帝王

所欲之事甚少,所惧之事甚多,此乃一种可悲的心态。然而这往往就是为帝王者之心理。他们已称孤道寡,至高无上,故而缺乏更高的企求,这便使他们心中多有苦思;但同时他们身边又总是险象环生,这又使他们心中少有宁静。此情亦是《圣经》曰"君王之心测不透"[①]的原因之一。因若无一种占支配地位的企望来规范妒羡戒疑等诸多感情,任何人的内心都难测或叵测。于是乎每每也有帝王替自己营造欲望,把心思寄托于一些琐事:或设计一座建筑;或新创一种祭礼;或栽培一位臣僚;或精于某种技艺,如尼禄之精于竖琴,图密善之精于射箭,康茂德之精于角斗,以及卡拉卡拉之精于驾车,[②]此类事例,不一而足。有人会觉得这似乎难以置信,殊不知此乃人之天性使然,即在小事上有所进取比在大业上停滞不前更使人心情舒畅,精神振奋。世人尚可看到,有些帝王早年东征西讨无往而不胜,但由于征服不可能无限,成功总有尽头,结果他们在晚年或变得迷信,或郁郁寡欢,例如亚历山大、戴克里先和世人尚记得的查理五世等等。[③]因习惯勇往直前者一旦

①《旧约·箴言》第25章3节云:"天之高,地之厚,君王之心测不透。"

②此四人均为罗马暴君。尼禄(在位期54—68)即位后曾师从当时的竖琴大师特尔普努斯,习成后常为自己举行演奏会;图密善(在位期81—96)因不好重武器而喜弓箭,相传他曾让一名奴隶站在百步开外举掌为靶,他射出的箭从其指间穿过而不伤其手;康茂德(在位期180—192)据说在竞技场参加过735场角斗,最终为一角斗士所杀;卡拉卡拉(在位期211—217)则喜欢驾战车,并宣称他此好是模仿太阳神阿波罗(神话中阿波罗每天驾载着太阳的金马车由东向西驶过天空)。

③马其顿国王亚历山大大帝(在位期公元前336—前323)曾先后征服希腊、埃及和波斯,建立亚历山大帝国,不幸死于疟疾,终年33岁,临终前还在筹划远征,虽普鲁塔克对他的迷信有所记述,但那并非在晚年,故培根以其为例似有不妥;罗马皇帝戴克里先(在位期284—305)当政21年后自行隐退,相传他8年后因忧于政局而自杀;神圣罗马帝国皇帝查理五世(在位期1519—1556)当政37年后隐退,两年后死于西班牙一修道院。

发现自己止步，往往会自暴自弃，不复故我。

接下来且说帝王权力之平衡。这种平衡很难保持，因为平衡和失衡均由王权和自由这对矛盾构成，不过平衡是让这对矛盾融为一体，失衡则是让这对矛盾交替出现。关于这点，阿波罗尼乌斯[①]给韦斯帕芗[②]的答复极富教益。后者问："尼禄因何被推翻？"前者答："尼禄虽善弹琴并善调琴，可治理帝国却时而把弦绷得太紧，时而把弦放得太松。"而毫无疑问，最有损于帝王权威者莫过于既不合时宜又极不均匀地使用权力，忽而滥施淫威，忽而放任自流。

不可否认，近代君王巩固霸业之智谋与其说是可防患于未然的真谋实策，不如说是待灾难临近时如何消灾避难的权宜之计；然而这纯粹是在同运气较量。君王们务须注意，别忽略或容忍欲作乱者备下柴薪，因为谁也没法阻止火星迸发，而且也难测火星会来自何方。君王巩固其霸业之困难既多又巨，但最大的困难往往是在他们心里。因为君王们想法矛盾是常有的事，(正如塔西佗所说)"为人君者之欲望通常都极其强烈但又互相矛盾"[③]；因既想达目的又不忍用其手段乃当权者之致命错误。

君王们不得不与之打交道者有其接壤邻邦、妻子儿女、高级教士、王公贵族、新贵士绅、市贾商人、平民百姓以及士卒兵丁，而为君者若稍有不慎，以上人等均会带来危险。

关于如何与邻国打交道，由于情况多变，故不可能有一成不变的规律，但有一条原则永远适用，即为君者须保持应有的戒备，勿让任何邻国(通过领土扩张、贸易垄断或重兵压境而)过分强大，以致给本国造成前所未有的威胁。预见并阻止上述情况之发生通常应是政府枢要的工作。在英王亨利八世、法王弗兰西斯一世和神圣罗马帝国皇帝查理五世三雄鼎立的年代，三国之间就这样互相监视，一方若得巴掌大一块领土，其余两方也会马上着手使之均衡，或以结盟之手段，必要时则诉诸战争，绝不会牺牲本国利益以换取和平。与上述情况相似的还有由那不勒斯王斐迪南、佛罗伦萨共和

①阿波罗尼乌斯，公元前 1 世纪希腊哲学家及著名术士，曾游历各国。

②韦斯帕芗，罗马皇帝 (在位期 69—79) 。

③此言非塔西佗所说，而是出自罗马历史学家萨卢斯提乌斯 (约前 86—前 35) 的《朱古达战记》。

国僭主洛伦佐·梅迪契和米兰大公卢多维卡·斯福尔扎结成的联盟(圭恰尔迪尼[①]称该联盟为意大利的安全保障)。某些经院哲学家对战争的见解并不可信,他们认为战争的原则是人不犯我,我不犯人,殊不知对潜在危险之恐惧亦是发动战争的正当理由,即使那种危险尚未变成现实。

说到帝王们的后妃,历史上不乏祸起后宫的残酷事例。莉维亚因毒死其丈夫而声名狼藉。[②]奥斯曼帝国苏丹苏里曼一世之宠后罗克娑拉娜不仅是害死太子穆斯塔法的罪魁,而且是扰乱皇家宫廷、混淆皇家血统的祸首。[③]英王爱德华二世之后亦是废黜并谋害她丈夫的主谋。[④]所以当后妃们密谋让自己的儿子继位,或者是当她们与人私通之时,君王尤须提防上述危险。

至于君王们的子嗣,由他们引发的祸乱也屡见不鲜,而不幸的悲剧通常都始于君王们对其子嗣的怀疑。上文提到的穆斯塔法之死对苏里曼家族就是一场灾难,因谢利姆二世被认为是其母的私生子,故时至今日世人还怀疑自苏里曼一世之后的历代土耳其君主均非正统。君士坦丁大帝处死年轻有为的大儿子克里斯普斯,这对他的家族亦是一场灾难,结果他的儿子康斯坦提努斯和康士坦斯都死于非命,他另一个儿子康斯坦提乌斯结局亦不见佳,因为他虽说是死于疾病,但那是在朱里安起兵反他之后。[⑤]马其顿国王腓力五世诛其子季米特里乌斯,后因发现系误杀而悔恨身亡。[⑥]历史上

①圭恰尔迪尼(1483—1540),佛罗伦萨史学家及政治家,所著20卷本《意大利史》打破邦国界限,勾勒出了1494—1534年尚未统一的意大利之全貌。

②罗马皇帝提比略(在位期14—37)之子德鲁苏斯被其妻莉维亚毒死;另相传奥古斯都之妻莉维亚为确保儿子提比略继位而加速了病重的奥古斯都之死亡。

③苏里曼一世受其后罗克娑拉娜挑唆杀死皇太子穆斯塔法(与前妻所生之长子),此事导致穆斯塔法的弟弟桑格尔自戮。罗克娑拉娜的亲生子巴耶塞特谋叛被诛,另一亲生子后继王位称谢利姆二世,但其相貌性格与苏里曼一世迥然不同,世人疑其并非皇家嫡传。

④爱德华二世之后乃法王腓力四世之女伊莎贝尔,她与情夫莫蒂默(马奇伯爵)共谋废黜并谋害了爱德华二世(1327年)。

⑤年仅17岁就被任命为恺撒的克里斯普斯是君士坦丁大帝与前妻米列尔维娜所生的唯一儿子,其后母法乌斯塔欲提携亲生子,诬告克里斯普斯调戏她,后者遂被其父处死。康斯坦提努斯死于与康士坦斯的火并,康士坦斯后被部下所杀。康斯坦提乌斯死于起兵征讨自封为奥古斯都的朱里安(他的堂弟)之途中。

⑥季米特里乌斯因被其兄伯尔修控犯叛国罪而被父王处死。培根在此误将腓力五世作腓力二世(亚历山大大帝之父,在女儿的婚礼上遇刺身亡),译文改之。

这类事例不胜枚举，但少见为父王者从对子嗣的猜疑中得到好处；不过儿子们公开举兵反叛当属例外，如苏里曼一世诛逆子巴耶塞特，又如英王亨利二世败其三个逆子[①]。

高级教士妄自尊大亦可给君王造成危险，如当年的两位坎特伯雷大主教安塞姆和贝克特，他俩曾试图用主教的权杖与君王的利剑抗衡，只是他们不得不与之抗衡的是几位顽强而自信的君王：威廉二世、亨利一世和亨利二世。这种危险并非由于教会本身，而是由于教会有国外势力[②]撑腰，或是由于神职人员之选任不是靠君王或有圣职授予权者的决定，而是靠平民百姓的拥戴。

说到王公贵族，对他们敬而远之并不为过。对贵族加以抑制虽可加强王权，但却会减少君王的高枕无忧，而且在实施其主张时也不那么随心所欲。笔者在拙著《英王亨利七世传》中对此已有过评述。亨利七世对贵族加以抑制，结果他执政时期充满了麻烦和骚乱，因为贵族们虽说继续忠于皇室，但对亨利进行的事业却不予合作，所以他实际上不得不日理万机。[③]

至于新贵士绅，鉴于他们只是个松散的阶层，故不会对君王形成多大危险。他们有时会高谈阔论，但那几乎无甚妨害。何况他们是一种中和力量，可使王公贵族的势力不致过于强大，而且由于他们是君王与平民间的直接纽带，所以他们最能缓和民愤。

至于市贾商人，他们好比国家的门静脉，若门静脉血量不盛，国家即使有健全的四肢也难免会出现血管供血不足的情况。对商人课重税于君王的岁收好处甚微，因为从小处所得将会失于大处，原因是若各项税率增加，商贸的总量反倒会减少。

平民百姓对君王几乎不构成危险，只要他们没有强有力的领头人物，或是君王不对他们的宗教、习俗和生活方式横加干涉。

至于士卒兵丁，若让他们建制不变、久驻一方并习惯于领赏，那对君王

---

①指 1172—1173 年亨利二世的三个儿子杰弗里、约翰和理查联合反叛那次。后理查终在 1189 年击败其父亲并夺得王位，称理查一世（诨号狮心王）。

②指教皇。

③实际上亨利七世打击封建贵族、重工重商的政策得到了除贵族之外的各阶层人民的支持，使当时已在英国萌芽的资本主义得到了发展。

将是一种危险。土耳其御林军之骄纵和古罗马禁卫军之贪残均可作为后事之师。防范之道是让兵无常帅、驻无常地，并不给赏赐，如此君王可高枕无忧。

帝王君主好比天上的星宿，可带来盛世，亦可造成浊世。他们受人崇拜，但却永不安宁。所有对君王的戒律实际上可归纳为两记：一是记住你是凡人，二是记住你是神或神的化身；前者约束君王的权力，后者则限制君王的欲望。

解析

一、帝王的悲哀之处在于——

1. 所欲之事甚少，所惧之事甚多；

2. 他们不得不为自己营造欲望；

3. 最后他们往往会变得“迷信或郁郁寡欢”。

二、帝王权力之平衡——

1. 保持一致（把矛盾融合而不是相互转换）；

2. 要尽量找出真正的祸端。

三、帝王危险的来源：

1. 外国入侵；

2. 不忠好妒的后妃们；

3. 心怀猜疑的子嗣；

4. 受国外拥戴的高级教士；

5. 没有得到充分尊重的贵族（新贵士绅很少造成危险）；

6. 宗教、习俗与生活方式受干涉的平民；

7. 易受贿的军队。

四、帝王应该扼制自己的权力与意志。

Of Empire

IT IS a miserable state of mind, to have few things to desire, and many things to fear; and yet that commonly is the case of kings; who, being at the highest, want matter of desire, which makes their minds more languishing; and have many representations of perils and shadows, which makes their minds the less clear. And this is one reason also, of that effect which the Scripture speaketh of, That the king's heart is inscrutable. For multitude of jealousies, and lack of some predominant desire, that should marshal and put in order all the rest, maketh any man's heart, hard to find or sound. Hence it comes likewise, that princes many times make themselves desires, and set their hearts upon toys; sometimes upon a building; sometimes upon erecting of an order; sometimes upon the advancing of a person; sometimes upon obtaining excellency in some art, or feat of the hand; as Nero for playing on the harp, Domitian for certainty of the hand with the arrow, Commodus for playing at fence, Caracalla for driving chariots, and the like. This seemeth incredible, unto those that know not the principle, that the mind of man, is more cheered and refreshed by profiting in small things, than by standing at a stay, in great. We see also that kings that have been fortunate conquerors, in their first years, it being not possible for them to go forward infinitely, but that they must have some check, or arrest in their fortunes, turn in their latter years to be superstitious, and melancholy; as did Alexander the Great; Diocletian; and in our memory, Charles the Fifth; and others: for he that is used to go forward, and findeth a stop, falleth out of his own favor, and is not the thing he was.

To speak now of the true temper of empire, it is a thing rare and hard to keep; for both temper, and distemper, consist of contraries. But it is one thing, to mingle contraries, another to interchange them. The answer of Apollonius to Vespasian, is full of excellent instruction. Vespasian asked him, What was Nero's overthrow? He answered, Nero could touch and tune the harp well; but in government, sometimes he used to wind the pins too high, sometimes to let them down too low. And certain it is, that nothing destroyeth authority so much, as the unequal and untimely interchange of power pressed too far, and relaxed too much.

This is true, that the wisdom of all these latter times, in princes' affairs, is rather fine deliveries, and shiftings of dangers and mischiefs, when they are near, than solid and grounded courses to keep them aloof. But this is but to try masteries with fortune. And let men beware, how they neglect and suffer matter of trouble to be prepared; for no man can forbid the spark, nor tell whence it may come. The difficulties in princes' business are many and great; but the greatest difficulty, is often in their own mind. For it is common with princes (saith Tacitus) to will contradictories, Sunt plerumque regum voluntates vehementes, et inter se contrariae. [①] For it is the solecism of power, to think to command the end, and yet not to endure the mean.

Kings have to deal with their neighbors, their wives, their children, their prelates or clergy, their nobles, their second-nobles or gentlemen, their merchants, their commons, and their men of war; and from all these arise dangers, if care and circumspection be not used.

First for their neighbors; there can no general rule be given (for occasions are so variable), save one, which ever holdeth, which is, that princes do keep due sentinel, that none of their neighbors do ever grow so (by increase of territory, by embracing of trade, by approaches, or the like), as they become more able to annoy them, than they were. And this is generally the work of standing counsels, to foresee and to hinder it. During that triumvirate of kings, King Henry the Eighth of England, Francis the First King of France, and Charles the Fifth Emperor, there was such a watch kept, that none of the three could win a palm of ground, but the other two would straightways balance it, either by confederation, or, if need were, by a war; and would not in any wise take up peace at interest. And the like was done by that league (which Guicciardini saith was the security of Italy) made between Ferdinando King of Naples, Lorenzius Medici, and Ludovicus Sforza, potentates, the one of Florence, the other of Milan. Neither is the opinion of some of the Schoolmen, to be received, that a war cannot justly be made, but upon a precedent injury or provocation. For there is no question, but a just fear of an imminent danger, though there be no blow given, is a lawful cause of a war.

For their wives; there are cruel examples of them. Livia is infamed, for the poisoning of her husband; Roxalana, Solyman's wife, was the destruction of that renowned prince, Sultan Mustapha, and otherwise troubled his house and succession; Edward the Second of England, his queen, had the principal hand in the deposing and murder of her husband. This kind of danger, is then to be feared chiefly, when the wives have plots, for the raising of their own children; or else that they be advoutresses.

For their children; the tragedies likewise of dangers from them, have been many. And generally, the entering of fathers into suspicion of their children, hath been ever unfortunate. The destruction of Mustapha (that we named before) was so fatal to Solyman's line, as the succession of the Turks,

---

①The desires of kings are for the most part violent and inconsistent with one another.

from Solyman until this day, is suspected to be untrue, and of strange blood; for that Selymus the Second, was thought to be suppositious. The destruction of Crispus, a young prince of rare towardness, by Constantinus the Great, his father, was in like manner fatal to his house; for both Constantinus and Constance, his sons, died violent deaths; and Constantius, his other son, did little better; who died indeed of sickness, but after that Julianus had taken arms against him. The destruction of Demetrius, son to Philip the Second of Macedon, turned upon the father, who died of repentance. And many like examples there are; but few or none, where the fathers had good by such distrust; except it were, where the sons were up in open arms against them; as was Selymus the First against Bajazet; and the three sons of Henry the Second, King of England.

For their prelates; when they are proud and great, there is also danger from them; as it was in the times of Anselmus, and Thomas Becket, Archbishops of Canterbury; who, with their croziers, did almost try it with the king's sword; and yet they had to deal with stout and haughty kings, William Rufus, Henry the First, and Henry the Second. The danger is not from that state, but where it hath a dependence of foreign authority; or where the churchmen come in and are elected, not by the collation of the king, or particular patrons, but by the people.

For their nobles; to keep them at a distance, it is not amiss; but to depress them, may make a king more absolute, but less safe; and less able to perform, anything that he desires. I have noted it, in my History of King Henry the Seventh of England, who depressed his nobility; whereupon it came to pass, that his times were full of difficulties and troubles; for the nobility, though they continued loyal unto him, yet did they not co-operate with him in his business. So that in effect, he was fain to do all things himself.

For their second-nobles; there is not much danger from them, being a body dispersed. They may sometimes discourse high, but that doth little hurt; besides, they are a counterpoise to the higher nobility, that they grow not too potent; and, lastly, being the most immediate in authority, with the common people, they do best temper popular commotions.

For their merchants; they are vena porta; and if they flourish not, a kingdom may have good limbs, but will have empty veins, and nourish little. Taxes and imposts upon them, do seldom good to the king's revenue; for that that he wins in the hundred, he leeseth in the shire; the particular rates being increased, but the total bulk of trading, rather decreased.

For their commons; there is little danger from them, except it be, where they have great and potent heads; or where you meddle with the point of religion, or their customs, or means of life.

For their men of war; it is a dangerous state, where they live and remain in a body, and are used to donatives; whereof we see examples in the janizaries, and pretorian bands of Rome; but trainings of men, and arming them in several places, and under several commanders, and without donatives, are things of defence, and no danger.

Princes are like to heavenly bodies, which cause good or evil times; and which have much veneration, but no rest. All precepts concerning kings, are in effect comprehended in those two remembrances: memento quod es homo;① and memento quod es Deus, or vice Dei; ② the one bridleth their power, and the other their will.

①Remember that you are a man.

②Remember that you are a god or god's deputy.

20.论进言与纳谏

人与人之间最大的信任莫过于接受诤言。因为在别的信托中，人所托付的只是其生活之一部分，如田地、财产、子女、信贷或某项具体事物；但对自己心目中的诤友或谏官，从谏者则往往是以身家性命或江山社稷相托；所以进言者务须是忠义两全。明智的君王不必以为求言从谏会有伤其龙颜或有损其君威。上帝若不倡从谏，就不会把“劝世者”这一称谓作为其圣子的诸多尊号之一。[①]所罗门曾曰“从谏如流方可长治久安”[②]。凡事都有其波动，只是或早或迟；若不任其颠簸于室议廷诤之中，它们就将颠簸于命运的波涛之上，而后一种颠簸犹如醉汉之蹒跚，说不定何时一个趔趄就摔跟头。正如所罗门深知从谏之必要，其子罗波安也领教了进言的力量，因那个上帝宠爱的王国当初就因为他听信狂言而南北分裂。[③]作为后事之师，今人往往可凭此谏例明察两种偏辞谵语：一是乳臭小儿议人之妄说，二是张狂之徒议事之狂言。

古人早已用形象的故事阐明：君王与智慧本是一体，君王的智慧与之巧纳忠言也密不可分。故事之一讲众神之王朱庇特曾娶智慧女神墨提斯，其寓意是说君权总与智谋联姻。故事之二是之一的延续，讲墨提斯与朱庇特结婚后珠胎暗结，但朱庇特不容她分娩便将她吞食，于是神王自己身怀六甲，最后从他头颅里生出了全身披挂的帕拉斯女神。[④]这段荒唐的故事中

①参见《旧约·以赛亚书》第9章6节。

②《旧约·箴言》第20章18节云：“从谏如流方可长治久安，多见听纳才能百战不殆。”

③据《旧约·列王纪上》第12章记载，所罗门之子罗波安拒绝老臣们要他善待北方十支臣民的忠告，反而听信一班少壮臣僚的狂言，结果北方十支以色列人分裂而成以色列国，只剩下南方二支称犹大国。

④神话讲朱庇特(或宙斯)的第一个妻子大洋女神墨提斯(Metis，字面意思乃智慧)怀孕时曾预言，说她将生下一个比朱庇特更强大的孩子。朱庇特为防患于未然将妻子吞下，但胎儿却在他体内继续生长，最后从他的头颅里生出了智慧女神及女战神雅典娜(后来又名帕拉斯·雅典娜)。

暗藏着一则君王治国的秘诀，即君王该如何利用朝议廷诤。他们首先应把欲决之事交顾问们讨论，这就好比最初结胎或曰受孕，但当所议之事已在智囊之子宫中孕育成形的时候，君王切不可让策士谋臣继续行分娩之事，不可显得行此事非智囊莫属，而应当把所议之事收回到自己手中，并让世人觉得最后颁布的敕令谕示均出自君王本人(这些谕旨因其深谋远虑和极富效力而可比那位全身披挂的智慧女神)，不仅出自君王的绝对权威，而且出自君王的足智多谋(如此更能提高君王的声望)。

接下来且谈谏议的弊病和除弊之法。求言纳谏之弊病已见者有三：其一是议事外传，于保密不利；其二是有损君威，显得他们并非无所不知；其三是有佞臣进谗言的危险，结果从谏对进言者比对纳言者有利。为除掉这三种弊端，意大利和法兰西的某些君主曾分别提倡或实行过秘室顾问会议，可这除弊之法比弊端本身更有危害。

说到保密，君王无须把欲决之事告诉每一位顾问，而是可以择善者而言之，何况征询该用何法者也无须言明他将用何法。只是君王们得当心，勿让自己的秘密从自己口中走漏。至于密室顾问会议，下面这句台词可谓一语道破天机，“我真是漏洞百出”①；因为只要有一个以饶舌为荣的白痴，其他人都懂沉默是金也乃白搭。毋庸置疑，有些事需要高度保密，知者除君王和一两名亲信外不可再有他人。进言者寡也并非不是好事，因为除有利于保密外，其所陈意见往往都精神一致而无分歧；不过在这种情形下，纳谏者须是既英明睿智又能独行其是的君王，进言者亦须是足智多谋之辈，尤其是得忠于君王的宏旨。此例可见于英王亨利七世，他每行大事总是秘而不宣，最多只与莫顿②和福克斯③商议。

说到有损君威，前文讲那则神话之寓意时已讲明了弥补之道。而且与其说君王坐进议事厅会有损其威望，不如说会增加其尊严。再说从不曾有

---

①语出古罗马喜剧作家泰伦提乌斯(Terentius，约前190—前159)之喜剧《阉奴》第1幕2场25行。

②莫顿(1420—1500)，亨利七世时期任过坎特伯雷大主教、大法官和牛津大学名誉校长等职。

③福克斯(1448—1528)，亨利七世时期任过威斯敏斯特主教、枢密院顾问、国务大臣和掌玺大臣等职。

哪位君王因与臣议事而丧失他独有的王权，除非有某位议臣羽毛过于丰满，或是有某些拉帮结派者过从甚密。但此类情况都容易发现并不难制止。

说到最后一弊，即有人进言是抱着私心。须知“他在这世间将难觅忠信”[①]之说无疑是就时代的风气而言，并非是就个人的天性而论。有些人天生就忠信两全，坦诚兼备，而非阴险狡诈，诡计多端，君王尤其要注意招纳这类忠义之士。另外谏官议臣通常并非抱成一团，反之他们往往是互相戒备，所以若有人为党派利益或个人目的而进言，真相多半都会传进君王的耳朵。不过最好的除弊之法是：为君者当如议臣知其君王般知其议臣。盖“君王之大德在于知人善任”[②]。而与之相反，进言者则不该过分探究君王的好恶。一名称职的议臣当通晓君王的事务，而非熟知君王的脾性，如此他方有可能直言进谏，而不会曲意逢迎。君王若能既私下求言又公开纳谏，其效益当会非常显著；因私下发表意见多直言不讳，公开提出规谏则多有顾忌。世人在私下里更勇于陈述己见，在公开场合则更容易人云亦云，故君王最好是兼而听之。求言冗官小吏于密室，以促其畅所欲言，征询高官大员于公堂，以保其出言谨慎。若君王只为用何法行事而广开言路，却不为用何人行事而集思广益，其求言纳谏也终归枉然；盖因欲行之事乃无生命之计划，其实施执行之活力全在于用之得人。考虑人选的品格素质不可仅凭其等级地位，正如不可仅凭自己的模糊记忆或他人的精确描述，因大错之铸成或大智之显示都在于人之选择。有至言道“死者乃最称职的谏官”，因即便生者因畏罪而结舌，书本也会直言进谏。故为君者博览群书不无裨益，尤其当读那些曾经也是君王的人所写的书。

今人议事多如亲友集会，对所议之事往往议而不辩，结果议题轻而易举就变成了议会的条例和法规。对重大问题之议论，最好是提前一天公布议题，待次日再付诸审议，俗话说“夜晚乃智谋的时辰”。“英格兰苏格兰合并事宜联合委员会”[③]就采用过这种做法，该委员会曾是个庄严而有序的立

①《新约·路加福音》第 18 章 8 节有云：“基督重临之日，他在世间将难觅忠信。”

②语出古罗马诗人马尔提阿利斯（Martialis，约 40—104）之《铭辞》第 8 卷 15 首 8 行。

③该委员会成立于 1604 年 10 月 20 日，同年 12 月 6 日解散。1603 年伊丽莎白一世驾崩后由其侄苏格兰国王詹姆斯六世继英格兰王位，称詹姆斯一世。当时任皇家法律顾问的培根极力主张两国合并，并促成了上述委员会之成立。委员会通过了《合并提案》，提案亦得到上议院批准，但合并之事终因他故而搁浅。直到 1707 年英格兰与苏格兰才正式合并。

法机构。笔者赞赏议院为请愿安排出日期，这种安排使请愿者更清楚他们何时可来议院，同时也让各类会议有工夫讨论国事，从而使当务之急得到及时处理。关于议会各临时委员会的人员，最好是选那些无偏无党的中立者，不应为造成一种均衡势态而选任对立双方的死党。笔者亦赞成建立一些常设性委员会，诸如负责贸易、金融、战争、诉讼和某些殖民地事务的委员会；因为既然有各种各样的议会特别会议，但却只有一个议会(和西班牙一样)，那么这些特别会议实际上就等于是常设委员会，只是它们的权力更大些而已。应该由各常设委员会先听取各相应行业人士(如律师业、航海业和皇家铸币厂的人士)向议会的报告，然后在适当的时机再提交议会；勿让报告者成群结队而来，亦不容他们慷慨激昂地陈词，因为那不是在向议会报告，而是在胁迫议会。安排会议座次或沿长桌、方桌，或绕墙置位，这看上去似乎只是形式问题，但却有实质上的不同；因若在长桌旁开会，坐首端的少数人实际上会左右整个议程，而若以其他形式排座，那位次较低者的意见便会多见采纳。君王主持会议时须当心，切莫就其提供讨论的问题表明自己的倾向，不然与会者只会投其所好，结果他听到的将不是各抒己见，而是一曲“吾将愉悦吾主”①。

解析

一、进谏事关——

1. 信任，与别的信托相比更为如此；

2. 必需——凡事皆有“波动”。

二、君王应该把从谏的结果归入自己的功劳。

三、谏议的弊病——

1. 议事外传；

2. 有损君威；

①戏引拉丁文本《圣经》(公元4世纪圣哲罗姆翻译)中《诗篇》第114篇9节语，英文本《圣经》可参阅第116篇。

3. 有佞臣进谗言的危险。

四、除弊之法：

1. （保密）君王必须有所保留，即使是对自己的顾问；
2. （有损君威）君王应小心取得所有诤言的功劳；
3. （误导）君王应了解进谏者的脾性。

五、采纳诤言最好的方法：

1. 不允许进谏者刨根问底；
2. 私下纳谏与公开纳谏相结合；
3. 纳谏既要关于事，又要关于人；
4. 从书中纳谏——它既不会紧张，也不会奉承；
5. 为请愿与其他事务安排固定的日期；
6. 选择无偏无党的进谏者而非妥协折中之人；
7. 听从专业人士的建议而非陈词；
8. 不要以为会议地点的陈设无关紧要。

Of Counsel

THE greatest trust, between man and man, is the trust of giving counsel. For in other confidences, men commit the parts of life; their lands, their goods, their children, their credit, some particular affair; but to such as they make their counsellors, they commit the whole: by how much the more, they are obliged to all faith and integrity. The wisest princes need not think it any diminution to their greatness, or derogation to their sufficiency, to rely upon counsel. God himself is not without, but hath made it one of the great names of his blessed Son: The Counsellor. Solomon hath pronounced, that in counsel is stability. Things will have their first, or second agitation: if they be not tossed upon the arguments of counsel, they will be tossed upon the waves of fortune; and be full of inconstancy, doing and undoing, like the reeling of a drunken man. Solomon's son found the force of counsel, as his father saw the necessity of it. For the beloved kingdom of God, was first rent, and broken, by ill counsel; upon which counsel, there are set for our instruction, the two marks whereby bad counsel is for ever best discerned; that it was young counsel, for the person; and violent counsel, for the matter.

The ancient times, do set forth in figure, both the incorporation, and inseparable conjunction, of counsel with kings, and the wise and politic use of counsel by kings: the one, in that they say Jupiter did marry Metis, which signifieth counsel; whereby they intend that Sovereignty, is married to Counsel: the other in that which followeth, which was thus: They say, after Jupiter was married to Metis, she conceived by him, and was with child, but Jupiter suffered her not to stay, till she brought forth, but eat her up; whereby he became himself with child, and was delivered of Pallas armed, out of his head. Which monstrous fable containeth a secret of empire; how kings are to make use of their counsel of state. That first, they ought to refer matters unto them, which is the first begetting, or impregnation; but when they are elaborate, moulded, and shaped in the womb of their counsel, and grow ripe, and be ready to be brought forth, that then they suffer not their counsel to go through with the resolution and direction, as if it depended on them; but take the matter back into their own hands, and make it appear to the world, that the decrees and final directions (which, because they come forth, with prudence and power, are resembled to Pallas armed) proceeded from themselves; and not only from their authority, but (the more to add reputation to themselves) from their head and device.

Let us now speak of the inconveniences of counsel, and of the remedies. The inconveniences that have been noted, in calling and using counsel, are three. First, the revealing of affairs, whereby they become less secret. Secondly, the weakening of the authority of princes, as if they were less of themselves. Thirdly, the danger of being unfaithfully counselled, and more for the good of them that counsel, than of him that is counselled. For which inconvenniences, the doctrine of Italy, and practice of France, in some kings' times, hath introduced cabinet counsels; a remedy worse than the disease.

As to secrecy; princes are not bound to communicate all matters, with all counsellors; but may extract and select. Neither is it necessary, that he that consulteth what he should do, should declare what he will do. But let princes beware, that the unsecreting of their affairs, comes not from themselves. And as for cabinet counsels, it may be their motto, plenus rimarum sum[①]: one futile person, that maketh it his glory to tell, will do more hurt than many, that know it their duty to conceal. It is true there be some affairs, which require extreme secrecy, which will hardly go beyond one or two persons, besides the king: neither are those counsels unprosperous; for, besides the secrecy, they commonly go on constantly, in one spirit of direction, without distraction. But

①I am full of chinks.

then it must be a prudent king, such as is able to grind with a handmill; and those inward counsellors need also be wise men, and especially true and trusty to the king's ends; as it was with King Henry the Seventh of England, who, in his great business, imparted himself to none, except it were to Morton and Fox.

For weakening of authority; the fable showeth the remedy. Nay, the majesty of kings, is rather exalted than diminished, when they are in the chair of counsel; neither was there ever prince, bereaved of his dependences, by his counsel, except where there hath been, either an over-greatness in one counsellor, or an over-strict combination in divers; which are things soon found, and holpen.

For the last inconvenience, that men will counsel, with an eye to themselves; certainly, non inveniet fidem super terram① is meant, of the nature of times, and not of all particular persons. There be, that are in nature faithful, and sincere, and plain, and direct; not crafty and involved; let princes, above all, draw to themselves such natures. Besides, counsellors are not commonly so united, but that one counsellor, keepeth sentinel over another; so that if any do counsel out of faction or private ends, it commonly comes to the king's ear. But the best remedy is, if princes know their counsellors, as well as their counsellors know them: Principis est virtus maxima nosse suos.② And on the other side, counsellors should not be too speculative into their sovereign's person. The true composition of a counsellor, is rather to be skilful in their master's business, than in his nature; for then he is like to advise him, and not feed his humor. It is of singular use to princes, if they take the opinions of their counsel, both separately and together. For private opinion is more free; but opinion before others, is more reverent. In private, men are more bold in their own humors; and in consort, men are more obnoxious to others' humors; therefore it is good to take both; and of the inferior sort, rather in private, to preserve freedom; of the greater, rather in consort, to preserve respect. It is in vain for princes, to take counsel concerning matters, if they take no counsel likewise concerning persons; for all matters are as dead images; and the life of the execution of affairs, resteth in the good choice of persons. Neither is it enough, to consult concerning persons secundum genera③, as in an idea, or mathematical description, what the kind and character of the person should be; for the greatest errors are committed, and the most judgment

①He shall not find faith upon earth.

②The greatest virtue in a prince is to know his people.

③according to their class

is shown, in the choice of individuals. It was truly said, optimi consiliarii mortui[①]: books will speak plain, when counsellors blanch. Therefore it is good to be conversant in them, specially the books of such as themselves have been actors upon the stage.

The counsels at this day, in most places, are but familiar meetings, where matters are rather talked on, than debated. And they run too swift, to the order, or act, of counsel. It were better that in causes of weight, the matter were propounded one day, and not spoken to till the next day; in nocte consilium.[②] So was it done in the Commission of Union, between England and Scotland; which was a grave and orderly assembly. I commend set days for petitions; for both it gives the suitors more certainty for their attendance, and it frees the meetings for matters of estate, that they may hoc agree[③]. In choice of committees; for ripening business for the counsel, it is better to choose indifferent persons, than to make an indifferency, by putting in those, that are strong on both sides. I commend also standing commissions; as for trade, for treasure, for war, for suits, for some provinces; for where there be divers particular counsels, and but one counsel of estate (as it is in Spain), they are, in effect, no more than standing commissions: save that they have greater authority. Let such as are to inform counsels, out of their particular professions (as lawyers, seamen, mintmen, and the like) be first heard before committees; and then, as occasion serves, before the counsel. And let them not come in multitudes, or in a tribunitious manner; for that is to clamor counsels, not to inform them. A long table and a square table, or seats about the walls, seem things of form, but are things of substance; for at a long table a few at the upper end, in effect, sway all the business; but in the other form, there is more use of the counsellors' opinions, that sit lower. A king, when he presides in counsel, let him beware how he opens his own inclination too much, in that which he propoundeth; for else counsellors will but take the wind of him, and instead of giving free counsel, sing him a song of placebo.

①The dead are the best counsellors.

②In the night comes counsel.

③do the business which is before them

21.说时机

时运每每就像集市，你若在那儿多逛一会儿，物价说不定就会下跌；但它有时又像西彼拉那套预言集[1]，开初以整套索价，然后烧掉其中几册，但索价依然如初。因为时机(恰如那句谚语所说)，她若给你额发你不抓，就只剩下光秃的后脑勺；[2]或者你至少知道这句格言：时者难得而易失，且失不再来。故凡事能把握住发轫之机无疑是大智。欲行事者须知，看上去不足惧的危险往往并非不足为惧，令人虚惊一场的危险则历来都多于逼迫人的危险。不仅如此，对某些危险最好是不等其逼近就迎头出击，而不能过久地对其逼临进行监视，因若监视时间太长，监视者很有可能会放松警惕。反之，被晕光幻影所迷惑而出击过早(在弯月低挂、敌影拖长时有过这种情况)，或是因打草惊蛇而导致"引蛇出洞"，则属于另一个极端。如上所言，时机成熟与否得时时悉心掂量。而一般说来，每行大事须派百眼巨人阿耳戈斯当先，再派百臂巨人布里阿柔斯随后，即首先明察秋毫，然后则雷厉风行；因为对明智者而言，普路同[3]那顶隐身帽便是议事之隐秘和行事之神速。事情一旦付诸实施，保密之最佳手段就是迅雷不及掩耳，犹如出膛的子弹，其追风逐日之速目力所不及也。

---

①又名《西卜林书》，是古罗马一部神谕集，相传由女预言家西彼拉所作并售与古罗马王政时代第七代王塔奎尼乌斯(Tarquinius，又译塔昆，约前534—前509)。传说西彼拉欲售书九卷于王，索重金，遭王拒，西焚书三卷后再售王，索价如初，遭拒后再焚三卷，此时王经占卜师点破方知该书是宝，遂以原价购残卷，藏于卡皮托尔山神庙。

②此喻最初见于古罗马作家加图(Dionysius Cato，约前3—前4世纪)的《道德箴言》第2卷，后世流传的拉丁文句为 Fronte capillata, post haec Occasio calva(时运女神前额有发，后脑光秃)。

③普路同是希腊罗马神话之冥王。

解析

一、拖延——

1. 有时会带来好处；

2. 往往是有害的(三个例子)。

二、真正的智慧在于把握好拖延的限度，因为——

1. 对危险未加准备是增大危险，然而——

2. 为危险做准备往往会导致危险。

三、准备应保密，实施应迅捷，如出膛的子弹。

Of Delays

FORTUNE is like the market; where many times if you can stay a little, the price will fall. Again, it is sometimes like Sibylla's offer; which at first, offereth the commodity at full, then consumeth part and part, and still holdeth up the price. For occasion (as it is in the common verse) turneth a bald noddle, after she hath presented her locks in front, and no hold taken; or at least turneth the handle of the bottle, first to be received, and after the belly, which is hard to clasp. There is surely no greater wisdom, than well to time the beginnings, and onsets, of things. Dangers are no more light, if they once seem light; and more dangers have deceived men, than forced them. Nay, it were better, to meet some dangers half way, though they come nothing near, than to keep too long a watch upon their approaches; for if a man watch too long, it is odds he will fall asleep. On the other side, to be deceived with too long shadows (as some have been, when the moon was low, and shone on their enemies' back), and so to shoot off before the time; or to teach dangers to come on, by over early buckling towards them; is another extreme. The ripeness, or unripeness, of the occasion (as we said) must ever be well weighed; and generally it is good, to commit the beginnings of all great actions to Argus, with his hundred eyes, and the ends to Briareus, with his hundred hands; first to watch, and then to speed. For the helmet of Pluto, which maketh the politic man go invisible, is secrecy in the counsel, and celerity in the execution. For when things are once come to the execution, there is no secrecy, comparable to celerity; like the motion of a bullet in the air, which flieth so swift, as it outruns the eye.

22.论狡诈

笔者以为狡诈乃一种邪恶或畸形的智慧。毋庸置疑，狡诈者与聪明人之间有天壤之别，其别不仅在于诚实，而且还在于能力。牌桌上有人善弄手脚，但论牌技却并非高手；官场上有人善游说拉票，结党营私，但除此之外就一无所长。须知人情练达是一回事，世事洞明则是另一回事；盖精于鉴貌辨色者大有人在，可这些人做大事却不甚能干，此乃只揣度他人之腹而不披览古今之书者的一大通病。这等人适合做收发文牍而不宜参政议事，他们也只在自家的球槽里才能滚出好球。若被送到陌生人中间，他们就会晕头转向；所以亚里斯提卜[①]那条老规则对他们刚好适用，那位先哲曾说：把两个人赤裸裸地置于陌生人中间，你便可从两人中分辨出上智下愚。鉴于狡诈者都像是些小商小贩，故说说他们店里的货色也并不为过。

与人交谈时注意察言观色乃狡诈之一要点，正如耶稣会[②]会士在其戒律中所规定的那样，因为许多聪明人心能保密但脸却无遮无掩。不过在察言观色时目光往往得假装谦恭，亦如耶稣会会士通常所做的那样。

另一个要点是，当你迫不及待地为获得某事某物而请求某人时，你得先拐弯抹角地东拉西扯让那人高兴，以免他因过于清醒而拒绝你的请求。我曾认识一位枢密院顾问兼国务大臣，他每次去请伊丽莎白女王签文件时，总要先引女王与他谈论国是，如此女王便不可能有更多的心思去注意她签署的文件。

①亚里斯提卜(约前435—前356)，古希腊哲学家，昔勒尼学派创始人。

②耶稣会是天主教一主要修会，1534年由西班牙贵族罗耀拉(Loyola，1491—1556)创建于巴黎，其目的是反对宗教改革，重振天主教会，维护教皇权威，其行动信条是为达上述目的可以不择手段。该会会士一般不穿教服，不住僧院，而是以各种职业为掩护广泛接触社会，从事阴谋活动，甚至暗杀不与教皇合作的政界要人(如法王亨利三世和亨利四世均被耶稣会刺杀)，故Jesuit(耶稣会会士)一词在西语中又有狡诈者、虚伪者和阴谋家等义。

与上一点相似，你亦可趁某人忙得不可开交时突然向他提出请求，这样他便无暇对你的请求加以仔细考虑。

如果你反对某人即将提出的某项提案，而你又觉得那人的论据之充分将足以使该提案有效通过，那你必须装出对该提案非常赞同，并在会上由自己将它提出，但当然要用一种能使之被否决的方式。

欲言之事刚说半截又戛然而止，仿佛你突然意识到自己失言，如此往往会引起听话人想听下半截话的欲望。

鉴于经问询而得知之事总比不打自招的话可信，你不妨设下诱饵引他人来探询你欲言之事，譬如说你装出一副与往日不同的表情，以便别人有机会问你脸色变化为何故，就像尼希米当年所为："我素来在王面前没有愁容。"①

欲言难以启齿且令人不快之事时，最好让某位人微言轻者先去把事情捅破，然后你再装作是碰巧介入该事，以便当事人向你提问以证实前者的通报。当年纳尔奇苏斯就曾用此法向克劳狄报告梅萨丽娜和西利乌斯的婚事。②

欲言某事又不想把自己牵扯于其中，狡诈者之一法是借用世人名义，你不妨说"人人都在议论"，或说"四下里都在传闻"。

笔者曾认识一人，此君写信时总把最要紧的事作为附言写在信末，仿佛那事是被附带提及似的。

笔者还认识一个人，此公发言时总把他最想说的话留在最后，往往是海阔天空地说上一阵后再谈正题，而且谈的方式就像他在讲一件差点儿被忘掉的事情。

有些人在其欲施加影响的客人来时爱佯装感到意外，仿佛来客是不期而至似的，这时他们往往是手里正捏着一封信，或是正在做某件他们不常

---

①见《旧约·尼希米记》，流亡于波斯宫廷的犹太领袖尼希米欲归（当时耶路撒冷被巴比伦毁），故在波斯王前露愁容，引王发问，表心迹后遂得归，重建耶路撒冷城垣。

②据塔西佗《编年史》第 11 卷 29—30 章记载，罗马皇帝克劳狄（在位期 41—51）的第三任妻子梅萨丽娜与情夫西利乌斯举行秘密婚礼，以释放奴身份任皇帝秘书的纳尔奇苏斯说服宫中两名女人向皇帝通风报信，然后再谒帝详陈，结果皇帝处死梅萨丽娜。可参见商务版《罗马十二帝王传》中之《克劳狄传》。

做的事情，其目的是想让客人就他们本来就想说的事情发问。

狡诈之又一要术是让某些话从自己口中道出，存心让他人拾此牙慧去调嘴学舌，从而占他的便宜。笔者认识两位伊丽莎白时代的旧同僚，他俩为国务大臣一职相争，但仍然保持交往，而且常就任职之事交换意见。其中一人说，在王权衰落的时代当大臣很伤脑筋，他可不想揽这种棘手的事情；另一位马上就捡过此话，并对其三朋四友说，他没理由要在这王权衰落的时代当一名大臣。最初说这话的那人抓住时机，设法让此话传进了女王的耳朵，"王权衰落"四字令女王大为光火，从此她再也不听那另一个人的请求。

另外还有一种狡诈，我们英国人管它叫"锅里翻饼"，其做法是一个人把他对另一个人说的话翻过来说成是另一个人对他所言。而实话实说，既然这事只有那两人才知道真相，所以要弄清这话出自谁人之口实属不易。

以败事有余的方式证明自己有资格替他人担保，从而置被担保人于不利境地，这也是某些人采用的伎俩，这就如同说"这等事叫我就不会干"。当年提格利努斯替布鲁斯说话就用过这种方式：他对陛下并无二心，只是想确保皇上平安。[①]

有些人备有一肚子的奇闻轶事，以致他无论想隐射什么，都可以让自己的话披上传闻的外衣，这样既可以保护自己，又可使听话人乐于去传播自己的话。

在自己的要求和措辞中体现出自己想要的答复，这也不失为一种狡诈之招，因为这样便可使答话人少些困惑。

有些人在言欲言之事前，所拖沓延宕之久、所绕的弯子之大，以及所东拉西扯之多都令人不可思议。这样做需要极大的耐心，但却往往收到奇效。

趁人不备时没头没脑地突然发问，往往可令对方措手不及，从而使其暴露无遗。这就像有个已改名换姓的人在圣保罗教堂[②]散步，另一个人突然在他身后直呼其真名，前者必然会回头一样。

此类狡诈之花招伎俩可谓不计其数，能为它们开出份清单实乃大功大

①布鲁斯是罗马禁卫军统帅，曾与塞内加一道当过尼禄的老师。尼禄荒淫无道，布鲁斯多次劝他弃恶扬善，终被尼禄毒死；提格利努斯系尼禄宠臣，此处所述他坑害布鲁斯一事见于塔西佗《编年史》第 14 卷。

②伦敦的圣保罗大教堂在培根时代是一个散步、聚会和谈生意的去处。

德；因为对国家来说，最大的危害莫过于把狡诈之徒当作明智之士。

但毋庸置疑，有些人就是只知事物的起始兴衰，但却弄不懂起始兴衰的缘由。这就像一座房子只有方便的楼梯和门户，但却没有一个像样的房间。所以世人可见，这等只知其然者在作判断时也许会歪打正着，但却绝无能力审时度势。然而他们却往往因其无能而得到好处，居然常常被认为是治国安民的精英。有些人步步高升与其说是凭自己坚实的努力，不如说是靠利用他人，或者(如笔者上文所述)是靠欺人骗人诓人诈人；但所罗门有言："智者之智在于明道，愚者之愚在于欺诈。"[①]

解析

一、狡诈乃一种邪恶或畸形的智慧，应当被揭露。

二、揭露狡诈的要点：

1. 与人交谈时察言观色；
2. 从你真正的需求上转移注意力；
3. 趁别人忙得不可开交时提出请求；
4. 利用表面同意的方式破坏提案；
5. 巧妙地制造对你希望的东西的兴趣；
6. 引诱你的听众探寻你欲言之事；
7. 用他人去说你欲言之事；
8. 将你欲言之事模糊地说成是大众传言；
9. 突出你想说的事情，却把它当成是——
   (1) 一个附记，
   (2) 一件差点被忘掉的事情，
   (3) 出乎意料提及之事；
10. 伤害竞争对手——
    (1) 引导他们说出一些有失判断的言论，

①语出《旧约·箴言》第14章8节。

(2)“锅里翻饼”,让人无法知道话是出自谁人之口;

11. 借自卫之名攻击对手;

12. 将你的真实意图隐藏在故事中;

13. 借对手之口说出你想要的回答;

14. 谨慎地言及自己所欲之事;

15. 趁人不备时突然发问。

三、所有这些小诡计都不是才能,智者避而远之。

Of Cunning

WE TAKE cunning for a sinister or crooked wisdom. And certainly there is a great difference, between a cunning man, and a wise man; not only in point of honesty, but in point of ability. There be, that can pack the cards, and yet cannot play well; so there are some that are good in canvasses and factions, that are otherwise weak men. Again, it is one thing to understand persons, and another thing to understand matters; for many are perfect in men's humors, that are not greatly capable of the real part of business; which is the constitution of one that hath studied men, more than books. Such men are fitter for practice, than for counsel; and they are good, but in their own alley: turn them to new men, and they have lost their aim; so as the old rule, to know a fool from a wise man, Mitte ambos nudos ad ignotos, et videbis, doth scarce hold for them.① And because these cunning men, are like haberdashers of small wares, it is not amiss to set forth their shop.

It is a point of cunning, to wait upon him with whom you speak, with your eye; as the Jesuits give it in precept: for there be many wise men, that have secret hearts, and transparent countenances. Yet this would be done with a demure abasing of your eye, sometimes, as the Jesuits also do use.

Another is, that when you have anything to obtain, of present despatch, you entertain and amuse the party, with whom you deal, with some other discourse; that he be not too much awake to make objections. I knew a counsellor and secretary, that never came to Queen Elizabeth of England, with bills to sign, but he would always first put her into some discourse of estate,

①Send them both unprepared among strangers, and you will see (the difference).

that she mought the less mind the bills.

The like surprise may be made by moving things, when the party is in haste, and cannot stay to consider advisedly of that is moved.

If a man would cross a business, that he doubts some other would handsomely and effectually move, let him pretend to wish it well, and move it himself in such sort as may foil it.

The breaking off, in the midst of that one was about to say, as if he took himself up, breeds a greater appetite in him with whom you confer, to know more.

And because it works better, when anything seemeth to be gotten from you by question, than if you offer it of yourself, you may lay a bait for a question, by showing another visage, and countenance, than you are wont; to the end to give occasion, for the party to ask, what the matter is of the change? As Nehemias did; And I had not before that time, been sad before the king.

In things that are tender and unpleasing, it is good to break the ice, by some whose words are of less weight, and to reserve the more weighty voice, to come in as by chance, so that he may be asked the question upon the other's speech: as Narcissus did, relating to Claudius the marriage of Messalina and Silius.

In things that a man would not be seen in himself, it is a point of cunning, to borrow the name of the world; as to say, The world says, or There is a speech abroad.

I knew one that, when he wrote a letter, he would put that, which was most material, in the postscript, as if it had been a by-matter.

I knew another that, when he came to have speech, he would pass over that, that he intended most; and go forth, and come back again, and speak of it as of a thing, that he had almost forgot.

Some procure themselves, to be surprised, at such times as it is like the party that they work upon, will suddenly come upon them; and to be found with a letter in their hand, or doing somewhat which they are not accustomed; to the end, they may be apposed of those things, which of themselves they are desirous to utter.

It is a point of cunning, to let fall those words in a man's own name, which he would have another man learn, and use, and thereupon take advantage. I knew two, that were competitors for the secretary's place in Queen Elizabeth's time, and yet kept good quarter between themselves; and would confer, one with another, upon the business; and the one of them said, That to be a secretary, in the declination of a monarchy, was a ticklish thing, and that he did not affect it: the other straight caught up those words, and discoursed with divers of his friends, that he had no reason to desire to be secretary, in the declination of a monarchy. The first man took hold of it, and found means it was told the Queen; who, hearing of a declination of a monarchy, took it so ill, as she would never after hear of the other's suit.

There is a cunning, which we in England call, the turning of the cat in the pan; which is, when that which a man says to another, he lays it as if another had said it to him. And to say the truth, it is not easy, when such a matter passed between two, to make it appear from which of them it first moved and began.

It is a way that some men have, to glance and dart at others, by justifying themselves by negatives; as to say, This I do not; as Tigellinus did towards Burrhus, Se non diversas spes, sed incolumitatem imperatoris simpliciter spectare.[①]

Some have in readiness so many tales and stories, as there is nothing they would insinuate, but they can wrap it into a tale; which serveth both to keep themselves more in guard, and to make others carry it with more pleasure.

It is a good point of cunning, for a man to shape the answer he would have, in his own words and propositions; for it makes the other party stick the less.

It is strange how long some men will lie in wait to speak somewhat they desire to say; and how far about they will fetch; and how many other matters they will beat over, to come near it. It is a thing of great patience, but yet of much use.

A sudden, bold, and unexpected question doth many times surprise a man, and lay him open. Like to him that, having changed his name, and walking in Paul's, another suddenly came behind him, and called him by his true name, whereat straightways he looked back.

But these small wares, and petty points, of cunning, are infinite; and it were a good deed to make a list of them; for that nothing doth more hurt in a state, than that cunning men pass for wise.

But certainly some there are that know the resorts and falls of business, that cannot sink into the main of it; like a house that hath convenient stairs and entries, but never a fair room. Therefore, you shall see them find out pretty looses in the conclusion, but are no ways able to examine or debate matters. And yet commonly they take advantage of their inability, and would be thought wits of direction. Some build rather upon the abusing of others,

---

①He, at any rate had no aims of his own, but regarded solely the Emperor's safety.

and (as we now say) putting tricks upon them, than upon soundness of their own proceedings. But Solomon saith, Prudens advertit ad gressus suos; stultus divertit ad dolos.[1]

---

[1]The prudent man pays heed to his goings, but the fool turns aside to deceit.

23.谈利己之聪明

若论为己营生，蚂蚁可谓一种聪明的动物，但对果园花圃来说，它却是一种祸害；而毋庸置疑，过分自私的人亦会有害于公众。故人应该理智地在私利与公利之间划出界限，不可因利己而有负于他人，尤其不可有负于君王和国家。常人之行为以自我为中心实乃不幸，因为那就像地球只绕其轴心而转，而与各重天道有亲和力的所有天体都绕别的中心而运动并有益于它们所围绕的中心。[①]一切以自我为中心，这于帝王君王尚情有可原，因为君王并不仅仅代表其自身，他们的祸福也与公众的安危息息相关；但于普通臣民或公民，一切以自我为中心则是一种大恶，因为凡事经这种人之手，他们都会使其适合自己的目的，而他们的目的往往都与君王和国家的目标背道而驰，由此可见，君王或国家不可选这种人作为臣仆或公仆，除非只让他们做一些无关紧要的琐事。谋私利的更大危害是使纲常失调。置臣利于君利之先已是违常乱纲，而为臣之小利损君之大利则更是大逆不道。然而这正是那些贪官污吏所为，腐败堕落的大臣、司库、使节和将军，无不为其蝇头小利而偏离正道，从而破坏其君王的宏图大业。而总的说来，这些人所获之利通常只与他们的财富相称，可他们为获私利而牺牲的公利则往往与其君王的财富成正比。为烤熟自家鸡蛋而不惜烧掉公家房屋，这无疑就是极端利己者的本性；然而这类利己者却往往得到主人的信任，因为他们的心思全在于如何讨好主人，如何替自己捞好处；他们可以为任何一点好处而抛弃主人的利益。

为利己而玩弄的诸多聪明，说到底是一种败坏的聪明。它是老鼠的聪明，因大屋将倾，鼠必先逃之；它是狐狸的聪明，因獾掘洞穴，狐占而居之；

---

①培根时代人们仍相信托勒密的“地心说”，而不相信哥白尼的“日心说”。另参见本书《论叛乱与骚动》一文关于“地球中心说”之注释。

它是鳄鱼的聪明,因其欲食之,必先哭之。但值得指出的是,那些除自己之外谁也不爱的人(如西塞罗笔下之庞培),到头来往往都可叹可悲;尽管他们总是为自己而牺牲他人,并自以为已用其聪明缚住了命运的翅翼,但他们终归也会变成无常命运的祭品。

解析

1. 利己与利他应相结合。
2. 对于君王,利己情有可原;对于下臣,利己极其有害。
3. 利己是一种败坏的聪明(类似于老鼠、狐狸与鳄鱼的聪明),对施行者也有灾难性的影响。

Of Wisdom for a Man's Self

AN ANT is a wise creature for itself, but it is a shrewd thing, in an orchard or garden. And certainly, men that are great lovers of themselves, waste the public. Divide with reason; between self-love and society; and be so true to thyself, as thou be not false to others; specially to thy king and country. It is a poor centre of a man's actions, himself. It is right earth. For that only stands fast upon his own centre; whereas all things, that have affinity with the heavens, move upon the centre of another, which they benefit. The referring of all to a man's self, is more tolerable in a sovereign prince; because themselves are not only themselves, but their good and evil is at the peril of the public fortune. But it is a desperate evil, in a servant to a prince, or a citizen in a republic. For whatsoever affairs pass such a man's hands, he crooketh them to his own ends; which must needs be often eccentric to the ends of his master, or state. Therefore, let princes, or states, choose such servants, as have not this mark; except they mean their service should be made but the accessory. That which maketh the effect more pernicious, is that all proportion is lost. It were disproportion enough, for the servant's good to be preferred before the master's; but yet it is a greater extreme, when a little good of the servant, shall carry things against a great good of the master's.

And yet that is the case of bad officers, treasurers, ambassadors, generals, and other false and corrupt servants; which set a bias upon their bowl, of their own petty ends and envies, to the overthrow of their master's great and important affairs. And for the most part, the good such servants receive, is after the model of their own fortune; but the hurt they sell for that good, is after the model of their master's fortune. And certainly it is the nature of extreme self-lovers, as they will set an house on fire, and it were but to roast their eggs; and yet these men many times hold credit with their masters, because their study is but to please them, and profit themselves; and for either respect, they will abandon the good of their affairs.

Wisdom for a man's self is, in many branches thereof, a depraved thing. It is the wisdom of rats, that will be sure to leave a house, somewhat before it fall. It is the wisdom of the fox, that thrusts out the badger, who digged and made room for him. It is the wisdom of crocodiles, that shed tears when they would devour. But that which is specially to be noted is, that those which (as Cicero says of Pompey) are sui amantes, sine rivali,[①] are many times unfortunate. And whereas they have, all their times, sacrificed to themselves, they become in the end, themselves sacrifices to the inconstancy of fortune, whose wings they thought, by their self-wisdom, to have pinioned.

①lovers of themselves without a rival

24.谈革新

犹如动物初生时都其貌不扬，新生事物刚出现时亦模样丑陋，因为新事物乃时间孕育的产儿。但尽管如此，如同最初使家族获荣誉者通常比保持荣誉的后人更值得尊敬一样，最初开创之(有益)先例通常亦非凭模仿便能获得。因为对误入歧途的人性来说，恶就像落体运动，越下落力量越大，而善则如抛物运动，只有起初那股力最强。毋庸置疑，每一种药物都是一项创新，不愿用新药者也得面临新的疾病，因为时间就是最伟大的创新者。如果时间循其正道使事物衰败，而人之智慧与灵性又不使其更新，那结局将会如何?但不可否认，由习惯形成的旧例虽欠优良，可至少还算适时合世，且长期并行的陈规旧俗似乎也相辅相成；而新生事物与之却难和谐融洽，虽说新东西因其效用而有助益，但也会因其令人不适而引起麻烦；再说新事物就像远方来客，往往是可敬而不可亲。然而千真万确的事情是，假设似箭如梭的时间停滞不前，那固守旧俗的做法也会像开创新风一般引起动荡；故对旧时代过分崇尚者只会成为新时代的笑柄。由此可见，世人之革新最好是循时间的榜样，时间之革故鼎新不可谓不大，但却进行得非常平缓，缓得几乎不为世人所察觉。如若不然，任何革新都会令人感到意外，而且对社会有所改良亦会有所损伤。受益者固然会视之为幸事并将其归功于时代，可受损者则会视之为犯罪并将其归咎于革新之人。而且最好别搞政体改革实验，除非情势万不得已，或是其功效十分明显。务须注意，革新应是可带来变化的改良，而非假装改良的喜新厌旧之变化。最后还须注意，虽说不可拒绝新鲜事物，但仍须对其有所质疑，正如《圣经》所言："我们停于古道，然后环顾四野，找出那条笔直的坦途，于是顺路前行。"[①]

---

①《旧约·耶利米书》第6章16节有言道："耶和华说，你们应停在路口察看，访求那些旧路古道，找出最好的坦途，然后行于其上，如此你们心中将得到安宁。"

解析

一、思考——

1. 赞成革新:

(1) 时代的变迁要求革新;

(2) 革新比模仿要好;

(3) 它们可以消除新弊端。

2. 反对革新:

(1) 被革新的东西虽然欠佳,但仍可行;

(2) 用来替代的新事物可敬而不可亲。

二、革新真正的模式:

1. 循时间的榜样,进展平缓;

2. 只在情势万不得已或功效十分明显时进行改革;

3. 革新应是可带来变化的改良,而非假装改良的喜新厌旧之变化;

4. 对新事物不可拒绝,但仍须对其有所质疑。

Of Innovations

AS THE births of living creatures, at first are ill-shapen, so are all innovations, which are the births of time. Yet notwithstanding, as those that first bring honor into their family, are commonly more worthy than most that succeed, so the first precedent (if it be good) is seldom attained by imitation. For ill, to man's nature, as it stands perverted, hath a natural motion, strongest in continuance; but good, as a forced motion, strongest at first. Surely every medicine is an innovation; and he that will not apply new remedies, must expect new evils; for time is the greatest innovator; and if time of course alter things to the worse, and wisdom and counsel shall not alter them to the better, what shall be the end? It is true, that what is settled by custom, though it be not good, yet at least it is fit; and those things which have long gone together, are, as it were, confederate within themselves; whereas new things piece not so well; but though they help by their utility, yet they trouble by their inconformity. Besides, they are like strangers; more admired, and less favored. All this is true, if time stood still; which contrariwise moveth so round, that a froward retention of custom, is as turbulent a thing as an innovation; and they that reverence too much old times, are but a scorn to the new. It were good, therefore, that men in their innovations would follow the example of time itself; which indeed innovateth greatly, but quietly, by degrees scarce to be perceived. For otherwise, whatsoever is new is unlooked for; and ever it mends some, and pairs others; and he that is holpen, takes it for a fortune, and thanks the time; and he that is hurt, for a wrong, and imputeth it to the author. It is good also, not to try experiments in states, except the necessity be urgent, or the utility evident; and well to beware, that it be the reformation, that draweth on the change, and not the desire of change, that pretendeth the reformation. And lastly, that the novelty, though it be not rejected, yet be held for a suspect; and, as the Scripture saith, that we make a stand upon the ancient way, and then look about us, and discover what is the straight and right way, and so to walk in it.

25. 谈求速

急于求成对于将行之事乃最危险的因素之一，因为那就像医家所谓的预先消化[①]，肯定会在体内留下许多没法吸收的物质，从而埋下难以察觉的病根。所以衡量办事之快慢不可凭耗时之多少，而应当根据事情的进展。一如奔跑之速度并不取决于跨步之大或抬足之高，办事之迅捷亦非取决于一次办理许多，而是取决于认真负责的办理。有人只关心以较短的时间办完公务，或是设法让事情看上去已经了结，如此他们便可显得办事利索。但是凭精打细算省时是一回事，靠偷工减料求速则是另一回事；须知如此了结之事并未真正了结，而以多次会议或数轮会期来了结之事通常都反反复复，磕磕绊绊。我认识的一位明白人曾有句口头禅，他见人急于求成时爱说："少安勿躁，这样我们可以早点了事。"

但另一方面，真正的求速求快则十分宝贵，因为正如金钱是商品价值的尺度，时间亦是办事效益的尺度；若办事慢条斯理，那办成事情所付出的代价就会高昂。斯巴达人和西班牙人以慢条斯理著称，故有"让我的死神从西班牙来"一说，因为如果那样的话，死亡肯定会姗姗来迟。

最好耐心地听取有关人士就有关事务的概要汇报，宁可在其汇报之前就发号施令，也不要在其汇报之中打断人家；因为被打断思路者往往会颠三倒四，重复前言，而比起他按自己的思路顺着讲，他这样边回忆边说更为冗长乏味；不过会议主席比发言者更令人讨厌的时候并不鲜见。

说话一再重复往往浪费时间，但有时节省时间的诀窍就是反复强调问题的要点，因为这样就消除了许多可能会随之而来的冗言赘语。发言拖泥带水就如同奔跑穿长袍披风。开场白、过渡语、客套话，以及关于发言者本人的空聊闲扯，都是对时间的极大浪费；它们听起来像是在谦虚，其实是在

---

①用模拟消化过程的加工方法对食物进行预先处理，一般用于伤病员。

自夸。不过应该注意，当与会者对你的发言可能有反对之意时，则不可开门见山地亮出观点，因为脑子里的偏见需要用开场白去消除，正如要让药膏之药性发作需要热敷一样。

最值得注意的是，有条不紊、各司其职和突出重点是办事迅捷的关键所在，而且分配职责不可过于粗略，因未分职责者对事情会不闻不问，分配职责过多者则会忙得不顾后果。选择好时机就是节约时间，而不合时宜的行动只是徒劳。凡事都须经三个步骤，即筹划、讨论(或曰审议)和实施。如若你要求速就得注意，唯讨论可使较多人参加，筹划和实施则只能由少数人担任。[①]某种书面形式的议事提纲可在很大程度上提高效率，即使提纲被完全否决，那些否决意见也比无纲可循的漫谈更有指导意义，正如柴灰比土尘更有利于植物生长一样。

解析

一、行事是否迅捷应根据最后节省的时间而非当前节省的时间来判断。

二、求速之办法——

1. 开始时需耐心；
2. 坚持围绕事情的要点，除非冗言赘语可能消除对方的反对之意；
3. 注意处理问题的方法与安排；
4. 筹划与实施应由少数人担任；
5. 预先准备议事提纲。

Of Dispatch

AFFECTED dispatch is one of the most dangerous things to business that can be. It is like that, which the physicians call predigestion, or hasty digestion; which is sure to fill the body full of crudities, and secret seeds of

①此句中的“你”、“较多人”和“少数人”当分别指当时的英国国王、国会和枢密院。

diseases. Therefore measure not dispatch, by the times of sitting, but by the advancement of the business. And as in races it is not the large stride or high lift that makes the speed; so in business, the keeping close to the matter, and not taking of it too much at once, procureth dispatch. It is the care of some, only to come off speedily for the time; or to contrive some false periods of business, because they may seem men of dispatch. But it is one thing, to abbreviate by contracting, another by cutting off. And business so handled, at several sittings or meetings, goeth commonly backward and forward in an unsteady manner. I knew a wise man that had it for a byword, when he saw men hasten to a conclusion, Stay a little, that we may make an end the sooner.

On the other side, true dispatch is a rich thing. For time is the measure of business, as money is of wares; and business is bought at a dear hand, where there is small dispatch. The Spartans and Spaniards have been noted to be of small dispatch; Mi venga la muerte de Spagna; Let my death come from Spain; for then it will be sure to be long in coming.

Give good hearing to those, that give the first information in business; and rather direct them in the beginning, than interrupt them in the continuance of their speeches; for he that is put out of his own order, will go forward and backward, and be more tedious, while he waits upon his memory, than he could have been, if he had gone on in his own course. But sometimes it is seen, that the moderator is more troublesome, than the actor.

Iterations are commonly loss of time. But there is no such gain of time, as to iterate often the state of the question; for it chaseth away many a frivolous speech, as it is coming forth. Long and curious speeches, are as fit for dispatch, as a robe or mantle, with a long train, is for race. Prefaces and passages, and excusations, and other speeches of reference to the person, are great wastes of time; and though they seem to proceed of modesty, they are bravery. Yet beware of being too material, when there is any impediment or obstruction in men's wills; for pre-occupation of mind ever requireth preface of speech; like a fomentation to make the unguent enter.

Above all things, order, and distribution, and singling out of parts, is the life of dispatch; so as the distribution be not too subtle: for he that doth not divide, will never enter well into business; and he that divideth too much, will never come out of it clearly. To choose time, is to save time; and an unseasonable motion, is but beating the air. There be three parts of business; the preparation, the debate or examination, and the perfection. Whereof, if you look for dispatch, let the middle only be the work of many, and the first and last the work of few. The proceeding upon somewhat conceived in writing, doth for the most part facilitate dispatch: for though it should be wholly rejected, yet that negative is more pregnant of direction, than an indefinite; as ashes are more generative than dust.

26.谈貌似聪明

世人历来有种看法，认为法国人实际上比看上去聪明，而西班牙人则看上去比实际上聪明。但且不论民族之间的这种差异到何等程度，人与人之间的情况可的确如此，因为正如圣保罗所说："有人虚有虔诚的外表，实无虔诚的内心。"[①]所以就智慧和能力而言，这世上当然就有些虽不会做事、很少做事，或只能"极其费力地做点小事"[②]的聪明能干之人。若能看出这类徒有其表者是用什么手段和方法使虚显实，使浅显深并使小显大，那明智之士都会觉得荒唐可笑，会觉得这等事真该写成篇讽刺文章。他们中有些人讳莫如深，以致他们的货色都只能在暗处出示，而且还总显得有所保留；这些人心头虽然也明白他们对自己所言之事通常都不甚了了，可表面上却装出他们懂得诸多也许难以言传的事理。有些人显得聪明完全是借助于表情手势，他们就像西塞罗所形容的庇索[③]："你回答说不赞成虐待之时，一道眉毛扬到了额顶，另一道则垂到了腮帮。"有些人以为凭吹牛说大话和专横独断就可以获得聪明，并进而以为只要被允许他们就可以担任其没有能力胜任的职务。有些人对自己弄不懂的一切都装出鄙薄的样子，或将其作为荒唐事古怪事睨而视之，以为如此便可使他们的无知显得像有见识。有些人凡事都有其与众不同的见解，并常常用诡辩糊弄世人以回避所谈论的问题。杰利乌斯曾为这种人下过定义，说他们是"用模棱两可的华丽词藻误大

---

①语出《新约·提摩太后书》第3章5节。

②语出古罗马喜剧作家泰伦提乌斯(Terentius，约前190—前159)之喜剧《自责者》第3幕5场8行。

③指鲁基乌斯·庇索(Lucius Piso)，恺撒之岳父，公元前58年任执政官时曾与保民官克劳狄乌斯一道控告西塞罗违法，使之流亡于希腊、马其顿等地，公元前57—前55年任马其顿总督，卸任后归罗马在元老院遭到西塞罗面劾，下文引言即出西塞罗面劾之词。

事的白痴”[1]；柏拉图也在其对话《普罗塔哥拉篇》中对这类人的代表普罗蒂库斯[2]进行过嘲讽，他让那位诡辩家发表了一篇从头到尾都用与众不同的见解构成的演说。一般说来，这种人在审议任何提案时都乐于持否定态度，并指望凭着表示反对和预言困难而获得声望；因为提案一经否决他们就万事大吉，而提案若被通过则需要一番新的工作。这种骗人的聪明实乃国家大业的祸害。总而言之，这些不学无术者一心要保住的就是他们精明能干的名声，正如负债的商人和破产的阔佬一心想保住他们富有的名声一样，不过若论为保名声而玩弄的花招之多，后者比之前者则可谓小巫见大巫。貌似聪明者也许会凭其手腕获得名声，但当政者千万别挑选他们担任要职；因不可否认，即便用那种稍显愚笨者也胜过任用这等徒有其表的聪明人。

解析

一、有些人，尽管不是所有人，努力使自己看上去比实际聪明。

二、达到这一目的常用的手段：

1. 假装有所保留；
2. 用表情手势佯装掩饰；
3. 专横独断、气势汹汹；
4. 假装鄙薄他们所言之事；
5. 字词上的诡辩；
6. 借助于否定他人言论的反对策略。

三、这等人不能选用，因为他们还不如那种十足的蠢材。

---

①此语出自古罗马修辞学家昆提利安（Quintilian，约 35—95）的《雄辩术教程》（又译《演说术原理》），而非出自古罗马作家杰利乌斯（Gellius，约 123—165）笔下。

②普罗塔哥拉和普罗蒂库斯均为公元前 5 世纪末至公元前 4 世纪初的希腊智者派哲学家，而智者派是柏拉图一生的主要政敌，他称该学派为诡辩派。

Of Seeming Wise

IT HATH been an opinion, that the French are wiser than they seem, and the Spaniards seem wiser than they are. But howsoever it be between nations, certainly it is so between man and man. For as the Apostle saith of godliness, Having a show of godliness, but denying the power thereof; so certainly there are, in point of wisdom and sufficiently, that do nothing or little very solemnly: magno conatu nugas①. It is a ridiculous thing, and fit for a satire to persons of judgment, to see what shifts these formalists have, and what prospectives to make superficies to seem body, that hath depth and bulk. Some are so close and reserved, as they will not show their wares, but by a dark light; and seem always to keep back somewhat; and when they know within themselves, they speak of that they do not know well, would nevertheless seem to others, to know of that which they may not well speak. Some help themselves with countenance and gesture, and are wise by signs; as Cicero saith of Piso, that when he answered him, he fetched one of his brows up to his forehead, and bent the other down to his chin; Respondes, altero ad frontem sublato, altero ad mentum depresso supercilio, crudelitatem tibi non placere. ② Some think to bear it by speaking a great word, and being peremptory; and go on, and take by admittance, that which they cannot make good. Some, whatsoever is beyond their reach, will seem to despise, or make light of it, as impertinent or curious; and so would have their ignorance seem judgment. Some are never without a difference, and commonly by amusing men with a subtilty, blanch the matter; of whom A. Gellius saith, Hominem delirum, qui verborum minutiis rerum frangit pondera③. Of which kind also, Plato, in his Protagoras, bringeth in Prodicus in scorn, and maketh him make a speech, that consisteth of distinction from the beginning to the end. Generally, such men in all deliberations find ease to be of the negative side, and affect a credit to object and foretell difficulties; for when propositions are denied, there is an end of them; but if they be allowed, it requireth a new work; which false point of wisdom is the bane of business. To conclude, there is no decaying merchant, or inward beggar, hath so many tricks to uphold the credit of their wealth, as these empty persons have, to maintain the credit of their sufficiency. Seeming wise men may make shift to get opinion; but let no man choose

①trifles with great effort

②You answer, with one eyebrow raised up to your chin, that cruelly does not please you.

③a senseless man, who tries to break down weighty matters with verbal quibbles them for employment; for certainly you were better to take for business, a man somewhat absurd, than over-formal.

27. 论友谊

喜欢孤独者非兽即神,[①]恐怕连说出这句名言的人也再难用别的寥寥数语如此高明地把真理和谬误混为一谈,因人对社会抱有的天生而隐秘的憎恶中固然有些许兽性,但若说那其中有神性则大谬不然,除非那憎恶并非出自乐于孤独,而是出自人对一种更崇高的生活之热爱和向往,这种更崇高的向往在传说中见于一些异教徒,如克里特岛人埃庇门笛斯、古罗马国王努马、西西里岛人恩培多克勒和蒂尔那人阿波罗尼乌斯,[②]在现实中则见于古代的许多隐士和教会中的众多神父。但普通人几乎不知何为孤独,亦不知孤独可蔓延多广。其实在没有爱心的地方,熙攘的人群并非伴侣,如流的面孔无非是条画廊,而交口攀谈也不过是铙钹作声。此情有句拉丁格言略能描绘:一座都市便是一片荒野。因为在都市里朋友分散,所以大多数人难觅可见于小镇上的那种友谊。但笔者不妨进而更确切地断言,没有真正的朋友才是一种纯粹而可悲的孤独,没有真正的友谊这个世界只是一片荒野;而即便是在这种意义上的荒野里,若有人天性中缺乏交友的倾向,那他的天性也是来自兽类,而非来自人类。

友谊的一个主要作用乃宣泄积压的感情,使心情舒畅,而喜怒哀乐均可导致情满欲溢的状态,世人皆知滞疴郁疾对人体最为危险,须知情感之郁积基本上亦复如此。人可用菝葜剂疏肝,用铁质丸浚脾,用硫磺粉宣肺,

---

①语出亚里士多德《政治学》第1章2节。

②埃庇门笛斯乃公元前6世纪希腊哲学家及诗人,相传他曾在洞中一觉睡了57年;努马乃古罗马王政时代的第二代国王(在位期前715—前673),相传他曾在一洞中受仙女埃吉丽亚教诲而创立宗教历法和各种宗教礼仪;恩培多克勒(约前490—前430)乃古希腊哲学家,传说他跳进埃特纳火山口而死,目的是这样突然消失会使世人以为他是神;阿波罗尼乌斯出生在土耳其蒂尔那,为公元1世纪哲学家,曾周游列国,后定居希腊,关于他有许多奇迹般的传说。

用海狸香通脑，可除了真正的朋友外，世上无任何灵丹妙药可以舒心。只有面对知心朋友，人才可能倾吐其忧伤、欢乐、恐惧、希望、猜疑、忠告，以及压在心头的任何感情，这就像一种教门外的世俗忏悔。

若知帝王君主们是多么看重笔者谈论的这种友谊，世人定会感到奇怪，因为君王们对这种友谊是如此看重，以致为求之而往往不顾自己的安全和高贵。鉴于帝王与臣仆间的地位之悬殊，他们本无可能得到这种友谊，除非(为使之可能)他们把某些人提升到几乎与自己平起平坐的地位，而这往往导致诸多麻烦。现代语管这种人叫宠信或亲信，仿佛他们之高升仅仅是因为得君王恩宠或与君王过从甚密；但古罗马语称这种人为“分忧者”，此名才算道出了他们的作用和高升的原因，惟其“分忧”能使君臣结成挚友。世人尚可清楚地看到，与臣下结莫逆之交者不止是那种软弱无能、多情善感的君主，而且还有那种具雄才大略、能称霸于世的帝王，这些帝王常与臣下交好，彼此之间以朋友相称，而且允许旁人在非公开场合用同样的方式称呼他们。

苏拉统治罗马时把庞培提升到高位(后来还授予他“伟大者”称号)，以致庞培自诩已胜过苏拉。因为有一次庞培不顾苏拉的好恶让自己的一个朋友当上了执政官，苏拉对此稍有不满，并开始以帝王的口吻说话，可庞培居然对他发怒，实际上还命令他免开尊口；毕竟“崇拜朝阳者比赞美落日者更多”[①]。德基摩斯·布鲁图也获得了可向恺撒施加影响的身份，以致后者在其遗嘱中指定他为继其甥外孙之后的第二顺序继承人，可正是此人具有把他拖向死亡的能力；因为当恺撒考虑到一些凶兆，尤其是考虑到妻子卡尔普尼娅的不祥之梦，正准备取消那次元老院会议时，是布鲁图挽住他的胳臂，轻轻地把他从坐椅上拉起，并说他不希望恺撒让元老们失望，不希望恺撒等妻子做了好梦后再让元老院开会。[②]此举足见他受宠之深，正如西塞罗在一篇抨击安东尼的演说中全文引述的一封安东尼的信所说的那样，安东尼在该信中把布鲁图称为巫师，仿佛他是用巫术迷惑了恺撒似的。奥古斯都曾把出身低微的阿格里巴[③]擢升到高位，以致当他就女儿尤丽娅的婚事问

①此话是公元前 81 年庞培率军从非洲回罗马后强迫苏拉为他举行凯旋式时所说。

②恺撒被刺前的详情可参阅商务印书馆 1995 年版的《罗马十二帝王传》41—43 页。

③阿格里巴 (约前 62—前 12)，平民出身的古罗马统帅，战功卓著，深得奥古斯都信任，两度出任执政官，并娶奥古斯都之女。

玛塞纳斯[①]时，后者直言答道："既然你已经使他如此显赫，那你若不把女儿嫁给他就只有杀掉他，此外没有第三条路可走。"在提比略当政时期，塞雅努斯[②]曾爬到极其显赫的位置，以致别人把他俩视为并称作一对朋友，提比略在一封写给他的信中说："鉴于我俩的友谊，我从未对你隐瞒过这些事情。"[③]为了对他俩的伟大友谊表示敬重，元老院还一致决定建了座友谊祭坛，就像是为一位女神建的祭坛一样。塞维鲁与普劳蒂亚努斯的关系如同上例，[④]或者说还有过之而无不及。因塞维鲁强迫自己的大儿子娶了普劳蒂亚努斯的女儿，并经常容忍普劳蒂亚努斯公开侮辱他儿子；他也在写给元老院的一封信中说："吾爱此人至深，愿他比朕长寿。"[⑤]如果上述诸位皇帝都像是图拉真或马可·奥勒留[⑥]，那世人尚可认定他们的所作所为是因为其天性太善良，可上述诸君全都属于狡诈诡谲、骁勇强悍、作风严厉且极端自私之辈，这就清楚地证明了虽说他们的大福大贵已到了世人不可企及的地步，可他们仍然觉得美中不足，除非能有个朋友使之完美；而尚需说明的是，这些帝王都有妻子、儿子和侄甥，但天伦之乐不能弥补友情之乐。

在此不应忽略的是康明[⑦]对其第一位主人勃艮第公爵查理的评述，他

①玛塞纳斯(约前70—前8)，古罗马政治家及艺术保护人，是贺拉斯、维吉尔和屋大维(即后来的奥古斯都)的挚友，在奥古斯都继位后成为他的顾问。

②塞雅努斯，古罗马政治家及阴谋家，提比略的宠臣，长期任禁卫军统帅(公元15—31)，公元31年出任执政官；曾与提比略的媳妇莉维亚合谋毒死提比略之子德鲁苏斯，后因对提比略构成威胁而被处死。

③语出塔西佗《编年史》第4卷40章。

④普劳蒂亚努斯和上例中的塞雅努斯情况相似，在塞维鲁当政(193—211)时任过禁卫军统帅，于204年密谋篡位未遂被诛。

⑤语出狄奥《罗马史》第75章15节。

⑥其实这两位罗马皇帝同样好穷兵黩武。图拉真(在位期98—117)被认为善良也许是因为他的处世态度比诸先帝温和，较为妥善地处理了国内社会矛盾，使罗马出现了一个"太平盛世"；马可·奥勒留(在位期161—180)政绩平平，可他是新斯多葛派哲学家，在行军中写成《沉思录》12篇，其论多善。

⑦康明(约1447—1511)，法国政治活动家及历史学家，曾先后事勃艮第公爵查理(勇敢者)、法王路易十一和查理八世，晚年写成《回忆录》八卷，颇具史料价值，已有多种语言译本，培根在此引用的评述即出自该书第5卷3章。

说查理从不向人吐露心中的隐秘，尤其是那些最使他烦恼的隐秘。接着他又说道：查理的守口如瓶到后来损伤了，或者说在一定程度上毁了他的判断力。毫无疑问，要是康明愿意，他也完全可以把这段评述一字不改地用于他的第二个主人路易十一，因这位国王之讳莫如深的确曾使他自己备受折磨。毕达哥拉斯那句三字格言虽晦涩难解但却一语破的：勿食心（Cor ne edito）；若勉为其难地将其说成明白话，那言下之意就是无朋友可吐露心迹者实乃食其心者。不过还有一点更令人惊奇(笔者就以此来结束关于友谊的第一种作用之讨论)，这就是向朋友倾述衷肠可产生两种相反的结果，一是使欢乐加倍，一是使烦忧减半；因为凡与朋友分享欢乐者都会感到其乐更甚，而凡是把忧愁告诉朋友者都会觉得忧愁顿减。所以友谊对人心所起的作用的确就像炼金术士的点金石对人体所起的作用，因为点金石对人体的作用也完全相反，但却都具有好的性质。[①]不过即使不替炼金术士鼓吹，通常也有一种明显的类似比喻，即任何物质之类聚均可增强并保持其天然作用，同时亦可削弱并减轻外力的影响；自然万物如斯，人之心亦然。

如友谊的第一种作用极有益于感情之健康一样，友谊的第二种作用极有益于理智之健全；因为友谊既可把感情之暴风骤雨变成丽日和风，亦可把理智之混沌暗夜变成朗朗白昼，这种变化不可仅仅被理解为是因为得到了朋友的忠告；其实在得到忠告前，任何百思缠其心者只要与旁人讨论沟通，他也会头脑更加开窍，心智更加豁朗，从而会更容易地表达其想法，更有序地整理其思路，并意识到自己的思想变成语言时是何模样，最后终于变得更为明智。这真可谓一小时交谈胜过一整天沉思。特米斯托克利[②]对波斯王那番话讲得极好，他说："语言犹如展开的挂毯，心象意念都显现在其图案之中；而思想则如未打开的挂毯，心象意念只是被裹在里面。"说到友谊开启理智这种作用，它也不仅仅限于那些可给予忠告的朋友(这种朋友的确最好)，因即使没有这样的朋友，人亦可听自己说话，可以亮出自己的思想，像磨刃于石一般对其进行磨砺，须知此刃不会伤此砺石。总而言

①传说中的点金石既可使人延年益寿，又可替人祛病除疾，前者为增，后者为减，但都有益处。

②特米斯托克利（约前 524—前 460），古雅典民主派政治家，曾任执政官，政绩显著，后遭贵族派用陶片放逐法放逐，辗转至波斯（前 471 年），波斯王予以善待。

之，人宁可对一尊塑像或一幅绘画吐露心迹，也不要让所思所想在心里窒息。

为了充分说明友谊的第二种作用，且让笔者再进一步说说那本身非常清楚但一般人却没说明白的一点，即朋友的忠告。赫拉克利特有句晦涩的名言：Dry light is ever the best。[①]而毫无疑问，与仅凭自己的理解判断得出的见解相比，据朋友的忠告形成的看法通常都更为公允，更为完善，因为一个人的理解力和判断力总是浸泡在自己的偏好和习惯之中。所以朋友的建议和自己的主张往往有极大差异，这就如同朋友的忠告和谄媚者的奉承有极大差异一样；因为最喜欢奉承自己的人莫过于自己，而医治自以为是的最佳良药又莫过于朋友的忠告。忠告一般分为两类，一类就品行而言，一类就事业而论。说到品行方面，保持心灵健康的最好药物就是朋友的谆谆告诫。严于责己有时难免会过于尖酸刻薄，读劝善说教之经籍又有点枯燥乏味，而以人为镜有时候又不合自身实情；所以最好的药物（亦是最起作用且最易服用的药物）就是朋友的药石之言。说来真叫人不可思议，许多先人（尤其是一些英雄豪杰）就因为没有能进忠言的朋友而铸下大谬极误，从而毁了自己的名声和好运；因为他们就像圣雅各说的那种人，有时也照照镜子，但转身就忘了自己的模样。[②]说到事业方面，一个人只要愿意，他尽可以去以为两双眼之所见并不多于一双眼之所见，或当局者总比旁观者清，或正在发怒者比默念过二十四个字母的人更为明智，[③]或步枪举在手上和放在架上都打得一样准，总而言之，他尽可以去发挥他幼稚而傲慢的想象，以为自己便是一切的一切；但等这一切都试过之后，他会发现只有忠告才能使事业去偏就正。如果有人认为，他乐意接受忠告，但只用零散的方式，即

①这是一句以讹传讹的格言（大概是因为赫拉克利特本来就有"晦涩哲人"之称），在从古希腊语译成拉丁语时已出现 lumen siccum (dry light) 二字。西方学者对此的解释历来众说纷纭，除培根的英译文外，这句格言的英译文还有"The dry soul is the wisest and best"、"The dry light is the wisest soul"、"The dry mind (uninfluenced by feelings and appetites) is the wisest and best"。本书译者将此格言理解为"不带个人偏见的看法往往最为明智"。

②圣雅各在《新约·雅各书》第 1 章 23—24 节中用此比喻来形容那些对基督的劝喻听之藐藐并不去实行的人。

③在培根时代，英语字母 i 和 j、u 和 v 尚无区别，故字母表中只有 24 个字母。另西方人认为发怒时默念一遍字母表足以息怒。

就一事同此人商量，就另一事与彼人讨论。这样当然也不错(就是说总比完全不请教人更好)，但他将冒两种风险：一是他可能得不到真正的忠告，因为除挚友至交外，少有人替人家出主意时不为自己的私利盘算；二是他得到的建议虽是出于好意，但却并不可靠甚至有害，即他得到的建议既是良药又是祸根。这就像你有病求医，找到一位善治你所患疾病但却不了解你身体状况的医生，结果他也许会治好你眼下的病，但同时却在另一方面毁掉你的健康，此乃所谓的治好疾病却杀了病人。但替你出谋划策的若是位熟悉你事业的朋友，他就会注意别为了办好你眼前的事务而替你招来其他麻烦。所以不要依赖零散的建议，它们往往只会引起混乱并造成误导，而很少能稳定事态并对其有所指引。

除上述两种可观的作用外(即除平息感情和加强理智外)，友谊还有一种作用，而这种作用犹如石榴，果内多籽，此喻的意思是说这种作用可见于各种日常行为和各种场合。在这一点上，要生动地说明友谊之种种益处，最好的办法就是看看生活中有多少事不能靠自己去做，如此一看便会觉得“朋友乃另一己身”这句古话说得过于谨慎，因为一个朋友远远多于一个己身。生死有命，多少人临终尚惦着某件放不下的心事，诸如子女之安顿、工作之完成等等。但若是临终者有位挚友，他便可以瞑目安息，因为他知道身后事自有人料理；而就其所惦念的事情而言，可以说这个人有了两次生命。一人只有一身，而一身不能同时在两地，但若是一个人在远方有朋友，就可以说那个地方为他和他的代理人提供了办事场所，因为他可以让他的朋友在那里做事。再说人一生有多少自己难以启齿或不宜去说的事?如人不能既自己表功又显得谦逊，更不用说对自己的功绩大吹大擂；又如人有时候不能低三下四地去央告或恳求。这类不宜自己去说的话实在太多，但这些自己说来会赧颜的话出自朋友之口则很得体。另外一个人的社会角色使他有许多没法摆脱的关系，如他对儿子说话得作为父亲，对妻子说话得作为丈夫，对他的敌人说话更须考虑自己的身份，但是朋友出面说话则可就事论事，不必考虑与听话人的关系。鉴于这类事例不胜枚举，笔者曾提供过一条规则：若是一个人在某方面不能得体地扮演自己的角色，而他又没有一个朋友，那他倒不如退下舞台。

解析

一、除非是有精神上的意图，否则孤独具有兽性，不管——

1. 是荒原似的孤独（即没有同伴），
2. 还是在众人中没有朋友。

二、友谊的功用：

1. 宣泄积压的感情。帝王伟人们最为需要，以致为求之而不顾自己的安危，如：
   苏拉与庞培，
   恺撒与布鲁图，
   奥古斯都与阿格里巴，
   提比略与塞雅努斯，
   塞维鲁与普劳蒂亚努斯。
   实际上，没有朋友是"食心的"。
2. 健全理智——
   （1）将混浊的理智变成清晰的语言；
   （2）可以借助朋友的忠告纠正愚蠢；
   （3）朋友可帮助完成身后未竟之业，即意味着自身生命的延长。

Of Friendship

IT HAD been hard for him that spake it to have put more truth and untruth together in few words, than in that speech, Whatsoever is delighted in solitude, is either a wild beast or a god. For it is most true, that a natural and secret hatred, and aversation towards society, in any man, hath somewhat of the savage beast; but it is most untrue, that it should have any character at all, of the divine nature; except it proceed, not out of a pleasure in solitude, but out of a love and desire to sequester a man's self, for a higher conversation: such as is found to have been falsely and feignedly in some of the heathen; as Epimenides the Candian, Numa the Roman, Empedocles the Sicilian, and Apollonius of Tyana; and truly and really, in divers of the ancient hermits and holy fathers of the church. But little do men perceive what solitude is, and how far it extendeth. For a crowd is not company; and faces are but a gallery of pictures; and talk but a tinkling cymbal, where there is no love. The Latin adage meeteth with it a little: Magna civitas, magna solitudo;① because in a great town friends are scattered; so that there is not that fellowship, for the most part, which is in less neighborhoods. But we may go further, and affirm most truly, that it is a mere and miserable solitude to want true friends; without which the world is but a wilderness; and even in this sense also of solitude, whosoever in the frame of his nature and affections, is unfit for friendship, he taketh it of the beast, and not from humanity.

A principal fruit of friendship, is the ease and discharge of the fulness and swellings of the heart, which passions of all kinds do cause and induce. We know diseases of stoppings, and suffocations, are the most dangerous in the body; and it is not much otherwise in the mind; you may take sarza to open the liver, steel to open the spleen, flowers of sulphur for the lungs, castoreum for the brain; but no receipt openeth the heart, but a true friend; to whom you may impart griefs, joys, fears, hopes, suspicions, counsels, and whatsoever lieth upon the heart to oppress it, in a kind of civil shrift or confession.

It is a strange thing to observe, how high a rate great kings and monarchs do set upon this fruit of friendship, whereof we speak: so great, as they purchase it, many times, at the hazard of their own safety and greatness. For princes, in regard of the distance of their fortune from that of their subjects and servants, cannot gather this fruit, except (to make themselves capable thereof) they raise some persons to be, as it were, companions and almost equals to themselves, which many times sorteth to inconvenience. The modern languages give unto such persons the name of favorites, or privadoes; as if it were a matter of grace, or conversation. But the Roman name attaineth the true use and cause thereof, naming them participes curarum②; for it is that which tieth the knot. And we see plainly that this hath been done, not by weak and passionate princes only, but by the wisest and most politic that ever reigned; who have oftentimes joined to themselves some of their servants; whom both themselves have called friends, and allowed other likewise to call them in the same manner; using the word which is received between private men.

L. Sylla, when he commanded Rome, raised Pompey (after surnamed the

①A great city is a great solitude.

②partners in their cares

Great) to that height, that Pompey vaunted himself for Sylla's overmatch. For when he had carried the consulship for a friend of his, against the pursuit of Sylla, and that Sylla did a little resent thereat, and began to speak great, Pompey turned upon him again, and in effect bade him be quiet; for that more men adored the sun rising, than the sun setting. With Julius Caesar, Decimus Brutus had obtained that interest as he set him down in his testament, for heir in remainder, after his nephew. And this was the man that had power with him, to draw him forth to his death. For when Caesar would have discharged the senate, in regard of some ill presages, and specially a dream of Calpurnia; this man lifted him gently by the arm out of his chair, telling him he hoped he would not dismiss the senate, till his wife had dreamt a better dream. And it seemeth his favor was so great, as Antonius, in a letter which is recited verbatim in one of Cicero's Philippics, calleth him venefica, witch; as if he had enchanted Caesar. Augustus raised Agrippa (though of mean birth) to that height, as when he consulted with Maecenas, about the marriage of his daughter Julia, Maecenas took the liberty to tell him, that he must either marry his daughter to Agrippa, or take away his life; there was no third way, he had made him so great. With Tiberius Caesar, Sejanus had ascended to that height, as they two were termed, and reckoned, as a pair of friends. Tiberius in a letter to him saith, Haec pro amicitia nostra non occultavi; [①]and the whole senate dedicated an altar to Friendship, as to a goddess, in respect of the great dearness of friendship, between them two. The like, or more, was between Septimius Severus and Plautianus. For he forced his eldest son to marry the daughter of Plautianus; and would often maintain Plautianus, in doing affronts to his son; and did write also in a letter to the senate, by these words: I love the man so well, as I wish he may overlive me. Now if these princes had been as a Trajan, or a Marcus Aurelius, a man might have thought that this had proceeded of an abundant goodness of nature; but being men so wise, of such strength and severity of mind, and so extreme lovers of themselves, as all these were, it proveth most plainly that they found their own felicity (though as great as ever happened to mortal men) but as an half piece, except they mought have a friend, to make it entire; and yet, which is more, they were princes that had wives, sons, nephews; and yet all these could not supply the comfort of friendship.

It is not to be forgotten, what Comineus observeth of his first master, Duke Charles the Hardy, namely, that he would communicate his secrets with none; and least of all, those secrets which troubled him most. Whereupon he

①These things in accordance with our friendship I have not concealed.

goeth on, and saith that towards his latter time, that closeness did impair, and a little perish his understanding. Surely Comineus mought have made the same judgment also, if it had pleased him, of his second master, Lewis the Eleventh, whose closeness was indeed his tormentor. The parable of Pythagoras is dark, but true; Cor ne edito; Eat not the heart. Certainly, if a man would give it a hard phrase, those that want friends, to open themselves unto, are cannibals of their own hearts. But one thing is most admirable (wherewith I will conclude this first fruit of friendship), which is, that this communicating of a man's self to his friend, works two contrary effects; for it redoubleth joys, and cutteth griefs in halves. For there is no man, that imparteth his joys to his friend, but he joyeth the more; and no man that imparteth his griefs to his friend, but he grieveth the less. So that it is in truth, of operation upon a man's mind, of like virtue as the alchemists use to attribute to their stone, for man's body; that it worketh all contrary effects, but still to the good and benefit of nature. But yet without praying in aid of alchemists, there is a manifest image of this, in the ordinary course of nature. For in bodies, union strengtheneth and cherisheth any natural action; and on the other side, weakeneth and dulleth any violent impression: and even so it is of minds.

The second fruit of friendship, is healthful and sovereign for the understanding, as the first is for the affections. For friendship maketh indeed a fair day in the affections, from storm and tempests; but it maketh daylight in the understanding, out of darkness, and confusion of thoughts. Neither is this to be understood only of faithful counsel, which a man receiveth from his friend; but before you come to that, certain it is, that whosoever hath his mind fraught with many thoughts, his wits and understanding do clarify and break up, in the communicating and discoursing with another; he tosseth his thoughts more easily; he marshalleth them more orderly, he seeth how they look when they are turned into words: finally, he waxeth wiser than himself; and that more by an hour's discourse, than by a day's meditation. It was well said by Themistocles, to the king of Persia, That speech was like cloth of Arras, opened and put abroad; whereby the imagery doth appear in figure; whereas in thoughts they lie but as in packs. Neither is this second fruit of friendship, in opening the understanding, restrained only to such friends as are able to give a man counsel; (they indeed are best;) but even without that, a man learneth of himself, and bringeth his own thoughts to light, and whetteth his wits as against a stone, which cuts itself not. In a word, a man were better relate himself to a statua, or picture, than to suffer his thoughts to pass in smother.

Add now, to make this second fruit of friendship complete, that other point, which lieth more open, and falleth within vulgar observation; which is faithful counsel from a friend. Heraclitus saith well in one of his enigmas, Dry light is ever the best. And certain it is, that the light that a man receiveth by counsel from another, is drier and purer, than that which cometh from his own understanding and judgment; which is ever infused, and drenched, in his affections and customs. So as there is as much difference between the counsel, that a friend giveth, and that a man giveth himself, as there is between the counsel of a friend, and of a flatterer. For there is no such flatterer as is a man's self; and there is no such remedy against flattery of a man's self, as the liberty of a friend. Counsel is of two sorts: the one concerning manners, the other concerning business. For the first, the best preservative to keep the mind in health, is the faithful admonition of a friend. The calling of a man's self to a strict account, is a medicine, sometime too piercing and corrosive. Reading good books of morality, is a little flat and dead. Observing our faults in others, is sometimes improper for our case. But the best receipt (best, I say, to work, and best to take) is the admonition of a friend. It is a strange thing to behold, what gross errors and extreme absurdities many (especially of the greater sort) do commit, for want of a friend to tell them of them; to the great damage both of their fame and fortune: for, as St. James saith, they are as men that look sometimes into a glass, and presently forget their own shape and favor. As for business, a man may think, if he win, that two eyes see no more than one; or that a gamester seeth always more than a looker-on; or that a man in anger, is as wise as he that hath said over the four and twenty letters; or that a musket may be shot off as well upon the arm, as upon a rest; and such other fond and high imaginations, to think himself all in all. But when all is done, the help of a good counsel, is that which setteth business straight. And if any man think that he will take counsel, but it shall be by pieces; asking counsel in one business, of one man, and in another business, of another man; it is well (that is to say, better, perhaps, than if he asked none at all); but he runneth two dangers: one, that he shall not be faithfully counselled; for it is a rare thing, except it be from a perfect and entire friend, to have counsel given, but such as shall be bowed and crooked to some ends, which he hath, that giveth it. The other, that he shall have counsel given, hurtful and unsafe (though with good meaning), and mixed partly of mischief and partly of remedy; even as if you would call a physician, that is thought good for the cure of the disease you complain of, but is unacquainted with your body; and therefore may put you in way for a present cure, but overthroweth your health in some other kind; and so cure the disease, and kill the patient. But a friend that is wholly acquainted with a man's estate, will beware, by furthering any present business, how he dasheth upon other inconvenience. And therefore rest not upon scattered counsels; they will rather distract and mislead, than settle and direct.

After these two noble fruits of friendship (peace in the affections, and support of the judgment), followeth the last fruit; which is like the pomegranate, full of many kernels; I mean aid, and bearing a part, in all actions and occasions. Here the best way to represent to life the manifold use of friendship, is to cast and see how many things there are, which a man cannot do himself; and then it will appear, that it was a sparing speech of the ancients, to say, that a friend is another himself; for that a friend is far more than himself. Men have their time, and die many times, in desire of some things which they principally take to heart; the bestowing of a child, the finishing of a work, or the like. If a man have a true friend, he may rest almost secure that the care of those things will continue after him. So that a man hath, as it were, two lives in his desires. A man hath a body, and that body is confined to a place; but where friendship is, all offices of life are as it were granted to him, and his deputy. For he may exercise them by his friend. How many things are there which a man cannot, with any face or comeliness, say or do himself? A man can scarce allege his own merits with modesty, much less extol them; a man cannot sometimes brook to supplicate or beg; and a number of the like. But all these things are graceful, in a friend's mouth, which are blushing in a man's own. So again, a man's person hath many proper relations, which he cannot put off. A man cannot speak to his son but as a father; to his wife but as a husband; to his enemy but upon terms: whereas a friend may speak as the case requires, and not as it sorteth with the person. But to enumerate these things were endless; I have given the rule, where a man cannot fitly play his own part; if he have not a friend, he may quit the stage.

28.谈消费

有钱是为了花钱，而花钱应当考虑荣誉和善行，鉴于此，大笔花销须以其用途之价值大小为度，须知为了祖国和为了天国都有人甘愿破产；而日常花销则应以个人的财产多少为度，须考虑量入为出，勿受仆人欺瞒，并尽可能安排得体面些，使实际花销低于外人的估计。毫无疑问，若一个人只想保持收支平衡，那他的日常花销应是他收入的一半，而如果他想变得富有，其日常花销则应是收入的三分之一。大人物问及并清查自己的财产不会有失身份。有人避免此举并不只是因为疏忽，而是怕发现自己破产而平添忧愁；但身体若有创伤而不检查，那就谈不上将其治愈。不清点自家财产者须用人得当，并且应该经常辞旧雇新，因新雇家仆多畏怯而少奸诈。不常清点自家财产者须对自己的收支作出明确的限定。在某方面花销较大者须在另一方面厉行节约，诸如膳食费用高者须在服饰方面节省，而居室耗资巨者须在马厩上减少花费；因处处都大手大脚就难免入不敷出，家道中落。过快地清偿债务和任其拖延太久一样有害，因为急于廉价推销通常和多付货物利息一样都会带来亏损。而且一次清偿债务者容易走借贷之老路，因为他发现自己摆脱困境后很可能故态复萌；但逐渐还清债务者往往会养成节俭的习惯，而这对他的头脑和家业都不无裨益。欲振兴家业者断不可轻视小节，须知减少零星花费通常比屈尊而求小利更为体面。对一旦开始就会持续的长期性支出须慎之又慎，但对一次性消费则不妨慷慨一些。

解析

一、有钱是为了花钱——特殊情况下可以不受限制，日常花销中须量入为出。

二、管理开支的方法：

1. 收入的固定比例用于日常花销(一半或三分之一)；

2. 切莫因为——

（1）妄自尊大，

（2）粗心大意，

（3）或过度担心

而不去关心自己的开支；

3. 须用人得当且经常辞旧雇新；

4. 明确地限定支出；

5. 在某方面花销较大应在另一方面厉行节约；

6. 在偿还旧债时，最好是有息借贷；

7. 减少零星花费；

8. 谨慎地对待长期性支出。

Of Expense

RICHES are for spending, and spending for honor and good actions. Therefore extraordinary expenses must be limited by the worth of the occasion; for voluntary undoing, may be as well for a man's country, as for the kingdom of heaven. But ordinary expense, ought to be limited by a man's estate; and governed with such regard, as it be within his compass; and not subject to deceit and abuse of servants; and ordered to the best show, that the bills may be less than the estimation abroad. Certainly, if a man will keep but of even hand, his ordinary expenses ought to be but to the half of his receipts; and if he think to wax rich, but to the third part. It is no baseness, for the greatest to descend and look into their own estate. Some forbear it, not upon negligence alone, but doubting to bring themselves into melancholy, in respect they shall find it broken. But wounds cannot be cured without searching. He that cannot look into his own estate at all, had need both choose well those whom he employeth, and change them often; for new are more timorous and less subtle. He that can look into his estate but seldom, it behooveth him to turn all to certainties. A man had need, if he be plentiful in some kind of expense, to be as saving again in some other. As if he be plentiful in diet, to be saving in apparel; if he be plentiful in the hall, to be saving in the stable; and the like. For he that is plentiful in expenses of all kinds, will hardly be preserved from decay. In clearing of a man's estate, he may as well hurt himself in being too sudden, as in letting it run on too long. For hasty selling, is commonly as disadvantageable as interest. Besides, he that clears at once will relapse; for finding himself out of straits, he will revert to his custom: but he that cleareth by degrees, induceth a habit of frugality, and gaineth as well upon his mind, as upon his estate. Certainly, who hath a state to repair, may not despise small things; and commonly it is less dishonorable, to abridge petty charges, than to stoop to petty gettings. A man ought warily to begin charges which once begun will continue; but in matters that return not, he may be more magnificent.

29.论国家之真正强盛

雅典人特米斯托克利的言论虽因过分替自己表功而显得傲气十足,但却历来都被视为真知灼见而广泛地适用于他人。有人曾在一次宴会上请他弹琴,他回答说:“鄙人不精琴艺,但却精于把小城变成大邦。”[①]稍稍借助于隐喻法,此言也许就可说明政府官员所具有的两种不同能耐;因为若对政府官员来一次认真的审查,国人便可发现,他们中(个别)能使小国变成大邦者都不会弹琴, 而大批精于弹琴者非但没有把小国变成大邦的能耐,反而具有一种相反的才能——即能把一个繁荣昌盛的国家引向衰败没落。而毋庸置疑,既然诸多官员就凭这种已蜕化的功夫和本事讨得君王的欢心并赢得百姓的喝彩,那这种功夫本事除“弹琴”外就不配再有更好的名称;因为此类雕虫小技只能讨人一时喜欢,使玩弄者自己觉得体面,但却无助于他们所服务的国家之繁荣进步。当然也有些高官要员可以被视为“称职”,他们能处理国家事务,使之不陷入危机和明显的麻烦,但却远远没有能力使国力增强,使国库充裕,使国运昌盛。不过官员们是何等人且由他们去,笔者在此只谈国事本身,即谈谈一个国家之真正强盛及强盛之道。此乃一番适合雄主明君一览的议论,其目的在于两个方面:一是让君主们别因高估其势力而热衷于徒劳的计划,二是让他们别因低估自己而屈从于怯懦的建议。

一国之疆土大小可由测量而知,岁收多少可经计算而晓,人口众寡可见于户籍名册,城镇数量可见于舆地图表;然而在国政事务中,对国力强弱之判断依然是最难做到正确无误并最容易出错的一个难点。天国没有被比

①据普鲁塔克《希腊罗马名人列传》记载,特米斯托克利酷爱虚荣,从不放过炫耀自己的机会,经常在公民大会上表功。此处引言即出自《列传》中之《特米斯托克利篇》第2章3节。另参见本书《论友谊》一文有关注释。

喻成任何硕大的果核，而是被比作一粒芥子，芥子比其他种子都小，但却具有生长快蔓延广的特性和活力。[①]所以有些国家虽幅员辽阔，但却不易扩张领土或控制他国；而有些国家虽只有弹丸之地，可那弹丸之地却易于成为庞大帝国之基础。

若一国之民缺乏英武骁勇的气概，那坚城、武库、骏马、战车、巨象和大炮之类都不过是披着狮皮的绵羊。而若一国之兵士气低落，那军队数量再多也无济于事，因为正如维吉尔所说："狼从不在乎面对的羊是多是少。"[②]当年埃尔比勒平原上的波斯军队如一片人海，以致亚历山大军中的将领也不免有几分惊惶，他们找到亚历山大，希望他下令夜间偷袭，可亚历山大回答说他不想偷取胜利，结果是马其顿人轻而易举就击溃了波斯军队。[③]亚美尼亚国王提格拉尼一世曾率四十万大军驻守一山头，当发现前来进攻的罗马军队不过一万四千人时，他取笑说："来者若是个使团则人数太多，若是支军队则人数太少。"但在那天太阳下山之前，他发现来者已足以屠宰他的军队并追得他丢盔弃甲。[④]此类以勇气胜过数量的战例不胜枚举，因此世人可以断言，任何国家强大之关键都在于要有一个英勇善战的民族。有人浅薄地认为战争的力量是金钱，殊不知士兵双臂的力量若因民族的卑微柔弱而衰退，金钱也没法为战争注入力量。当克罗伊斯[⑤]得意洋洋地向梭伦[⑥]炫耀其黄金时，梭伦曾善意地对他说："陛下，若有他人前来，且来者的钢铁比你的更硬，那他就将成为这些黄金的主人。"由此可见，若非本国军队皆由

①此喻见于《新约·马太福音》第 13 章 31 节。

②引自维吉尔《牧歌》第 7 首 52 行。

③此例所述乃公元前 331 年的埃尔比勒战役，亚历山大大帝在此役中以少胜多彻底击败了大流士三世。此役的实际战场是埃尔比勒古城（位于今伊拉克北部）以西不远的高加米拉（Gaugamela），故又称高加米拉战役。

④此例所述乃史家所谓的第三次米特拉达悌战争中之一役，此役的罗马军队统帅是执政官卢库鲁斯（Lucullus，约前 117—前 56）。

⑤克罗伊斯乃小亚细亚古国吕底亚之末代国王（约前 560—前 546），其王国于约公元前 546 年被波斯国王居鲁士所灭。传说他是古代巨富，其名 Croesus 已成为"富豪"的同义词。

⑥梭伦（约前 638—前 559），古雅典政治家及诗人，"希腊七贤"之一，公元前 594 年任执政官，进行过积极的政治改革（即"梭伦立法"），任满后出国旅行，到过小亚细亚。

品格优良且英勇善战的国民组成，任何君王或政府都不可过高地估计其国力；但另一方面，若一国之臣民具有尚武的性格，其君王则须确信自己的力量，除非他的臣民在其他方面有缺陷。至于用钱从国外招募军队，虽说这也不失为一种补救措施，但所有的先例都证明，依靠雇佣军的国家或君王都只能得意一时，不久就会威风扫地。

犹大和以萨迦的天命不可能重合，同一个部族或民族不可能既是威武之狮又是负重之驴；[①]与此同理，一个赋税过重的民族不可能成为勇敢尚武的民族。但经国民代表同意的征税对士气民心影响较小乃不争的事实，此例明显地见于荷兰的国内货物税[②]，在某种程度上也见于英国的王室特别税[③]。读者须注意，此处讨论的是民气问题而非钱包问题；所以虽说自愿缴纳或强迫征收的税款都出自同一钱包，但对民心士气的影响却截然不同。由此可有如下结论：帝国的臣民不宜负担过重的捐税。

凡旨在图强的国家均须注意，勿让本国的贵族和缙绅增长过速；因为那样会使平民阶级渐渐沦为萎靡不振的雇农和贱民，实际上成为上流阶级的奴仆。这种情形可见于萌芽林之培养，如果你把优势木树苗留得太密，那你永远也别想见到中间木或被压木，因为优势木下将只有灌丛荆棘。所以一国的缙绅太多，自由民就会变得低下卑微，其结果将是百人之中难有一人宜戴军盔，更不用说充当步兵，而步兵乃一国军队之主力，那时就会出现民众而势微的情形。笔者以上所论之最好例证就是英法两国间的比较，论疆土和人口英国都远不及法国，然而英国从来就是法国最强劲的对手，其原因就是英国的中产阶级可造就优秀的士兵，而法国的乡农村夫则断然不能。英王亨利七世在这方面的策略可谓深谋远虑，值得赞赏(关于这点笔者在拙著《英王亨利七世传》中已有详尽的论述)：为农庄和牧户规定一个标准，即为他们保留一定比例的土地，使他们能生活在富裕的条件下，而非在

①《旧约·创世记》第 49 章记载：犹太人的祖先雅各临终前把 12 个儿子召到床前，预言他们及其后代的命运 (他们的后代成为以色列的 12 个部族)，预言说犹大将是威武之狮，以萨迦将为负重之驴。

②尼德兰联省共和国政府 (三级会议) 征收的一种间接税，用于国家和军队的开支。当时前宗主国西班牙的威胁尚未完全消除，尼德兰人民仍同仇敌忾，故无人抱怨这项重税。

③当时由英国议会代征并发给王室的一种特别津贴。

奴隶般的境况中，并使耕者都有其田，而非仅仅是雇农。[①]如此励精图治，国家便可达到维吉尔所形容的古意大利那种盛况：一个有强兵沃土的国家。[②]

还有一个社会阶层也不应忽略(据笔者所知，这个阶层几乎为英国所独有，也许还存在于波兰，除此在任何地方都不存在)，笔者指的是贵族和缙绅家中具有自由民身份的仆从阶层，因为论从军打仗，他们与自耕农子弟相比也毫不逊色。所以毫无疑问，贵族豪绅家所习惯的豪华阔绰、殷勤好客及使用大批随从的确有助于恢弘尚武精神；而与之相反，贵族豪绅家有节制的封闭生活方式则会导致兵源的匮乏。

无论如何也得让尼布甲尼撒梦中那棵王国之树的树干健壮得足以承受其枝叶[③]；此喻是说一国之本土臣民与该国统治的异族臣民须形成合理的比例。所以那些对异族臣民之归化持开明态度的国家都易于成为帝国。因不难想象，一个小民族即便因其智勇绝伦而获得广阔的疆土，它也只能维持一时，不久就会骤然崩溃。斯巴达人在外族人归化问题上持歧视态度，所以当他们固守本土时能坚不可摧，可一旦对外扩张其树干就不堪承受其枝叶，到头来终于像风吹果落一般突然消亡。在接纳外族人入籍这一点上，任何国家都比不上古罗马开明，因此罗马人一帆风顺，渐渐形成了世界上最庞大的帝国。他们的做法是授予外族人罗马国籍(他们称之为公民权)，而且是最充分地授予，即不仅授予财产权、通婚权和继承权，而且还授予选举权和被选举权，这种公民权不止是向个人授予，同样还授予整个家庭、整座城市，有时甚至是整个民族。加之罗马人惯于殖民，把罗马的籽苗移入异国他乡的土壤，并使不同的习俗合二为一，因此可以说并非罗马人向世界扩张，而是世界向罗马蔓延，这正是最稳妥的强国之道。笔者有时对西班牙感到惊异，不知那么少的西班牙人何以获得并保持那么大的宗主权；不过西班牙本土无疑是一株巨大的树干，远远胜过罗马和斯巴达兴国之初。除

①15世纪末，由于圈地盛行，大批英国农民被赶出家园，沦为流浪者，造成社会动荡，纳税人和兵源也锐减，为此亨利七世统治下的政府于1489年首次颁布《反圈地条例》，提出退牧还农，保护领有20英亩份地的农民，规定牧主的羊群不得超过两千头。

②引自维吉尔《埃涅阿斯纪》第1卷531行。

③据《旧约·但以理书》第4章记载，巴比伦王尼布甲尼撒梦见一参天大树枝繁叶茂，果实累累……忽有一天他宣布将该树伐倒，希伯来先知但以理说此梦乃亡国之兆。

此之外，虽说他们从来没有让异族人自由入籍的惯例，但他们有一种仅次于授予国籍的措施，那就是他们几乎一视同仁地招募各族士兵，而且有时候还让异族人当高级将领；不仅如此，从西班牙国王刚颁布的国事诏书来看，他们此刻似乎也意识到了本土人丁不旺之缺陷。[1]

毋庸置疑，凡需在室内久坐不动的技术性行当和(只需动指头而无需用臂力的)精巧细工都在本质上与军人的禀性格格不入。一般而论，尚武的民族都有几分懒散，都乐于冒险而不思劳作；而若要保持他们的尚武精神，就不可过分改变其懒散习性。所以古代的斯巴达、雅典、罗马诸国都使用奴隶，这对他们有极大好处，因为上述既费时又无益于强身的工作一般都由奴隶去完成。但由于基督教的戒律，蓄奴制基本上已不复存在。如今与蓄奴制最相近的做法就是把上述行道留给异族人去从事(异族人因此也更易于在移居国容身)，从而把绝大多数本国平民限于三种职业，一是有耕地的农夫，二是有自由民身份的仆从，三是适于男子汉充当的工匠，如铁匠、木匠和砖瓦匠等。此处未计职业军人。

但若要真正成为强大的帝国，至关重要的一点就是国家须公开承认尚武从军乃最大荣耀、最高目标和最佳职业；因为上文所论都不过是进行战争的能力，但若无目标和行动，能力又有何用呢？根据罗马人的传说，罗穆卢斯在升天后曾给过他们一道神谕，[2]告诉他们最重要的事是致力于战争，这样便可建成世界上最强大的帝国。斯巴达国家之组织结构完全是为了适应扩张帝国的目的(虽说那种结构并不明智)。[3]波斯人和马其顿人曾一度建起庞大的帝国。高卢人、日耳曼人、哥特人、撒克逊人、诺曼人以及其他一些民族也都曾强盛一时。土耳其人今天还拥有奥斯曼帝国，尽管其国势已大大衰微。在当今欧洲的基督教国家中，拥有帝国势力的实际上只有西班

①西班牙国王腓力四世(Philip Ⅳ，在位期1621—1665)于1622年颁布国事诏书，授予已婚的西班牙本土居民某些特权，并进一步豁免有六个孩子以上的家庭之国民义务。

②罗穆卢斯相传为特洛伊英雄埃涅阿斯的后代，罗马城的创建者，“王政时代”的第一代国王。传说他尚未去世就已升天，被罗马人尊奉为神。此处提及的神谕一事见于李维《罗马史》第1卷16章。

③如斯巴达实行双王制，一个国王专管国内事务，一个国王专管统兵征战。

牙[1];不过人人都是在其最专注的事业上获利,此理显而易见,不必多论。笔者只须指出:一个国家若不直截了当地宣称尚武,它就别指望尝到强盛的滋味;另一方面,(若像古罗马人和土耳其人那样)坚持不懈地兴戎起衅,任何国家都可以创造奇迹,此乃时间给予的一道最可靠的神谕;至于那些只在某一时期尚武的国家,虽说它们通常只会在该时期获得强国地位,但那种地位在其军事活动衰减后仍可长期地保护它们。

伴随上述要点而来的是一种需要,即国家需要有可提供(说得出口的)战争理由的法律或惯例,因为人的正义感与生俱有,所以若无某些至少是显得公正的理由,人们一般不会投入(将导致无穷灾难的)战争。土耳其人常以传播其宗教为由兴师征战,那是他们随时都可以使用的战争借口。罗马人虽说把拓展帝国疆域视为建此大功的统帅们之殊荣,但他们并非只凭这一个理由对外发动战争。鉴于此,欲尚武图强的国家须做到以下两点:其一是对他国施加于本国边境居民、过境商人或外交使节的无礼行为要非常敏感,并且对如何处置挑衅不可讨论太久;其二是随时准备以最快的速度出兵援助盟国,就像当年罗马人所做的那样。当年罗马人的原则是,若一受外敌入侵的盟国与其他国家也订有防御盟约并分别向多国求援,罗马人的援军总是最先赶到,绝不把这份荣誉留给他国。至于古人为了某党某派或某国的政府性质而进行的战争,笔者也不知如何证明其理由正当,如罗马人为希腊的自由而进行的一场战争[2],又如斯巴达人和雅典人为在希腊各城邦建立或推翻民主政体或寡头政体而进行的战争[3],再如一国或以主持公道,或以提供保护,或以解救他国受专制压迫的国民为理由而发动的战争等等。总而言之,凡不敏于找兴兵之由的国家都别指望强盛。

人体不运动不健壮,政体不运动不强盛;而对国家来说,师出有名的体面战争无疑就是最好的运动。国内战争固然如同感冒发烧,可对外战争的确就像运动发热,有益于保持身体健康;因为在歌舞升平中,民气易变阴

---

①当时的西班牙不仅占有美洲的墨西哥、秘鲁、智利、哥伦比亚、西印度群岛和亚洲的菲律宾群岛,而且在欧洲也拥有霸主地位。

②指第二次马其顿战争(前200—前197)。

③指伯罗奔尼撒战争(前431—前404)。修昔的底斯《伯罗奔尼撒战争史》对这次战争有翔实的记载。

柔，民风易趋堕落。但不管尚武对升平康乐有何影响，它对国家之强盛都有利无弊；它可使国家保持一支常备军，虽说维持一支劲旅耗资不菲，但它通常能使一国对邻国发号施令，或至少在邻国中保持强国的名声。此例可见于西班牙，它在欧洲各地驻扎精兵差不多已有一百二十年历史。

拥有海上霸权是一个强国的象征。西塞罗在致阿提库斯的信中曾谈及庞培准备对付恺撒的计划，他说："庞培的计划显然是特米斯托克利当年采用的策略，因为他认为谁控制了海洋谁就控制了一切。"而毫无疑问，若庞培不因过于自负而弃舟登陆，他肯定能拖垮恺撒。[①]海战之重大影响世人皆知。亚克兴战役决定了罗马帝国的归属。[②]勒班陀海战则抑制了土耳其人的扩张。[③]以海战决战争胜负的例子不可胜数，这固然是因为各国君王或政府历来就推崇并依赖海战。但至此可以肯定的是，拥有海上霸权者也拥有了战争的主动权，战与不战或战多战少均可随心所欲；而那些只拥有强大陆军的国家仍常常陷入进退维谷的境地。不可否认，当今之欧洲占有极大的海上优势(这种优势亦是大不列颠王国得天独厚的一个方面)，这一是因为欧洲国家多半不是内陆国，它们的国界大多濒海，二是因为东西印度[④]的财富似乎在很大程度上只是海上霸权的附属品。

与古代战争赋予军人的光彩荣耀相比，现代战争都未免显得黯然失色。如今也有些为鼓舞士气而设立的骑士称号和勋位，但却往往被不加区别地授予军人和非军人；此外也许还有诸如荣誉纪念册和伤残军人医院之类的东西。然而在古代，他们有在战场上竖起的纪念碑，有在葬礼上吟诵的追悼颂词，有为阵亡将士建立的纪念馆，有奖给个人的花环和花冠，有后来被各大国君主借用的emperor这一称号[⑤]，有将帅们班师时的凯旋仪式，

①庞培终在法萨罗战役（约公元前48年）败于恺撒，史家认为庞培的败因乃指挥失当和贻误战机，因为当时他的势力优于恺撒，决战时尚有60艘舰船停在海上未动用。

②亚克兴战役发生在公元前31年，古罗马屋大维在此役中击败了安东尼及助阵的埃及女王克娄巴特拉。此役结束了罗马内战，屋大维成为罗马帝国的第一个皇帝（即奥古斯都）。

③勒班陀海战发生于1571年10月，西班牙威尼斯联合舰队在此役中大败土耳其舰队。

④"东印度"乃西方人使用的一个不确切的地理名称，一般指印度、中南半岛、马来半岛和马来群岛；"西印度"是由哥伦布之误而产生的一个地区名，后来欧洲殖民者借以称南北美洲。

⑤古罗马士兵在胜利后习惯向他们的统帅欢呼，呼之为imperator（英语作emperor，意为"统帅"或"凯旋将军"），奥古斯都建帝国后用此称号作终身头衔，此词遂转义为"皇帝"。

还有遣散军队时的慷慨赏赐。这一切都能激发士兵们的勇武精神，但其中最值得一提的是古罗马人的凯旋式，那种仪式并非显摆或炫耀，而是曾有过的一种最为明智且高贵的习俗。因为凯旋式包括三项内容，一是给凯旋将军以荣耀，二是用战利品充实国库，三是给士兵们以赏赐。不过这种荣耀也许不适合君主国，除非获此殊荣者是君王本人或他们的子嗣，就像发生在罗马帝国时代的情况一样，皇帝们把凯旋式据为己有，只为自己和儿子们取得的胜利举行凯旋式，对获胜归来的部将则只给予凯旋服饰。[①]

综上所述，虽说（如《圣经》所言）人不可能凭操操心就使自己的身体长高一寸[②]，但对国家政体而言，使国土更广国势更盛则在于君王或政府的能力；因为只要让上文谈及的那些策略、规则和惯例得以实施，他们便可为子孙后代播下强盛的种子。无奈此等大事通常都被忽略，只能任其听天命。

解析

一、关于政治家：

1. 很多皆为无力胜任者；

2. 一些能维持已稳定的政权；

3. 极少能使小城变成大邦。

二、一国之真正强盛——

1. 不在于坚城、武库等，

2. 不在于数字意义上的军力，

3. 而在于国民英武骁勇的气概（举例：埃尔比勒战役，提格拉尼，所

①在罗马共和国时代，所有在对外战争中大获全胜的将领均可得到凯旋式，届时凯旋将军穿王家紫边阔袍，乘饰有月桂枝的战车，由执政官和众元老引路进城，身后是战利品、俘虏和班师军队等，队伍游行至卡匹托儿山上的朱庇特神庙，然后举行献祭和俘虏等活动，仪式以宴会告终。但进入帝国时代后，除奥古斯都曾慷慨地为三十余名将军举行过正式的凯旋式外，后来的得胜将军只能获凯旋服饰荣誉，即获得穿凯旋服、戴桂冠、坐象牙圈椅和塑像的权利。

②参见《新约·马太福音》第 6 章 27 节及《路加福音》第 12 章 25 节。

罗门)。

三、如何变得强盛:

1. 赋税不能过重;
2. 鼓励自耕农与有自由身份的仆从;
3. 推动异族移民,在这方面要吸取斯巴达人的教训,学习罗马人的经验;
4. 将在室内久坐不动的技术性行当和精巧细工留给外族人;
5. 让国民学会尚武从军;
6. 抓住每一次正义宣战的机会;
7. 拥有海上霸权;
8. 赋予军人荣耀与名望。

四、通过战争,君王可以扩充疆土,强盛国势。

Of the True Greatness of Kingdoms and Estates

THE speech of Themistocles the Athenian, which was haughty and arrogant, in taking so much to himself, had been a grave and wise observation and censure, applied at large to others. Desired at a feast to touch a lute, he said, He could not fiddle, but yet he could make a small town, a great city. These words (holpen a little with a metaphor) may express two differing abilities, in those that deal in business of estate. For if a true survey be taken of counsellors and statesmen, there may be found (though rarely) those which can make a small state great, and yet cannot fiddle; as on the other side, there will be found a great many, that can fiddle very cunningly, but yet are so far from being able to make a small state great, as their gift lieth the other way; to bring a great and flourishing estate, to ruin and decay. And certainly whose degenerate arts and shifts, whereby many counsellors and governors gain both favor with their masters, and estimation with the vulgar, deserve no better name than fiddling; being things rather pleasing for the time, and graceful to themselves only, than tending to the weal and advancement of the state which they serve. There are also (no doubt) counsellors and governors which may be held sufficient (negotiis pares[1]), able to manage affairs, and to

①equal to their business

keep them from precipices and manifest inconveniences; which nevertheless are far from the ability to raise and amplify an estate in power, means, and fortune. But be the workmen what they may be, let us speak of the work; that is, the true greatness of kingdoms and estates, and the means thereof. An argument fit for great and mighty princes to have in their hand; to the end that neither by over-measuring their forces, they leese themselves in vain enterprises; nor on the other side, by undervaluing them, they descend to fearful and pusillanimous counsels.

The greatness of an estate, in bulk and territory, doth fall under measure; and the greatness of finances and revenue, doth fall under computation. The population may appear by musters; and the number and greatness of cities and towns by cards and maps. But yet there is not anything amongst civil affairs more subject to error, than the right valuation and true judgment concerning the power and forces of an estate. The kingdom of heaven is compared, not to any great kernel or nut, but to a grain of mustard-seed: which is one of the least grains, but hath in it a property and spirit hastily to get up and spread. So are there states, great in territory, and yet not apt to enlarge or command; and some that have but a small dimension of stem, and yet apt to be the foundations of great monarchies.

Walled towns, stored arsenals and armories, goodly races of horse, chariots of war, elephants, ordnance, artillery, and the like; all this is but a sheep in a lion's skin, except the breed and disposition of the people, be stout and warlike. Nay, number (itself) in armies importeth not much, where the people is of weak courage; for (as Virgil saith) It never troubles a wolf, how many the sheep be. The army of the Persians, in the plains of Arbela, was such a vast sea of people, as it did somewhat astonish the commanders in Alexander's army; who came to him therefore, and wished him to set upon them by night; and he answered, He would not pilfer the victory. And the defeat was easy. When Tigranes the Armenian, being encamped upon a hill with four hundred thousand men, discovered the army of the Romans, being not above fourteen thousand, marching towards him, he made himself merry with it, and said, Yonder men are too many for an embassage, and too few for a fight. But before the sun set, he found them enow to give him the chase with infinite slaughter. Many are the examples of the great odds, between number and courage; so that a man may truly make a judgment, that the principal point of greatness in any state, is to have a race of military men. Neither is money the sinews of war (as it is trivially said), where the sinews of men's arms, in base and effeminate people, are failing. For Solon said well to Croesus (when in ostentation he showed him his gold), Sir, if any other come, that hath better iron, than you, he will be master of all this gold. Therefore let any prince or state think solely of his forces, except his militia of natives be of good and valiant soldiers. And let princes, on the other side, that have subjects of martial disposition, know their own strength; unless they be otherwise wanting unto themselves. As for mercenary forces (which is the help in this case), all examples show, that whatsoever estate or prince doth rest upon them, he may spread his feathers for a time, but he will mew them soon after.

The blessing of Judah and Issachar will never meet; that the same people, or nation, should be both the lion's whelp and the ass between burthens; neither will it be, that a people overlaid with taxes, should ever become valiant and martial. It is true that taxes levied by consent of the estate, do abate men's courage less: as it hath been seen notably, in the excises of the Low Countries; and, in some degree, in the subsidies of England. For you must note, that we speak now of the heart, and not of the purse. So that although the same tribute and tax, laid by consent or by imposing, be all one to the purse, yet it works diversely upon the courage. So that you may conclude, that no people overcharged with tribute, is fit for empire.

Let states that aim at greatness, take heed how their nobility and gentlemen do multiply too fast. For that maketh the common subject, grow to be a peasant and base swain, driven out of heart, and in effect but the gentleman's laborer. Even as you may see in coppice woods; if you leave your staddles too thick, you shall never have clean underwood, but shrubs and bushes. So in countries, if the gentlemen be too many, the commons will be base; and you will bring it to that, that not the hundred poll, will be fit for an helmet; especially as to the infantry, which is the nerve of an army; and so there will be great population, and little strength. This which I speak of, hath been nowhere better seen, than by comparing of England and France; whereof England, though far less in territory and population, hath been (nevertheless) an overmatch; in regard the middle people of England make good soldiers, which the peasants of France do not. And herein the device of King Henry the Seventh (whereof I have spoken largely in the History of His Life) was profound and admirable; in making farms and houses of husbandry of a standard; that is, maintained with such a proportion of land unto them, as may breed a subject to live in convenient plenty and no servile condition; and to keep the plough in the hands of the owners, and not mere hirelings. And thus indeed you shall attain to Virgil's character which he gives to ancient Italy: Terra potens armis atque ubere glebae[①].

---

①a land mighty in arms and in fruitfulness

Neither is that state (which, for anything I know, is almost peculiar to England, and hardly to be found anywhere else, except it be perhaps in Poland) to be passed over; I mean the state of free servants, and attendants upon noblemen and gentlemen; which are no ways inferior unto the yeomanry for arms. And therefore out of all questions, the splendor and magnificence, and great retinues and hospitality, of noblemen and gentlemen, received into custom, doth much conduce unto martial greatness. Whereas, contrariwise, the close and reserved living of noblemen and gentlemen, causeth a penury of military forces.

By all means it is to be procured, that the trunk of Nebuchadnezzar's tree of monarchy, be great enough to bear the branches and the boughs; that is, that the natural subjects of the crown or state, bear a sufficient proportion to the stranger subjects, that they govern. Therefore all states that are liberal of naturalization towards strangers, are fit for empire. For to think that an handful of people can, with the greatest courage and policy in the world, embrace too large extent of dominion, it may hold for a time, but it will fail suddenly. The Spartans were a nice people in point of naturalization; whereby, while they kept their compass, they stood firm; but when they did spread, and their boughs were becomen too great for their stem, they became a windfall, upon the sudden. Never any state was in this point so open to receive strangers into their body, as were the Romans. Therefore it sorted with them accordingly; for they grew to the greatest monarchy. Their manner was to grant naturali-zation (which they called jus civitatis①), and to grant it in the highest degree; that is, not only jus commercii, jus connubii, jus haereditatis; but also jus suffragii, and jus honorum.② And this not to singular persons alone, but likewise to whole families; yea to cities, and sometimes to nations. Add to this their custom of plantation of colonies; whereby the Roman plant was removed into the soil of other nations. And putting both constitutions together, you will say that it was not the Romans that spread upon the world, but it was the world that spread upon the Romans; and that was the sure way of greatness. I have marvelled, sometimes, at Spain, how they clasp and contain so large dominions, with so few natural Spaniards; but sure the whole compass of Spain, is a very great body of a tree; far above Rome and Sparta at the first. And besides, though they have not had that usage, to naturalize liberally, yet they have that which is next to it; that is, to employ, almost indifferently, all nations in

①the right of citizenship

②the right of trading, the right of intermarriage, the right of inheritance, the right of voting, and the right of candidature for civil office their militia of ordinary soldiers; yea, and sometimes in their highest commands. Nay, it seemeth at this instant they are sensible, of this want of natives; as by the Pragmatical Sanction, now published, appeareth.

It is certain that sedentary, and within-door arts, and delicate manufactures (that require rather the finger than the arm), have, in their nature, a contrariety to a military disposition. And generally, all warlike people are a little idle, and love danger better than travail. Neither must they be too much broken of it, if they shall be preserved in vigor. Therefore it was great advantage, in the ancient states of Sparta, Athens, Rome, and others, that they had the use of slaves, which commonly did rid those manufactures. But that is abolished, in greatest part, by the Christian law. That which cometh nearest to it, is to leave those arts chiefly to strangers (which, for that purpose, are the more easily to be received), and to contain the principal bulk of the vulgar natives, within those three kinds: tillers of the ground; free servants; and handicraftsmen of strong and manly arts, as smiths, masons, carpenters, etc.; not reckoning professed soldiers.

But above all, for empire and greatness, it importeth most, that a nation do profess arms, as their principal honor, study, and occupation. For the things which we formerly have spoken of, are but habilitations towards arms; and what is habilitation without intention and act? Romulus, after his death (as they report or feign), sent a present to the Romans, that above all, they should intend arms; and then they should prove the greatest empire of the world. The fabric of the state of Sparta was wholly (though not wisely) framed and composed, to that scope and end. The Persians and Macedonians had it for a flash. The Gauls, Germans, Goths, Saxons, Normans, and others, had it for a time. The Turks have it at this day, though in great declination. Of Christian Europe, they that have it are, in effect, only the Spaniards. But it is so plain, that every man profiteth in that, he most intendeth, that it needeth not to be stood upon. It is enough to point at it; that no nation which doth not directly profess arms, may look to have greatness fall into their mouths. And on the other side, it is a most certain oracle of time, that those states that continue long in that profession (as the Romans and Turks principally have done) do wonders. And those that have professed arms but for an age, have, notwithstanding, commonly attained that greatness, in that age, which maintained them long after, when their profession and exercise of arms hath grown to decay.

Incident to this point is, for a state to have those laws or customs, which may reach forth unto them just occasions (as may be pretended) of war. For there is that justice, imprinted in the nature of men, that they enter not upon wars (whereof so many calamities do ensue) but upon some, at the least specious, grounds and quarrels. The Turk hath at hand, for cause of war, the propagation of his law or sect; a quarrel that he may always command. The Romans, though they esteemed the extending the limits of their empire, to be great honor to their generals, when it was done, yet they never rested upon that alone, to begin a war. First, therefore, let nations that pretend to greatness have this; that they be sensible of wrongs, either upon borderers, merchants, or politic ministers; and that they sit not too long upon a provocation. Secondly, let them be prest, and ready to give aids and succors, to their confederates; as it ever was with the Romans; insomuch, as if the confederate had leagues defensive, with divers other states, and, upon invasion offered, did implore their aids severally, yet the Romans would ever be the foremost, and leave it to none other to have the honor. As for the wars which were anciently made, on the behalf of a kind of party, or tacit conformity of estate, I do not see how they may be well justified: as when the Romans made a war, for the liberty of Grecia; or when the Lacedaemonians and Athenians, made wars to set up or pull down democracies and oligarchies; or when wars were made by foreigners, under the pretence of justice or protection, to deliver the subjects of others, from tyranny and oppression; and the like. Let it suffice, that no estate expect to be great, that is not awake upon any just occasion of arming.

Nobody can be healthful without exercise, neither natural body nor politic; and certainly to a kingdom or estate, a just and honorable war, is the true exercise. A civil war, indeed, is like the heat of a fever; but a foreign war is like the heat of exercise, and serveth to keep the body in health; for in a slothful peace, both courages will effeminate, and manners corrupt. But howsoever it be for happiness, without all question, for greatness, it maketh to be still for the most part in arms; and the strength of a veteran army (though it be a chargeable business) always on foot, is that which commonly giveth the law, or at least the reputation, amongst all neighbor states; as may well be seen in Spain, which hath had, in one part or other, a veteran army almost continually, now by the space of six score years.

To be master of the sea, is an abridgment of a monarchy. Cicero, writing to Atticus of Pompey his preparation against Caesar, saith, Consilium Pompeii plane Themistocleum est; putat enim, qui mari potitur, eum rerum potiri.[①] And, without doubt, Pompey had tired out Caesar, if upon vain confidence,

①Pompey's policy is clearly that of Themistocles; for he considers that the man who commands the sea commands the situation.

he had not left that way. We see the great effects of battles by sea. The battle of Actium, decided the empire of the world. The battle of Lepanto, arrested the greatness of the Turk. There be many examples, where sea-fights have been final to the war; but this is when princes or states have set up their rest, upon the battles. But thus much is certain, that he that commands the sea, is at great liberty, and may take as much, and as little, of the war as he will. Whereas those that be strongest by land, are many times nevertheless in great straits. Surely, at this day, with us of Europe, the vantage of strength at sea (which is one of the principal dowries of this kingdom of Great Britain) is great; both because most of the kingdoms of Europe, are not merely inland, but girt with the sea most part of their compass; and because the wealth of both Indies seems in great part, but an accessory to the command of the seas.

The wars of latter ages seem to be made in the dark, in respect of the glory, and honor, which reflected upon men from the wars, in ancient time. There be now, for martial encouragement, some degrees and orders of chivalry; which nevertheless are conferred promiscuously, upon soldiers and no soldiers; and some remembrance perhaps, upon the scutcheon; and some hospitals for maimed soldiers; and such like things. But in ancient times, the trophies erected upon the place of the victory; the funeral laudatives and monuments for those that died in the wars; the crowns and garlands personal; the style of emperor, which the great kings of the world after borrowed; the triumphs of the generals, upon their return; the great donatives and largesses, upon the disbanding of the armies; were things able to inflame all men's courages. But above all, that of the triumph, amongst the Romans, was not pageants or gaudery, but one of the wisest and noblest institutions, that ever was. For it contained three things: honor to the general; riches to the treasury out of the spoils; and donatives to the army. But that honor, perhaps were not fit for monarchies; except it be in the person of the monarch himself, or his sons; as it came to pass in the times of the Roman emperors, who did impropriate the actual triumphs to themselves, and their sons, for such wars as they did achieve in person; and left only, for wars achieved by subjects, some triumphal garments and ensigns to the general.

To conclude: no man can by care taking (as the Scripture saith) add a cubit to his stature, in this little model of a man's body; but in the great frame of kingdoms and commonwealths, it is in the power of princes or estates, to add amplitude and greatness to their kingdoms; for by introducing such ordinances, constitutions, and customs, as we have now touched, they may sow greatness to their posterity and succession. But these things are commonly not observed, but left to take their chance.

30.谈养生之道

此道中有一种医家规则没有包含的智慧。什么有益健康,什么会伤身体,人对此的自我观察才是保健之最佳良药;不过更安全的观察结论应该是“这于我不甚相宜,所以我将弃之”,而不应该是“我觉得这对我无妨,所以我要用之”。须知少时的血气方刚往往纵容过度行为,而行为无度终将欠下一笔年老时须还的旧债。应该意识到年龄的增长,别老想做事不减当年,因为岁月毕竟不饶人。对主食之骤然改变须非常谨慎,如果非改不可,则副食品亦须有相应改变;须知自然之道和治国之道有一个相同的秘诀,即百事之更新比一事之鼎革更为安全。[①]应经常审视你衣食住行等方面的习惯,若判定某种习气有害,则须设法逐渐将其戒除;但若发现因改变某习性而引起不适,你也不妨故态复萌;因为很难区分何为公认的有益于健康的习惯,何为对你个人有益并相宜的习性。日常生活中应该无忧无虑,自得其乐,此乃延年益寿的秘诀之一。至于人之所感所思,当避免忌妒、焦虑、忧愤以及过度欣喜和暗自悲伤,亦当避免思其力之所不及、其智之所不能。应该让心中怀有憧憬,怀有并非狂喜的愉悦和并不过量的多种情趣,并怀有仰慕和惊叹以及由此产生的新奇感;还应让头脑中充满庄重而多彩的思考对象,如历史、神话以及对自然的研究。若你从不用药物维护健康,当你一旦须用药物时身体将不适应;而若你平时使用药物太多,生病时用药则不会有显著疗效。笔者赞成按季节变换食品,而不赞成经常服用药物,除非服药已成为一种习惯;须知营养食品对身体多有调护而少有伤害。对身体的异常情况不可掉以轻心,而须及时请医求诊。生病时应注重调养,健康时应注重锻炼,因为平时注重锻炼者患微恙一般都不必求医,只须注意饮食和调养便可痊愈。塞尔苏斯若非一个哲人而只是一名医生,那他就绝不可能把

---

①马基雅弗利在其《论李维》第1卷26篇曰:“新君即位须革新百事。”

以下见解作为健康长寿的要领:人应交替采用截然不同的生活方式,不过应倾向更宜人的一种,如时而节食时而饱餐,但更多时是饱餐;时而熬夜时而早眠,但更多时是早眠;时而静养时而运动,但更多的是运动;诸如此类,不一而足。①这样生理机能可得到呵护,同时亦可防止疾病。有些医生对病人的脾气过于迁就,以致不坚持正确的治疗措施;有些医生则过分遵循医书药理,以致对病人的体质情况不予充分的考虑。应该请那种介于这二者之间的医生,若此等良医难觅,则各请一名综合之。最后别忘了,有病时既要请医道高明的名医,又要请熟悉你身体状况的大夫。

解析

保持健康的方法:

1. 摒弃于你不相宜的东西;
2. 逐步改变饮食、锻炼、衣着等方面的习惯;
3. 培养愉悦的情绪,避免过度激动或愤怒;
4. 使用药物,但须控制用量(宁愿相信饮食),需要的时候及时求诊;
5. 交替采用不同的生活方式,不要放弃于你有益的东西;
6. 选择一位精于医道且熟悉你身体状况的医生。

Of Regiment of Health

THERE is a wisdom in this; beyond the rules of physic: a man's own observation, what he finds good of, and what he finds hurt of, is the best physic to preserve health. But it is a safer conclusion to say, This agreeth not well with me, therefore, I will not continue it; than this, I find no offence of this,

①塞尔苏斯是公元1世纪罗马作家及编纂家,所编百科全书只有《医学篇》流传于世,该书被公认为一部优秀的医学文献。培根这段话引自《医学篇》第1章1节,但与塞尔苏斯的原话原义有很大出入。

therefore I may use it. For strength of nature in youth, passeth over many excesses, which are owing a man till his age. Discern of the coming on of years, and think not to do the same things still; for age will not be defied. Beware of sudden change, in any great point of diet, and, if necessity enforce it, fit the rest to it. For it is a secret both in nature and state, that it is safer to change many things, than one. Examine thy customs of diet, sleep, exercise, apparel, and the like; and try, if any thing thou shalt judge hurtful, to discontinue it, by little and little; but so, as if thou dost find any inconvenience by the change, thou come back to it again: for it is hard to distinguish that which is generally held good and wholesome, from that which is good particularly, and fit for thine own body. To be free-minded and cheerfully disposed, at hours of meat, and of sleep, and of exercise, is one of the best precepts of long lasting. As for the passions, and studies of the mind; avoid envy, anxious fears; anger fretting inwards; subtle and knotty inquisitions; joys and exhilarations in excess; sadness not communicated. Entertain hopes; mirth rather than joy; variety of delights, rather than surfeit of them; wonder and admiration, and therefore novelties; studies that fill the mind with splendid and illustrious objects, as histories, fables, and contemplations of nature. If you fly physic in health altogether, it will be too strange for your body, when you shall need it. If you make it too familiar, it will work no extraordinary effect, when sickness cometh. I commend rather some diet for certain seasons, than frequent use of physic, except it be grown into a custom. For those diets alter the body more, and trouble it less. Despise no new accident in your body, but ask opinion of it. In sickness, respect health principally; and in health, action. For those that put their bodies to endure in health, may in most sicknesses, which are not very sharp, be cured only with diet, and tendering. Celsus could never have spoken it as a physician, had he not been a wise man withal, when he giveth it for one of the great precepts of health and lasting, that a man do vary, and interchange contraries, but with an inclination to the more benign extreme: use fasting and full eating, but rather full eating; watching and sleep, but rather sleep; sitting and exercise, but rather exercise; and the like. So shall nature be cherished, and yet taught masteries. Physicians are, some of them, so pleasing and conformable to the humor of the patient, as they press not the true cure of the disease; and some other are so regular, in proceeding according to the art for the disease, as they respect not sufficiently the condition of the patient. Take one of a middle temper; or if it may not be found in one man, combine two of either sort; and forget not to call as well, the best acquainted with your body, as the best reputed of for his faculty.

31.说疑心

疑心犹如蝙蝠,总在黄昏时出现。不可否认,疑心应该被消除,至少应该加以抑制,因为它会蒙蔽大脑,破坏友谊并有碍公务,从而使事业不能顺利进行。疑心使君王易施暴政,使丈夫易生妒忌,并使智者也优柔寡断,心绪郁结。然疑心并非心病,而是脑疾,因为连性格最坚强者也难免不生疑心,英王亨利七世就是一例。论疑心之重和性格之坚都无人堪比亨利七世,而要是具有那样一种禀性,疑心就不会造成大害;因为具有那种禀性的人通常不会轻信自己的猜疑,而是会对其严加审视,辨明真伪。但对胆小怕事者来说,疑心一生便会很快地越来越重。最容易使人生疑的事莫过于对实情知之甚少,所以消除疑心的办法应是多了解情况,而不该让疑窦藏在迷雾之中。世人干吗要多疑呢?难道他们以为他们所雇所交之人都该是圣贤?难道他们以为别人就不应该替自己打算?难道他们以为别人不该更忠于自己而该更忠于他们?由此可见,减轻疑心的最好办法是一方面把疑点视为真从而加以提防,一方面又将其视为假从而对疑心加以抑制;因为至此人只应将猜疑用作一种防范措施,应想到所疑之事即便是真,它也有可能不造成任何伤害。头脑中自然滋生的疑团不过是嗡嗡蜂鸣,但由流言蜚语人工合成的疑云通常却布满螫刺。驱散这种疑云的最佳方法就是开诚布公把自己的疑心告诉被怀疑者, 这样疑者对被疑者肯定会有比以往更多的了解,同时亦可使被怀疑者今后小心,别再因言行不慎而引人生疑。但开诚布公不宜用于天性卑劣者,因为那种人一旦发现自己被人怀疑,从此以后就不会再有真诚。意大利人爱说"疑心是忠诚的护照",仿佛猜疑真是忠诚离去的通行证似的;其实猜疑更应该激发忠诚证明自身之无可置疑。

解析

一、疑心的弊病：影响行事，于胆小者或性格坚强者皆如此——如亨利七世。

二、减轻疑心的办法：

1. 尽可能多地了解情况；
2. 尽管希望它们为假，但仍要知道它们也有可能为真并对之做好准备；
3. 避免人为加以夸张；
4. 开诚布公，对天性卑劣者除外。

Of Suspicion

SUSPICIONS amongst thoughts, are like bats amongst birds, they ever fly by twilight. Certainly they are to be repressed, or at least well guarded: for they cloud the mind; they leese friends; and they check with business, whereby business cannot go on currently and constantly. They dispose kings to tyranny, husbands to jealousy, wise men to irresolution and melancholy. They are defects, not in the heart, but in the brain; for they take place in the stoutest natures; as in the example of Henry the Seventh of England. There was not a more suspicious man, nor a more stout. And in such a composition they do small hurt. For commonly they are not admitted, but with examination, whether they be likely or no. But in fearful natures they gain ground too fast. There is nothing makes a man suspect much, more than to know little; and therefore men should remedy suspicion, by procuring to know more, and not to keep their suspicions in smother. What would men have? Do they think, those they employ and deal with, are saints? Do they not think, they will have their own ends, and be truer to themselves, than to them? Therefore there is no better way, to moderate suspicions, than to account upon such suspicions as true, and yet to bridle them as false. For so far a man ought to make use of his suspicions, as to provide, as if that should be true, that he suspects, yet it may do him no hurt. Suspicions that the mind of itself gathers, are but buzzes; but suspicions that are artificially nourished, and put into men's heads, by the tales and whisperings of others, have stings. Certainly, the best mean, to clear the way in this same wood of suspicions, is frankly to communicate them with the party, that he suspects; for thereby he shall be sure to know more of the truth of them, than he did before; and withal shall make that party more circumspect, not to give further cause of suspicion. But this would not be done to men of base natures; for they, if they find themselves once suspected, will never be true. The Italian says, Sospetto licentia fede;[①] as if suspicion, did give a passport to faith; but it ought, rather, to kindle it to discharge itself.

①Suspicion bids loyalty go.

32.谈辞令

某些人在言谈中更欣赏能自圆其说的趣言妙语，而不注重可辨明真伪的判断能力，仿佛值得赞赏的应该是知其所言，而不应该是知其所思。某些人熟谙一些老生常谈，并善于就此高谈阔论而少有发挥，这种贫乏之辞多半都单调沉闷，而且一经察觉会显得荒唐可笑。善于辞令者的可贵之处在于能提起话头、缓和话锋并转移话题，这种人可谓是交谈的指挥。言谈话语最好能有抑扬张弛，如在时事中加以论证，在铺叙中夹以推理，忽而提问忽而酬答，有时调侃有时认真，因为老用一种腔调平铺直叙会令人感到乏味，就如人们时下爱说的“简直没劲儿”。说到调侃，须注意有些事不可成为调侃的对象，如宗教、国务、伟人，以及任何人的当务之急和任何值得同情的病症；然而有些人以为言辞不刻薄就不足以显示其风趣，这是一种应加以制止的倾向，“小伙子哟，请少用鞭子，多拉缰绳。”[①]况且一般说来，听话人应该能辨出何为风趣何为尖刻。所以好冷嘲热讽者固然会使别人怕他的妙语，但他也肯定有必要担心人家的记忆。交谈中善于提问者不仅自己会获益匪浅，而且可使他人也得到满足，尤其是当他针对别人的专长提问之时，因这样他就使别人乐于开口，而他自己则可不断地获取知识；但所提的问题不可太难，因为太难的问题只适合老师考学生。若作为席谈的主人，务必保证让人人都有说话的机会，如果有人谈锋过健，悬河滔滔而不绝，就应设法转移话题，引其他人加入交谈，就像当年乐师们对付加利亚舞[②]舞迷所做的那样。若对别人确信你懂得的事偶尔佯装不知，那下次你对不懂之事保持沉默别人也会以为你懂。交谈中应少提自己，提及时应出言谨慎。我曾认识的某人爱说一句风凉话，曰：“过多言及自己的人肯定是智者。”只有在一

---

①语出奥维德《变形记》第2章127行。

②加利亚舞是一种轻快活泼的三节拍双人舞，在伊丽莎白时代曾风靡一时。

种情况下人可以既称赞自己又不失体面，那就是在谈另一个人的优点之时，尤其是所谈的那种优点说话人本身也具有。议论应尽量避免针对具体的个人，因为交谈应像一片原野纵横阡陌，没有直达某人家的专道。我曾认识两位贵族，都是英格兰西部人，其中一位有嘲弄人的癖好，但却爱在家中设华宴款待宾客；而另一位则爱问去过他家的赴宴者："请说实话，难道席间没人被他讽刺挖苦？"客人们常常回答有诸如此类的事情发生，于是问话的一位常说："我早料到他会糟践那桌佳肴。"慎言胜过雄辩，所以与人交谈时，话语中听比妙语如珠或有板有眼更为重要。善滔滔大论而不善酬答显反应迟钝；善应答酬对而不善侃侃长谈则显浅陋单薄。就像世人在动物界所见，不善久奔者多敏于腾挪转身，一如猎犬和野兔之分别。谈要点之前铺陈太多会令人生厌，但毫无铺陈又显得生硬。

解析

一、好的交谈毁于——

1. 注重所言胜过所思；
2. 对众所周知的陈词滥调进行滑稽冗长的重复。

二、好的谈话的原则：

1. 不独霸谈话，而是能领导话题、转移话题，并引导众人的参与；
2. 不调侃某些不能调侃的对象；
3. 除了陈述自己的观点，还应提出问题——不仅可使自己得到启发，还能使他人得到满足；
4. 若对自己懂得的事佯装不知，那么下次你对不懂之事保持沉默别人也会以为你懂；
5. 不过多提及自己，提及时也应避免攻击别人；
6. 尽量让你的谈话迎合别人的喜好，避免单调和繁复冗长的废话。

Of Discourse

SOME, in their discourse, desire rather commendation of wit, in being able to hold all arguments, than of judgment, in discerning what is true; as if it were a praise, to know what might be said, and not, what should be thought. Some have certain common places, and themes, wherein they are good and want variety; which kind of poverty is for the most part tedious, and when it is once perceived, ridiculous. The honorablest part of talk, is to give the occasion; and again to moderate, and pass to somewhat else; for then a man leads the dance. It is good, in discourse and speech of conversation, to vary and intermingle speech of the present occasion, with arguments, tales with reasons, asking of questions, with telling of opinions, and jest with earnest: for it is a dull thing to tire, and, as we say now, to jade, anything too far. As for jest, there be certain things, which ought to be privileged from it; namely, religion, matters of state, great persons, any man's present business of importance, and any case that deserveth pity. Yet there be some, that think their wits have been asleep, except they dart out somewhat that is piquant, and to the quick. That is a vein which would be bridled: Parce, puer, stimulis, et fortius utere loris. ① And generally, men ought to find the difference, between saltness and bitterness. Certainly, he that hath a satirical vein, as he maketh others afraid of his wit, so he had need be afraid of others' memory. He that questioneth much, shall learn much, and content much; but especially, if he apply his questions to the skill of the persons whom he asketh; for he shall give them occasion, to please themselves in speaking, and himself shall continually gather knowledge. But let his questions not be troublesome; for that is fit for a poser. And let him be sure to leave other men, their turns to speak. Nay, if there be any, that would reign and take up all the time, let him find means to take them off, and to bring others on; as musicians use to do, with those that dance too long galliards. If you dissemble, sometimes, your knowledge of that you are thought to know, you shall be thought, another time, to know that you know not. Speech of a man's self ought to be seldom, and well chosen. I knew one, was wont to say in scorn, He must needs be a wise man, he speaks so much of himself: and there is but one case, wherein a man may commend himself with good grace; and that is in commending virtue in another; especially if it be such a virtue, whereunto himself pretendeth. Speech of touch towards others, should be sparingly used; for discourse ought to be as a field, without coming home to any man. I knew two

①Spare the goad, boy, and pull more firmly with the reins.

noblemen, of the west part of England, whereof the one was given to scoff, but kept ever royal cheer in his house; the other would ask, of those that had been at the other's table, Tell truly, was there never a flout or dry blow given? To which the guest would answer, Such and such a thing passed. The lord would say, I thought, he would mar a good dinner. Discretion of speech, is more than eloquence; and to speak agreeably to him, with whom we deal, is more than to speak in good words, or in good order. A good continued speech, without a good speech of interlocution, shows slowness: and a good reply or second speech, without a good settled speech, showeth shallowness and weakness. As we see in beasts, that those that are weakest in the course, are yet nimblest in the turn; as it is betwixt the greyhound and the hare. To use too many circumstances, ere one come to the matter, is wearisome; to use none at all, is blunt.

33.谈殖民地

建殖民地乃古代先民的英雄业绩之一。[①]当世界年轻的时候，它生育过众多儿女，但如今世界已年迈，所生子女也稀少，故笔者不妨将新建的殖民地视为旧有的国家所生育的儿女。余以为殖民地最好是建在处女地上，如此便不会为了殖民而将原有居民根除，因为那样做与其说是殖民，不如说是屠民。建立殖民地犹如人工造林，必须估计到投资二十年后方会有利可图。许多殖民地毁灭的原因主要就在于殖民初期的急功近利。当然对早期获利也不应一概弃之，但限度是符合殖民地的良性发展，决不可超越这一限度。

把流氓恶棍囚犯送去殖民地充居民，这种做法不仅可耻可恶，而且将对殖民地造成损害。因为那种人将继续过其败类的生活，终日游手好闲，不务正业，滋事启衅，白耗粮食，并很快又玩得不耐烦，于是便写信回母国败坏殖民地的声誉。殖民地的首批居民应该是一些园丁、农民、小工、铁匠、木匠、渔夫、猎手，以及少量的厨师、医生、药剂师和面包师。初到一殖民地区，首先应考察当地出产什么可食之物，如栗子、胡桃、菠萝、橄榄、枣椰、梅子、樱桃和野蜂蜜等等，并对这些现成食物加以利用；其次应考虑在当地种植生长周期较短的一年生作物或蔬菜，如欧洲萝卜、胡萝卜、芜菁、洋葱、四季萝卜、洋蓟和玉米等等。至于小麦、大麦和燕麦，它们费工太多，但不妨先种些豌豆和蚕豆，一则它们费工少，二则它们既可鲜食又可做面包；稻谷也生长极快，而且也是一种主食。不过最要紧的是运去足够的饼干、燕麦片、面粉和玉米粉等食物，直到能在当地生产出面包为止。至于家畜家禽，主要应选带那些既不易生病又繁殖迅速的品种，如猪、羊、鸡、鹅、火鸡和家鸽等

---

①如公元前8—前6世纪希腊在海外大规模建立殖民城邦；罗马共和国和罗马帝国所建立的大批行省实际上也是一种殖民地。

等。殖民地初期的食品消耗应和围城中的情形一样，即按一定标准定量分配；应把菜园和玉米地出产之大部作为公共储备并善加储存，然后按计划比例进行分发，上述园地不包括个人为自家用度而不得不开垦耕种的零星土地。同时应考虑开发适于殖民地土壤生长的经济作物，以期在某种程度上减轻殖民地的负担，但不可像前文所说的那样急功近利，从而不合时宜地损害主业，就像在弗吉尼亚种植烟草[①]的结果那样。殖民地通常都有丰富的森林资源，故木材可作为一种经济产品；若森林茂密处有铁矿和适宜建厂的河流，炼铁也不失为一种经济产业；在气候允许的地方可尝试生产海盐；任何纤维作物都有潜在的开发价值；松杉茂密的地方不会缺乏树脂和焦油；药材和月桂[②]亦不会不产生极大利润；另外白蜡树和其他物产也可以考虑开发；但勿花太多精力在地下折腾，因为发现矿藏的希望极其渺茫，而且探矿往往使移民懒于其他劳作。

说到殖民地的管理，应由一人总督，若干顾问辅之，而且应授权殖民地政府在必要时实行有限的军事管制。尤其重要的是，要让移民们获得身居旷野的那种益处，让他们觉得上帝及其佑助时时刻刻都近在眼前。[③]殖民地的管理不可过多地依赖母国的受托管理人和特许承包人，这种人的数量应有限制，而且最好是贵族缙绅而非商人，因为商人总是只顾眼前利益。在殖民地巩固之前，不应对其征收关税，而且除因特殊的安全原因外，应允许殖民地将产品出口到任何最能使其获利的地方。为避免殖民地人满为患，勿急着一批接一批地送去移民，而应根据其人员消耗按比例进行补充。总之殖民地人口数量应以人人都能安居为度，不可让他们因人口过多而陷入贫困。有些移民区建在海岸河滨的沼泽地带，其恶劣的环境一直危害着移民

①英国于 1584 年在北美建立弗吉尼亚殖民地，开发该殖民地的公司一心想迅速发财，只准移民种植和加工伦敦市场需要的产品，却不让他们种植生活必需的农作物。烟草虽成了弗吉尼亚的主要财源，但同时也制约了其他方面的发展，如种烟的土地几年后就变得贫瘠，农民不得不经常移居，到培根写这篇文章时(1625 年)，弗吉尼亚殖民地尚没有一座城镇，连所谓的首府詹姆斯敦也只有几户人家。

②月桂之叶和果均可提取芳香油。

③约翰曾在犹太的旷野上替人施洗，耶稣曾在加利利的旷野中经受住魔鬼的诱惑。参见《新约·马太福音》第 3—4 章。

的健康；所以初时择低地而居虽可避免运输和其他方面的不便，但从长远看仍然应把居所建在高处。储备足够的食盐同样关系到移民的健康，因为必要时他们可用其腌制食品。若在有土著的地区殖民，不可只用华而不实的小玩意儿讨他们的欢心，而应在有充分防范的前提下待之以公平与友好。不可为取悦他们而助其侵犯他们的敌人，但帮助他们抵御入侵则不为过。应经常选送一些土著到殖民地之母国，让他们亲眼目睹一种优于他们的生活环境，以便他们回去后现身说法。待殖民地巩固之后，就可不仅接纳男丁，亦接纳妇女，让移民一代代繁衍生息，而非永远从母国补充。抛弃正在发展的殖民地是世间最大的罪恶，因为那不仅是母国的耻辱，亦葬送掉许多可怜的移民。

解析

一、建殖民地是“古老的、原始的、英雄的”。

二、建立一块殖民地需要避免的做法：

1. 驱赶或消灭原有居民；
2. 急功近利；
3. 把流氓恶棍送去殖民地充当居民，而不是有用的、有技艺的工匠。

三、开拓殖民地应注意的事项：

1. 维持生存：
   (1) 好好利用当地出产的现成食物；
   (2) 引进生长期较短的作物与蔬菜，以及一些繁殖迅速的动物品种；
   (3) 谨慎经济地分配所获得的产品。
2. 开展贸易：
   (1) 发展与出口必需品而不是奢侈品；
   (2) 依赖农业而不是矿业。
3. 管理方面：

（1）一人总督，若干顾问辅之，施行某种形式的军事管制；

（2）暂时免除进出口关税。

4. 维护健康：

（1）避免人口过多；

（2）把住所建在高处，而非海岸河滨的沼泽地带；

（3）有足够的食盐储备。

5. 综合管理：

（1）公平、友好地对待土著；

（2）殖民地稳定、繁荣以后，应接纳妇女；

（3）不抛弃正在发展的殖民地。

Of Plantations

PLANTATIONS are amongst ancient, primitive, and heroical works. When the world was young, it begat more children; but now it is old, it begets fewer: for I may justly account new plantations, to be the children of former kingdoms. I like a plantation in a pure soil; that is, where people are not displanted, to the end, to plant in others. For else it is rather an extirpation, than a plantation. Planting of countries, is like planting of woods; for you must make account to leese almost twenty years' profit, and expect your recompense in the end. For the principal thing, that hath been the destruction of most plantations, hath been the base and hasty drawing of a profit, in the first years. It is true, speedy profit is not to be neglected, as far as may stand with the good of the plantation, but no further.

It is a shameful and unblessed thing, to take the scum of people, and wicked condemned men, to be the people with whom you plant; and not only so, but it spoileth the plantation; for they will ever live like rogues, and not fall to work, but be lazy, and do mischief, and spend victuals, and be quickly weary, and then certify over to their country, to the discredit of the plantation. The people wherewith you plant ought to be gardeners, ploughmen, laborers, smiths, carpenters, joiners, fishermen, fowlers, with some few apothecaries, surgeons, cooks, and bakers. In a country of plantation, first look about, what kind of victual the country yields of itself to hand; as chestnuts, walnuts, pineapples, olives, dates, plums, cherries, wild honey, and the like;

and make use of them. Then consider what victual or esculent things there are, which grow speedily, and within the year; as parsnips, carrots, turnips, onions, radish, artichokes of Hierusalem, maize, and the like. For wheat, barley, and oats, they ask too much labor; but with pease and beans you may begin, both because they ask less labor, and because they serve for meat, as well as for bread. And of rice, likewise cometh a great increase, and it is a kind of meat. Above all, there ought to be brought store of biscuit, oat-meal, flour, meal, and the like, in the beginning, till bread may be had. For beasts, or birds, take chiefly such as are least subject to diseases, and multiply fastest; as swine, goats, cocks, hens, turkeys, geese, house-doves, and the like. The victual in plantations, ought to be expended almost as in a besieged town; that is, with certain allowance. And let the main part of the ground, employed to gardens or corn, be to a common stock; and to be laid in, and stored up, and then delivered out in proportion; besides some spots of ground, that any particular person will manure for his own private. Consider likewise what commodities, the soil where the plantation is, doth naturally yield, that they may some way help to defray the charge of the plantation (so it be not, as was said, to the untimely prejudice of the main business), as it hath fared with tobacco in Virginia. Wood commonly aboundeth but too much; and therefore timber is fit to be one. If there be iron ore, and streams whereupon to set the mills, iron is a brave commodity where wood aboundeth. Making of bay-salt, if the climate be proper for it, would be put in experience. Growing silk likewise, if any be, is a likely commodity. Pitch and tar, where store of firs and pines are, will not fail. So drugs and sweet woods, where they are, cannot but yield great profit. Soap-ashes likewise, and other things that may be thought of. But moil not too much under ground; for the hope of mines is very uncertain, and useth to make the planters lazy, in other things.

For government; let it be in the hands of one, assisted with some counsel; and let them have commission to exercise martial laws, with some limitation. And above all, let men make that profit, of being in the wilderness, as they have God always, and his service, before their eyes. Let not the government of the plantation, depend upon too many counsellors, and undertakers, in the country that planteth, but upon a temperate number; and let those be rather noblemen and gentlemen, than merchants; for they look ever to the present gain. Let there be freedom from custom, till the plantation be of strength; and not only freedom from custom, but freedom to carry their commodities, where they may make their best of them, except there be some special cause of caution. Cram not in people, by sending too fast company after company; but rather harken how they waste, and send supplies proportionably; but so, as the number may live well in the plantation, and not by surcharge be in penury. It hath been a great endangering to the health of some plantations, that they have built along the sea and rivers, in marish and unwholesome grounds. Therefore, though you begin there, to avoid carriage and like discommodities, yet build still rather upwards from the streams, than along. It concerneth likewise the health of the plantation, that they have good store of salt with them, that they may use it in their victuals, when it shall be necessary. If you plant where savages are, do not only entertain them, with trifles and gingles, but use them justly and graciously, with sufficient guard nevertheless; and do not win their favor, by helping them to invade their enemies, but for their defence it is not amiss; and send oft of them, over to the country that plants, that they may see a better condition than their own, and commend it when they return. When the plantation grows to strength, then it is time to plant with women, as well as with men; that the plantation may spread into generations, and not be ever pieced from without. It is the sinfullest thing in the world, to forsake or destitute a plantation once in forwardness; for besides the dishonor, it is the guiltiness of blood of many commiserable persons.

34.论财富

笔者认为财富不过是德行的包袱。包袱一词用拉丁字眼 impedimenta[①]更好,因为财富之于德行,不啻辎重之于军队。辎重不可缺少,亦不可滞后,但它每每有碍行军,有时为顾辎重甚至会贻误战机或妨碍胜利。巨额财富无什么真正的用处,除修斋布施之外,其他用途均属幻想。因此所罗门有言:“财物越多,食者越众;除了饱饱眼福,财主得何益呢?”[②]任何人的个人享用都不可能达到非要巨额钱财的地步, 有巨额钱财者只是保管着钱财,或拥有施舍捐赠的权利,或享有富豪的名声,但钱财于他们并无实在的用处。君不见有人为几粒石子或罕见之物开出天价?君不见有人为使巨额财富显得有用而着手某些铺张的工程?不过读者也许会说,钱财可以替人消灾化难,正如所罗门之言:“钱财在富人心里就像一座城堡。”[③]然此言正好道破天机,那城堡是在心里,而绝非在现实之中;因为不可否认,钱财替人招灾致祸的时候远远多于替人消灾化难的时候。千万别为摆阔炫耀而追求财富,只挣你取之有道、用之有度、施之有乐且遗之有慰的钱财。但也别像修道士那样不食人间烟火,对金钱全然不屑一顾。只是挣钱要分清有道无道,就像西塞罗当年替波斯图穆斯辩护时所说:“他追求财富增加显然不是为满足其贪婪之心,而是为了得到行善的资力。”[④]还应听从所罗门的教诲,别急欲发财,“急欲发财者将失去其清白”[⑤]。

在诗人的虚构中, 财神普路图斯受天帝朱庇特派遣时总是磨磨蹭蹭,

---

①impedimenta 有“障碍”、“包袱”、“辎重”等义。

②语出《旧约·传道书》第 5 章 11 节。

③语出《旧约·箴言》第 18 章 11 节。

④语出西塞罗《为波斯图穆斯辩之二》。波斯图穆斯是公元前 1 世纪罗马银行家及元老院元老。不过西塞罗所说的“他”并非指波斯图穆斯本人,而是指他父亲。

⑤语出《旧约·箴言》第 28 章 20 节。

而受冥王普路同差遣时却跑得飞快。[1]这段虚构的寓意是，靠诚实和汗水致富通常很慢，但靠他人的死亡发财（如继承遗产之类）则快如钱财从天而降。但若把普路同视为魔鬼，这种虚构也恰如其分；因为当财富来自魔鬼时（如靠欺诈、压迫和其他不公正的手段获取财富），的确来得很快。致富的途径千条万条，可多半都是邪门歪道。其中吝啬最为清白，但也并非清白无瑕，因为它阻止世人乐善好施。利用土地致富是最合理的生财之道，因土地提供的财富乃大地之母的恩赐，只是走这条路致富较慢。但已有万贯家财者若肯屈尊经营土地，其家财定会成倍增加。笔者曾识一位英格兰贵族，他当时需审计的账目为全国之最，因为他拥有大片的麦田、林场、牧场和羊群，还拥有巨大的煤矿、铅矿、铁矿和诸如此类的产业，所以大地于他就像是一片财源滚滚且永不枯竭的海洋。

有人[2]说他挣小钱很难赚大钱却很容易，此话一点不假。因为一个人若像他那样拥有雄厚的资金，便可囤积居奇，恃强凌弱并与人合伙经营年轻人的行当[3]，这样他非赚大钱不可。一般行当和职业挣的是老实钱，其挣钱手段主要有二：一是勤劳奋勉，二是童叟无欺。但靠讲盘议价而盈利，其公道就令人生疑；凡乘人急需而漫天要价，凡贿赂雇员和代理人而招揽生意，或是耍手腕排挤其他可能更公平的商人等等，都是奸诈卑劣之举。至于做投机买卖，即购物并非为自己所用，而是为了再高价出售，这对原卖主和二手顾客都可谓敲诈。如果选择的搭档可靠，合伙经营通常有大利可图。放债取息乃最可靠的发财之路，但也是最有害的邪路，因放债取息者不仅让别人流汗自己吃面包[4]，而且还在安息日盈利[5]。不过放债取息虽说可靠，但也并非没有风险，因公证人和中间人常常为了私利替没有偿还能力的人作信誉担保。若有幸率先获得某项发明或某项专利，有时候也可大发横财，如最

---

①古希腊作家卢奇安在其《厌世者泰门》中就有过这样的虚构。

②指普鲁塔克在其《道德论集》中提到一个名叫兰庞（Lampon）的富商。

③指有利可图的娱乐业。

④据《旧约·创世记》第 3 章 19 节载，上帝对即将被逐出伊甸园的亚当说："你必须汗流满面才有面包可吃。"

⑤"摩西十诫"之第四诫即为当守安息日（停止一切劳作），参见《旧约·出埃及记》第 20 章 8—11 节。

先在加那利群岛建糖厂的那人。因此，一个人若能充当真正的逻辑学家，即善于发现又善于判断[①]，那他就可以大捞一把，尤其是遇上走运得幸之时。靠固定收入生活者终归难成巨富，而倾其所有投机者又往往会倾家荡产；所以最好是有份固定收入作投机冒险的后盾，这样即使投机失败也有退路。在没有法律限制的地方，垄断商品并囤积待售乃发财之重要手段，在当事者能预见何种商品将供不应求，从而事先囤积时更是如此。出仕受禄固然最为风光，但若俸禄之获取是靠阿谀奉承、偷合苟容或其他奴颜婢膝的行径，那这种钱亦可列为最卑污之类。至于攫取遗嘱及遗嘱执行人身份（像塔西佗所说的塞内加那样用网捕捞遗嘱和遗孤监护权[②]），这比前者更为卑污；因前者讨好的毕竟是公侯君王，而后者得讨好一些卑鄙小人。

别太相信那些看上去蔑视财富的人，他们之所以蔑视财富乃因他们对发财已不抱希望；他们一旦发财仍然会惜财。别在小钱上精打细算，须知钱财长有翅膀，有时它们会自己飞走，有时你得放它们飞走，以便带来更多财富。人们通常把财产留给儿女或捐给社会，但或留或捐都以数额适中为妙。若子嗣年少，尚缺乏见识，留给他一大份家业不啻是留下了一块诱饵，将招来各种猛禽对他进行围攻。同样，为虚名而馈赠的捐款和基金就像没加盐的祭品[③]，不过是善行之涂金抹彩的墓冢，里面很快就会开始腐烂[④]。因此勿用数量作你捐赠的标准，而要用标准来规定你捐赠的用途；并且不可把捐赠之事拖到弥留之时，因平心而论，死到临头才捐赠那无疑是在慷他人之慨。

---

①法国逻辑学家拉米斯（Petrus Ramus，1515—1572）在其《逻辑学》第1章2节中称："逻辑之组成部分有二，即发现和判断。"

②见塔西佗《编年史》第13卷42章。王义铸、崔妙因译本（商务馆1997年版）将此句译作"那些没有子嗣的人和他们的遗产，都很难逃出他的罗网"。

③《旧约·利未记》第2章13节云："献给上帝的所有祭品都要加盐。"

④《新约·马太福音》第23章27节云："你们这班道学先生和法利赛人将大祸临头，因为你们就像一座座经粉饰的墓冢，外表富丽堂皇，里面却塞满了死人骨头和各种污秽。"

解析

一、财富的害处：

1. 阻碍德行；
2. 对持有人的享乐无真正的用处；
3. 它消灾化难的功用只存在于“想象中”。

二、对渴望财富之人的忠告：

1. 不能贪财；
2. 不急于发财，因为来得太快的钱财绝非来自天堂，它来自普路同，代表的不是死亡就是魔鬼。

三、致富的途径（有千万条，但多半都是邪门歪道）：

1. 吝啬；
2. 土地，致富较慢，除非投资巨大；
3. 一般行当，普通职业；
4. 讲盘议价；
5. 合伙经营；
6. 放债取息；
7. 率先发明；
8. 垄断商品并囤积待售；
9. 出仕受禄；
10. 奴颜婢膝，攫取遗产。

四、对拥有财富之人的忠告：

1. 不要相信那些看上去蔑视财富的人；
2. 别在小钱上精打细算；
3. 分配遗产要谨慎；
4. 不要死到临头才捐赠。

Of Riches

I CANNOT call riches better than the baggage of virtue. The Roman word is better, impedimenta. For as the baggage is to an army, so is riches to virtue. It cannot be spared, nor left behind, but it hindereth the march; yea, and the care of it, sometimes loseth or disturbeth the victory. Of great riches there is no real use, except it be in the distribution; the rest is but conceit. So saith Solomon, Where much is, there are many to consume it; and what hath the owner, but the sight of it with his eyes? The personal fruition in any man, cannot reach to feel great riches: there is a custody of them; or a power of dole, and donative of them; or a fame of them; but no solid use to the owner. Do you not see what feigned prices, are set upon little stones and rarities? and what works of ostentation are undertaken, because there might seem to be some use of great riches? But then you will say, they may be of use, to buy men out of dangers or troubles. As Solomon saith, Riches are as a strong hold, in the imagination of the rich man. But this is excellently expressed, that it is in the imagination, and not always in fact. For certainly great riches, have sold more men, than they have bought out. Seek not proud riches, but such as thou mayest get justly, use soberly, distribute cheerfully, and leave contentedly. Yet have no abstract nor friarly contempt of them. But distinguish, as Cicero saith well of Rabirius Posthumus, In studio rei amplificandae apparebat, non avaritiae praedam, sed instrumentum bonitati quaeri. ① Harken also to Solomon, and beware of hasty gathering of riches; Qui festinat ad divitias, non erit insons.②

The poets feign, that when Plutus (which is Riches) is sent from Jupiter, he limps and goes slowly; but when he is sent from Pluto, he runs, and is swift of foot. Meaning that riches gotten by good means, and just labor, pace slowly; but when they come by the death of others (as by the course of inheritance, testaments, and the like), they come tumbling upon a man. But it mought be applied likewise to Pluto, taking him for the devil. For when riches come from the devil (as by fraud and oppression, and unjust means), they come upon speed. The ways to enrich are many, and most of them foul. Parsimony is one of the best, and yet is not innocent; for it withholdeth men from works of liberality and charity. The improvement of the ground, is the most natural obtaining of riches; for it is our great mother's blessing, the

---

①In his keenness to increase his wealth it was clear that he sought not the gratification of avarice but the means to do good.

②He who hastens to get riches will not be guiltless.

earth's; but it is slow. And yet where men of great wealth do stoop to husbandry, it multiplieth riches exceedingly. I knew a nobleman in England, that had the greatest audits of any man in my time; a great grazier, a great sheep-master, a great timber man, a great collier, a great corn-master, a great lead-man, and so of iron, and a number of the like points of husbandry. So as the earth seemed a sea to him, in respect of the perpetual importation.

It was truly observed by one, that himself came very hardly, to a little riches, and very easily, to great riches. For when a man's stock is come to that, that he can expect the prime of markets, and overcome those bargains, which for their greatness are few men's money, and be partner in the industries of younger men, he cannot but increase mainly. The gains of ordinary trades and vocations are honest; and furthered by two things chiefly: by diligence, and by a good name, for good and fair dealing. But the gains of bargains, are of a more doubtful nature; when men shall wait upon others' necessity, broke by servants and instruments to draw them on, put off others cunningly, that would be better chapmen, and the like practices, which are crafty and naught. As for the chopping of bargains, when a man buys not to hold but to sell over again, that commonly grindeth double, both upon the seller, and upon the buyer. Sharings do greatly enrich, if the hands be well chosen, that are trusted. Usury is the certainest means of gain, though one of the worst; as that whereby a man doth eat his bread, in sudore vultus alieni①; and besides, doth plough upon Sundays. And yet certain though it be, it hath flaws; for that the scriveners and brokers do value unsound men, to serve their own turn. The fortune in being the first, in an invention or in a privilege, doth cause sometimes a wonderful overgrowth in riches; as it was with the first sugar man, in the Canaries. Therefore if a man can play the true logician, to have as well judgment, as invention, he may do great matters; especially if the times be fit. He that resteth upon gains certain, shall hardly grow to great riches; and he that puts all upon adventures, doth oftentimes break and come to poverty: it is good, therefore, to guard adventures with certainties, that may uphold losses. Monopolies, and coemption of wares for re-sale, where they are not restrained, are great means to enrich; especially if the party have intelligence, what things are like to come into request, and so store himself beforehand. Riches gotten by service, though it be of the best rise, yet when they are gotten by flattery, feeding humors, and other servile conditions, they may be placed amongst the worst. As for fishing for testaments and executorships (as Tacitus saith of Seneca, testamenta et orbos tamquam indagine

①in the sweat of another's brow

capi[1]), it is yet worse; by how much men submit themselves to meaner persons, than in service.

Believe not much, them that seem to despise riches; for they despise them, that despair of them; and none worse, when they come to them. Be not penny-wise; riches have wings, and sometimes they fly away of themselves, sometimes they must be set flying, to bring in more. Men leave their riches, either to their kindred, or to the public; and moderate portions, prosper best in both. A great state left to an heir, is as a lure to all the birds of prey round about, to seize on him, if he be not the better stablished in years and judgment. Likewise glorious gifts and foundations, are like sacrifices without salt; and but the painted sepulchres of alms, which soon will putrefy, and corrupt inwardly. Therefore measure not thine advancements, by quantity, but frame them by measure: and defer not charities till death; for, certainly, if a man weigh it rightly, he that doth so, is rather liberal of another man's, than of his own.

①Wills and childless men were caught in a net as it were.

35.论预言

笔者欲在此谈论的不是神灵的启示，不是异教徒的谶语，亦不是大自然的预兆，而只是某些在世人的记忆中已应验但却不明来由的预言。如女巫曾对扫罗说："明日汝及诸子将与吾同在。"[①]维吉尔曾从荷马借得如下诗句：埃涅阿斯的族人将统治所有的国土，／直到他儿子的儿子，后世的子子孙孙。[②]这两行诗似乎预言了罗马帝国的兴起。[③]悲剧诗人塞内加曾写下这些诗行：

> 在遥远的将来会有那么一天，
> 大海将解开束缚世界的锁链，
> 一片广阔的陆地将为人所知，
> 另一位忒菲斯将发现新世界，
> 极地图勒将不再是地角天边。[④]

这些诗行似乎预言了美洲之发现。波吕克拉特的女儿曾梦见朱庇特替她父亲沐浴，阿波罗替她父亲涂油，结果她父亲果然被钉在十字架上，有大雨浇

---

①据《旧约·撒母耳记上》第28章记载，此预言实际上出自女巫招来的已故希伯来先知撒母耳之口，后应验为扫罗在与非利士人争战时负伤自杀，三个儿子也同时阵亡。

②引自维吉尔《埃涅阿斯纪》第3卷97—98行，荷马的原诗为："埃涅阿斯的力量统治特洛伊人，／直到他儿子的儿子，后世的子子孙孙。"（《伊利亚特》第20卷307—308行）

③相传英雄埃涅阿斯带领战败的特洛伊人出海寻觅新的国土，最后在意大利建立了罗马。

④引自塞内加的悲剧《美狄亚》第2幕374—378行。诗中的忒菲斯乃希腊神话中的阿耳戈船英雄之一，英雄们寻取金羊毛时即由他引航。极地图勒是古代地理学家对挪威、冰岛等地的称呼，泛指极北地区。

淋他的身子,有太阳晒得他汗流浃背。[1]马其顿国王腓力二世曾梦见他封闭了妻子的腹腔,于是他自己解梦说他妻子将不会生育,但预言家亚里斯坦德却说是他妻子已有了身孕,因为人们通常不会封闭空着的器皿。[2]一个出现在布鲁图帐中的鬼魂对他说:"你我将在腓力比再会。"[3]提比略曾对伽尔巴说:"你将来也会尝到当皇帝的滋味。"[4]在韦斯帕芗时代,东方曾流传着一个预言,说从犹太地来的人将统治世界,尽管这预言可能是说我们的耶稣基督,但塔西佗解释说是指韦斯帕芗。[5]图密善在被刺的前一夜曾做一梦,梦见自己的颈背上长出了一颗金头颅,结果他的后继者们果然使罗马帝国出现了一个持续多年的"黄金时代"。[6]英王亨利六世曾指着为他端水的少年伯爵对人说:"这小伙子将戴上我们所争夺的这顶王冠。"后来那少年果然成了英国国王,称亨利七世。[7]笔者在法国的时候听一位叫佩纳的医生讲,笃信占星术的法国王太后曾用假名让占星术士替她丈夫算命,术士预言她丈夫将死于决斗,当时还是王后的王太后闻言大笑,心想没有人敢向国王挑战要求决斗,但后来她丈夫死于一次马上比武,因为与他交手的卫队长蒙哥马利的矛杆裂片刺入了他的护面具。[8]笔者在年幼之时,也就是

①见希罗多德《历史》第3卷124—125节。波吕克拉特是公元前6世纪萨默斯岛的统治者,以在爱琴海上从事海盗活动而臭名昭著,公元前522年被波斯帝国驻吕底亚总督奥瑞忒斯(Oroetes)诱擒,钉于十字架上而死。

②见普鲁塔克《列传·亚历山大篇》。此梦应验在腓力二世之妻生下后来的亚历山大大帝。

③见普鲁塔克《列传·布鲁图篇》。鬼魂之言应验在布鲁图在腓力比战役中败于屋大维安东尼联军并自杀身亡。

④见苏维托尼乌斯《伽尔巴传》,但文中引语实为奥古斯都所言。《伽尔巴传》第4章1节记载道,"众所周知,当小伽尔巴同一群孩子向奥古斯都问安时,奥古斯都捏了一下他的脸蛋说:'孩子,你将来也会尝到当皇帝的滋味。'而提比略得知这一预言后只是说:'好哇,让他活到那一天吧,那时他与我们已不再相干。'"

⑤见塔西佗《历史》第5卷13章和苏维托尼乌斯《韦斯帕芗传》第4章5节。当时韦斯帕芗正统兵在东方镇压耶路撒冷的犹太人起义。

⑥见苏维托尼乌斯《图密善传》第23章2节。"黄金时代"指公元96—192年罗马帝国安敦尼王朝统治时期的"太平盛世"。

⑦事见英国史学家霍林希德的《英格兰、苏格兰、爱尔兰编年史》,莎士比亚曾从该书取材写成《亨利六世》三联剧,培根列举之事可参见莎翁《亨利六世下篇》第4幕6场68—70行。

⑧法王亨利二世于1559年因比武受伤,不治而亡。

伊丽莎白女王还年轻的时候，曾听见过一则广为流传的预言：大麻一旦被纺，英格兰就灭亡。当时人们一般以为，这预言是说等都铎王朝的几位君王统治结束以后，英格兰就会陷入大乱。[①]感谢上帝，这预言后来只应在称号的改变上，因为当今王上的称号已不再是英格兰国王，而是不列颠国王[②]。在1588年以前流传过一则民谣，对此笔者迄今尚不甚明了。民谣说：

有朝一日你将看见，
在巴岛与梅岛之间，
挪威黑舰队的舰船。
等黑舰队一朝覆亡，
英格兰将修屋造房，
因从此再不会打仗。

人们曾普遍认为这首民谣说的是1588年来犯的西班牙舰队[③]，因为据说那位西班牙国王的小名就叫挪威。另外雷乔蒙塔努斯[④]那句“88年将是奇迹年”的预言也同样被认为应验于西班牙大舰队之远征，因为那是有史以来在海面上出现的最强大的舰队，虽说数量不是最多，但力量却堪称最强。至于克里昂那个梦，笔者认为只是一种调侃，调侃者说克里昂梦见他被一条长龙吞噬，而梦中的长龙被解释成惹他极度烦恼的腊肠贩子。[⑤]若把梦兆和占星术士的谶语都给算上，这类预言之多可谓数不胜数，不过笔者只记下

---

①把都铎王朝的 Henry Ⅶ（亨利七世）、Edward Ⅵ（爱德华六世）、Mary Ⅰ（玛丽一世）、Philip II（玛丽一世之夫、西班牙国王腓力二世）和 Elizabeth Ⅰ（伊丽莎白一世）名字的第一个字母连在一起即为 Hempe（大麻）。

②詹姆斯一世虽称不列颠国王，但当时英格兰与苏格兰尚未真正合并。

③西班牙无敌舰队于1588年5月远征英国，在英吉利海峡遭英国海军阻击，损失惨重，剩余舰船被迫北上绕苏格兰返航，途中有可能穿过巴（斯）岛与梅岛之间（在弗斯湾）。

④雷乔蒙塔努斯（1436—1476，原名 Johannes Müller），德国数学家及天文学家，他早在1472年就观测出了后来被命名为“哈雷”的那颗彗星，著有《预言》一书。

⑤希腊喜剧诗人阿里斯托芬曾写《骑士》一剧对雅典统帅克里昂（?—前422）进行讽刺。该剧把克里昂写成一个家奴，而他的顶头上司管家则是位灌制腊肠的小贩。

上述较有根据者作为范例。我以为对此类预言应一笑置之,只应将其作为冬日里围炉聚谈的话题;但我说一笑置之是就信与不信而言,而非就其他方面而论,譬如对这类预言之散布和流传就不可置之不理,而且笔者亦见多国法律对其严加禁止。预言被人接受并相信有三个原因。其一是世人只注意其应验而不注意其落空,人们对梦兆之注意亦是如此。其二是有充分根据的推测或意义含混的传说到头来往往都会被变成预言,因为人爱预测未来的天性使他们认为把自己的推测作为预言公布并无什么妨害,如前文所引塞内加的诗行就是一例;因当时已有许多理论可以证明,在大西洋以外地球还有广大区域,而那些区域很可能并非一片汪洋,[①]另外柏拉图在其对话《蒂默亚篇》和《克利托篇》中对大西岛[②]之描述,也足以鼓励世人将上述推测变成一种预言。最后是第三个(亦是最重要的一个)原因,即那些数不胜数的预言差不多全是冒牌货,它们不过是由一些无聊的机灵鬼在事情发生之后精心编造的谎言。

解析

一、预言的定义:不是神灵的启示,不是异教徒的谶语,亦不是大自然的预兆,而是在历史上应验却不明来由的预言。

二、此类预言的例子:

女巫对扫罗所言;

塞内加——美洲的发现;

波吕克拉特的女儿;

马其顿国王腓力二世之梦;

---

①如古希腊地理学家埃拉托色尼(Erastothenes,前 275—前 195)的《地理学》一书就对此有较为科学的论述。

②大西岛(又译亚特兰蒂斯)乃古代传说中的岛屿,据说位于大西洋直布罗陀海峡以西,后来沉没。柏拉图在其两篇对话中描述了该岛上的高度文明,故大西岛又被视为“乌托邦”的同义词。

布鲁图看见的“鬼魂”；

提比略对伽尔巴所言；

关于朱迪亚流传的信仰；

图密善的梦；

亨利六世对亨利七世的预言；

法王亨利二世之死；

英国都铎王朝的灭亡；

西班牙无敌舰队；

克里昂的梦。

三、这些作为预言并无重要性，如果不是对相信它们的人产生了恶劣的影响。

四、预言产生影响的原因：

1. 人们只注意到它们偶尔的应验，而忽略它们大部分情况下的落空；

2. 它们中不少都是有充分根据的推测，并不是预言；

3. 它们中不少都是事后编造出来的厚颜无耻的谎言。

Of Prophecies

I MEAN not to speak of divine prophecies; nor of heathen oracles; nor of natural predictions; but only of prophecies that have been of certain memory, and from hidden causes. Saith the Pythonissa to Saul, To-morrow thou and thy son shall be with me. Homer hath these verses: At domus Aeneae cunctis dominabitur oris, / Et nati natorum, et qui nascentur ab illis. ① A prophecy, as it seems, of the Roman empire. Seneca the tragedian hath these verses:

—Venient annis
Saecula seris, quibus Oceanus
Vincula rerum laxet, et ingens
Pateat Tellus, Tiphysque novos
Detegat orbes; nec sit terris

①But the house of Aeneas shall lord it over all lands, they and their sons' sons and the generations after them.

Ultima Thule:①

a prophecy of the discovery of America. The daughter of Polycrates, dreamed that Jupiter bathed her father, and Apollo anointed him; and it came to pass, that he was crucified in an open place, where the sun made his body run with sweat, and the rain washed it. Philip of Macedon dreamed, he sealed up his wife's belly; whereby he did expound it, that his wife should be barren; but Aristander the soothsayer, told him his wife was with child, because men do not use to seal vessels, that are empty. A phantasm that appeared to M. Brutus, in his tent, said to him, Philippis iterum me videbis. ② Tiberius said to Galba, Tu quoque, Galba, degustabis imperium. ③ In Vespasian's time, there went a prophecy in the East, that those that should come forth of Judea, should reign over the world: which though it may be was meant of our Savior; yet Tacitus expounds it of Vespasian. Domitian dreamed, the night before he was slain, that a golden head was growing, out of the nape of his neck: and indeed, the succession that followed him for many years, made golden times. Henry the Sixth of England, said of Henry the Seventh, when he was a lad, and gave him water, This is the lad that shall enjoy the crown, for which we strive. When I was in France, I heard from one Dr. Pena, that the Queen Mother, who was given to curious arts, caused the King her husband's nativity to be calculated, under a false name; and the astrologer gave a judgment, that he should be killed in a duel; at which the Queen laughed, thinking her husband to be above challenges and duels: but he was slain upon a course at tilt, the splinters of the staff of Montgomery going in at his beaver. The trivial prophecy, which I heard when I was a child, and Queen Elizabeth was in the flower of her years, was, When hempe is spun England's done: whereby it was generally conceived, that after the princes had reigned, which had the principal letters of that word hempe (which were Henry, Edward, Mary, Philip, and Elizabeth), England should come to utter confusion; which, thanks be to God, is verified only in the change of the name; for that the King's style, is now no more of England but of Britain. There was also another prophecy, before the year of '88, which I do not well understand.

---

①A time shall come after the passing of years, when Ocean shall loose the bonds of the world, a vast land shall appear, and Tiphys shall discover new worlds; nor shall Thule be the end of the earth.

②Thou shalt see me again at Philippi.

③You too, Galba, will taste imperial power.

There shall be seen upon a day,
Between the Baugh and the May, The black fleet of Norway.
When that that is come and gone,
England build houses of lime and stone,
For after wars shall you have none.

It was generally conceived to be meant, of the Spanish fleet that came in '88: for that the king of Spain's surname, as they say, is Norway. The prediction of Regiomontanus, Octogesimus octavus mirabilis annus, ① was thought likewise accomplished in the sending of that great fleet, being the greatest in strength, though not in number, of all that ever swam upon the sea. As for Cleon's dream, I think it was a jest. It was, that he was devoured of a long dragon; and it was expounded of a maker of sausages, that troubled him exceedingly. There are numbers of the like kind; especially if you include dreams, and predictions of astrology. But I have set down these few only, of certain credit, for example. My judgment is, that they ought all to be despised; and ought to serve but for winter talk by the fireside. Though when I say despised, I mean it as for belief; for otherwise, the spreading, or publishing, of them, is in no sort to be despised. For they have done much mischief; and I see many severe laws made, to suppress them. That that hath given them grace, and some credit, consisteth in three things. First, that men mark when they hit, and never mark when they miss; as they do generally also of dreams. The second is, that probable conjectures, or obscure traditions, many times turn themselves into prophecies; while the nature of man, which coveteth divination, thinks it no peril to foretell that which indeed they do but collect. As that of Seneca's verse. For so much was then subject to demonstration, that the globe of the earth had great parts beyond the Atlantic, which mought be probably conceived not to be all sea: and adding thereto the tradition in Plato's Timaeus, and his Atlanticus, it mought encourage one to turn it to a prediction. The third and last (which is the great one) is, that almost all of them, being infinite in number, have been impostures, and by idle and crafty brains merely contrived and feigned, after the event past.

①Eighty-eight will be a wonderful year.

36.论野心

野心就像体液之一的胆汁，当其分泌不受阻时，可使人敏捷、热情、振奋并陶然欣然；但当其一旦受阻，无道可泄，便会造成胆汁郁滞，肝气不顺，从而使人肝起怒火，胆生恶意。[①]野心勃勃的人亦是这般，当其发现仕途坦荡，觉得还有望升迁之时，他们非但没有危险，而且还勤于公务；但当其欲望一旦受阻，他们就会变得满腹牢骚，看人看事都用一双毒眼，睥睨国是，幸灾乐祸，而这无论于君主国之下臣还是于共和国之公仆，都是一种最恶劣的品质。鉴于此，君王如果要任用野心勃勃者，就得做到让他们一直步步升迁而不遭谪降，可这种做法难免不引起麻烦，所以对这类野心家最好完全弃之不用；须知这种人若不能随其职位步步高升，就会设法让其职权随他们一道堕落。但既然笔者是说对这种人最好不用，那就说明还真有对他们非用不可的例外，因此谈谈该在何时用他们也就成了理所当然。

战争时必须择良将而用，不管他们有何等勃勃野心；因为用其所长之利可弥补其他弊端，再说没有野心的军人就等于没有鞭策的战马。当君王遇到危险或遭受妒忌时，可用有野心之人作为屏障；因为除了这种像瞎眼鸽一样因看不见周围事态而只顾往上蹿的人外，谁也不愿意充当挡箭牌的角色。君王还可以利用有野心者除掉任何拥权自重的大臣，就像当年提比略用马克罗除掉塞雅努斯[②]一样。由此可见，既然在上述情况下对有野心者非用不可，那就有必要再谈谈如何对这种人加以控制，以便把他们的危险

①古代西方医家认为人体内有四种体液（血、黏液、黄胆汁、黑胆汁），这四种体液的多寡决定一个人的气质（多血质、黏液质、胆汁质、抑郁质），气质在一定程度上可因体液之变化而变化。

②塞雅努斯，古罗马政治家及阴谋家，提比略的宠臣，长期任禁卫军统帅（公元 15—31），公元 31 年出任执政官，拥权自重，对提比略构成威胁，被处死；在除掉塞雅努斯的行动中立功的马克罗被升为禁卫军统帅，但此人后来参与了谋害提比略的阴谋。

性减少到最低程度。就这种人的危险性而论，出身低微者比出身高贵者更小，严厉苛刻者比宽厚随和者更小，新被擢升者比树大根深者更小。有人把豢养心腹亲信视为君王的一种缺点，殊不知此乃对付野心家们的最佳良策，因为既然讨好或触怒君王的路子都在这些亲信的脚边，那其他任何人都不可能变得过于位高权重。限制野心家们的又一办法是让另一些心高气傲者与他们势均力敌，但此时朝中须有一股中间势力以保持事态平稳，因为航船若无压舱物会颠簸得太厉害。君王至少可鼓励一些出身低微者，使他们在一定程度上习惯于同野心家们作对。至于说设法让有野心的人时时感到如履薄冰，这对那些生性怯懦者也许是可行的良策，但对那些胆大妄为者则可能适得其反，会促使他们图谋生乱。至于说当情势需要君王对野心家们加以铲除，而一时又没有可一举成功的可靠手段，那唯一的办法就是不断地对他们恩威并施，赏罚并行，使他们仿佛身处密林而不知该取何路。

就野心本身而言，只想在大事上占先的野心比事事都想露脸的野心危害更小，因为后者往往造成混乱，妨碍公务；但与那种想八面威风、一呼百诺的野心相比，这种只会扰乱公务的野心又危害较小。那种试图在能人俊士中超凡出众的野心虽说很难实现，但对于公众却永远都有益无害；而那种企图在蠢材白痴中鹤立鸡群的野心则会导致整个时代的衰退。欲求高位者可怀有三种动机：一是想获得佐政济世的条件，二是想获得攀龙附凤的机会，三是想获得发财致富的时运。抱着第一种动机入仕者才是值得信任的良臣，而能甄别分辨这三种动机的君王才算有道明君。一般说来，君王和政府在选拔要员时，应挑选那些更注重其职责者，而非那些更注重其职位者；应挑选那些为了良心而热爱公务者，而非那些为了炫耀而热衷公务者；总而言之，要分清乐于报国的雄心和好管百事的野心。

解析

一、有野心的人欲望一旦受阻，就会变得危险；因此除了一些特殊情况，君王不该用此类人。

二、在下列情况中可以用他们：

1. 战争时；

2. 易遭嫉妒的工作，作为君王的挡箭牌；

3. 用以取代拥权自重的大臣。

三、如何对这种人加以控制：

1. 他们的危险性在下列情况中较小——

(1) 出身低微，或者

(2) 严厉苛刻，或者

(3) 新被擢升；

2. 他们与下列人物可相互抗衡——

(1) 宠臣，

(2) 竞争对手；

3. 让他们感到半信半疑和不知所措是为良策；

4. 想在大事上占先的野心比事事都想露脸的野心危害更小。

四、君王们应该仔细辨别——

1. 有德行的野心，目的是：

(1) 获得佐政济世的条件，

(2) 获得攀龙附凤的机会；

2. 可耻的野心，它是自私的——目的是想获得发财致富的时运。

Of Ambition

AMBITION is like choler; which is an humor that maketh men active, earnest, full of alacrity, and stirring, if it be not stopped. But if it be stopped, and cannot have his way, it becometh adust, and thereby malign and venomous. So ambitious men, if they find the way open for their rising, and still get forward, they are rather busy than dangerous; but if they be checked in their desires, they become secretly discontent, and look upon men and matters with an evil eye, and are best pleased, when things go backward; which is the worst property in a servant of a prince, or state. Therefore it is good for princes, if they use ambitious men, to handle it, so as they be still progressive and not retrograde; which, because it cannot be without inconvenience, it is good not to use such natures at all. For if they rise not with their service, they will take order, to make their service fall with them. But since we have said, it were good not to use men of ambitious natures, except it be upon necessity, it is fit we speak, in what cases they are of necessity.

Good commanders in the wars must be taken, be they never so ambitious; for the use of their service, dispenseth with the rest; and to take a soldier without ambition, is to pull off his spurs. There is also great use of ambitious men, in being screens to princes in matters of danger and envy; for no man will take that part, except he be like a seeled dove, that mounts and mounts, because he cannot see about him. There is use also of ambitious men, in pulling down the greatness of any subject that overtops; as Tiberius used Marco, in the pulling down of Sejanus. Since, therefore, they must be used in such cases, there resteth to speak, how they are to be bridled, that they may be less dangerous. There is less danger of them, if they be of mean birth, than if they be noble; and if they be rather harsh of nature, than gracious and popular: and if they be rather new raised, than grown cunning, and fortified, in their greatness. It is counted by some, a weakness in princes, to have favorites; but it is, of all others, the best remedy against ambitious great-ones. For when the way of pleasuring, and displeasuring, lieth by the favorite, it is impossible any other should be overgreat. Another means to curb them, is to balance them by others, as proud as they. But then there must be some middle counsellors, to keep things steady; for without that ballast, the ship will roll too much. At the least, a prince may animate and inure some meaner persons, to be as it were scourges, to ambitions men. As for the having of them obnoxious to ruin; if they be of fearful natures, it may do well; but if they be stout and daring, it may precipitate their designs, and prove dangerous. As for the pulling of them down, if the affairs require it, and that it may not be done with safety suddenly, the only way is the interchange, continually, of favors and disgraces; whereby they may not know what to expect, and be, as it were, in a wood.

Of ambitions, it is less harmful, the ambition to prevail in great things, than that other, to appear in everything; for that breeds confusion, and mars business. But yet it is less danger, to have an ambitious man stirring in business, than great in dependences. He that seeketh to be eminent amongst able men, hath a great task; but that is ever good for the public. But he, that plots to be the only figure amongst ciphers, is the decay of a whole age. Honor hath three things in it: the vantage ground to do good; the approach to kings and principal persons; and the raising of a man's own fortunes. He that hath the best of these intentions, when he aspireth, is an honest man; and that prince, that can discern of these intentions in another that aspireth, is a wise prince. Generally, let princes and states choose such ministers, as are more sensible of duty than of using; and such as love business rather upon conscience, than upon bravery, and let them discern a busy nature, from a willing mind.

37.谈假面剧[①]和比武会

与本书其他严肃的篇什相比,此文所谈不过是消遣寻乐,但既然君王们惯于用这些方式解闷,那就当以考究来使其优美典雅,而不该用铺张来使其靡丽俗艳。随歌起舞这种形式既庄重又入耳悦目。我认为声乐应该是合唱,唱班的位置应在廊台,有出色的分解音乐[②]伴奏,而且曲调须适合剧情。剧中歌者伴以动作,尤其是在对唱时,会产生一种出神入化的优雅;我是说动作,不是说舞蹈(因为歌者手舞足蹈俗不可耐)。对唱的声音应铿锵,应有阳刚之气(亦一个低音和一个次中音,不可用最高音部),唱词应高雅严肃,不可妖艳或娇媚。数个唱班,分列于廊台之相对位置,像唱圣诗一般以多声部轮唱,其效果当如闻天籁。至于舞者变化其队形以排出数码或字母[③],笔者认为那是一种幼稚的把戏。概而言之,须注意笔者在此提到的表演均应自然而然地悦人感官,而不可刻意哗众取宠。

毋庸置疑,布景之变换只要能做得无声无息,的确能增加美感和乐趣,因为换景可消除眼睛因久视一物而产生的疲劳, 会使人感到赏心悦目。布景应该明亮,尤其是色彩应富于变化;演员下台前应在紧靠布景之亮处做些动作,因为这特别能吸引观者的目光,会使人怀着极大的兴趣想看清其实没法看清的细微之处。歌声应嘹亮而欢快,不应轻柔而哀伤。音乐也应轻

---

①英国的假面剧承袭 16 世纪上半叶唱诗班歌童音乐剧的传统, 到 17 世纪初已成为一种复杂的宫廷娱乐形式,融诗歌、舞蹈、声乐和器乐于一炉,包括布景、服装和舞台装置。随着众多著名诗人、作家和音乐家加入假面剧的创作,至培根写这篇短文时 (1625 年) ,假面剧已开始向歌剧靠拢。

②一般用术语“康索特” (consort) ,只有培根和莎士比亚用“分解音乐” (broken music) ,指流行于 16 世纪和 17 世纪的一种室内重奏,“康索特”指同类乐器的重奏 (即“完整康索特”) ,“分解音乐”可能包括不同类乐器的重奏 (即被错误命名的“分解康索特”) 。

③用数码和字母代表君王或某位王室成员的生日或姓名,此乃宫廷假面剧中常有的表演。

快而激越，并起止得当。在烛光下最出效果的颜色是白色、粉红色和一种海绿色。金箔之类的装饰虽不值钱，但却显得光彩夺目。而昂贵的刺绣织品在烛光下则不显其精致华丽。演员的服装应优雅，应在摘下面具后仍显得合身，而且别采用人们所熟悉的土耳其装、水手装和军装等式样。幕间的滑稽节目宜短不宜长，这类过场节目里通常可有弄臣、萨堤尔①、笨人、狂人、小丑、野兽、鬼怪、女巫、黑人、侏儒、乡巴佬、小仙人、小仙女、小爱神和活动塑像②等等。但把安琪儿们放进过场节目并不够滑稽，正如魔鬼巨怪等丑恶形象不宜放在正剧中一样。但首先应使过场音乐具有娱乐性，有某些奇妙的变化。若能使紧张激动的观众中间突然飘过阵阵清香，但头顶上却无任何水珠滴下，那定会使人觉得格外神清气爽。让绅士和淑女同时登台演出，可使场面更为隆重并多彩多姿。③但倘若演出的场馆欠干净整洁，那上述一切努力都将是白搭。

至于马上斗矛和徒步斗剑等比武盛会，其壮观之处主要在于挑战者们进入比武场时乘坐的战车，尤其是当战车由狮、熊、骆驼等奇兽拖曳之时；或在于入场式之排场，或在于武士们的随从服饰之斑斓，或在于马具和铠甲之光亮。然此类装饰点缀已足矣。

解析

一、假面剧与比武会只是消遣寻乐的方式，但既然这种方式经常使用，就应该让它们考究得体。

二、假面剧的原则：

1. 用分解音乐来伴随舞蹈与表演，但不要过于繁复；

---

①希腊神话中最低级的林神，半人半羊状，其形象早在古代希腊悲剧演出时就被作为幕间过场角色。

②一种滑稽节目，演者原地转圈，听到信号即停，以造成各种各样滑稽别扭的姿势。

③按照传统，一出假面剧的演员皆为同性；另假面剧之正剧多由宫中绅士淑女业余演出，而幕间滑稽节目则由职业优伶表演。

2. 布景可以变化，但一定要明亮，色彩也应富于变化，昂贵的刺绣品在烛光下不显其精致华丽；
3. 演员的服装应优雅；
4. 幕间的滑稽节目宜短不宜长，其中的形象可以离奇有趣，但不能令人憎恶；
5. 芳香与绅士淑女同时登台都可以，但前提是演出场馆必须干净整洁。

三、比武会：

1. 主要有马上斗矛与徒步斗剑等；
2. 它们的趣味不在于打斗，而在于场面的雄伟华丽。

Of Masques and Triumphs

THESE things are but toys, to come amongst such serious observations. But yet, since princes will have such things, it is better they should be graced with elegancy, than daubed with cost. Dancing to song, is a thing of great state and pleasure. I understand it, that the song be in quire, placed aloft, and accompanied with some broken music; and the ditty fitted to the device. Acting in song, especially in dialogues, hath an extreme good grace; I say acting, not dancing (for that is a mean and vulgar thing); and the voices of the dialogue would be strong and manly (a base and a tenor; no treble); and the ditty high and tragical; not nice or dainty. Several quires, placed one over against another, and taking the voice by catches, anthem-wise, give great pleasure. Turning dances into figure, is a childish curiosity. And generally let it be noted, that those things which I here set down, are such as do naturally take the sense, and not respect petty wonderments.

It is true, the alterations of scenes, so it be quietly and without noise, are things of great beauty and pleasure; for they feed and relieve the eye, before it be full of the same object. Let the scenes abound with light, specially colored and varied; and let the masquers, or any other, that are to come down from the scene, have some motions upon the scene itself, before their coming down; for it draws the eye strangely, and makes it, with great pleasure, to desire to see, that it cannot perfectly discern. Let the songs be loud and cheerful, and not chirpings or pulings. Let the music likewise be sharp and loud, and well placed. The colors that show best by candle-light are white, carnation, and a kind of seawater-green; and oes, or spangs, as they are of no great cost, so they are of most glory. As for rich embroidery, it is lost and not discerned. Let the suits of the masquers be graceful, and such as become the person, when the vizors are off; not after examples of known attires; Turke, soldiers, mariners, and the like. Let anti-masques not be long; they have been commonly of fools, satyrs, baboons, wild-men, antics, beasts, sprites, witches, Ethiops, pigmies, turquets, nymphs, rustics, Cupids, statuas moving, and the like. As for angels, it is not comical enough, to put them in anti-masques; and anything that is hideous, as devils, giants, is on the other side as unfit. But chiefly, let the music of them be recreative, and with some strange changes. Some sweet odors suddenly coming forth, without any drops falling, are, in such a company as there is steam and heat, things of great pleasure and refreshment. Double masques, one of men, another of ladies, addeth state and variety. But all is nothing except the room be kept clear and neat.

For justs, and tourneys, and barriers; the glories of them are chiefly in the chariots, wherein the challengers make their entry; especially if they be drawn with strange beasts: as lions, bears, camels, and the like; or in the devices of their entrance; or in the bravery of their liveries; or in the goodly furniture of their horses and armor. But enough of these toys.

38.说人之本性

本性往往藏而不露，它有时可被压抑，但很少能被易移。强行压抑只会使本性越发强烈，谈经论道仅可使本性稍有收敛，唯有长期养成的习惯才能改变和制服人之本性。欲彻底改变本性者为自己规定的改变举措不可太多或太少，举措太多往往顾此失彼，从而使人灰心丧气；举措太少虽说易于实施，但却难以达到习与性成。培养新习惯之初可寻求一些帮助，就像初学游泳者借助漂浮物一样；但过些时候就应该在不利条件下培养，就像舞蹈家故意穿厚底鞋练舞一般，因所练所习难于日常所用，用时便会更显熟能生巧、习以为常。若本性根深蒂固，难以根除，改变之举措就须循序渐进：起初可练习及时克制自己的感情，就像易怒者每每默念二十四个字母那样；然后开始减少对痼习之纵容，如欲戒酒者把一杯之量减少到一口之量；到最后再一举革除旧习。但若是一个人有足够的决心和毅力，能在一次尝试中就脱胎换骨，那当然是最理想的情况，毕竟"最维护其精神自由者才能断然砸碎束缚其心灵的锁链，／从而一劳永逸地免除烦忧"[1]。有古训认为矫枉不妨过正，可用完全相反的习惯来匡正痼习，此训亦不失为一种良策，只要那相反的习惯不是恶习。人不可强迫自己一鼓作气地养成一种新的习性，这过程中需要有所间歇，其原因有二，一是停下来反省可巩固这新的开端，二是这样做可避免新养成的习性良恶兼备，因若是一个人的本性并不完美，那他一鼓作气养成的新习性也可能良恶兼而有之。人不可过分相信自己已革除旧习，因为本性会长期潜伏，一有机会或一受到诱惑又会故态复萌；这就像伊索寓言中那位猫变的姑娘，她本一直娴静地坐在桌子一端，可当老鼠从她跟前蹿过时她马上就旧性复发。因此欲除旧习者要么完全避开可诱发其本性的机会，要么就天天与之打交道，这样他也许会因见惯不

---

①语出奥维德《爱之治疗》293—294行。

惊而不再受其诱惑。人之本性最见于独处幽居之时、感情强烈之际和新的尝试之中，因独居时不必矫揉造作，激动时会忘掉其清规戒律，而在新的尝试中则无惯例可援引。其本性适于其职业者乃幸运之人，而与之相反，那些所从事的职业与其本性所好不相合者则只能悲叹："我的心久久地寄人篱下。"[①]在治学方面，人若强迫自己研究某一学科，他得为此安排出固定时间，但若研究某一学科符合他的习性，他就无须为固定时间费神，因为他的心思会自然而然地尽可能花在那上面，只要做其他事务或研究的时间允许。人之性格可长成芳草亦可长成杂莠，故须适时浇灌前者而芟除后者。

解析

一、只有长期养成的习惯才能改变和制服人的本性。

二、怎样利用习惯去支配人的本性——

1. 规定的改变举措既不太多也不太少，但必要时——
   （1）循序渐进；
   （2）即时彻底地脱胎换骨；
   （3）用完全相反的习惯来匡正痼习。
2. 让新习惯的培养有所间歇。
3. 要么完全避开可诱发其本性的机会，要么天天与之打交道，让其见惯不惊。
4. 抛开习惯，人的真正本性最常见于——
   （1）独处幽居之时；
   （2）感情强烈之际；
   （3）新的尝试之中。
5. 习惯无须强迫人发展自己天生的爱好。
6. 人之性格可形成芳草，亦可长成杂莠。

①语出圣哲罗姆译拉丁文本《旧约·诗篇》第 120 篇 6 节；英文 1611 年钦定本《圣经》同篇 6—7 节云："我长久地寄居于那憎恨和平者的家中，我天性爱和平，但我言和平他们却言战争。"

Of Nature in Man

NATURE is often hidden; sometimes overcome; seldom extinguished. Force, maketh nature more violent in the return; doctrine and discourse, maketh nature less importune; but custom only doth alter and subdue nature. He that seeketh victory over his nature, let him not set himself too great, nor too small tasks; for the first will make him dejected by often failings; and the second will make him a small proceeder, though by often prevailings. And at the first let him practise with helps, as swimmers do with bladders or rushes; but after a time let him practise with disadvantages, as dancers do with thick shoes. For it breeds great perfection, if the practice be harder than the use. Where nature is mighty, and therefore the victory hard, the degrees had need be, first to stay and arrest nature in time; like to him that would say over the four and twenty letters when he was angry; then to go less in quantity; as if one should, in forbearing wine, come from drinking healths, to a draught at a meal; and lastly, to discontinue altogether. But if a man have the fortitude, and resolution, to enfranchise himself at once, that is the best: Optimus ille animi vindex laedentia pectus / Vincula qui rupit, dedoluitque semel. ① Neither is the ancient rule amiss, to bend nature, as a wand, to a contrary extreme, whereby to set it right, understanding it, where the contrary extreme is no vice. Let not a man force a habit upon himself, with a perpetual continuance, but with some intermission. For both the pause reinforceth the new onset; and if a man that is not perfect, be ever in practice, he shall as well practise his errors, as his abilities, and induce one habit of both; and there is no means to help this, but by seasonable intermissions. But let not a man trust his victory over his nature, too far; for nature will lay buried a great time, and yet revive, upon the occasion or temptation. Like as it was with Aesop's damsel, turned from a cat to a woman, who sat very demurely at the board's end, till a mouse ran before her. Therefore, let a man either avoid the occasion altogether; or put himself often to it, that he may be little moved with it. A man's nature is best perceived in privateness, for there is no affectation; in passion, for that putteth a man out of his precepts; and in a new case or experiment, for there custom leaveth him. They are happy men, whose natures sort with their vocations; otherwise they may say, multum incola fuit anima

---

①He best frees his spirit who bursts the bonds that hurt his heart and end his pain once and for all.

mea; ① when they converse in those things, they do not affect. In studies, whatsoever a man commandeth upon himself, let him set hours for it; but whatsoever is agreeable to his nature, let him take no care for any set times; for his thoughts will fly to it, of themselves; so as the spaces of other business, or studies, will suffice. A man's nature, runs either to herbs or weeds; therefore let him seasonably water the one, and destroy the other.

①My soul has long been a sojourner.

39.谈习惯和教育

人的思维多取决于性格上的倾向，其言论多取决于被灌输的知识和主张，但其行为却多取决于他们长期养成的习惯。所以马基雅弗利理所当然地指出(尽管是在谈一桩丑恶的事情时指出)，不可信性格的力量，不可信言辞之豪迈，除非它们能被习惯证明。[①]这位史学家所谈的事例是：若要使刺杀君王的阴谋获得成功，主谋者就不可只信赖行刺者性格之凶残或誓言之豪迈，而须挑选一名双手已沾过鲜血的杀手。然而马基雅弗利不知会有位克莱芒，不知会有位拉瓦亚克，不知会有位若雷吉，亦不知会有位热拉尔。[②]但尽管如此，他的话仍然基本正确，性格的力量不如习惯的力量强大，只是对誓言的力量已应刮目相看。如今宗教狂热如火如荼，以致从未闻过血腥的人提起刀来也和职业屠夫一样毫不手软，在暗杀行刺方面，誓言的力量已同习惯的力量旗鼓相当。不过在其他方面，习惯的支配地位仍随处可见，以致你会惊讶地发现，世人在宣誓、保证、许诺和夸口之后，依然一如既往，一仍旧贯，仿佛他们是一些傀儡或机械，全凭习惯的轮子驱动。此外我们还可见到习俗惯例的统治或专横，其影响之大令人不可思议。印度的天衣教[③]信徒竟会平静地卧于柴堆上，然后自焚以献祭[④]，而且他们的妻子也都追求与丈夫一道葬身火堆。古代的斯巴达男孩习惯在狄安娜祭坛上受

①此说见于《论李维》第3卷6篇，马基雅弗利在这一节中谈论了刺杀君王的种种难处。

②克莱芒(1567—1589)于1589年刺杀法王亨利三世；拉瓦亚克(1578—1610)于1610年刺杀法王亨利四世；若雷吉于1582年行刺奥伦治亲王威廉(当时任刚成立的尼德兰联省共和国首任执政)未遂；热拉尔(1558—1584)于1584年步若雷吉之后刺杀威廉成功。以上刺客均非职业杀手，这数桩有名的谋杀都发生在马基雅弗利(1469—1527)去世多年之后。

③天衣教为印度耆那教(Gina)之一派，除耆那教正统的“三正五戒”和苦行主义之外，该派还主张以天为衣(裸体)，靠乞食为生。

④此乃培根之误解，因耆那教的特征之一就是反对祭祀。

鞭笞，甚至挨打的时候一声不吭。[①]我还记得在伊丽莎白女王时代之初，曾有位被判死刑的爱尔兰叛逆者上书总督，要求吊死他时用藤条而不用绞索，因为依照爱尔兰惯例，绞死叛逆者都用藤条。俄罗斯的东正教徒为了赎罪，会在盛满凉水的大盆里坐上一夜，直到身子被冰冻住。关于习俗对人精神和肉体的强大作用，可举的例子还有很多。由此可见，既然习惯可主宰人的生活，那世人务须努力培养良好的习惯。

毋庸置疑，形成于青少年时期的习惯最为良好。我们把这种习惯之形成称为教育，其实那不过是一种早期习惯。如我们所知，青少年舌头更灵活，四肢更柔软，他们更易模仿各种声音腔调，更易学会各种运动技艺，而成年人在这方面比青少年逊色乃不争之事实；虽说有些才智出众者从来不僵化，他们终生都能保持灵活柔软，随时都能接受可使之更完美的东西，但这种人毕竟太少。如果说单纯而独立的个人习惯力量已不小，那相互结合而成的集体力量则可谓强大无比；因为在集体中有榜样的教导、同伴的鼓励、竞争的鞭策和荣誉的指引，以致习惯的力量在那儿可登峰造极。不可否认，要让人类习性中的优点得以增加，关键在于各社会团体[②]之规章严明和风纪纯正，因为国家和政府只鼓励已经形成的美德，而不改良美德的种子；但如今育种的最有效手段正被用来达到各种最不应该向往的目标，这种现状实乃可叹可悲。

解析

一、人的行为多取决于他们长期养成的习惯。

二、然而，迷信通常会帮助没有经验的人去做大事，如：

克莱芒修士；

拉瓦亚克；

①这种鞭笞的目的是为了锻炼意志。古代斯巴达男子从7岁起就得接受这类严酷的锻炼，18岁接受军训，20岁成为军人，30岁结婚（婚后大部分时间仍住军营），60岁退伍。

②此处的社会团体当指各教会教派及其控制的学校。

若雷吉；

热拉尔。

三、习俗惯例的统治与专横：

印度天衣教信徒；

斯巴达男孩；

被判死刑的爱尔兰青年；

俄罗斯的东正教徒。

四、获得好习惯的途径：

1. 让其形成于青少年时期，即所谓教育；

2. 让其不局限于个人，而是以明确良好的目的形成社会的基础。

Of Custom and Education

MEN'S thoughts, are much according to their inclination; their discourse and speeches, according to their learning and infused opinions; but their deeds, are after as they have been accustomed. And therefore, as Machiavel well noteth (though in an evil-favored instance), there is no trusting to the force of nature, nor to the bravery of words, except it be corroborate by custom. His instance is, that for the achieving of a desperate conspiracy, a man should not rest upon the fierceness of any man's nature, or his resolute undertakings; but take such an one, as hath had his hands formerly in blood. But Machiavel knew not of a Friar Clement, nor a Ravillac, nor a Jaureguy, nor a Baltazar Gerard; yet his rule holdeth still, that nature, nor the engagement of words, are not so forcible, as custom. Only superstition is now so well advanced, that men of the first blood, are as firm as butchers by occupation; and votary resolution, is made equipollent to custom, even in matter of blood. In other things, the predominancy of custom is everywhere visible; insomuch as a man would wonder, to hear men profess, protest, engage, give great words, and then do, just as they had done before; as if they were dead images, and engines moved only by the wheels of custom. We see also the reign or tyranny of custom, what it is. The Indians lay themselves quietly upon a stock of wood, and so sacrifice themselves by fire. Nay, the wives strive to be burned, with the corpses of their husbands. The lads of Sparta, of ancient time, were wont to be scourged upon the altar of Diana, without so much as queching. I remember, in the beginning of Queen Elizabeth's time of England, an Irish rebel condemned, put up a petition to the deputy, that he might be hanged in a withe, and not in an halter; because it had been so used, with former rebels. There be monks in Russia, for penance, that will sit a whole night in a vessel of water, till they be engaged with hard ice. Many examples may be put of the force of custom, both upon mind and body. Therefore, since custom is the principal magistrate of man's life, let men by all means endeavor, to obtain good customs.

Certainly custom is most perfect, when it beginneth in young years: this we call education; which is, in effect, but an early custom. So we see, in languages, the tongue is more pliant to all expressions and sounds, the joints are more supple, to all feats of activity and motions, in youth than afterwards. For it is true, that late learners cannot so well take the ply; except it be in some minds, that have not suffered themselves to fix, but have kept themselves open, and prepared to receive continual amendment, which is exceeding rare. But if the force of custom simple and separate, be great, the force of custom copulate and conjoined and collegiate, is far greater. For there example teacheth, company comforteth, emulation quickeneth, glory raiseth: so as in such places the force of custom is in his exaltation. Certainly the great multiplication of virtues upon human nature, resteth upon societies well ordained and disciplined. For commonwealths, and good governments, do nourish virtue grown but do not much mend the deeds. But the misery is, that the most effectual means, are now applied to the ends, least to be desired.

40.谈走运

不可否认，外在的偶然因素经常影响人的命运，如相貌、时机、他人的死亡和施展才能的机会等等；但人的命运主要还是掌握在自己手中，所以有位诗人说："每个人都是自己命运的设计师。"[①]最经常出现的上述外因乃某人所干的蠢事，因为它每每造成另一个人走运；须知最快捷的成功就是靠他人出错而取得的成功，蛇必须吞食其他蛇才能变成巨龙[②]。显而易见的优点固然令人称道，但使人走运的往往却是些隐而不显的长处，或曰一个人表现自己的有效方式。这些方式莫可名状，难以言传，也许西班牙字眼disemboltura 可将其道出三分，这三分意思就是：只有当人的天性中没有立场和倔强作梗的时候，他的心机之轮方可与命运之轮同步。正因为如此，李维在形容加图时虽然先说："此人体魄如此健壮，心智如此健全，因此他无论生在何等家庭都能使自己交上好运。"[③]但他最后还是发现此人有一种"灵性"。所以一个人只要睁大眼睛留神张望，他就会看见命运女神；须知这位女神虽蒙着双眼[④]，但她并非无形无踪。命运之路就像天上的银河，银河是无数星星的会聚或结合，但看上去并非星星点点，而是一条完整的光带；与此相似，使人走运的亦是人身上那许许多多几乎无法辨清的小小的优点或长处，更准确地说是一些能力和习性。其中一些世人简直想象不到，但意大利人对此却明察秋毫。当意大利人谈论某位从不会出错的幸运儿时，他

①语出拉丁诗人阿比乌斯·克劳狄乌斯（约公元前 3 世纪）。

②希腊谚语，瑞士博物学家格斯纳（Konrad von Gesner，1516—1565）曾在其《动物志》中引用。

③见李维《罗马史》第 39 卷 40 章。加图出身于农民家庭，这在公元前 3 世纪的罗马属于出身低贱，只有跻身于贵族阶层才算走运。

④在西方绘画作品中，命运女神总是蒙着双眼（表示不偏不倚）、脚踏圆轮（象征祸福无常），一手持丰裕之角，一手在抛撒钱币。

们通常会加上这么一句："此人倒会几分装疯卖傻。"而毋庸置疑，最经常使人走运的习性只有两种，一是会几分装疯卖傻，二是少几分朴质真诚。所以极端的忠君爱国者从来都不走运，而且永远也不会走运，因为当一个人毫不考虑自我的时候，他当然不会只顾走自己的路。轻易到手的幸运只会造就出冒险家和鲁莽汉(法国人对这类幸运儿的称呼更妙，曰"胆大妄为者"和"惹是生非者")，但经过磨难的幸运则会造就出能人俊杰。幸运应该受人尊重被人崇尚，即便仅仅是为了她的两个女儿，这两姐妹分别叫"自信"和"声誉"，前者生在幸运者的心中，后者则生在知晓幸运者的他人心里。智者们为避免他人对其优点的妒忌，都习惯于把自己的长处归因于上帝和命运女神，如此他们便可更充分地发挥其长处；另外神灵的庇佑也足以使他们显其不凡。于是恺撒在暴风雨中对舵工说："你的船不仅载着恺撒，还载着恺撒的运气。"[①]所以苏拉替自己选称号为"幸运的苏拉"，而不是"伟大的苏拉"。[②]并且世人历来都注意到，凡是把成就过分地归功于自己的聪明才智者，其结局往往都很不幸。据史书记载，雅典将军提谟修斯在向其政府述职时每每爱说："这次胜利绝非是凭运气。"结果他后来再也没建立过什么功勋。[③]不可否认，有些人的运气就像荷马的诗行，而众所周知荷马的诗比其他人的都更顺畅；普鲁塔克在把提摩列昂的运气与阿偈西劳和伊巴密浓达的运气作比较的时候，就曾用过这个比方。[④]人与人运气不同乃天经地义，但运气主要取决于一个人本身也确凿无疑。

---

①见普鲁塔克《列传·恺撒篇》第 38 章 3 节。

②见普鲁塔克《列传·苏拉篇》第 34 章 2 节。

③见普鲁塔克《列传·苏拉篇》第 6 章 3—4 节。提谟修斯 (?—前 354) 在与斯巴达人和波斯人的战争中屡建战功，但终因在同盟战争 (前 357—前 355) 中指挥不当而被逐出雅典，死于流亡之中。

④见普鲁塔克《列传·提摩列昂篇》第 36 章 1—3 节。普鲁塔克在此记述说提摩列昂 (?—前 337，古希腊科林斯将军) 打胜仗易如反掌。阿偈西劳 (约前 444—前 360，斯巴达国王) 和伊巴密浓达 (约前 420—前 362，古希腊底比斯将军) 也都战功卓著，但不幸均死于征战。

解析

一、人是自己命运的设计师。

二、外在的偶然因素会产生极大的影响:

相貌;

时机;

他人的死亡;

施展才能的机会;

他人所干的愚蠢事。

三、能使人走运的长处:

1. 随机应变(disemboltura)

如:李维对加图的评价。

2. 许许多多几乎无法辨清的长处:

(1) 被认为是装疯卖傻之人;

(2) 不追求轻易到手的运气;

(3) 之前的成功所带来的自信与声誉。

四、应把智慧归功于神的眷顾。

例子:恺撒与苏拉;另一方面,提谟修斯。

五、不管运气好坏与否,它都取决于一个人本身。

Of Fortune

IT CANNOT be denied, but outward accidents conduce much to fortune; favor, opportunity, death of others, occasion fitting virtue. But chiefly, the mould of a man's fortune is in his own hands. Faber quisque fortunae suae,① saith the poet. And the most frequent of external causes is, that the folly of one man, is the fortune of another. For no man prospers so suddenly, as by others' errors. Serpens nisi serpentem comederit non fit draco. ② Overt and

①Every man is the maker of his own fortune.

②A serpent, unless it first eats a serpent, does not become a dragon.

apparent virtues, bring forth praise; but there be secret and hidden virtues, that bring forth fortune; certain deliveries of a man's self, which have no name. The Spanish name, desemboltura, partly expresseth them; when there be not stonds nor restiveness in a man's nature; but that the wheels of his mind, keep way with the wheels of his fortune. For so Livy (after he had described Cato Major in these words, In illo viro tantum robur corporis et animi fuit, ut quocunque loco natus esset, fortunam sibi facturus videretur.①) falleth upon that, that he had versatile ingenium②. Therefore if a man look sharply and attentively, he shall see Fortune: for though she be blind, yet she is not invisible. The way of fortune, is like the Milken Way in the sky; which is a meeting or knot of a number of small stars; not seen asunder, but giving light together. So are there a number of little, and scarce discerned virtues, or rather faculties and customs, that make men fortunate. The Italians note some of them, such as a man would little think. When they speak of one that cannot do amiss, they will throw in, into his other conditions, that he hath Poco di matto③. And certainly there be not two more fortunate properties, than to have a little of the fool, and not too much of the honest. Therefore extreme lovers of their country or masters, were never fortunate, neither can they be. For when a man placeth his thoughts without himself, he goeth not his own way. A hasty fortune maketh an enterpriser and remover (the French hath it better, entreprenant, or remuant); but the exercised fortune maketh the able man. Fortune is to be honored and respected, and it be but for her daughters, Confidence and Reputation. For those two, Felicity breedeth; the first within a man's self, the latter in others towards him. All wise men, to decline the envy of their own virtues, use to ascribe them to Providence and Fortune; for so they may the better assume them: and, besides, it is greatness in a man, to be the care of the higher powers. So Caesar said to the pilot in the tempest, Caesarem portas, et fortunam ejus.④ So Sylla chose the name of Felix, and not of Magnus⑤. And it hath been noted, that those who ascribe openly too much to their own wisdom and policy, end infortunate. It is written that Timotheus the Athenian, after he had, in the account he gave to the state of his government, often interlaced this speech, and in this, Fortune had no part, never

①There was in that man such power both physical and mental that in whatever circumstance he had started life he seemed bound to achieve success.

②a versatile genius

③little of the fool

④You carry Caesar and his fortune.

⑤"the Fortunate" not "the Great"

prospered in anything, he undertook afterwards. Certainly there be, whose fortunes are like Homer's verses, that have a slide and easiness more than the verses of other poets; as Plutarch saith of Timoleon's fortune, in respect of that of Agesilaus or Epaminondas. And that this should be, no doubt it is much, in a man's self.

41.论有息借贷

有许多人都措辞巧妙地抨击过有息借贷。[①]有人说放债取息可悲,竟让魔鬼得到了上帝的份额,即十分之一[②]。有人说放债取息者是最不守安息日的人,因为他们每个礼拜天都在赢利。[③]有人说放债取息者就是维吉尔所说的那种雄蜂,而维吉尔在诗中写道:"把那些好逸恶劳的雄蜂赶出蜂房。"[④]有人说放债取息者触犯了亚当夏娃堕落后上帝为人类制定的第一条法律,即"必须汗流满面才有面包可吃"[⑤],而放债者是让别人流汗而自己吃面包。有人说放债取息者都应该戴上黄帽子,因为他们已变成了犹太人。[⑥]还有人说让钱生钱有悖天道。[⑦]诸如此类的抨击不胜枚举,然笔者认为有息借贷只不过是对世人铁石心肠的一种让步,因为借钱贷款不可避免,而人的心肠又硬得不肯把钱白白借给他人,所以有息借贷就必须得到允许。另有一些人已不无疑虑地对银行、个人财产申报及其他新举措提出了巧妙的主张,

---

①有息借贷古已有之,但也一直被人视为不义之举。英王亨利八世(在位期 1509—1547)使有息借贷合法化,规定最高利率为 10%。其子爱德华六世废除了这一规定,严禁放债取息。后伊丽莎白一世恢复亨利八世旧例,但当时人们对放债取息的合理性仍争论不休。

②据《旧约·利未记》第 27 章 30—31 节中的"什输其一"法规定,凡大地所产(包括粮食、瓜果、牛羊等)之十分之一均属于上帝,西欧教会据此从公元 8 世纪起便向人们征收"什一税"。

③"摩西十诫"之第四诫即为当守安息日(是日停止一切劳作),参见《旧约·出埃及记》第 20 章 8—11 节。

④引自维吉尔《农事诗》第 4 卷 168 行。

⑤据《旧约·创世记》第 3 章 19 节载,上帝对即将被逐出伊甸园的亚当说:"你必须汗流满面才有面包可吃。"

⑥中世纪的许多欧洲国家都曾规定犹太人必须戴黄色小帽。另犹太人中多有放债取息者。

⑦此乃亚里士多德在其《政治学》中所持的观点,莎士比亚在其《威尼斯商人》中对此观点进行了生动形象的阐释。

但却几乎没人对有息借贷发表过任何建设性的意见。而有益的做法是将有息借贷的弊与利都摆到大家面前，使它的好处有可能被认真考虑，被仔细挑出，并被谨慎地加以利用，以便我们在找到更好的做法前不致陷入更糟的境地。

有息借贷存在如下弊端：弊端之一是使商人减少，须知若无放债这种坐收利息的行当，货币就不会躺在钱箱里不动，其中大部分都会被用于商业贸易，而商业贸易乃国家财源的门静脉；弊端之二是使商人变劣，因为像农牧场主若能坐享高额地租就不会用心经营其土地一样，商人若能用资金放债牟利亦不会专心经营其买卖；弊端之三是之一之二的必然后果，那就是君王或国家的税收将会减少，须知税收的涨落与商业的兴衰成正比；弊端之四是一国的财富将被聚敛到少数人手中，因为放债人总能稳稳当当地坐收利息，而借债人却没有把握将本图利，所以到头来大部分钱都会装进放债人的钱柜，而一国之繁荣昌盛往往都是在财富分配较均匀的时期；弊端之五是使土地的价格下跌，因为金钱之大部分应用于商业流通和购置地产，可有息借贷使这两条渠道都受阻；弊端之六是有碍于工业企业、改良改革和发明创造，因为若无有息借贷作梗，金钱应该在这些方面发挥其积极作用；最后的一个弊端是，有息借贷将使许多人破产，从而渐渐造成一种全民贫困。

但从另一角度来看，有息借贷也不无其好处。首先，虽说它在某些方面对商业有所阻碍，可它同时也在另一些方面对其有所促进；因不可否认，如今的绝大部分贸易都是由一些靠有息借贷作资本的年轻商人在进行，所以如果放债人要求还清借款或不再贷出资金，那商业贸易无疑将马上陷于停顿。其二，若无这种容易到手的有息借贷，那人们一时之窘迫亦会导致他们突然破产，因为他们将不得不以极低的价格卖掉他们的资产(不管是土地还是货物)，所以有息贷款固然会啃食借款人，但不景气的市场却会把他们一口吞掉。至于说抵押典当，那几乎也于事无补，因为受押人要么是拒收没有用的典押物，要么就是巴不得抵押人到期赎不回抵押品，从而将其收归己有。笔者记得有位狠心的乡下阔佬就爱嘀咕：“让这有息借贷见鬼去吧，它使我们老留不住押在手里的物品和地契房契。”第三点亦是最后一点，这就是如今借钱不付利息已是一种空想，而且限制借贷将带来的诸多不便也令人无法想象，因此言取消有息借贷只是徒费口舌；再说所有国家都存在这种借贷方式，只不过种类和利率略有差别，所以取消有息借贷的建议只能向“乌托邦”提交。

现在且容笔者谈谈有息借贷的改进和规范，谈谈如何尽量避免其弊端，保持其好处。权衡一下上文所说的利弊，有息借贷中似乎有两点需要改进：一是要磨钝有息借贷的牙齿，使之别把借款人啃得太厉害；二是要允许用一种公开的方式鼓励有钱人贷款给商人，从而使商业贸易能持久并快速地发展。要做到这点就必须采用两种不同的借贷，一种利息较低，一种利息较高，因为若把贷款都降成低息，那虽说一般人借钱容易，可经商之人却难以弄到资金；同时应该注意到，商业贸易最有利可图，因此商人可承受较高的利息，而其他借债人却不能承受。

要实现上文所说的两点改进，其做法大致应该如下：为有息借贷设定两种利率，一种是为所有人设立的不受限制的普通利率，一种是为某些人在某些地区从事商业活动而设立的有限制的特种利率。因此首先应将普通年利率降至百分之五，宣布以此利率放债不受限制，并且国家应保证不对这种借贷施与处罚。此举将防止借贷活动全面停止或消失，将减轻这个国家无数借债人的负担，并将在很大程度上提高土地的价格，因为以相当于十六年租金的价格购置的土地每年可产生百分之六或更高一点的纯利润，而贷款利息仅为百分之五。因为这同样的原因，此举亦将刺激工业的发展和改良改革的进行，因为许多人会宁愿把钱投入这些方面，而不愿用其放债收百分之五的利息，尤其那些习惯了收取高利息的人更是如此。其次，应允许一些人以较高的利率借钱给已知的商人，不过这一特许之实施须保证做到以下几点：一、即便借款者是商人，这种借款的利息也应比他们从前所付的稍微低点，从而使所有借款人(不管是不是商人)均可因这一改进而多少减轻负担；二、放债人不能是银行或者说公共资金的保管者，而应该是货币的实际拥有者，这并非因为笔者完全不喜欢银行，而是因为考虑到某些令人生疑的银行活动，所以不能给予它们这种特许；三、国家应对这种特许放债征收少量税款，而把大部分利润留给债主，因放债人不会因减少这一小点利润而失去信心，举例来说，一个从前取百分之十或百分之九利息的放债人宁愿把收益降到百分之八，也不愿放弃这稳稳当当的收益转行去赚取其他有风险的利润;四、对这些特许的放债人数量上不应限制,但应把他们的借贷活动限制在某些重要的商业城镇,这样他们就不可能把别人的钱当自己的钱用,即不可能以百分之五的利息借进普通贷款,然后以百分之九的特许利息贷出,因为谁也不愿把钱借到远方,借到不知根底的人手中。

如果有人反对,说这样一来就在某种程度上正式认可了有息借贷,而以前它只是在某些地区被人容忍,那笔者的回答是:对于有息借贷,与其默认其存在从而任其流行,不如公开宣布其合法从而对其加以约制。

解析

一、古已有之的阻止有息借贷的努力:

1. 抨击;

2. “巧妙的主张”:

(1) 银行,

(2) 个人财产申报等。

二、有息借贷的弊端:

1. 造成货币流通的停滞;

2. 使商人变劣;

3. 君王或国家税收的减少;

4. 国家的财富被聚敛到少数人手中;

5. 削低地价;

6. 有碍于工业发展、改良改革和发明创造;

7. 使许多人破产,进而造成一种全民贫困。

三、有息借贷的好处:

1. 给予年轻商人以鼓励与帮助;

2. 挽救一时窘迫之人以免他们突然破产;

3. 取消有息借贷的想法是不切实际的。

四、有息借贷的改进与规范:

1. 两点改进：

(1) 限制有息借贷的利率；

(2) 推动商业贸易的发展。

2. 具体的做法：

(1) 让普通利率的有息借贷合法化，这样会——

(a) 刺激贸易；

(b) 减轻借债人的负担；

(c) 提高土地的价格；

(d) 刺激工业的发展与改良改革的进行。

(2) 允许有些人以较高的利率借债给已知的商人，条件是——

(a) 利息仍要比他们从前所付的低；

(b) 不许银行或公共资金的保管者放债；

(c) 对这种特许放债征收少量税款；

(d) 不限制特许放债人的数量，但限制他们借贷活动的地点。

五、对有息借贷加以约制比默认其存在从而任其流行好得多。

Of Usury

MANY have made witty invectives against usury. They say that it is a pity, the devil should have God's part, which is the tithe. That the usurer is the greatest Sabbath-breaker, because his plough goeth every Sunday. That the usurer is the drone, that Virgil speaketh of; Ignavum fucos pecus a praesepibus arcent. [①] That the usurer breaketh the first law, that was made for mankind after the fall, which was, in sudore vultus tui comedes panem tuum; not, in sudore vultus alieni. [②] That usurers should have orange-tawny bonnets, because they do Judaize. That it is against nature for money to beget money; and the like. I say this only, that usury is a concessum propter duritiem cordis[③]; for since there must be borrowing and lending, and men are so hard of heart, as they will not lend freely, usury must be permitted. Some

①The idle pack of drones they keep from the hive.

②In the sweat of thy brow thou shalt eat thy bread, not in the sweat of another's brow.

③a thing allowed by reason of the hardness of men's hearts

others, have made suspicious and cunning propositions of banks, discovery of men's estates, and other inventions. But few have spoken of usury usefully. It is good to set before us, the incommodities and commodities of usury, that the good, may be either weighed out or culled out; and warily to provide, that while we make forth to that which is better, we meet not with that which is worse.

The discommodities of usury are, First, that it makes fewer merchants. For were it not for this lazy trade of usury, money would not be still, but would in great part be employed upon merchandizing; which is the vena porta of wealth in a state. The second, that it makes poor merchants. For, as a farmer cannot husband his ground so well, if he sit at a great rent; so the merchant cannot drive his trade so well, if he sit at great usury. The third is incident to the other two; and that is the decay of customs of kings or states, which ebb or flow, with merchandizing. The fourth, that it bringeth the treasure of a realm, or state, into a few hands. For the usurer being at certainties, and others at uncertainties, at the end of the game, most of the money will be in the box; and ever a state flourisheth, when wealth is more equally spread. The fifth, that it beats down the price of land; for the employment of money, is chiefly either merchandizing or purchasing; and usury waylays both. The sixth, that it doth dull and damp all industries, improvements, and new inventions, wherein money would be stirring, if it were not for this slug. The last, that it is the canker and ruin of many men's estates; which, in process of time, breeds a public poverty.

On the other side, the commodities of usury are, first, that howsoever usury in some respect hindereth merchandizing, yet in some other it advanceth it; for it is certain that the greatest part of trade is driven by young merchants, upon borrowing at interest; so as if the usurer either call in, or keep back his money, there will ensue, presently, a great stand of trade. The second is, that were it not for this easy borrowing upon interest, men's necessities would draw upon them a most sudden undoing; in that they would be forced to sell their means (be it lands or goods) far under foot; and so, whereas usury doth but gnaw upon them, bad markets would swallow them quite up. As for mortgaging or pawning, it will little mend the matter: for either men will not take pawns without use; or if they do, they will look precisely for the forfeiture. I remember a cruel moneyed man in the country, that would say, The devil take this usury, it keeps us from forfeitures, of mortgages and bonds. The third and last is, that it is a vanity to conceive, that there would be ordinary borrowing without profit; and it is impossible to conceive, the number of inconveniences that will ensue, if borrowing be cramped. Therefore to speak of the abolishing of usury is idle. All states have ever had it, in one kind or rate, or other. So as that opinion must be sent to Utopia.

To speak now of the reformation, and reiglement, of usury; how the discommodities of it may be best avoided, and the commodities retained. It appears, by the balance of commodities and discommodities of usury, two things are to be reconciled. The one, that the tooth of usury be grinded, that it bite not too much; the other, that there be left open a means, to invite moneyed men to lend to the merchants, for the continuing and quickening of trade. This cannot be done, except you introduce two several sorts of usury, a less and a greater. For if you reduce usury to one low rate, it will ease the common borrower, but the merchant will be to seek for money. And it is to be noted, that the trade of merchandize, being the most lucrative, may bear usury at a good rate; other contracts not so.

To serve both intentions, the way would be briefly thus. That there be two rates of usury: the one free, and general for all; the other under license only, to certain persons, and in certain places of merchandizing. First, therefore, let usury in general, be reduced to five in the hundred; and let that rate be proclaimed, to be free and current; and let the state shut itself out, to take any penalty for the same. This will preserve borrowing, from any general stop or dryness. This will ease infinite borrowers in the country. This will, in good part, raise the price of land, because land purchased at sixteen years' purchase will yield six in the hundred, and somewhat more; whereas this rate of interest, yields but five. This by like reason will encourage, and edge, industrious and profitable improvements; because many will rather venture in that kind, than take five in the hundred, especially having been used to greater profit. Secondly, let there be certain persons licensed, to lend to known merchants, upon usury at a higher rate; and let it be with the cautions following. Let the rate be, even with the merchant himself, somewhat more easy than that he used formerly to pay; for by that means, all borrowers, shall have some ease by this reformation, be he merchant, or whosoever. Let it be no bank or common stock, but every man be master of his own money. Not that I altogether mislike banks, but they will hardly be brooked, in regard of certain suspicions. Let the state be answered some small matter for the license, and the rest left to the lender; for if the abatement be but small, it will no whit discourage the lender. For he, for example, that took before ten or nine in the hundred, will sooner descend to eight in the hundred than give over his trade of usury, and go from certain gains, to gains of hazard. Let these licensed lenders be in number indefinite, but restrained to certain principal cities and towns of merchandizing; for then they will be hardly able to color other men's moneys in the country: so as the license of nine will not suck away the current rate of five; for no man will send his moneys far off, nor put them into unknown hands.

If it be objected that this doth in a sort authorize usury, which before, was in some places but permissive; the answer is, that it is better to mitigate usury, by declaration, than to suffer it to rage, by connivance.

42.论青年与老年

年少者也有可能老成持重，只要他不曾虚度光阴，然这种少年老成毕竟罕见。一般说来，青年就好比最初形成的想法，总不如经过深思熟虑的见解明智；因为正如在年岁上有青春时代，在思想上亦有幼稚阶段。但年轻人的创造力比年长者的更富生机，各种想象会源源不断地涌进他们的头脑，而且可以说他们更多地受到神的启迪。凡天生热情奔放、欲望强烈且易恼易怒者，都要等过了盛年才可成就大事，恺撒和塞维鲁二人即是明证。[1]关于后者有人曾说："他年轻时放浪形骸，甚至疯疯癫癫。"[2]然而他几乎可以算是罗马皇帝中最能干的一位。凡性格稳重者都可在年轻时就建功立业，例如罗马皇帝奥古斯都、佛罗伦萨大公科西莫，以及勒莫尔公爵加斯东等等。[3]但另一方面，老年时的热情开朗对事业来说亦是一种极好的性格。青年人更适合创造而非判断，更适合执行而非决策，更适合新举新措而非旧事陈规；老年人富于经验，凡经验之内的事他们做起来都轻车熟路，但遇到新情况他们就可能误入歧途。年轻人出错往往会使事情毁于一旦，年长者出错则只是使本来可做得更多更快的事情做得少点慢点。

在实施计划和指挥行动方面，年轻人往往会自不量力，好大喜功，会不考虑方式方法和轻重缓急而直奔目标，会可笑地实行某些他们偶然发现的什么主义，会因为求变不慎而招致莫名其妙的麻烦，矫枉纠偏时会一开始

---

①恺撒 42 岁（约公元前 58 年）出任高卢总督，51 岁（约公元前 49 年）夺得罗马政权，52 岁才彻底击败庞培，当上终身独裁官；塞维鲁亦是大器晚成，到 47 岁（公元 193 年）才当上罗马皇帝。

②见斯巴提亚努斯（Spartianus）的《塞维鲁传》。

③奥古斯都在 33 岁（公元前 30 年）击败安东尼后就实际上成了罗马唯一的统治者；科西莫（1519—1574）18 岁就当上了大公；而法国的勒莫尔公爵加斯东（1489—1512）也是年纪轻轻就当上了法国驻意大利军队的统帅，因用兵神速而闻名并被载入史册。

就用极端手段，而且弄得错上加错也不知悔改，不知回头，就像训练无素的马，不知何时该停步，何时该转弯。但老年人持事则往往提议太多，商量太久，冒险太少，后悔太快，并且很少把一件事做得干净利落，完全彻底，而总是满足于一种平庸的结果。不可否认，用人之道应是老少兼用。这样做有益于眼下，因为老少双方的优点可弥补各自之不足；这样做有益于今后，因为当年长者唱主角时年轻人可以效尤；这样做还有益于处理民间事务，因为年长者总是具有权威，而年轻人则总是受人欢迎。不过在道德风貌方面，年轻人应占主导地位，正如年长者在政治关系方面占支配地位一样。有位犹太拉比[①]在讲“你们的少年人要见异象，老年人要做异梦”[②]这句经文时指出，这说明年轻人比老年人离上帝更近，因为异象是比异梦更清楚的一种启示；而毫无疑问，人在这世上活得越久，在世俗中就陷得越深，因年岁使人受益的是处世方面的能力增强，而非情感方面的美德增多。世上有些人过早成熟，然而早熟也往往早衰。这类早熟早衰的人有三种。第一种早年才智过人，但很快就才竭智枯，如修辞学家希摩热内斯，他的修辞著作精妙绝伦，但他后来渐渐变成了白痴。[③]第二种人具有某些天生气质，可那些气质只能为青春添彩而不能为老年增光，如说话声音优美且词藻华丽就只适合青年而不适合老年，所以西塞罗评奥滕修斯时说：“他风格依旧，但那种风格已不再适合于他。”[④]第三种人在建功之初就赢得太高的名望，以致后来难以维持其赫赫声威，大西庇阿就属于这种人物，结果李维评道：“他后期的作为比不上他早期的功绩。”[⑤]

①指著名犹太神学家阿卜拉巴勒(Issac Abrabanel，1437—1508)。

②语出《新约·使徒列传》第2章17节；《旧约·约珥书》第2章28节中亦有此句，措辞为：“你们的老年人要做异梦，少年人要见异象。”

③希摩热内斯是公元2世纪希腊修辞学家，所著修辞文论曾被广泛用作教科书，据说他在25岁时丧失了记忆。

④语出西塞罗《布鲁图斯》第95章。奥滕修斯(前114—前50)是古罗马律师及雄辩家，因在“维列斯审判”(前70年)中充当西塞罗的辩论对手而闻名。

⑤语出李维《罗马史》第38卷53章。大西庇阿(前236—约前184)是第二次布匿战争中古罗马的主要将领，20岁时任军团副将参加著名的坎尼战役，34岁时率军攻占迦太基从而结束第二次布匿战争，并因此获得“阿非利加征服者”称号，但后来遭奴隶主民主派攻击，愤然离开罗马，隐居故里，直到逝世。

解析

一、青年与老年优缺点的比较——

1. 青年的特点：

(1) 缺乏深思熟虑的见解，但极富创造力与想象力；

(2) 性格强烈者行为不成熟，性格稳重者行为成熟；

(3) 更适合创造而非判断，更适合执行而非决策，更适合新举新措而非旧事陈规；

(4) 青年的错误往往致命，因为他们——

(a) 好大喜功，

(b) 不考虑方式方法而直奔目标，

(c) 坚持一些欠考虑的原则，

(d) 革新轻率，

(e) 采用极端手段，

(f) 从不承认错误；

2. 老年的典型缺点：

(1) 太喜欢提出异议；

(2) 太害怕冒险；

(3) 满足于一种平庸的结果。

二、因此，最好的用人之道是老少兼用，这样可以保证——

1. 有益于眼下；

2. 有益于今后，因为年长者唱主角时年轻人可以效尤；

3. 有助于处理民间事务，因为可以将权威和亲民相结合；

4. 将年轻人在道德风貌上的主导地位与年长者在政治关系上的支配地位相结合。

三、青年有时无法实现其诺言——

1. 才智无法持久(希摩热内斯)；

2. 某些天赋只能为青春添彩而不能为老年增光(奥滕修斯)；

3. 建功之初就赢得太高的声望(大西庇阿)。

Of Youth and Age

A MAN that is young in years, may be old in hours, if he have lost no time. But that happeneth rarely. Generally, youth is like the first cogitations, not so wise as the second. For there is a youth in thoughts, as well as in ages. And yet the invention of young men, is more lively than that of old; and imaginations stream into their minds better, and, as it were, more divinely. Natures that have much heat, and great and violent desires and perturbations, are not ripe for action, till they have passed the meridian of their years; as it was with Julius Caesar and Septimius Severus. Of the latter, of whom it is said, Juventutem egit erroribus, imo furoribus, plenam. ① And yet he was the ablest emperor, almost, of all the list. But reposed natures may do well in youth. As it is seen in Augustus Caesar, Cosmus Duke of Florence, Gaston de Foix, and others. On the other side, heat and vivacity in age, is an excellent composition for business. Young men are fitter to invent, than to judge; fitter for execution, than for counsel; and fitter for new projects, than for settled business. For the experience of age, in things that fall within the compass of it, directeth them; but in new things, abuseth them. The errors of young men, are the ruin of business; but the errors of aged men, amount but to this, that more might have been done, or sooner.

Young men, in the conduct and manage of actions, embrace more than they can hold; stir more than they can quiet; fly to the end, without consideration of the means and degrees; pursue some few principles, which they have chanced upon absurdly; care not to innovate, which draws unknown inconveniences; use extreme remedies at first; and, that which doubleth all errors, will not acknowledge or retract them; like an unready horse, that will neither stop nor turn. Men of age object too much, consult too long, adventure too little, repent too soon, and seldom drive business home to the full period, but content themselves with a mediocrity of success. Certainly it is good to compound employments of both; for that will be good for the present, because the virtues of either age, may correct the defects of both; and good for succession, that young men may be learners, while men in age are actors; and, lastly, good for extern accidents, because authority followeth old men, and favor and popularity, youth. But for the moral part, perhaps youth will have the pre-eminence, as age hath for the politic. A certain rabbin, upon the text, Your young men shall see visions, and your old men shall dream dreams, inferreth

①His youth was full of blunders, or rather acts of madness.

that young men, are admitted nearer to God than old, because vision, is a clearer revelation, than a dream. And certainly, the more a man drinketh of the world, the more it intoxicateth; and age doth profit rather in the powers of understanding, than in the virtues of the will and affections. There be some, have an over-early ripeness in their years, which fadeth betimes. These are, first, such as have brittle wits, the edge whereof is soon turned; such as was Hermogenes the rhetorician, whose books are exceeding subtle; who afterwards waxed stupid. A second sort, is of those that have some natural dispositions which have better grace in youth, than in age; such as is a fluent and luxuriant speech; which becomes youth well, but not age: so Tully saith of Hortensius, Idem manebat, neque idem decebat.① The third is of such, as take too high a strain at the first, and are magnanimous, more than tract of years can uphold. As was Scipio Africanus, of whom Livy saith in effect, Ultima primis cedebant.②

---

①He remained the same, but the same was no longer becoming to him.

②The end was not equal to the beginning.

43.论美

善犹如宝石，以镶嵌自然为美；而善附于美者无疑最美，不过这美者倒不必相貌俊秀，只须气度端庄，仪态宜人。世人难见绝美者兼而至善，仿佛造物主宁愿专心于不出差错，也不肯努力创造出美善兼备之上品。故世间美男子多有身躯之完美而无精神之高贵，多注重其行而不注重其德。但此论并非放之四海而皆准，因古罗马皇帝奥古斯都和韦斯帕芗、法兰西国王腓力四世、英格兰国王爱德华四世、古雅典将军亚西比德，以及伊朗国王伊思迈尔一世皆为志存高远者，但也都是当时的冠玉美男。至于美女，天生容貌胜过粉黛胭脂，而优雅举止又胜过天生容貌。优雅之态乃美之极致，非丹青妙笔所能绘之，亦非乍眼一看所能识之。绝色者之形体比例定有异处。世人难断阿佩利斯[①]和丢勒[②]谁更可笑，后者画人像总是按几何比例，前者则将诸多面孔的最美之处汇于一颜[③]。笔者以为除画家本人之外，此等画像谁也不会喜欢。虽说笔者认为画家可以画出比真颜更美的容貌，但他必须得靠神来之笔，而非凭借什么规则尺度，这就像音乐家谱写妙曲得靠灵感一般。世人可见这样的面庞，若将其五官分而视之则一无是处，但合在一起却堪称花容玉颜。倘美之要素果真在于仪态之优雅，那长者比少者更美就不足为奇，须知美人之秋亦美。假如不把春青视为优雅得体之补足，年少者多半都难称俊秀。美貌如夏日鲜果易腐难存，而且它每每使年少者放荡，并给年长者几分难堪；但笔者开篇所言仍然不谬，若美貌依附于善者，便会使善举光彩夺目，使恶行无地自容。

---

①阿佩利斯是公元前4世纪希腊画家，曾为马其顿国王腓力二世和亚历山大大帝的宫廷画师，善画肖像。

②丢勒（1471—1528）乃德国画家，著有《人体比例研究》一书。

③培根在此处也许误将阿佩利斯记成了另一名古希腊画家宙克西斯（Zeuxis，约前464—前389），相传宙克西斯曾汇五位美女的长处于一身，绘成海伦像。

解析

美的基本原则：

一、善自然镶嵌于美为最美。

二、绝美之人很难兼而至善。

不过也有值得注意的例外：

奥古斯都·恺撒；

提图斯·韦斯帕芗；

法兰西国王腓力四世；

英格兰国王爱德华四世；

雅典的亚西比德；

波斯的伊思迈尔一世。

三、行为举止之美胜过天生容貌之美。

四、绝色者之形体比例定有异常处。

（因为忽略了这一点，阿佩利斯与丢勒犯了错误。）

五、美体现在统一的整体上，而非分开的个体中。

六、长者比少者更美。

七、美（1）易腐难存；

（2）对善可能有害而非有益。

Of Beauty

VIRTUE is like a rich stone, best plain set; and surely virtue is best, in a body that is comely, though not of delicate features; and that hath rather dignity of presence, than beauty of aspect. Neither is it almost seen, that very beautiful persons are otherwise of great virtue; as if nature were rather busy, not to err, than in labor to produce excellency. And therefore they prove accomplished, but not of great spirit; and study rather behavior, than virtue. But this holds not always: for Augustus Caesar, Titus Vespasianus, Philip le Belle of France, Edward the Fourth of England, Alcibiades of Athens, Ismael the Sophy of Persia, were all high and great spirits; and yet the most beautiful men of their times. In beauty, that of favor, is more than that of color; and that of decent and gracious motion, more than that of favor. That is the best part of beauty, which a picture cannot express; no, nor the first sight of the life. There is no excellent beauty, that hath not some strangeness in the proportion. A man cannot tell whether Apelles, or Albert Durer, were the more trifler; whereof the one, would make a personage by geometrical proportions; the other, by taking the best parts out of divers faces, to make one excellent. Such personages, I think, would please nobody, but the painter that made them. Not but I think a painter may make a better face than ever was; but he must do it by a kind of felicity (as a musician that maketh an excellent air in music), and not by rule. A man shall see faces, that if you examine them part by part, you shall find never a good; and yet altogether do well. If it be true that the principal part of beauty is in decent motion, certainly it is no marvel, though persons in years seem many times more amiable; pulchrorum autumnus pulcher;① for no youth can be comely but by pardon, and considering the youth, as to make up the comeliness. Beauty is as summer fruits, which are easy to corrupt, and cannot last; and for the most part it makes a dissolute youth, and an age a little out of countenance; but yet certainly again, if it light well, it maketh virtue shine, and vices blush.

①The autumn of the beautiful is beautiful.

44.论残疾

残疾者通常会向造物主实施报复。既然造物主对他们已不公,他们对造物主也会不义。由于残疾者大多(都如《圣经》所言)“缺乏自然亲情”[①],所以他们对造物主都怀有报复之心。毋庸置疑,肉体与精神之间应该有一种平衡,故造物主在一方面弄出差错,那她就得在另一方面担当风险。但由于精神之构筑可以由人选择,不像肉体之形态只能听天由命,所以决定性格倾向的命星有时可被修炼和德行的太阳遮掩。由此可见,最好别把残疾视为一个人更可欺的标志,而应该将其看作十之八九会产生结果的动因。凡身上有引人轻视之处者无不具有一种欲使自己免遭白眼的永恒动力,因此所有的残疾人都异常勇敢。这种勇敢起初是为了在被人嘲弄时进行自卫,但久而久之就形成了一种习性。身体之缺陷还往往激起残疾人之勤奋,尤其是勤于观察他人的弱点,以期能发现什么可实施报复之处。另外残疾人可消除占优势者对他们的妒忌,因他们在健康人眼中不过是可任意轻蔑的对象;残疾人亦可麻痹其竞争对手,因后者绝不会相信残疾人居然可能得到提升,直到他们目睹提升成为事实。因此总的来说,一个大智者的生理缺陷可能成为他们升迁的有利因素。古代(和现代某些国家)的君王都惯于宠信宦官,其原因是对天下人都怀有妒忌之心的宦官更乐于服从并效忠君王一人;不过君王对宦官的宠信与其说是把他们视为合格的行政官员,不如说是看作称职的耳目密探。宦官的情况与残疾人非常相似。二者的共同之处是,如若其智所能,他们都将努力消除别人对自己的轻视,而消除的手段非善即恶。所以若偶见残疾者原来是出类拔萃的人物,千万别感到惊讶好奇,须知他们中已有过斯巴达国王阿偈西劳[②]、苏里曼一世之子桑格尔[③]、寓

①见《新约·罗马书》第1章31节。

②阿偈西劳天生瘸腿,有“跛足国王”之称。

③桑格尔绰号“驼背”。另参见本书《论帝王》中关于苏里曼一世之注。

言大师伊索[1]和秘鲁总督加斯卡[2]，而且连苏格拉底[3]和其他一些人也可以归入他们的行列。

解析

一、身体的残疾往往会导致性格的缺陷。

二、然而残疾人往往能克服自己的缺陷而获得成功，因为残疾——

1. 能够激发能量与勇猛(首先用于自卫，之后形成一种习性)；
2. 使他们易发现并利用他人的弱点；
3. 减轻优势者与竞争对手对他们的猜疑与敌意。

三、因此，君王往往会让残疾人作为自己的宠臣与密探。

四、所有的残疾人都会设法弥补自己的缺陷，借助于——

1. 恶行；
2. 出众的美德。

Of Deformity

DEFORMED persons are commonly even with nature; for as nature hath done ill by them, so do they by nature; being for the most part (as the Scripture saith) void of natural affection; and so they have their revenge of nature. Certainly there is a consent, between the body and the mind; and where nature erreth in the one, she ventureth in the other. Ubi peccat in uno, periclitatur in altero. But because there is, in man, an election touching the frame of his mind, and a necessity in the frame of his body, the stars of natural

①据 13 世纪发现的一部手抄本《伊索传》记载，伊索之形体丑陋不堪。

②加斯卡 (1485—1567)，西班牙天主教教士，1547 年被派往秘鲁恢复殖民地秩序，1548 年击败叛逆的皮萨罗并将其处死，1550 年返回西班牙任锡古恩萨及帕伦西亚主教。据说此人四肢奇长。

③苏格拉底貌丑，但并不畸残。

inclination are sometimes obscured, by the sun of discipline and virtue. Therefore it is good to consider of deformity, not as a sign, which is more deceivable; but as a cause, which seldom faileth of the effect. Whosoever hath anything fixed in his person, that doth induce contempt, hath also a perpetual spur in himself, to rescue and deliver himself from scorn. Therefore all deformed persons, are extreme bold. First, as in their own defence, as being exposed to scorn; but in process of time, by a general habit. Also it stirreth in them industry, and especially of this kind, to watch and observe the weakness of others, that they may have somewhat to repay. Again, in their superiors, it quencheth jealousy towards them, as persons that they think they may, at pleasure, despise: and it layeth their competitors and emulators asleep; as never believing they should be in possibility of advancement, till they see them in possession. So that upon the matter, in a great wit, deformity is an advantage to rising. Kings in ancient times (and at this present in some countries) were wont to put great trust in eunuchs; because they that are envious towards all are more obnoxious and officious, towards one. But yet their trust towards them, hath rather been as to good spials, and good whisperers, than good magistrates and officers. And much like is the reason of deformed persons. Still the ground is, they will, if they be of free spirit, seek to free themselves from scorn; which must be either by virtue or malice; and therefore let it not be marvelled, if sometimes they prove excellent persons; as was Agesilaus, Zanger the son of Solyman, Aesop, Gasca, President of Peru; and Socrates may go likewise amongst them; with others.

45.说建房

建房子是为了居住,而不是为了观赏,所以应首先考虑其适用,然后再顾及其美观,除非美观适用可兼而得之。只讲究美观的建房设计应该留给诗人,因为诗人们善于用很少的花销建造富丽堂皇的魔宫。把一幢漂亮的房子建在糟糕的环境中不啻是让自己住进牢笼。我说的糟糕环境不仅是指空气有害于健康之处,而且也指空气流通不均匀的地方。如世人所见,许多漂亮的住宅都建于四周有山峦环绕的一盆地中之较高处,可太阳的热量在盆地里不易散发,风聚盆地也易如水集低谷,结果居者会感到骤冷骤热之巨大温差,仿佛是居住在几个不同的地方。使一地不宜建房者不仅有空气之恶劣,还有交通之不便和购物之困难,而如果你愿意听从莫摩斯的意见,那有坏邻居的地方也不宜建房。[①]另有诸多不宜因素我在此就不详说,如雨水缺乏,林木稀少,土壤贫瘠,地形单调,无可观之风景,无开阔之平地,无逐猎放鹰跑马之适当场所,离海太远或太近,无通航河流之便利,或有河水泛滥之隐患。此外要想到别离大城市太远,因为那样会有碍公务;但也别离大城市太近,因为大城市消耗日用品多,会使任何东西都昂贵。最后还须考虑在何处能置得连片的地产,在何处此举会受到限制。以上不利因素也许不可能完全避免,但最好对它们有所了解并加以考虑,以便在选址时能尽量获得有利条件,而且一个人要是有若干居所,他也可以照此考虑加以安排,从而使一处欠缺的条件可在另一处得到弥补。当年卢库鲁斯答庞培那番话就很说明问题,那是在庞培参观他一处私宅的时候,庞培见那所房子有高大壮观的门廊和宽敞明亮的房间,就说:“这真是一座消夏别墅,可你冬天怎么办呢?”卢库鲁斯答道:“难道你以为我不如一些鸟儿聪明?连它们

①莫摩斯乃希腊神话中专管吹毛求疵的神,因挑不出美神阿佛洛狄忒的毛病而活活气死。传说他曾指摘智慧女神雅典娜不为其住房安装轮子,因而无法避开难以相处的邻居。

在冬天快来时也会挪窝。”①

从建房选址谈到建房本身，笔者欲采用西塞罗谈演讲艺术的方法，西塞罗曾写下三卷本的《论演说艺术》，又写了一本《演说家》，前者论这门艺术的基本规律，后者则谈演说之实践。所以笔者欲在此描绘一座豪华宅邸，以期创造出一个简明的样板。须知在当今之欧洲，连在梵蒂冈宫和埃斯科里亚尔宫②这等宏伟的建筑里也难觅一个非常漂亮的房间，这种情形实在奇怪。

所以我首先得说，如果你想建一座完美的府邸，那这府邸就必须得有两个分隔的部分，一部分是《以斯帖记》中所述的那种设宴场所③，一部分是家人居住的地方；前者用于宴会娱乐，后者用于居家度日。我以为这两个部分不一定非得是侧厅，亦可是建筑的正面部分，虽说内部分间不同，但外墙造型统一。这两部分可位于建筑正面居中的塔状主楼两边，看上去像是那座壮观的主楼把它们连在一起。在宴会厅一侧朝外的楼上，我喜欢只要一间宽敞的大厅，大厅约四十英尺高，楼下应有一个可用于化装或准备的房间，以备有时举行演出庆典等活动时用。而在另一侧，也就是居住的一侧，我希望首先隔出一个客厅和一间祈祷室，二者均应整洁而宽敞，但不必占据该侧的整个长度，而应在远端布置出两个分别供冬夏使用的小客厅，两厅都须布置优雅；在这些厅室下面应有一个漂亮而宽大的酒窖，此外还应有几间专用厨房、食品贮藏室和配餐室。至于正中塔楼，我认为它应比两侧翼楼高出两层，每层高度为十八英尺，应用上等铅皮铺屋顶，屋顶周围应有栏杆，栏杆柱上应间隔相宜地装饰雕像。这塔楼也应按可想到的用途隔出房间，亦有楼梯上楼，楼梯可采用绕墙旋转式样④，配以古铜色的雕木栏杆，而且顶端有非常漂亮的楼梯平台。但采用这种楼梯就不能把下层的任何一

①这段对话见于普鲁塔克《列传·卢库鲁斯篇》第 39 章 4 节。

②马德里西北约四十公里处一西班牙皇家行宫建筑群，于 1563 年至 1567 年由著名的建筑师托莱多 (Juan Bautista de Toledo) 设计并建造。

③《旧约·以斯帖记》第 1 章 1—8 节记述波斯王亚哈随鲁在书珊城王家御园设宴七日款待万民之场景。

④一般的旋转楼梯有中柱，英文中称为 newel 或 solid newel；绕墙旋转楼梯没有中柱，其支撑是墙体，英文中称为 open newel 或 hollow newel。

个房间作为仆人的餐室，不然有时你吃过饭后又得陪着仆人再吃一顿，因为这种楼梯就像烟囱通道，饭菜的气味会顺着楼梯上飘。关于房子的正面部分就描绘到此，只是我认为第一段楼梯的高度应为十六英尺，这亦是底层房间之高度。

穿过这正面部分应有一个漂亮的庭院，庭院其余三面的房屋应远远低于正面建筑。该庭院的四角有美观的楼梯，只是这些楼梯只连接凸外的角楼，而非通往建筑本身。那些角楼不可与正面的塔楼一般高，而应与庭院周围的低矮房屋成比例。庭院之地面不宜铺砖石，因砖石会使院内夏天太热，冬天太冷。除四周和院中的十字小径外，其余地面均应铺成草坪，草坪应经常修剪，但不宜剪得太短。靠宴会厅一侧的厢房可全部作为陈列室，这排厢房要显得壮观，要有三五个等距的穹顶，还要有图案各异的彩绘玻璃窗。居室一侧的厢房可设若干会客和便宴的厅堂，另设若干卧室。这左右两边厢房和与主楼相对的那溜配房都应隔成内外层，只单面采光，这样你上午或下午都可拥有不受日光直射的房间。你尚可按冬夏不同的需要设计出不同的房间，让夏天用的房间多荫，冬天用的房间保暖。不可像有些人那样把一幢漂亮的房子装满玻璃窗，那会叫人不知往何处躲避日晒或寒冷。至于凸窗，我认为非常适用，可作为朋友聚谈之僻静之处(当然，在城里建房得考虑临街一面的统一性，故采用平窗更为合适)；另外凸窗还可避开日晒风吹，射入室内的阳光或穿堂而过的风都几乎对其没有影响。不过凸窗宜少不宜多，上述庭院中可有四扇分设两边厢房。

穿过这庭院还应有一个内院，其面积与外院一般大，地面亦与外院水平，周围房屋前环以花园，花园内圈设漂亮的拱形回廊，回廊应与二楼一般高，朝向花园的下层应建成洞穴式的消夏避暑之处，洞口或窗户均应朝向花园，并高出地面以避潮气。此院之中央应有一座喷泉，或是一组精致的雕像，院内地面亦铺草坪，唯有砖石小径纵横其间；两边的厢房可作专用客房，底端的一排则作为私人画廊，不过应想到把其中一单元留作医疗室用，以防府邸主人或某位贵宾突然犯病。此医疗室应设在二楼，有卧室、接见室、候见室及内室与之相连。这排房子的一楼和三楼均应有一个用立柱支撑的凸外露台，以便观赏风景和呼吸花园里的新鲜空气。在左右与两侧厢房相接的两个角上应有两座精美华丽的楼阁，地面铺精美的花砖，墙头饰艳丽的挂毯，窗户安装水晶玻璃，上方是富丽堂皇的穹顶，再配以其他所能想到的优雅装饰。如果条件允许，我还想要几股清泉从上层露台墙体的不同处涌出，并配以精巧的出水口。以上便是这座府邸的大致模样，不过在进入这座府邸前还得穿过三个庭院：第一个只铺绿草并围以垣墙；第二个与第一个相似，但可在垣墙上点缀些小角楼，或只对垣墙稍加装饰；第三个庭院与建筑正面围成一个正方形，但两边没有房屋或垣墙，而是围以造型优美的阶梯式露台，露台内侧建柱式回廊，柱与柱之间不加拱饰。至于马厩和洗衣房等附属建筑，应将其建在稍远的地方，由一些简易走廊与府邸相连。

解析

一、建房时，应首先考虑适用而不是美观。

二、开始选址时常犯的错误：

1. 空气流通不均匀、有害于健康的环境；
2. 交通不便、购物困难或有坏邻居的地方；
3. 诸多其他不宜因素，如未考虑到——

(1) 雨水，

(2) 林木，

(3) 肥沃的土壤，

(4) 视线，

(5) 运动，

(6) 接近大海、河流与城镇。

对于一座房屋，以上因素不可能完全避免。

三、房屋设计的原则：

1. 正面要有：

(1) 两个分开的侧厅——

(a) 设宴场所：上面一个大房间，下面一些更衣室；

(b) 居家之处：

客厅,

祈祷室,

小客厅;

(2) 正中塔楼;

(3) 旋转楼梯,下面不能有仆人的食堂。

2. 后面:

(1) 庭院,除四周和院中的十字小径外铺设草皮;

(2) 围着庭院三面的建筑物,均为两间房进深,一面作陈列室,另外两面作私人房间;

(3) 几个弧形凸窗——最多四扇。

3. 内院:

(1) 被一座花园包围,有回廊装饰;

(2) 中间有喷泉或其他装饰;

(3) 有作为私人住房、医务室等的房间;

(4) 角上应有装饰华丽的楼阁,多处皆设喷泉。

4. 三个前院:

(1) 第一个只铺绿草并围以垣墙;

(2) 第二个点缀以角楼;

(3) 第三个有露台与回廊。

5. 附属建筑应保持距离,用一些简易回廊相连。

Of Building

HOUSES are built to live in, and not to look on; therefore let use be preferred before uniformity, except where both may be had. Leave the goodly fabrics of houses, for beauty only, to the enchanted palaces of the poets; who build them with small cost. He that builds a fair house, upon an ill seat, committeth himself to prison. Neither do I reckon it an ill seat, only where the air is unwholesome; but likewise where the air is unequal; as you shall see many fine seats set upon a knap of ground, environed with higher hills round about it; whereby the heat of the sun is pent in, and the wind gathereth as in troughs; so as you shall have, and that suddenly, as great diversity of heat and cold as if you dwelt in several places. Neither is it ill air only that maketh an ill seat, but ill ways, ill markets; and, if you will consult with Momus, ill neighbors. I speak not of many more; want of water; want of wood, shade, and shelter; want of fruitfulness, and mixture of grounds of several natures; want of prospect; want of level grounds; want of places at some near distance for sports of hunting, hawking, and races; too near the sea, too remote; having the commodity of navigable rivers, or the discommodity of their overflowing; too far off from great cities, which may hinder business, or too near them, which lurcheth all provisions, and maketh everything dear; where a man hath a great living laid together, and where he is scanted: all of which, as it is impossible perhaps to find together, so it is good to know them, and think of them, that a man may take as many as he can; and if he have several dwellings, that he sort them so that what he wanteth in the one, he may find in the other. Lucullus answered Pompey well; who, when he saw his stately galleries, and rooms so large and lightsome, in one of his houses, said, Surely an excellent place for summer, but how do you in winter? Lucullus answered, Why, do you not think me as wise as some fowl are, that ever change their abode towards the winter?

To pass from the seat, to the house itself; we will do as Cicero doth in the orator's art; who writes books De Oratore, and a book he entitles Orator; whereof the former, delivers the precepts of the art, and the latter, the perfection. We will therefore describe a princely palace, making a brief model thereof. For it is strange to see, now in Europe, such huge buildings as the Vatican and Escurial and some others be, and yet scarce a very fair room in them.

First, therefore, I say you cannot have a perfect palace except you have two several sides; a side for the banquet, as it is spoken of in the book of Hester, and a side for the household; the one for feasts and triumphs, and the other for dwelling. I understand both these sides to be not only returns, but parts of the front; and to be uniform without, though severally partitioned within; and to be on both sides of a great and stately tower, in the midst of the front, that, as it were, joineth them together on either hand. I would have on the side of the banquet, in front, one only goodly room above stairs, of some forty foot high; and under it a room for a dressing, or preparing place, at times of triumphs. On the other side, which is the household side, I wish it divided at the first, into a hall and a chapel (with a partition between); both of good state and bigness; and those not to go all the length, but to have at the further end, a winter and a summer parlor, both fair. And under these rooms, a fair and large cellar, sunk under ground; and likewise some privy kitchens, with butteries and pantries, and the like. As for the tower, I would have it two stories, of eighteen foot high apiece, above the two wings; and a goodly leads upon the top, railed with statuas interposed; and the same tower to be divided into rooms, as shall be thought fit. The stairs likewise to the upper rooms, let them be upon a fair open newel, and finely railed in, with images of wood, cast into a brass color; and a very fair landing-place at the top. But this to be, if you do not point any of the lower rooms, for a dining place of servants. For otherwise, you shall have the servants' dinner after your own: for the steam of it, will come up as in a tunnel. And so much for the front. Only I understand the height of the first stairs to be sixteen foot, which is the height of the lower room.

Beyond this front, is there to be a fair court, but three sides of it, of a far lower building than the front. And in all the four corners of that court, fair staircases, cast into turrets, on the outside, and not within the row of buildings themselves. But those towers, are not to be of the height of the front, but rather proportionable to the lower building. Let the court not be paved, for that striketh up a great heat in summer, and much cold in winter. But only some side alleys, with a cross, and the quarters to graze, being kept shorn, but not too near shorn. The row of return on the banquet side, let it be all stately galleries: in which galleries let there be three, or five, fine cupolas in the length of it, placed at equal distance; and fine colored windows of several works. On the household side, chambers of presence and ordinary entertainments, with some bed-chambers; and let all three sides be a double house, without thorough lights on the sides, that you may have rooms from the sun, both for forenoon and afternoon. Cast it also, that you may have rooms, both for summer and winter; shady for summer, and warm for winter. You shall have sometimes fair houses so full of glass, that one cannot tell where to become, to be out of the sun or cold. For inbowed windows, I hold them of good use (in cities, indeed, upright do better, in respect of the uniformity towards the street); for they be pretty retiring places for conference; and besides, they keep both the wind and sun off; for that which would strike almost through the room, doth scarce pass the window. But let them be but few, four in the court, on the sides only.

Beyond this court, let there be an inward court, of the same square and height; which is to be environed with the garden on all sides; and in the inside, cloistered on all sides, upon decent and beautiful arches, as high as the first story. On the under story, towards the garden, let it be turned to a grotto, or a place of shade, or estivation. And only have opening and windows towards the garden; and be level upon the floor, no whit sunken under ground, to avoid all dampishness. And let there be a fountain, or some fair work of statuas, in the midst of this court; and to be paved as the other court was. These buildings to be for privy lodgings on both sides; and the end for privy galleries. Whereof you must foresee that one of them be for an infirmary, if the prince or any special person should be sick, with chambers, bed-chamber, antecamera, and recamera joining to it. This upon the second story. Upon the ground story, a fair gallery, open, upon pillars; and upon the third story likewise, an open gallery, upon pillars, to take the prospect and freshness of the garden. At both corners of the further side, by way of return, let there be two delicate or rich cabinets, daintily paved, richly hanged, glazed with crystalline glass, and a rich cupola in the midst; and all the other elegancy that may be thought upon. In the upper gallery too, I wish that there may be, if the place will yield it, some fountains running in divers places from the wall, with some fine avoidances. And thus much for the model of the palace; save that you must have, before you come to the front, three courts. A green court plain, with a wall about it; a second court of the same, but more garnished, with little turrets, or rather embellishments, upon the wall; and a third court, to make a square with the front, but not to be built, nor yet enclosed with a naked wall, but enclosed with terraces, leaded aloft, and fairly garnished, on the three sides; and cloistered on the inside, with pillars, and not with arches below. As for offices, let them stand at distance, with some low galleries, to pass from them to the palace itself.

46.说园林

万能的上帝乃营造园林之创始者。[1]种植花木实乃人类最无瑕的消遣，亦是最令人神清气爽的一种娱乐。若无园林花圃映衬，玉殿广厦将只剩人工雕琢之粗俗，而不见自然天工之妙趣。世人可见，凡在崇尚文明与优雅的年代，人们总是一修高楼大厦就必建精美花园，仿佛唯有花圃园林可使建筑完美。就王公贵族家的花园布局而言，我认为应考虑到一年中之所有月份，让四季都有美丽的花草树木。为避免十一月底和十二月及一月的园景萧瑟，园中须栽培一些在冬天也青翠的植物，如四季青、常春藤、月桂、杜松、香柏、紫杉、松树、冷杉、迷迭香、熏衣草、各色夹竹桃、留兰香、鸢尾花、橘树、柠檬树，此外还可用保温法栽种桃金娘，在向阳处栽种墨角兰。在一月底和二月份应有正值花期的欧瑞香、黄色和白色的香菖兰，以及报春花、银莲花、郁金香、风信子、蝴蝶花和龟头花。三月可观赏的应有花期最早的那种单瓣紫罗兰，以及黄水仙、雏菊、杏花、桃花、山茱萸花和多花蔷薇。四月里应有重瓣白香堇、桂竹香、康乃馨、黄花樱草、矮株鸢尾、各种百合、迷迭香花、郁金香、重瓣牡丹、白水仙、法国杜鹃、樱桃花、大马士革李花和欧洲李花，以及正抽叶的英国山楂和丁香树。五月和六月可观赏的应有各种石竹，尤其是红石竹，有除晚开的麝香玫瑰之外的各种玫瑰，有忍冬花、林石草、牛舌花、白花耧斗菜、万寿菊、金盏花、茶藨子、挂果的樱桃树和无花果树、覆盆子、葡萄花、正开花的熏衣草、白花林神草、碎花香草、天香百合和满树繁花的苹果树。七月里应有各色香石竹、麝香玫瑰、开花的欧椴树，以及挂果的梨树、李树和苹果树。八月份应有各种硕果累累的李树、梨树和杏树，有黄花浆果、欧洲榛果和甜瓜香瓜，还有各种颜色的僧冠花。九月里可观赏成熟的葡萄、苹果、黄桃、蜜桃、山茱萸、冬梨、榅桲，以及五颜六色的

---

[1] 《旧约·创世记》第2章8节云："上帝在东方的伊甸辟一园圃，将所造之人安置于此。"

罂粟花。十月和十一月初则应有成熟的花楸果、欧山楂和大马士革李子，有用嫁接或移植的方法使花期推迟的玫瑰，还有蜀葵等等。以上花木之栽培是就伦敦的气候而言，但笔者的意图显而易见，那就是你可以因地制宜地营造出“永恒的春天”。

鉴于自然散发的花木之香远比提炼到手中的芳香油更沁人心脾(花香飘溢犹如音乐荡漾)，所以要增添踏园觅香之乐，最正确的方法是先了解哪些花木最容易造成满园芳菲。叙利亚大红玫瑰最会暗藏其幽香，以致贴着身子从它们跟前走过也不觉其香味，甚至在晨露浸润时亦是如此。生长中的月桂同样不泄漏其芳泽，迷迭香和墨角兰散发的香味也不浓郁。[①]最能使空气中弥漫其香味的当数三色堇，尤其是重瓣白花的那种，此花一年开两次，一次在四月中旬，一次在圣巴托罗缪节前后[②]；其次当数麝香玫瑰；再其次是叶片开始枯萎时的林石草，它会散发一种有兴奋作用的香气；然后是葡萄花，其花像柔荑草的穗状花一样如一团粉尘，开在刚抽出的簇状果柄上；然后是多花蔷薇和桂竹香，它们若被种在客厅或楼下卧室的窗外会非常讨人喜欢；然后是各种石竹，尤其是丛生石竹和麝香石竹；然后是欧椴花；最后是忍冬花，不过嗅其香味得稍稍站远一点。关于各种豆花我姑且不谈，因为它们不属于观赏花卉。但有三种不属观赏花的植物值得一提，它们往往使空气中充满诱人的清香，但闻其香不是从它们旁边走过之时，而是把它们踩在脚下的时候，这三种植物是小地榆、野百里香和水薄荷；因此你尽可以把它们栽遍园中小径，这样当你漫步于小径时便可足下生香。

至于花园本身(记住笔者所谈的是王公贵族家的大花园，正如前文所论的是王公贵族的府邸一样)，其面积不应少于三十英亩，并且应该分成三个部分，即入口处的一块草坪，花园尽头的一片荒野，或称旷野，和位于这两者之间的正园，此外还有正园两边的树篱小径。我以为草坪应占地四英亩。旷野占地六英亩，正园两侧各有四英亩的辅园，正园本身占地十二英亩。这块草坪将使人感受到两种乐趣，其一是修剪得平平展展的绿草最令人悦目，其二是草坪中间可提供一条干干净净的通道，你可沿此通道直达围绕正园的一圈高高的篱墙。不过因为这条通道稍长了一点，而在大热天

①以上四种花木均是提取芳香油的好原料。

②即8月24日前后。

你不该为了进园纳凉而先在草坪上受热，所以你应在草坪两侧各建一条十二英尺高的木制廊道，如此你便可在荫蔽下进入正园。至于在朝向花园的那排房舍窗下用各色泥土铺出几何图案，我以为那只是雕虫小技，因为你在水果馅饼上就常常见到十分美妙的图案。正园最好是四方形，周围环以刚才提到的那圈篱墙，篱墙上有许多拱洞，拱洞用木柱支撑，其高应为十英尺，宽为六英尺，拱洞的宽度亦是拱洞与拱洞之间的距离。篱墙应高出拱洞四英尺，也就是说拱洞之上的四英尺篱墙应是完整的一圈，这一圈仍由木工筑架造型，在每一个拱洞上面建一个小小的角楼，其大小应足以容纳一个鸟笼；另在两拱洞之间的顶部再构筑某种造型，其外表贴上大片大片的圆形彩色玻璃，以反射绚丽的阳光；我打算把这道篱墙建在一圈斜坡上，斜坡不陡，而是非常平缓，从底到顶六英尺高，坡上遍植鲜花。我还以为这个四方形正园不应占据整个大花园的宽度，而应当在两侧留出足够的空间以建各种树篱幽径，草坪两侧的廊道应与这些幽径相接；但在正园里边不可有被树篱遮掩的横向小径，因前端的树篱会阻挡你透过拱洞看草坪的视线，后端的树篱则会使你看不见那片旷野。

至于大篱墙之内的园林布置，各人可随心所欲地安排；但笔者在此有一点忠告，那就是不管将园子布置成什么模样，你都得做到别让花木太密，或对其雕琢太甚；譬如我就不喜欢把杜松或别的什么庭园树修剪成人或动物的形象，因为那只适合小孩儿的口味。我很欣赏低矮的小树篱，修剪得像圆圆的镶边，其间再修剪出一座座小小的金字塔，在一些地方可借助木制框架，使植物长成一根美丽的圆柱。我还喜欢园中的人行道宽敞而美观。虽说在两侧辅园中你可以有被遮得密不透风的幽径，但正园中的通道不可被遮掩。我还希望在正园中央有一座美丽的小山，有三段通往山顶的台阶，每段台阶顶上有一条可容四人并行的环山小径，我认为环山小径应成正圆，两旁无任何碍目障眼之物；小山应高三十英尺，山上应建一座优雅的宴会厅，厅内应有造型简洁的壁炉，不要装太多的玻璃窗户。

清泉乃园林妙景，令人赏心悦目；但水塘则会使一切都大为减色，因为塘中会滋生蚊蝇虫蛙，从而破坏园内的清纯明净。我以为泉景可有两种，一种是飞雾喷泉，一种是碧池涌泉，后者须建一三十英尺至四十英尺见方的泉池，但池中不可有鱼，亦不可有泥土淤积。飞雾喷泉的装饰柱可采用一直都时兴的雕像，镀金铜像或大理石像均可。但关键的问题是如何巧妙地排水，使之不积在雕像下的凹处；切不可让水因积在凹处而变浑，从而呈现出偏红偏绿等不正常的颜色，或生出苔藓或藏污纳垢。除设计上的措施外，每天还得用人工保持喷泉之清洁。另外喷泉基座可建上几级台阶，周围地面也应精心铺砌。至于那种我们可称之为“浴池”的池形涌泉，因它可接受更多奇妙而美丽的装饰，所以我们不必为它多费脑筋；比如说可在池底用花砖铺出精美的图案，池边亦可同样铺砌，并饰以彩色玻璃和类似的闪光材料，另外再围上一圈低矮的石砌雕栏。但关键问题仍然是要使水不断流动；水源应来自较高处，由一些铺设精巧的喷管引入泉池，然后由一些泄量与引入量相等的泄孔从地下排出，这样水在池中就只稍作停留。使水喷涌的装置应设计巧妙，可使水凸出池面而不外溢，或高高涌起如鸟状、杯状或华盖状等等，毕竟这是供人观赏的泉池，而非治病养身的真正的汤泉。

作为大花园三部分之一的那片旷野，我希望能营造得尽可能像一片天然荒地，那儿不可有高大乔木，只应有一些以多花蔷薇和忍冬构成的灌木丛，另有一些野藤纠缠其间；地面可播种些三色堇、林石草和欧洲樱花，因为这几种花草香气宜人，而且适于在阴凉处生长；这些花草应星星点点地随意撒播，不可有任何条理顺序。我还喜欢在这片旷野上堆出一些类似鼢鼠丘一样的土丘(就像在天然旷野中所见到的那种)。在一些土丘上分别栽种花形美丽的百里香、香石竹和留兰香；在另一些土丘上则分别栽种虽不名贵但却又香又美的花草，如长春花、堇堇菜、林石草、牛舌花、雏菊、红玫瑰、天香百合、美洲石竹和熊掌嚏根草等等。有些土丘顶上可有独丛灌木，有些则不必有。作独丛灌木的可有玫瑰、杜松、冬青、黄花浆果(只用于点缀，因其花味浓而不香)、红穗醋栗、茶藨子、迷迭香、灌状月桂和多花玫瑰等等。不过这些独丛灌木得加以修剪，以免长得过分凌乱。

至于正园两侧的辅园，你尽可在其中铺建各种有树篱掩映的幽径，让园中充满荫凉处。有些小径可完全被植物遮蔽，从任何方向都射不进阳光；有些小径可建成避风通道，遇疾风乍起时你行于其间也犹如行于室内走廊。遮阳的小径亦须在两端竖以树篱，以阻挡厉风长驱直入；避风的通道则须用沙砾精心铺路，以免长草带露弄湿鞋袜。在许多小径两边的狭长花坛上可种植各类果木，附墙攀援类和直立成行类皆可，但通常应该注意，种果树的花坛应较宽并较矮，若有斜面也不能太陡，其中可栽一些名贵花草，但要栽得稀朗，以免与果树争肥。在这两个辅园的尽头，我认为应各有一座小山，其高度以人站其上胸部高过篱墙为宜，以便观赏园外的田野风光。

至于上文已描绘过的正园，我也不反对其中有一些两旁栽有果树的小径，有一些栽有果树并建有带座凉亭的山丘，但这些小径山丘须安排得当，无论如何不能让正园的布局过于繁缛，不能让那里显得拥塞幽闭，要让其中的空气流通无阻。因为若要荫蔽，我建议你利用辅园中那些幽僻小径。如果你愿意，你尽可以在大热天上那儿去散步；但须考虑到正园之设计主要是为一年中较凉爽的季节，在盛夏季节则只适用于清晨傍晚或阴天。

我不喜欢在花园里设大型鸟笼，除非那笼子大得足以在里面铺草坪并栽种各类树木，这样鸟儿便可有较宽阔的活动空间和较自然的栖息之处，而且地面上也见不到鸟粪污秽。

以上就是笔者对王公贵族家的大花园的一种设想，这设想一半是规划，一半是描绘，所规划描绘出的并非一个模型，而只是一个大致轮廓。在设想中我没有考虑费用问题，但这个问题对王公贵族来说并不重要，他们通常是采纳工匠们的各种建议，七拼八凑地弄出一座花园，其费用也许并不比我设想的花园更便宜，有时候他们还为了富丽堂皇而增加雕塑之类，但那无助于真正的园林雅趣。

解析

一、园林艺术高于建筑艺术。

二、一座好的园林应该——

1. 一年中所有月份皆有美景；

2. 满园芳菲。

三、建造一座三十英亩花园的原则：

1. 草坪（四英亩）——

（1）既要令人悦目，又要走上去舒适；

（2）周围有一条可提供荫蔽的木制廊道；

(3) 最好不设花哨的泥土建的花坛;

(4) 花木不能太密,也不能被修剪得奇形怪状的树木煞了风景;

(5) 正园中央应有一座三十英尺高的小山;

(6) 可利用飞雾喷泉与碧池涌泉作为泉景。

2. 旷野(六英亩)与两个辅园(各四英亩)——

(1) 尽可能营造得像一片天然荒地;

(2) 只应有灌木,不能有高大乔木;

(3) 堆出一些类似鼢鼠丘一样的小土丘;

(4) 辅园——

(a) 提供遮阳避风的地方,

(b) 通道用沙砾精心铺就,

(c) 种植各类果木,

(d) 尽头有座小山,高度以人站在山上胸部高过篱墙为宜。

3. 主园(十二英亩)——

(1) 栽种果树,建有带座凉亭的山丘;

(2) 布局不能显得繁缛、拥塞、幽闭;

(3) 不设大型鸟笼,除非大且自然。

Of Gardens

GOD Almighty first planted a garden. And indeed it is the purest of human pleasures. It is the greatest refreshment to the spirits of man; without which, buildings and palaces are but gross handiworks; and a man shall ever see, that when ages grow to civility and elegancy, men come to build stately sooner than to garden finely; as if gardening were the greater perfection. I do hold it, in the royal ordering of gardens, there ought to be gardens, for all the months in the year; in which severally things of beauty may be then in season. For December, and January, and the latter part of November, you must take such things as are green all winter: holly; ivy; bays; juniper; cypress-trees; yew; pineapple-trees; fir-trees; rosemary; lavender; periwinkle, the white, the purple, and the blue; germander; flags; orange-trees; lemon-trees; and myrtles, if they be stoved; and sweet marjoram, warm set.

There followeth, for the latter part of January and February, the mezereon-tree, which then blossoms; crocus vernus, both the yellow and the grey; primroses, anemones; the early tulippa; hyacinthus orientalis; chamairis; fritellaria. For March, there come violets, specially the single blue, which are the earliest; the yellow daffodil; the daisy; the almond-tree in blossom; the peach-tree in blossom; the cornelian-tree in blossom; sweet-briar. In April follow the double white violet; the wallflower; the stock-gilliflower; the cowslip; flower-delices, and lilies of all natures; rosemary-flowers; the tulippa; the double peony; the pale daffodil; the French honeysuckle; the cherry-tree in blossom; the damson and plum-trees in blossom; the white thorn in leaf; the lilac-tree. In May and June come pinks of all sorts, specially the blushpink; roses of all kinds, except the musk, which comes later; honeysuckles; strawberries; bugloss; columbine; the French marigold, flos Africanus; cherry-tree in fruit; ribes; figs in fruit; rasps; vineflowers; lavender in flowers; the sweet satyrian, with the white flower; herba muscaria; lilium convallium; the apple-tree in blossom. In July come gilliflowers of all varieties; musk-roses; the lime-tree in blossom; early pears and plums in fruit; jennetings, codlins. In August come plums of all sorts in fruit; pears; apricocks; berberries; filberds; musk-melons; monks-hoods, of all colors. In September come grapes; apples; poppies of all colors; peaches; melocotones; nectarines; cornelians; wardens; quinces. In October and the beginning of November come services; medlars; bullaces; roses cut or removed to come late; hollyhocks; and such like. These particulars are for the climate of London; but my meaning is perceived, that you may have ver perpetuum①, as the place affords.

And because the breath of flowers is far sweeter in the air (where it comes and goes like the warbling of music) than in the hand, therefore nothing is more fit for that delight, than to know what be the flowers and plants that do best perfume the air. Roses, damask and red, are fast flowers of their smells; so that you may walk by a whole row of them, and find nothing of their sweetness; yea though it be in a morning's dew. Bays likewise yield no smell as they grow. Rosemary little; nor sweet marjoram. That which above all others yields the sweetest smell in the air is the violet, specially the white double violet, which comes twice a year; about the middle of April, and about Bartholomew-tide. Next to that is the musk-rose. Then the strawberry-leaves dying, which yield a most excellent cordial smell. Then the flower of vines; it is a little dust, like the dust of a bent, which grows upon the cluster in the first coming forth. Then sweet-briar. Then wall-flowers, which are very

①perpetual spring

delightful to be set under a parlor or lower chamber window. Then pinks and gilliflowers, especially the matted pink and clove gilliflower. Then the flowers of the lime-tree. Then the honeysuckles, so they be somewhat afar off. Of beanflowers I speak not, because they are field flowers. But those which perfume the air most delightfully, not passed by as the rest, but being trodden upon and crushed, are three; that is, burnet, wildthyme, and watermints. Therefore you are to set whole alleys of them, to have the pleasure when you walk or tread.

For gardens (speaking of those which are indeed princelike, as we have done of buildings), the contents ought not well to be under thirty acres of ground; and to be divided into three parts; a green in the entrance; a heath or desert in the going forth; and the main garden in the midst; besides alleys on both sides. And I like well that four acres of ground be assigned to the green; six to the heath; four and four to either side; and twelve to the main garden. The green hath two pleasures: the one, because nothing is more pleasant to the eye than green grass kept finely shorn; the other, because it will give you a fair alley in the midst, by which you may go in front upon a stately hedge, which is to enclose the garden. But because the alley will be long, and, in great heat of the year or day, you ought not to buy the shade in the garden, by going in the sun through the green, therefore you are, of either side the green, to plant a covert alley upon carpenter's work, about twelve foot in height, by which you may go in shade into the garden. As for the making of knots or figures, with divers colored earths, that they may lie under the windows of the house on that side which the garden stands, they be but toys; you may see as good sights, many times, in tarts. The garden is best to be square, encompassed on all the four sides with a stately arched hedge. The arches to be upon pillars of carpenter's work, of some ten foot high, and six foot broad; and the spaces between of the same dimension with the breadth of the arch. Over the arches let there be an entire hedge of some four foot high, framed also upon carpenter's work; and upon the upper hedge, over every arch, a little turret, with a belly, enough to receive a cage of birds: and over every space between the arches some other little figure, with broad plates of round colored glass gilt, for the sun to play upon. But this hedge I intend to be raised upon a bank, not steep, but gently slope, of some six foot, set all with flowers. Also I understand, that this square of the garden, should not be the whole breadth of the ground, but to leave on either side, ground enough for diversity of side alleys; unto which the two covert alleys of the green, may deliver you. But there must be no alleys with hedges, at either end of this great enclosure; not at the hither end, for letting your prospect upon this fair hedge from the green; nor at the further end, for letting your prospect from the hedge, through the arches upon the heath.

For the ordering of the ground, within the great hedge, I leave it to variety of device; advising nevertheless, that whatsoever form you cast it into, first, it be not too busy, or full of work. Wherein I, for my part, do not like images cut out in juniper or other garden stuff; they be for children. Little low hedges, round, like welts, with some pretty pyramids, I like well; and in some places, fair columns upon frames of carpenter's work. I would also have the alleys, spacious and fair. You may have closer alleys, upon the side grounds, but none in the main garden. I wish also, in the very middle, a fair mount, with three ascents, and alleys, enough for four to walk abreast; which I would have to be perfect circles, without any bulwarks or embossments; and the whole mount to be thirty foot high; and some fine banqueting-house, with some chimneys neatly cast, and without too much glass.

For fountains, they are a great beauty and refreshment; but pools mar all, and make the garden unwholesome, and full of flies and frogs. Fountains I intend to be of two natures: the one that sprinkleth or spouteth water; the other a fair receipt of water, of some thirty or forty foot square, but without fish, or slime, or mud. For the first, the ornaments of images gilt, or of marble, which are in use, do well: but the main matter is so to convey the water, as it never stay, either in the bowls or in the cistern; that the water be never by rest discolored, green or red or the like; or gather any mossiness or putrefaction. Besides that, it is to be cleansed every day by the hand. Also some steps up to it, and some fine pavement about it, doth well. As for the other kind of fountain, which we may call a bathing pool, it may admit much curiosity and beauty; wherewith we will not trouble ourselves: as, that the bottom be finely paved, and with images; the sides likewise; and withal embellished with colored glass, and such things of lustre; encompassed also with fine rails of low statuas. But the main point is the same which we mentioned in the former kind of fountain; which is, that the water be in perpetual motion, fed by a water higher than the pool, and delivered into it by fair spouts, and then discharged away under ground, by some equality of bores, that it stay little. And for fine devices, of arching water without spilling, and making it rise in several forms (of feathers, drinking glasses, canopies, and the like), they be pretty things to look up on, but nothing to health and sweetness.

For the heath, which was the third part of our plot, I wish it to be framed, as much as may be, to a natural wildness. Trees I would have none in it, but some thickets made only of sweet-briar and honeysuckle, and some wild vine amongst; and the ground set with violets, strawberries, and primroses. For these are sweet, and prosper in the shade. And these to be in the heath, here and there, not in any order. I like also little heaps, in the nature of mole-hills (such as are in wild heaths), to be set, some with wild thyme; some with pinks; some with germander, that gives a good flower to the eye; some with periwinkle; some with violets; some with strawberries; some with cowslips; some with daisies; some with red roses; some with lilium convallium; some with sweet-williams red; some with bear's-foot: and the like low flowers, being withal sweet and sightly. Part of which heaps, are to be with standards of little bushes pricked upon their top, and part without. The standards to be roses; juniper; holly; berberries (but here and there, because of the smell of their blossoms); red currants; gooseberries; rosemary; bays; sweetbriar; and such like. But these standards to be kept with cutting, that they grow not out of course.

For the side grounds, you are to fill them with variety of alleys, private, to give a full shade, some of them, wheresoever the sun be. You are to frame some of them, likewise, for shelter, that when the wind blows sharp you may walk as in a gallery. And those alleys must be likewise hedged at both ends, to keep out the wind; and these closer alleys must be ever finely gravelled, and no grass, because of going wet. In many of these alleys, likewise, you are to set fruit-trees of all sorts; as well upon the walls, as in ranges. And this would be generally observed, that the borders wherein you plant your fruit-trees, be fair and large, and low, and not steep; and set with fine flowers, but thin and sparingly, lest they deceive the trees. At the end of both the side grounds, I would have a mount of some pretty height, leaving the wall of the enclosure breast high, to look abroad into the fields.

For the main garden, I do not deny, but there should be some fair alleys ranged on both sides, with fruit-trees; and some pretty tufts of fruit-trees, and arbors with seats, set in some decent order; but these to be by no means set too thick; but to leave the main garden so as it be not too close, but the air open and free. For as for shade, I would have you rest upon the alleys of the side grounds, there to walk, if you be disposed, in the heat of the year or day; but to make account, that the main garden is for the more temperate parts of the year; and in the heat of summer, for the morning and the evening, or overcast days.

For aviaries, I like them not, except they be of that largeness as they may be turfed, and have living plants and bushes set in them; that the birds may have more scope, and natural nesting, and that no foulness appear in the floor of the aviary.

So I have made a platform of a princely garden, partly by precept, partly by drawing, not a model, but some general lines of it; and in this I have spared for no cost. But it is nothing for great princes, that for the most part taking advice with workmen, with no less cost set their things together; and sometimes add statuas and such things for state and magnificence, but nothing to the true pleasure of a garden.

47.说洽谈

就一般情况而论，当面洽谈比书面洽谈更好，而由第三者出面谈比本人出面谈更好。宜用书面洽谈的情况有：当一个人想得到书面答复的时候，当自己的洽谈信函日后可作为正当凭证的时候，或当面谈有可能受阻或被断章取义的时候。宜当面洽谈的情况有：当一个人的威信会令对方起敬的时候(如与身份较低者洽谈)；当所谈之事微妙，须观察对方的表情方知说话分寸的时候；更通常的是当一个人想对自己的话保留否认或解释之自由的时候。在挑选替自己出面洽谈事务的人时，最好挑那些爽快耿直的人，因为他们一般都受人之托就忠人之事，会向你如实汇报洽谈结果；千万别挑那些狡狯之徒，因为他们会利用替上等人办事的机会抬高自己，而且往往报喜不报忧以博取欢心。另须注意挑选那种乐意去谈你所托之事的人，这样会使洽谈事半功倍；同时亦须注意所选之人得适合所谈之事，如要告诫某人须挑敢说敢言者，要劝说某人须挑善甜言蜜语者，要探询某人须挑心眼灵活者，而要洽谈某项违情悖理的事时，则须挑选那种死心眼的人。还应注意选用那些曾受你之托去洽谈并有幸在洽谈中占上风的人，因为以往的成功会增加他们的自信，从而他们会努力坚持自己提出的条件。

洽谈时最好先婉转地探询对方的意图，不要直截了当地开门见山，除非你是想给对方来个出其不意。须知有求于人的洽谈对手比无所欲求的洽谈对手更容易对付。如果一个人与对方已达成初步协议，那该谁先履行协议就成了最重要的问题，而要合情合理地要求对方先履行义务，通常须具备三个条件：一是该协议的性质需要对方先履行义务，二是能使对方相信自己在另外某件事上还需要他的合作，三是能证明自己是最讲信用的人。洽谈的全部策略技巧就是观察对方并利用对方。人们暴露自己的时候往往是受人信任之时、兴奋激动之时、疏于防范之时、万不得已之时，或当想做某事而又找不到适当借口之时。如果你想左右对方，那你就必须了解其习性癖好从而引之，或了解其目的意图从而诱之，或了解其弱点短处从而迫之，要么就是了解到能影响对方的人和事，从而对其加以控制。与狡诈者洽谈必须断定他的真实意图，从而正确理解他的言语，记住在这种人面前应少说为佳，而且说的话要尽可能出乎其意料。在洽谈遇到困难时不要急于求成，但必须为洽谈成功做好准备，以期达成协议的时机逐渐成熟。

解析

一、洽谈——当面或第三者出面，比书面或本人出面更好。

二、书面或本人出面也有其好处：

1. 用信函——

(1) 可得到书面答复；

(2) 信函可作为日后凭证；

(3) 可保证连续、完整的陈述。

2. 本人出面——

(1) 与身份较低者，可以得到对方的敬重；

(2) 容易知道说话的分寸；

(3) 可以对自己的话保留否认或解释的自由。

三、如何挑选为自己出面洽谈之人：

1. 爽快耿直之人而非狡猾之徒；

2. 乐意去谈你所托之事的人；

3. 所选之人得适合所谈之事；

4. 曾经受托去洽谈并占上风的人。

四、洽谈的一般原则：

1. 先仔细探询对方意图，再进入正题。

2. 与有求于人的人洽谈更容易。

3. 要求对方先履行义务，三个条件——

(1)是协议的要求，或

(2)使对方相信在其他事情上也有求于他,或

(3)证明自己讲信用。

4. 洽谈的策略技巧:

(1)观察对方,人们暴露自己的情况——

(a)受人信任之时;

(b)兴奋激动之时;

(c)疏于防范之时;

(d)想做某事又找不到借口之时。

(2)利用对方,你必须——

(a)了解其习性癖好,从而引之;

(b)了解其目的意图,从而诱之;

(c)了解其弱点短处,从而迫之;

(d)了解能影响对方的人与事,从而对其加以控制。

5. 与狡诈者洽谈时应少说为佳,且说的话要尽可能出乎其意料。

6. 在洽谈遇到困难时不要急于求成。

Of Negotiating

IT IS generally better to deal by speech than by letter; and by the mediation of a third than by a man's self. Letters are good, when a man would draw an answer by letter back again; or when it may serve for a man's justification afterwards to produce his own letter; or where it may be danger to be interrupted, or heard by pieces. To deal in person is good, when a man's face breedeth regard, as commonly with inferiors; or in tender cases, where a man's eye, upon the countenance of him with whom he speaketh, may give him a direction how far to go; and generally, where a man will reserve to himself liberty, either to disavow or to expound. In choice of instruments, it is better to choose men of a plainer sort, that are like to do that, that is committed to them, and to report back again faithfully the success, than those that are cunning, to contrive, out of other men's business, somewhat to grace themselves, and will help the matter in report for satisfaction's sake. Use also such persons as affect the business, wherein they are employed; for that quickeneth much; and such, as are fit for the matter; as bold men for expostulation, fair-spoken men for persuasion, crafty men for inquiry and observation, froward, and absurd men, for business that doth not well bear out itself. Use also such as have been lucky, and prevailed before, in things wherein you have employed them; for that breeds confidence, and they will strive to maintain their prescription.

It is better to sound a person, with whom one deals afar off, than to fall upon the point at first; except you mean to surprise him by some short question. It is better dealing with men in appetite, than with those that are where they would be. If a man deal with another upon conditions, the start or first performance is all; which a man cannot reasonably demand, except either the nature of the thing be such, which must go before; or else a man can persuade the other party, that he shall still need him in some other thing; or else that he be counted the honester man. All practice is to discover, or to work. Men discover themselves in trust, in passion, at unawares, and of necessity, when they would have somewhat done, and cannot find an apt pretext. If you would work any man, you must either know his nature and fashions, and so lead him; or his ends, and so persuade him; or his weakness and disadvantages, and so awe him; or those that have interest in him, and so govern him. In dealing with cunning persons, we must ever consider their ends, to interpret their speeches; and it is good to say little to them, and that which they least look for. In all negotiations of difficulty, a man may not look to sow and reap at once; but must prepare business, and so ripen it by degrees.

48.谈门客与朋友

不可喜欢身价太高的门客,只怕那会使你像孔雀一样长了尾巴短了翅膀。我说身价太高并非仅指那种消耗钱财者,也指那些令人厌倦者和纠缠不休者。须知除主人提供的赞助、推荐和庇护之外,一般门客不应再提出更高的要求。而那些好拉帮结派的门客更不可喜欢,因为他们来投靠你门下并非出于对你的敬慕,而是出于对另外某人心怀不满,于是接踵而来的就往往是我们常见的大人物之间的误会。那种爱替主人当吹鼓手的门客也往往会招来麻烦,因为他们只顾吹嘘而不知保密,结果会成事不足败事有余,不仅有损主人的名望,而且为主人招来妒忌。还有一种门客也很危险,他们实际上是密探,善于打探主人家的秘密并将其告诉别人,然而这种人每每最受宠信,因为他们既殷勤又谦恭,而且常常能告诉主人他们用主人家的秘密交换而来的他人的秘密。至于说某位大人物被一些与其职业身份相符的人追随(比如某位参加过战争的要人被军人追随),这一直都被视为民间常事,即使在君主制国家也无可厚非,只要被追随者不过分炫耀或过于深孚众望。但被追随者中之最可敬者莫过于那种意欲使各种人的美德都得以发挥的人;然若是追随者们的德行无明显差异,则宁可收纳那种才能尚可者也不要那种精明能干的人。而且毋庸讳言,若在人心不古的年代,积极行动者比才智出众者更为有用。当然,君王对政府中的同级官员应一视同仁,此乃天经地义之举,因若是不顾惯例对某人格外器重,那被器重者未免会趾高气扬,而其他同级官员则会产生不满,因为他们有权要求公平对待;但豢养门客的情况却恰好相反,对待他们有亲疏之别才是上策,因为这会使受器重者更感知遇之恩,而其他人对你则会更加殷勤,毕竟一切都取决于主人的欢心。对初接纳的任何门客都须谨慎,不可对其言听计从,因为此时你还掌握不好分寸。而一旦(像人们所说的)被某人牵着鼻子走,那你就将身处险境，须知这种情形会显出你的软弱，使对你的诬蔑诽谤肆意流行，因为连那些平时不直接说三道四的人也会更大胆地言及主人之不是，从而损害主人的名声。不过对众多门客都言听计从会比这更糟，因为那会使你的见解变成印刷清样，已经经过多次校改。听取某几位朋友的意见永远是可敬之举，因为旁观者往往比当局者看得清，身在谷底者更识山之面目。世间少有真正的友谊，而在势均力敌者之间这种友谊更罕见，惺惺惜惺惺不过是世人惯常的夸张。真正的友谊只存在于身份地位有上下之别者之间，这种朋友才可能风雨同舟，休戚与共。

解析

一、不招人喜欢的门客：

1. 身价太高的门客，因为他们——
   (1) 消耗太多钱财；
   (2) 要求过高。
2. 一般门客，除非他们只要求——
   (1) 赞助；
   (2) 推荐；
   (3) 庇护。
3. 好拉帮结派的门客，因为他们会导致不和。
4. 爱替主人当吹鼓手的门客——
   (1) 不能保密，容易坏事；
   (2) 有损主人名望，为主人招来忌妒。
5. 密探性质的门客，他们到处扩散秘密，却因为其既殷勤又谦恭而最受宠信。

二、应当接纳的门客：

1. 主人的追随者；
2. 才能尚可者而非精明能干者，因为——
   (1) 他们深感知遇之恩，

（2）会让其余的人更加殷勤。

三、豢养门客的一般原则：

1. 对初接纳的门客都须谨慎；

2. 避免——

（1）被某人牵着鼻子走，

（2）对众多门客都言听计从。

四、友谊：

1. 听取几位朋友的意见是可敬之举；

2. 真正的友谊仅存在于身份地位有上下之别者之间。

Of Followers and Friends

COSTLY followers are not to be liked; lest while a man maketh his train longer, he make his wings shorter. I reckon to be costly, not them alone which charge the purse, but which are wearisome, and importune in suits. Ordinary followers ought to challenge no higher conditions, than countenance, recommendation, and protection from wrongs. Factious followers are worse to be liked, which follow not upon affection to him, with whom they range themselves, but upon discontentment conceived against some other; whereupon commonly ensueth that ill intelligence, that we many times see between great personages. Likewise glorious followers, who make themselves as trumpets of the commendation of those they follow, are full of inconvenience; for they taint business through want of secrecy; and they export honor from a man, and make him a return in envy. There is a kind of followers likewise, which are dangerous, being indeed espials; which inquire the secrets of the house, and bear tales of them, to others. Yet such men, many times, are in great favor; for they are officious, and commonly exchange tales. The following by certain estates of men, answerable to that, which a great person himself professeth (as of soldiers, to him that hath been employed in the wars, and the like), hath ever been a thing civil, and well taken, even in monarchies; so it be without too much pomp or popularity. But the most honorable kind of following, is to be followed as one, that apprehendeth to advance virtue, and desert, in all sorts of persons. And yet, where there is no eminent odds in sufficiency, it is better to take with the more passable, than with the more able. And besides, to speak truth, in base times, active men are of more use than virtuous. It is true that in government, it is good to use men of one rank equally: for to countenance some extraordinarily, is to make them insolent, and the rest discontent; because they may claim a due. But contrariwise, in favor, to use men with much difference and election is good; for it maketh the persons preferred more thankful, and the rest more officious: because all is of favor. It is good discretion, not to make too much of any man at the first; because one cannot hold out that proportion. To be governed (as we call it) by one is not safe; for it shows softness, and gives a freedom, to scandal and disreputation; for those, that would not censure or speak ill of a man immediately, will talk more boldly of those that are so great with them, and thereby wound their honor. Yet to be distracted with many is worse; for it makes men to be of the last impression, and full of change. To take advice of some few friends, is ever honorable; for lookers-on many times see more than gamesters; and the vale best discovereth the hill. There is little friendship in the world, and least of all between equals, which was wont to be magnified. That that is, is between superior and inferior, whose fortunes may comprehend the one the other.

49. 谈求情说项[①]

许多极不正当的请求也有人答应代呈，可见私下请托的确有损公益。许多正当的请求常被卑污的官员接手转呈，而我说的卑污官员不仅指腐败堕落者，也指那些老奸巨猾者，这种人只想受人之托而无意替人办事。有些人答应替人说项时并不想尽心尽力去说，但若发现该事由于他人说情而有办成的希望时，他们又极想得到请托人的酬谢，或是分到部分酬金，或至少会在事情办成之前利用请托人的希望。有些人答应代转请求只是想借机去见到某人，或去探听什么消息，因为除受托之事外他们找不到其他的适当借口。待自己的目的达到后，他们丝毫不关心那项请求的成败。概而言之，这种人是把他人委托之事当作自己过河之桥。更有甚者，有些人接受人家的委托是一心想让那受托之事砸锅，以此来讨好请求者的冤家或竞争对手。

毋庸置疑，可以说每接手一项请求就获得了一种权利。若请求者是想通过托人打点而赢得某场官司，那受托人就获得了主持公道的权利；若请求人是想通过请人说项而竞争某个职位，那受托人就获得了评功鉴才的权利。倘受托人之感情在前例中偏向无理的一方，那他最好利用其受托之机使纠纷在私下化解，而不要让其对簿公堂；倘受托人之感情在后例中偏向较为逊色的某人，那他在成全此人时最好别诋毁那位更有资格升迁者，从而断了人家的后路。若对别人所托之事不甚了然，那最好去咨询某位对该事有见识的朋友，他也许会告诉受托人接办此事是否体面；不过选择咨询人得小心谨慎，以免被人家牵着鼻子走。求人办事者最恨受托人敷衍欺骗，

①在培根时代，拜托有权势者向朝廷，甚至直接向君王提出请求并代为说项(为谋求某个职位、某块领地或某种特许等)乃正常之事，只要请求者提出的要求不太过分，如培根本人就曾央托其身居高位的姨父塞西尔勋爵和伊丽莎白女王的宠臣埃塞克斯伯爵替他向女王求官。

所以待之以坦诚实乃上策，要么一开始就拒绝接受委托，要么就应及时告诉人家事情进展的情况，而且事成之后不可索要额外的报酬，这种坦诚如今已不仅是一种体面，而且也是一种礼貌。若有人第一个来托情谋求某项特许[1]，而受托人觉得来者几乎不该获得该项权利，在这种情况下他应考虑到来者对他的信任，而且如果不通过来者他本来并不可能知道有那项特许，所以他不应该利用这个情报，而应该让来者另找途径去达到目的，这也算是回报了人家的信任。不知所求之事的价值大小是头脑简单，而不问所求之事正当与否则是缺乏良知。在说项过程中保守秘密是成功的主要手段之一，因为若大肆张扬，让人家知道自己的事有望办成，这固然会使其他一些说项人死心，但也有可能促使另一些人加紧活动，甚至招来新的竞争对手。不过掌握好时机才是说项成功的关键，须知掌握时机不仅要考虑到那位有权批准请求的要人，而且要考虑到那些有可能阻挠该请求获得批准的角色。请求者在选中介人的时候，与其选权位更高者，不如选更适合其请求事项的人；与其选统管全局者，不如选分管具体事务的人。一个人若在第一次说项遭拒后既不沮丧也不埋怨，那他第二次提出同样的请求有时可能获得恩准。对特别受宠者而言，欲得一寸先求一尺是一条适用的规则，但对情况相反者来说，他最好想要一尺时也先只求一寸，因为施恩者往往敢于失去一个初次讨情者，但却不愿失去已获得过恩惠的说情者以及先前已经赐予的恩惠。一般人以为求大人物写封举荐信不过是烦他举手之劳，殊不知若是那举荐理由不充分，那将极大地损害他的名誉。求情说项者中最可恶者莫过于那些以此为生的专业户，因为他们就是妨害国家秩序的毒药和病菌。

①这种特许包括获得被处决的阴谋分子的地产，或获得到海外经营某个殖民地的权利，伊丽莎白女王甚至经常把某种进口商品关税的包收权或某种商品的专卖权作为特许赏赐给下臣（获利的下臣当然也会有所回报）。

解析

一、不正当的请求有两种:

1. 请托本身就有损公益;
2. 由卑污的官员(包括不尽心尽力者与只想达到自身目的之人)接手转呈。

二、请求受托人的原则:

1. 尽力发现每一项请求的公正性。
2. 如果受托人的情感与公正相悖,至少该向公正作出让步。
3. 若对所托之事不甚了然,最好去咨询某位有见识的朋友。
4. 不能用以下方式欺骗请托者——
   (1) 假装接受委托;
   (2) 过度抬高请托者对成功的希望;
   (3) 事成之后索要额外的报酬。
5. 支持请托不问先后,而应根据对请托的判断,不能别有居心地利用请托。

三、请托者的原则:

1. 不可大肆张扬自己请托的内容与进展,要掌握好时机;
2. 选中介人时,宁可选适合的,不要选权位更高的;
3. 在首次说项被拒后不埋怨,也许以后提出同样的请求会获得恩准;
4. 根据不同的受宠程度决定是先求一寸还是先求一尺;
5. 不要因为一封大人物的举荐信而坏事;
6. 决不能用那种以此为生的求情说项者。

Of Suitors

MANY ill matters and projects are undertaken; and private suits do putrefy the public good. Many good matters, are undertaken with bad minds; I mean not only corrupt minds, but crafty minds, that intend not performance. Some embrace suits, which never mean to deal effectually in them; but if they see there may be life in the matter, by some other mean, they will be content to win a thank, or take a second reward, or at least to make use, in the meantime, of the suitor's hopes. Some take hold of suits, only for an occasion to cross some other; or to make an information, whereof they could not otherwise have apt pretext; without care what become of the suit, when that turn is served; or, generally, to make other men's business a kind of entertainment, to bring in their own. Nay, some undertake suits, with a full purpose to let them fall; to the end to gratify the adverse party, or competitor.

Surely there is in some sort a right in every suit; either a right of equity, if it be a suit of controversy; or a right of desert, if it be a suit of petition. If affection lead a man to favor the wrong side in justice, let him rather use his countenance to compound the matter, than to carry it. If affection lead a man to favor the less worthy in desert, let him do it, without depraving or disabling the better deserver. In suits which a man doth not well understand, it is good to refer them to some friend of trust and judgment, that may report, whether he may deal in them with honor: but let him choose well his referendaries, for else he may be led by the nose. Suitors are so distasted with delays and abuses, that plain dealing, in denying to deal in suits at first, and reporting the success barely, and in challenging no more thanks than one hath deserved, is grown not only honorable, but also gracious. In suits of favor, the first coming ought to take little place: so far forth, consideration may be had of his trust, that if intelligence of the matter could not otherwise have been had, but by him, advantage be not taken of the note, but the party left to his other means; and in some sort recompensed, for his discovery. To be ignorant of the value of a suit, is simplicity; as well as to be ignorant of the right thereof, is want of conscience. Secrecy in suits, is a great mean of obtaining; for voicing them to be in forwardness, may discourage some kind of suitors, but doth quicken and awake others. But timing of the suit is the principal. Timing, I say, not only in respect of the person that should grant it, but in respect of those, which are like to cross it. Let a man, in the choice of his mean, rather choose the fittest mean, than the greatest mean; and rather them that deal in certain things, than those that are general. The reparation of a denial, is sometimes equal to the first grant; if a man show himself neither dejected nor discontented. Iniquum petas ut aequum feras[①] is a good rule, where a man hath strength of favor: but otherwise, a man were better rise in his suit; for he, that would have ventured at first to have lost the suitor, will not in the conclusion lose both the suitor, and his own former favor. Nothing is thought

①Ask more than you due, that you may get your due.

so easy a request to a great person, as his letter; and yet, if it be not in a good cause, it is so much out of his reputation. There are no worse instruments, than these general contrivers of suits; for they are but a kind of poison, and infection, to the public proceedings.

50. 谈读书

读书之用有三：一为怡神旷心，二为增趣添雅，三为长才益智。怡神旷心最见于蛰伏幽居，增趣添雅最见于高谈雄辩，而长才益智则最见于处事辩理。虽说有经验者能就一事一理进行处置或分辨，但若要通观全局并运筹帷幄，则还是博览群书者最能胜任。读书费时太多者皆因懒散，寻章摘句过甚者显矫揉造作，全凭书中教条断事者则乃学究书痴。天资之改善须靠读书，而学识之完美须靠实践；因天生资质犹如自然花木，需要用学识对其加以修剪，而书中所示则往往漫无边际，必须用经验和阅历界定其经纬。讲究实际者鄙薄读书，头脑简单者仰慕读书，唯英明睿智者运用读书，这并非由于书不示人其用法，而是因为其用法乃一种在书之外并高于书本的智慧，只有靠观察方可得之。读书不可存心吹毛求疵，不可尽信书中之论，亦不可为己言掠辞夺句，而应该斟酌推敲，钩深致远。有些书可浅尝辄止，有些书可囫囵吞枣，但有少量书则须细细咀嚼，慢慢消化；换言之，有些书可只读其章节，有些书可大致浏览，有少量书则须通篇细读并认真领悟。有些书还可以请人代阅，只取代阅人所作摘录节要；但此法只适用于次要和无关紧要的书，因浓缩之书如蒸馏之水淡而无味。读书可使人充实，讨论可使人敏锐，笔记则可使人严谨；故不常做笔记者须有过目不忘之记忆，不常讨论者须有通权达变之天资，而不常读书者则须有狡诈诡谲之伎俩，方可显其无知为卓有见识。读史使人明智，读诗使人灵透，数学使人精细，物理学使人深沉，伦理学使人庄重，逻辑修辞则使人善辩，正如古人所云："学皆成性。"[①]不仅如此，连心智上的各种障碍都可以读适当之书而令其开豁。身体之百病皆有相宜的调养运动，如滚球有益于膀胱和肾脏，射箭有益于肺部和胸腔，散步有益于肠胃，骑马有益于大脑等等。与此相似，若有人难聚神

---

①语出奥维德《列女志》第 15 篇 83 行。

思，可令其研习数学，因在演算求证中稍一走神就得重来一遍；若有人不善辨异，可令其读经院哲学，因该派哲学家之条分缕析可令人不胜其烦；而若是有人不善由果溯因之归纳，或不善由因及果之演绎，则可令其阅读律师之案卷；如此心智上之各种毛病皆有特效妙方。

解析

一、读书之用：

1. 怡神旷心——蛰伏幽居之时；
2. 增趣添雅——高谈雄辩之时；
3. 长才益智——处世辨理之时。

二、读书的陋习：

1. 费时太多（"懒散"）；
2. 寻章摘句过甚（"矫揉造作"）；
3. 全凭书中教条断事（"学究书痴"）。

三、读书的原则：

1. 读书要斟酌推敲。
2. 对要读的书区别对待——
   (1) 只读其章节（"浅尝辄止"）；
   (2) 大致浏览（"囫囵吞枣"）；
   (3) 通篇细读并认真领悟（"细细咀嚼、慢慢消化"）；
   (4) 请代阅人摘录节要。
3. 谨慎运用——
   (1) 不同的学习方法：
      (a) 阅读——使人充实；
      (b) 讨论——使人敏锐；
      (c) 笔记——使人严谨。
   (2) 各门学科的价值：
      (a) 历史——使人明智；

(b) 诗歌——使人灵透；

(c) 数学——使人精细；

(d) 科学——

自然——使人深沉；

伦理——使人庄重；

(e) 逻辑学——使人善辩。

4. 如同锻炼可消除身体疾病，学习可以消除心智上的障碍。

(1) 体育锻炼：

(a) 滚球——有益肾脏；

(b) 射箭——有益心肺；

(c) 散步——有益消化；

(d) 骑马——有益大脑。

(2) 心智锻炼：

(a) 数学——有助于集中神思；

(b) 经院哲学——有助于辨义；

(c) 律师的案卷——可改善记忆迟钝。

Of Studies

STUDIES serve for delight, for ornament, and for ability. Their chief use for delight, is in privateness and retiring; for ornament, is in discourse; and for ability, is in the judgment, and disposition of business. For expert men can execute, and perhaps judge of particulars, one by one; but the general counsels, and the plots and marshalling of affairs, come best, from those that are learned. To spend too much time in studies is sloth; to use them too much for ornament, is affectation; to make judgment wholly by their rules, is the humor of a scholar. They perfect nature, and are perfected by experience: for natural abilities are like natural plants, that need proyning, by study; and studies themselves, do give forth directions too much at large, except they be bounded in by experience. Crafty men contemn studies, simple men admire them, and wise men use them; for they teach not their own use; but that is a wisdom without them, and above them, won by observation. Read not to contradict and confute; nor to believe and take for granted; nor to find talk and discourse; but to weigh and consider. Some books are to be tasted, others to be swallowed, and some few to be chewed and digested; that is, some books are to be read only in parts; others to be read, but not curiously; and some few to be read wholly, and with diligence and attention. Some books also may be read by deputy, and extracts made of them by others; but that would be only in the less important arguments, and the meaner sort of books, else distilled books are like common distilled waters, flashy things. Reading maketh a full man; conference a ready man; and writing an exact man. And therefore, if a man write little, he had need have a great memory; if he confer little, he had need have a present wit; and if he read little, he had need have much cunning, to seem to know, that he doth not. Histories make men wise; poets witty; the mathematics subtile; natural philosophy deep; moral grave; logic and rhetoric able to contend. Abeunt studia in mores. ① Nay, there is no stond or impediment in the wit, but may be wrought out by fit studies; like as diseases of the body, may have appropriate exercises. Bowling is good for the stone and reins; shooting for the lungs and breast; gentle walking for the stomach; riding for the head; and the like. So if a man's wit be wandering, let him study the mathematics; for in demonstrations, if his wit be called away never so little, he must begin again. If his wit be not apt to distinguish or find differences, let him study the Schoolmen; for they are cymini sectores②. If he be not apt to beat over matters, and to call up one thing to prove and illustrate another, let him study the lawyers' cases. So every defect of the mind, may have a special receipt.

①Studies pass into character.

②dividers of cumin-seeds

51.论党派

许多人都抱有一种不明智的看法,认为对君王或大臣来说,治国处事中的主要策略应当着眼于与各党各派的关系;殊不知正确的策略恰好相反,安排处理符合国家总利益的大事要事,使各党各派都不得不赞成拥护,对待每个具体的人只考虑其个人身份而不考虑其党派,这才是君王和大臣的最明智之举。但笔者并非是说对党派的考虑可以完全忽略。出身低微者在升迁途中须有党派依附,但本身已有力量的大人物则最好无党无朋。初时依附某党派者不可死心塌地,应使自己成为该党中最能为他党所容忍的成员,此举通常能铺就一条最佳仕途。人少势微的党派往往更为团结,所以世人常见毫不妥协的小党拖垮较为温和的大党。相争的两党中有一党被击败后,获胜的党又会自行分裂。如当年庞培和恺撒曾结党与包括卢库鲁斯在内的元老院抗衡,但当元老院势衰后,恺撒和庞培马上就兵戎相见;安东尼和屋大维也曾结为一党与以布鲁图和卡西乌为首的共和派对阵,但当布、卡二人兵败自戕后,安东尼与屋大维也分道扬镳并反目为仇。以上二例都与战争有关,但非公开的党派斗争情况亦是如此;因此当获胜党再行分裂时,那些曾居次要地位的干将虽多有成为新党领袖者,但他们被人当作垃圾扔掉的情况也屡见不鲜,因为许多人的长处就在于与对手争斗,如果对手消失,他们也就不再有用。世人常见,有些人一旦借助某党派而获得权位,马上就开始与该党派的对立派系接触;这些人的心思多半是:既然前一个党派已抓到手,现在就该准备抓点新的东西。派系斗争的倒戈者往往能轻而易举地捞到好处,因为当两派的争斗久久相持不下时,争取到某人倒戈就会导致天平倾向一边,而这获胜的一边对倒戈者会感激不尽。在两党间持中立态度者并非人人都主张中庸调和,实际上有人是出于替自己打算,一心只想坐收渔人之利。不可否认,意大利人对教皇的不偏不倚就有所

怀疑，虽说他们嘴边常挂着“众教之父”这个字眼，但却认为这字眼指的是想把众人的一切都归于自家之伟大的那种人。为君王者务须当心，不可使自己偏向一方，不可使自己成为某党某派之一员；对君主制国家来说，政府中的党派永远都有害无益，因为党派要求其成员尽一种义务，而这种义务往往高于对君王应尽的义务，并且党派会把君王视为“我们中的一员”，这种情况曾见于法国的天主教同盟[①]。若党派之争愈演愈烈并甚嚣尘上，那就表明君王软弱无力，而这会极大地损害其权威及朝政。君主制国家的党派活动应像天文学家所说的内侧行星之运动，它们虽说可以有适当的自转，但其公转运动仍暗中受着来自第一运动的更高运动之支配。[②]

解析

一、党派的用途，虽然没有被轻视，但——

1. 不是正确策略的组成部分；
2. 是出身低微者在升迁途中可借用的工具(但这种利用也应适度)。

二、关于党派的一些真相：

1. 人少势微的党派往往更加强大，且易取得成功。
2. 两派相争，一派的失败往往造成另一派的灭亡，例如：
   (1) 卢库鲁斯对抗恺撒与庞培；
   (2) 安东尼与屋大维对抗布鲁图与卡西乌。
   规则：这种状况一旦发生，居次位的干将或者成为伟人，或者被当作垃圾扔掉。
3. 借助于某党派获得升迁的人往往成功后就抛弃该党派，一般说来，这么做有助于他们进一步的攀升。
4. 中立往往是自私的表现。

①法国胡格诺战争期间由部分天主教教士和贵族结成的同盟，目的是与胡格诺教派争雄并削弱王权，当时的法王亨利三世(在位期 1574—1589)在两派之间摇摆不定，对天主教同盟忽而禁止，忽而加盟，终招杀身之祸。

②请参阅本书《论叛乱与骚动》第 4 段正文及注释。

三、君王不应该偏袒任一党派，而应像第一运动那样保证自己的权力。

Of Faction

MANY have an opinion not wise, that for a prince to govern his estate, or for a great person to govern his proceedings, according to the respect of factions, is a principal part of policy; whereas contrariwise, the chiefest wisdom, is either in ordering those things which are general, and wherein men of several factions do nevertheless agree; or in dealing with correspondence to particular persons, one by one. But I say not that the considerations of factions, is to be neglected. Mean men, in their rising, must adhere; but great men, that have strength in themselves, were better to maintain themselves indifferent, and neutral. Yet even in beginners, to adhere so moderately, as he be a man of the one faction, which is most passable with the other, commonly giveth the best way. The lower and weaker faction, is the firmer in conjunction; and it is often seen, that a few that are stiff, do tire out a greater number, that are more moderate. When one of the factions is extinguished, the remaining subdivideth; as the faction between Lucullus, and the rest of the nobles of the senate (which they called Optimates) held out awhile, against the faction of Pompey and Caesar; but when the senate's authority was pulled down, Caesar and Pompey soon after brake. The faction or party of Antonius and Octavianus Caesar, against Brutus and Cassius, held out likewise for a time; but when Brutus and Cassius were overthrown, then soon after, Antonius and Octavianus brake and subdivided. These examples are of wars, but the same holdeth in private factions. And therefore, those that are seconds in factions, do many times, when the faction subdivideth, prove principals; but many times also, they prove ciphers and cashiered; for many a man's strength is in opposition; and when that faileth, he groweth out of use. It is commonly seen, that men, once placed, take in with the contrary faction, to that by which they enter: thinking belike, that they have the first sure, and now are ready for a new purchase. The traitor in faction, lightly goeth away with it; for when matters have stuck long in balancing, the winning of some one man casteth them, and he getteth all the thanks. The even carriage between two factions, proceedeth not always of moderation, but of a trueness to a man's self, with end to make use of both. Certainly in Italy, they hold it a little suspect in popes, when they have often in their mouth Padre commune: and take it to be a sign of one, that meaneth to refer all to the greatness of his own house. Kings had need beware, how they side themselves, and make themselves as of a faction or party; for leagues within the state, are ever pernicious to monarchies: for they raise an obligation, paramount to obligation of sovereignty, and make the king tanquam unus ex nobis[①]; as was to be seen in the League of France. When factions are carried too high and too violently, it is a sign of weakness in princes; and much to the prejudice, both of their authority and business. The motions of factions under kings ought to be, like the motions (as the astronomers speak) of the inferior orbs, which may have their proper motions, but yet still are quietly carried, by the higher motion of primum mobile.

①as if he were one of us

52.谈礼节与俗套

待人不拘礼节者须有非凡之大德，正如镶嵌时不用衬箔的宝石须十分珍贵。但若仔细观察就会发现，世人获得好名声的情形就如同赚钱获利的情况。须知小钱装满大钱袋是句不谬的格言，因为小钱可常得，而大利不常来。与此同理，小小的优点可赢得大大的赞扬，因为小优点可天天显示并为人注意，而展示大德的机会却如同过节。由此可见，讲究礼仪小节可替人增添美名，正如伊莎贝拉女王[①]所说："举止优雅乃永不过时的推荐信。"而要获得这种推荐信，你只须对它不小瞧就差不多可以到手，因为这样你就会留心他人的优雅举止，此外你还须做的就是自信；须知一个人若是在言谈举止上太煞费苦心，他就会失去其应有的风度和魅力，因为风度魅力之展现必须自然大方而无矫揉造作。有人的举手投足活像每个音节都推敲过的诗行，可一个在鸡毛蒜皮上绞脑汁的人又何以能领悟宏旨大义？

全然不讲礼节不啻是教别人待自己也非礼怠慢，亦等于是叫人对自己不必尊重。所以待人接物不可免礼，尤其在同陌生人或讲究礼仪者交往的时候；但过分强调礼节，把礼仪俗套看得高于一切，那不仅会使说话人显得可笑，而且会减少人家对他的信任。无可置疑，礼仪俗套之运用有一种效果极佳并令人难忘的方式，若能将其发现，必可行之有效。在同辈之间有的是亲热随便，故不妨保持几分庄重。在下属面前肯定会受到尊敬，故不妨显出几分随和。不分场合地过于讲礼会使人感到厌腻，从而会使自己显得庸俗。专心注意某人本身并无不妥，但须让对方知道你是出于敬重而非出于轻率。附和他人通常是一条有益的规则，但附和时须加上自己的主见。如同意他人的见解须加上点不同看法，赞成他人的提议须附上个先决条件，而认

①卡斯蒂利亚王国女王(1474—1504)及阿拉贡王国女王(1479—1504)，1479年使两国合并，为统一西班牙奠定了基础，曾资助哥伦布航海。

可他人的计划则须提出进一步的理由。在恭维人时须注意别太过分，不然你即使在别的方面都无可挑剔，你的嫉妒者也会说你善于阿谀奉承，从而贬低你其他更为可贵的优点。在处理大事时不可过分拘泥于俗套，在观察机会时亦不可过于谨小慎微，因为这二者皆为失措。须知所罗门有言："望风者难以下种，看云者不得收获。"[①]聪明人更多的是创造机会而非寻找机会。人的举止行为应像其衣着服饰，不可过分拘泥讲究，以便行动能轻松自如。

解析

一、优雅的举止时时有用，就像一封永不过时的推荐信。

二、举止优雅的原则：

1. 留心观察他人的举止，这样可以让你自然大方而不矫揉造作。
2. 自己不讲究礼节会导致别人对你不尊重；对细枝末节的过度追求则会引起怀疑。
3. 对待同辈要讲究礼节，对待下属要随和，不让自己在任何人面前显得庸俗。
4. 附和他人时应注意维护自己的独立，办法是——
   (1) 附和别人的意见时加上自己的看法；
   (2) 赞成他人的提议时加上先决条件。
5. 恭维别人时不能太过分。
6. 让你的举止行为像衣着服饰一样宽松自如。

Of Ceremonies and Respects

HE THAT is only real, had need have exceeding great parts of virtue; as

①语出《旧约·传道书》第 11 章 4 节。

the stone had need to be rich, that is set without foil. But if a man mark it well, it is, in praise and commendation of men, as it is in gettings and gains: for the proverb is true, That light gains make heavy purses; for light gains come thick, whereas great, come but now and then. So it is true, that small matters win great commendation, because they are continually in use and in note: whereas the occasion of any great virtue, cometh but on festivals. Therefore it doth much add to a man's reputation, and is (as Queen Isabella said) like perpetual letters commendatory, to have good forms. To attain them, it almost sufficeth not to despise them; for so shall a man observe them in others; and let him trust himself with the rest. For if he labor too much to express them, he shall lose their grace; which is to be natural and unaffected. Some men's behavior is like a verse, wherein every syllable is measured; how can a man comprehend great matters, that breaketh his mind too much, to small observations?

Not to use ceremonies at all, is to teach others not to use them again; and so diminisheth respect to himself; especially they be not to be omitted, to strangers and formal natures; but the dwelling upon them, and exalting them above the moon, is not only tedious, but doth diminish the faith and credit of him that speaks. And certainly, there is a kind of conveying, of effectual and imprinting passages amongst compliments, which is of singular use, if a man can hit upon it. Amongst a man's peers, a man shall be sure of familiarity; and therefore it is good, a little to keep state. Amongst a man's inferiors one shall be sure of reverence; and therefore it is good, a little to be familiar. He that is too much in anything, so that he giveth another occasion of satiety, maketh himself cheap. To apply one's self to others, is good; so it be with demonstration, that a man doth it upon regard, and not upon facility. It is a good precept generally, in seconding another, yet to add somewhat of one's own: as if you will grant his opinion, let it be with some distinction; if you will follow his motion, let it be with condition; if you allow his counsel, let it be with alleging further reason. Men had need beware, how they be too perfect in compliments; for be they never so sufficient otherwise, their enviers will be sure to give them that attribute, to the disadvantage of their greater virtues. It is loss also in business, to be too full of respects, or to be curious, in observing times and opportunities. Solomon saith, He that considereth the wind, shall not sow, and he that looketh to the clouds, shall not reap. A wise man will make more opportunities, than he finds. Men's behavior should be, like their apparel, not too strait or point device, but free for exercise or motion.

53.谈赞誉

赞誉乃德行之反映,但它亦是令人反思的镜鉴。倘若赞誉来自庸众,那它往往都是毫无价值的谬奖,而且通常只追随贪图虚荣者,而非德高品正者,因为平庸之人每每不知流光厚德为何物。薄德令他们叹赏,私德令他们惊羡,但对真正的大德伟德他们却浑然不识,唯有虚饰炫耀的假德行才最对他们的胃口。不可否认,庸众的口碑就像一条只漂虚名浮誉而不载厚重德望的河川。但倘若异口同声的赞赏来自有识之士,那就如《圣经》所言,"美名犹如香膏"[①],这种美名可远扬四方并久久不散,因为香膏之芳泽比鲜花之芳菲更能持久。

歌功颂德有如此多不实之处, 以致世人可理直气壮地对其加以怀疑。有些称颂褒扬已纯粹是为了阿谀奉承。如果谄媚者稍欠火候,他会做出一堆通用的高帽子,见谁都可以戴上一顶。如果献媚者有几分心计,他就会将心比心地揣摩自己欲攀附的贵人之心理,然后对其最自鸣得意之处大加吹捧。但如果那狐媚者是个厚颜无耻之徒,他便会找出一个人自己最感难堪的缺陷,然后硬把那缺陷说成优点,叫那被吹捧者也不得不鄙视自己的感觉。有些赞誉是出于良好的愿望和敬意,此乃对君王和要人们应有的一种礼貌;这种赞誉可谓"以赞为训",因为赞誉者所颂扬之处正是他们希望君王和要人们能做到的地方。有些赞誉就像裹上糖衣的毒箭,实际上是要为被赞誉者招来妒忌,这真可谓最可怕的敌人就是当面说好话的敌人;不过希腊人有这样一句格言:"口蜜腹剑的赞美者将鼻梁生疮。"[②]这就像我们英语中说撒谎者舌尖会起疮一样。毋庸置疑,有益的赞誉应适度、适时,并不

①参见《旧约·传道书》第7章1节。英文钦定本此句中"犹如"作"胜过"。

②此言化自古希腊诗人忒奥克里托斯(Theocritus,约前310—前250)的《田园诗》第12首23—24行:"我赞美你哟,美丽的人儿,/我不会因此而鼻上生疮。"

流于庸俗。所罗门曰:“早起而对朋友大加赞美，那不啻是对朋友大加诅咒。”[①]对人对事的赞扬过分夸张只会招人反感,并且会招来嫉妒和嘲笑。除个别情况之外,自吹自擂不可能显得合宜得体;但一个人若是赞美自己的工作或使命,他便可以显得非常体面,甚至显出一种崇高。那些身为神学家或经院神学家的罗马红衣主教就自命不凡,对世俗事务极其鄙薄,因为他们把所有的将军、大使、法官和其他非神职官员都叫做“代理执政官”,仿佛他们不过是在代行职权,然而这些“代理执政官”之所为往往比主教们高深的思辨更于人有益。圣保罗在夸耀时屡屡说“恕我妄言”[②],但当他言及其工作时却说“我要赞美我的使命”[③]。

解析

一、赞誉乃德行之反映——

1. 受到提出赞誉者人格的限制。
2. 来自庸众的赞誉往往都是毫无价值的谬奖,因为他们——
   (1) 对最低级的德行赞赏不已;
   (2) 对一般德行惊奇艳羡;
   (3) 对大德伟德反而浑然不识。

二、因为赞誉有如此多不实之处,所以要熟悉它的特点:

1. 阿谀奉承者的赞誉是平凡的,狡诈的,无耻的;
2. 出于敬意的赞誉对被赞者会有启发作用;
3. 出于恶意的赞誉往往带来不幸;
4. 自吹自擂不得体,但对自己工作的赞誉体面崇高。

---

①参见《旧约·箴言》第 27 章 14 节。英文钦定本此句中“赞美”为“祝福”。

②见《新约·哥林多后书》第 11 章 21—23 节。

③语出《新约·罗马书》第 11 章 13 节。

Of Praise

PRAISE is the reflection of virtue; but it is as the glass or body, which giveth the reflection. If it be from the common people, it is commonly false and naught; and rather followeth vain persons, than virtuous. For the common people understand not many excellent virtues. The lowest virtues draw praise from them; the middle virtues work in them astonishment or admiration; but of the highest virtues, they have no sense of perceiving at all. But shows, and species virtutibus similes①, serve best with them. Certainly fame is like a river, that beareth up things light and swoln, and drowns the weighty and solid. But if persons of quality and judgment concur, then it is (as the Scripture saith) nomen bonum instar unguenti fragrantis②. It fireth all round about, and will not easily away. For the odors of ointments are more durable, than those of flowers.

There be so many false points of praise, that a man may justly hold it a suspect. Some praises proceed merely of flattery; and if he be an ordinary flatterer, he will have certain common attributes, which may serve every man; if he be a cunning flatterer, he will follow the archflatterer, which is a man's self; and wherein a man thinketh best of himself, therein the flatterer will uphold him most: but if he be an impudent flatterer, look wherein a man is conscious to himself, that he is most defective, and is most out of countenance in himself, that will the flatterer entitle him to perforce, spreta conscientia③. Some praises come of good wishes and respects, which is a form due, in civility, to kings and great persons, laudando praecipere④, when by telling men what they are, they represent to them, what they should be. Some men are praised maliciously, to their hurt, thereby to stir envy and jealousy towards them: pessimum genus inimicorum laudantium;⑤ inasmuch as it was a proverb, amongst the Grecians, that he that was praised to his hurt, should have a push rise upon his nose; as we say, that a blister will rise upon one's tongue, that tells a lie. Certainly moderate praise, used with opportunity, and not vulgar, is that which doth the good. Solomon saith, He that praiseth his

①pretences appearing like virtues

②A good name is like sweet smelling ointment.

③defying conscience

④to advise by praising

⑤Those who praise are the worst kind of enemies.

friend aloud, rising early, it shall be to him no better than a curse. Too much magnifying of man or matter, doth irritate contradiction, and procure envy and scorn. To praise a man's self, cannot be decent, except it be in rare cases; but to praise a man's office or profession, he may do it with good grace, and with a kind of magnanimity. The cardinals of Rome, which are theologues, and friars, and Schoolmen, have a phrase of notable contempt and scorn towards civil business: for they call all temporal business of wars, embassages, judicature, and other employments, sbirrerie, which is under-sheriffries; as if they were but matters, for under-sheriffs and catchpoles: though many times those under-sheriffries do more good, than their high speculations. St. Paul, when he boasts of himself, he doth oft interlace, I speak like a fool; but speaking of his calling, he saith, magnificabo apostolatum meum.[①]

①I will magnify my apostleship.

54.论虚荣

伊索有则寓言讲得甚妙，停落在大车轮轴上的苍蝇说："看我把尘土扬得多高!"世上亦有这么一些爱虚荣的人，无论何事有进展，也不管这进展是由能力更强者在推动，只要此事与他们挨得上边，他们便以为其进展全凭他们的力量。好虚荣者必好派系之争，因为自我夸耀须借助比短论长。好自夸者都必然言辞激烈，以证明他们的吹嘘属实。而好吹嘘的人必然不能保密，故他们往往成事不足，败事有余。这种人正好应了一句法国格言——大吹大擂者做得最少。

但不可否认，吹嘘在国家事务中也有其用处。譬如说要为某种德行制造舆论，或者说需要为某人歌功颂德，上述好吹嘘者就可充当挺好的吹鼓手。再如李维谈及安条克三世与埃托里亚人结盟时就指出："说客对其游说的双方之交叉吹嘘，有时候可以收到奇效。"[①]因为，要是一名说客在两位君王间游说，想把他们拉入一场对第三者的战争，那他往往会分别对这两位君主夸大其未来盟友的力量，以达到促使二者结盟的目的。在两人间奔走的说士也往往会分别在这两人跟前夸大自己对另一方的影响，从而加深那两人对自己的信任。诸如此类的夸大其词常产生无中生有之奇效，因为高调大话足以诱发信念，而信念可转化成物质力量。

虚荣心对军人来说必不可少，正如剑与剑可以互相磨砺，将士们亦可利用虚荣心互相激励。说到那种须付出代价并担当风险的伟业，一批酷爱虚荣的人可使其大张旗鼓，而那些老成持重者则宜做压舱物而不宜做风帆。说到学者的名望，若无几片虚饰的羽毛，谁都难以名扬天下。"那些写书

①参见李维《罗马史》第35卷12章、17章和18章。公元前192年，塞琉西王国国王安条克三世应埃托里亚联盟(古希腊部分城邦以埃托里亚为中心结成的反马其顿同盟)之邀进入希腊，次年被向东扩张的罗马击败。两者的结盟自有其政治背景，但说客对两者力量的交叉吹嘘也促成了双方结盟的决心。

说名望如粪土者都没忘记把他们的大名印在扉页。"[①]就连苏格拉底、亚里士多德和盖仑[②]也喜欢露才扬己。无可否认,虚荣心的确可助人青史留名,因为功德被世人承认往往并不因其自身圆满,而是由于人性之好德之心,故名垂青史者多半都通过第二途径。若是西塞罗、塞内加和小普林尼不曾替自己涂脂抹粉,他们的名声也难传到今天。这种涂脂抹粉就好比替镶板刷漆,不仅可使其光彩照人,而且可使其经年累月。但在以上所论的虚荣中,笔者尚未触及到塔西佗为穆奇阿努斯界定的那种特性。塔西佗说:"此人有一种可使其以往的全部言行都获得赞赏的表现技巧。"[③]须知这种技巧并非产生于虚荣之心,而是产生于自然得体的宽容和谨慎。这种宽容和谨慎于某些人不仅自然得体,而且还使其显得雍容大雅,因为谦恭、宽谅和让步若能被精妙地运用,它们也都是吹捧自己的技艺。而在此类技巧中,最精妙不过的就是小普林尼曾谈及的那种,即如果你发现某人有与你自身相似的优点或成就,那你应该非常慷慨地对其大加赞赏。小普林尼的原话说得十分巧妙:"赞赏别人就是褒扬自己,因为别人被你赞赏之处要么比你出色,要么比你逊色。而如果他比你逊色而受到夸奖,那你就更加值得夸奖;如果他比你出色而未受到称颂,那你就更不值得称颂。"[④]为虚荣而自夸者乃有识之士鄙薄的人物、庸人白痴赞美的对象、寄生食客崇拜的神祇,同时也是他自己谎言大话之奴隶。

解析

一、虚荣之人必定——

①语出西塞罗《图斯库兰谈话录》第1卷15章。

②盖仑(约129—199),古希腊生理学家及哲学家,曾根据动物解剖推论人体结构,并用亚里士多德的目的论阐述人体功能。

③语出塔西佗《历史》第2卷80章。暴君尼禄死后,罗马帝国驻各地军团纷纷拥立新皇帝。曾三度出任执政官并握有重兵的叙利亚总督穆奇阿努斯审时度势,抛弃自己的敌意和妒忌心,答应把军队交给已被美西亚军团、犹太军团和埃及军团拥戴的韦斯帕芗,帮助后者登上了皇位。此举令他留名史册。

④语出小普林尼《书信集》第6卷17篇4节。

1. 好派系之争；

2. 言辞激烈；

3. 聒噪吵闹。

二、然而吹嘘也有其用处——

1. 在国家事务中——制造舆论，甚至可以利用互相矛盾的谎言。

2. 在军队事务中——为“须付出代价并担当风险的伟业”注入活力。

3. 在做学问上——

喜欢露才扬己之人：苏格拉底，亚里士多德，盖仑；

有些许虚荣之人：西塞罗，塞内加，小普林尼。

三、然而有益的虚荣——

1. 出自宽容而非虚荣之心；

2. 自然得体且雍容大雅。

四、好吹捧的人——

1. 为有识之士所鄙薄；

2. 为庸人白痴所赞美；

3. 是寄生食客崇拜的神祇；

4. 是自己谎言大话的奴隶。

Of Vainglory

IT WAS prettily devised of Aesop, The fly sat upon the axle-tree of the chariot wheel, and said, What a dust I do raise! So are there some vain persons, that whatsoever goeth alone, or moveth upon greater means, if they have never so little hand in it, they think it is they that carry it. They that are glorious, must needs be factious; for all bravery stands upon comparisons. They must needs be violent, to make good their own vaunts. Neither can they be secret, and therefore not effectual; but according to the French proverb, Beaucoup de bruit, peu de fruit; Much bruit little fruit.

Yet certainly, there is use of this quality in civil affairs. Where there is an opinion and fame to be created, either of virtue or greatness, these men are good trumpeters. Again, as Titus Livius noteth, in the case of Antiochus and the Aetolians, There are sometimes great effects, of cross lies; as if a man, that negotiates between two princes, to draw them to join in a war against the third, doth extol the forces of either of them, above measure, the one to the other: and sometimes he that deals between man and man, raiseth his own credit with both, by pretending greater interest than he hath in either. And in these and the like kinds, it often falls out, that somewhat is produced of nothing; for lies are sufficient to breed opinion, and opinion brings on substance.

In militar commanders and soldiers, vainglory is an essential point; for as iron sharpens iron, so by glory, one courage sharpeneth another. In cases of great enterprise upon charge and adventure, a composition of glorious natures, doth put life into business; and those that are of solid and sober natures, have more of the ballast, than of the sail. In fame of learning, the flight will be slow without some feathers of ostentation. Qui de contemnenda gloria libros scribunt, nomen, suum inscribunt.[①] Socrates, Aristotle, Galen, were men full of ostentation. Certainly vainglory helpeth to perpetuate a man's memory; and virtue was never so beholding to human nature, as it received his due at the second hand. Neither had the fame of Cicero, Seneca, Plinius Secundus, borne her age so well, if it had not been joined with some vanity in themselves; like unto varnish, that makes ceilings not only shine but last. But all this while, when I speak of vainglory, I mean not of that property, that Tacitus doth attribute to Mucianus; Omnium quae dixerat feceratque arte quadam ostentator[②]: for that proceeds not of vanity, but of natural magnanimity and discretion; and in some persons, is not only comely, but gracious. For excusations, cessions, modesty itself well governed, are but arts of ostentation. And amongst those arts, there is none better than that which Plinius Secundus speaketh of, which is to be liberal of praise and commendation to others, in that, wherein a man's self hath any perfection. For saith Pliny, very wittily, In commending another, you do yourself right; for he that you commend, is either superior to you in that you commend, or inferior. If he be inferior, if he be to be commended, you much more; if he be superior, if he be not to be commended, you much less. Glorious men are the scorn of wise men, the admiration of fools, the idols of parasites, and the slaves of their own vaunts.

---

①Those who write books on content of vainglory, put their own names on the title page.

②one who was almost an artist in making known what he had said and done

55.谈荣誉与名声

荣誉之获得不过是个人之美德和价值未遭毁损而得以昭然。须知有些人的全部所为就是为了追逐名誉，结果他们常常被公众挂在嘴边，但却很少赢得人们的真心崇敬。在另一方面，有些人在展示其美德时总是有所遮掩，所以舆论往往都低估了他们的价值。若有人能成就一项从未被人尝试过，或尝试过但未成功，或成功了却不甚圆满的事业，那与完成一项虽更为艰巨或高尚但已有人曾圆满完成的业绩相比，前者应获得更高的荣誉。若有人行事讲究中庸，结果他的某项中庸之举使各党派、政派、教派、学派都感到满意，那为他唱出的赞歌就会更加圆润。如果一个人在着手行事时不善珍惜自己的名声，那失败对他名誉的毁损将远远多于成功为他们带来的荣誉。因战胜他人而获得的荣誉最为光彩夺目，犹如经过琢磨的钻石；所以应力争战胜任何有声望的竞争对手，如果可能，最好在他们擅长的方面胜过他们。谨言慎行的门客和家仆能极大地助长主人的名声，[①]毕竟"主人的名声出自仆人之口"[②]。嫉妒是荣誉的天敌，所以必须消除他人对自己的嫉妒之心，方法是表明自己所追求的是功绩而非名望，并把自己的成就归功于上帝和命运，而非归因于自己的聪明才智。

对帝王君主或最高统治者而言，其荣誉可分为以下五等。第一等荣誉应归于那些江山社稷的创立者，诸如罗穆卢斯[③]、居鲁士大帝[④]、恺撒大帝[⑤]、

---

①英谚曰："仆人眼中无英雄。"(No man is a hero to his valet.)

②语出西塞罗《执政官竞选手记》第5章。

③罗穆卢斯乃罗马城之创建者、古罗马王政时代的第一代国王。

④居鲁士大帝乃波斯阿契美尼德王朝开国之君(在位期前559—前530)。

⑤恺撒大帝乃罗马共和国和罗马帝国的过渡者(当政期前49—前44)。

奥斯曼一世[①]和伊思迈尔一世[②]。第二等荣誉应归于那些立法者，他们亦被称作第二奠基人或“万世之君”，因为他们创立的法典在他们死后仍在治理国家。这类统治者有莱克格斯[③]、梭伦[④]、查士丁尼一世[⑤]、埃德加[⑥]和编纂并颁行《七法全书》的阿方索十世[⑦]。第三等荣誉应归于那些国家的解救者或曰救星，他们或结束了使人民受苦的长期内战，或从异族或暴君的奴役下拯救了祖国。这类雄主有奥古斯都[⑧]、韦斯帕芗[⑨]、奥勒良[⑩]、狄奥多里克[⑪]、英王亨利七世[⑫]和法王亨利四世[⑬]。第四等荣誉应归于国家的拓展者和保卫者，他们或在体面的战争中扩展了自己国家的疆土，或在高贵的战争中击败了敌人的入侵。第五等荣誉应归于有道明君，即那些在秉政期励精图治、创造出太平盛世的君王。这后两类君王不可悉数，无须枚举。

属于为臣者的荣誉可分为四等。第一等应归于分忧之臣，即那些能替君王分担重任的大臣，亦即世人所谓的左辅右弼。第二等应归于统兵之臣，即那些能代替君王率军出征并屡建战功的将帅。第三等应归于心腹之臣，即那些能够给君王以慰藉但不祸国殃民的内臣。第四等应归于称职之臣，

---

①奥斯曼一世乃奥斯曼帝国之缔造者（在位期 1281—1326）。

②伊思迈尔一世乃伊朗萨非王朝之创建者（在位期 1502—1524）。

③莱克格斯（又译来库古），约生活在公元前 9—前 8 世纪，相传为古斯巴达的立法者。

④梭伦是古雅典政治家，公元前 594 年任首席执政官时曾主持修改宪法并制定新的法典，史称“梭伦立法”。

⑤查士丁尼一世乃拜占庭帝国皇帝（在位期 527—565），曾主持编纂《查士丁尼法典》。

⑥埃德加为古英格兰撒克逊系第 12 代王（在位期 959—975），英格兰第一位立法者。

⑦阿方索十世乃西班牙卡斯蒂利亚及莱昂王国之国王（在位期 1252—1284）。

⑧奥古斯都即屋大维，是他结束了恺撒死后群雄混战的局面，使分裂的罗马又重归统一。

⑨韦斯帕芗结束了尼禄死后罗马帝国的内乱。

⑩奥勒良（在位期 270—275）结束了罗马塞维鲁王朝覆灭后“三十僭主”时期的内乱并击败了异族的入侵，恢复了罗马帝国的统一，赢得了“世界光复者”的称号。

⑪狄奥多里克于公元 495 年击败统治意大利的“蛮族”将领鄂多亚克（Odaocer），建立东哥特王国，其国家管理多沿袭罗马旧制。

⑫英王亨利七世于1485 年结束历时 30 年的玫瑰战争，开始都铎王朝的统治。

⑬法王亨利四世结束了胡格诺战争，于 1598 年颁布《南特敕令》，宣布天主教为国教，同时保证胡格诺教徒享有信教自由等权利，在欧洲开创了宗教宽容之先例。

即那些身居高位而效忠君王、日理万机且应付裕如的能臣。此外还有一等堪称最高的荣誉，这种少有的殊荣当属那些勇于为国家利益捐躯或赴汤蹈火的忠臣，如雷古卢斯[①]和德西乌斯父子[②]。

解析

一、真正荣誉之获得是追逐名誉与遮掩美德之间的中庸。

二、获得荣誉的方法：

1. 成为某项伟业的创始者；
2. 能取悦各个阶层；
3. 避免做失败了会有损声誉的事情；
4. 努力在竞争中赢得荣誉；
5. 利用谨言慎行的门客和家仆；
6. 表明自己追求的是功绩而非名望；
7. 把自己的成就归功于上帝和命运。

三、荣誉的等级：

1. 对统治者而言：
    （1）江山社稷的创立者；
    （2）立法者；
    （3）国家的解救者；
    （4）国家的拓展者和保卫者；
    （5）有道明君。
2. 对为臣者而言：
    （1）分忧之臣；

①雷古卢斯（?—约前249），古罗马将军，在第一次布匿战争中被迦太基人俘虏（公元前255年），后随迦太基使团赴罗马议和，趁机力促元老院继续对迦太基的战争，然后遵守自己事先立下的议和不成即回迦太基为囚的诺言，重返迦太基，被杀。

②德西乌斯父子同名，均任过古罗马执政官并均在萨莫奈战争中为国捐躯。父亲战死于坎巴尼亚战役（公元前340年），儿子阵亡于森提努姆战役（公元前295年）。

（2）统兵之臣；

（3）心腹之臣；

（4）称职之臣；

（5）但最高的荣誉应属于那些自我牺牲的忠臣。

Of Honor and Reputation

THE winning of honor, is but the revealing of a man's virtue and worth, without disadvantage. For some in their actions, do woo and effect honor and reputation, which sort of men, are commonly much talked of, but inwardly little admired. And some, contrariwise, darken their virtue in the show of it; so as they be undervalued in opinion. If a man perform that, which hath not been attempted before; or attempted and given over; or hath been achieved, but not with so good circumstance; he shall purchase more honor, than by effecting a matter of greater difficulty or virtue, wherein he is but a follower. If a man so temper his actions, as in some one of them he doth content every faction, or combination of people, the music will be the fuller. A man is an ill husband of his honor, that entereth into any action, the failing wherein may disgrace him, more than the carrying of it through, can honor him. Honor that is gained and broken upon another, hath the quickest reflection, like diamonds cut with facets. And therefore, let a man contend to excel any competitors of his in honor, in outshooting them, if he can, in their own bow. Discreet followers and servants, help much to reputation. Omnis fama a domesticis emanat.① Envy, which is the canker of honor, is best extinguished by declaring a man's self in his ends, rather to seek merit than fame; and by attributing a man's successes, rather to divine Providence and felicity, than to his own virtue or policy.

The true marshalling of the degrees of sovereign honor, are these: In the first place are conditores imperiorum, founders of states and commonwealths; such as were Romulus, Cyrus, Caesar, Ottoman, Ismael. In the second place are legislatores, lawgivers; which are also called second founders, or perpetui principes②, because they govern by their ordinances after they are gone; such were Lycurgus, Solon, Justinian, Eadgar, Alphonsus of Castile, the Wise, that

①All reputation comes from a man's own household.

②perpetual rulers

made the Siete Partidas. In the third place are liberatores, or salvatores, such as compound the long miseries of civil wars, or deliver their countries from servitude of strangers or tyrants; as Augustus Caesar, Vespasianus, Aurelianus, Theodoricus, King Henry the Seventh of England, King Henry the Fourth of France. In the fourth place are propagatores or propugnatores imperii①; such as in honorable wars enlarge their territories, or make noble defence against invaders. And in the last place are patres patriae②; which reign justly, and make the times good wherein they live. Both which last kinds need no examples, they are in such number.

Degrees of honor, in subjects, are, first participes curarum③, those upon whom, princes do discharge the greatest weight of their affairs; their right hands, as we call them. The next are duces belli④, great leaders in war; such as are princes' lieutenants, and do them notable services in the wars. The third are gratiosi, favorites; such as exceed not this scantling, to be solace to the sovereign, and harmless to the people. And the fourth, negotiis pares⑤; such as have great places under princes, and execute their places, with sufficiency. There is an honor, likewise, which may be ranked amongst the greatest, which happeneth rarely; that is, of such as sacrifice themselves to death or danger for the good of their country; as was M. Regulus, and the two Decii.

---

①enlargers or defenders of an empire

②fathers of their country

③partners in the cares of government

④leaders in war

⑤men who are equal to their business

56.论法官的职责

为法官者应当记住，他们的职责是司法，而非立法；他们只能解释法律，而不能制定或修改法律。不然司法权就会变成罗马教会声称其拥有的那种权力，即以阐释《圣经》为名，不惜对其进行增添或改动，甚至宣布在《圣经》里找不到依据的法规，假借古典，暗行新法。[①]法官应该足智多谋，但更应该博古通今；应该为人称道，但更应该受人尊敬；应该自信不疑，但更应该谨言慎行。而最最重要的是，刚正不阿应是他们固有的天性和美德。摩西律法说："挪移邻舍地界者必遭诅咒。"[②]偷挪界石者当然该受惩罚，但法官若在地产归属诉讼中错判误决，那他就是偷挪界石的首犯。一桩误判比多桩犯罪还更有害，因犯罪只是搅浑河水，可误判却是搅浑水源。故此所罗门说："姑息恶人的善人就好比污井浊泉。"[③]法官的职责要涉及到诉讼当事人、控辩双方律师、手下的书记员和执达吏，以及在上的君王和政府。以下笔者就逐一谈论这四方面的关系。

第一，关于诉讼当事人。《圣经》说："有人把审判变成苦艾。"[④]想必还有人会把审判变成醯醋；须知偏私左袒会使审判变苦，而拖延耽搁则会使审判变酸。法官的主要职责是惩治暴行和诈骗，因暴行张狂时可致人于死地，诈骗诡秘时亦可谋财害命。至于那些只为争长论短的鸡毛官司，法庭应视为公务之妨碍不予受理。要作出公正的判决，法官首先应该替自己铺平道

①罗马天主教会声称其有权解释《圣经》的依据是《新约·马太福音》第16章19节，即耶稣对西门说的那段话："我要给你天国的钥匙，凡你在地上禁止的，天上也要禁止；凡你在地上准许的，天上也要准许。"

②语出《旧约·申命记》第27章17节。

③语出《旧约·箴言》第25章26节。

④《旧约·阿摩司书》第5章7节云："你们把审判变成苦艾，把公正善良弃之于地。"

路，就像上帝削山填壑铺平大道那样。[1]所以遇一方当事人专横跋扈、栽赃诬告、施计耍奸、合谋串证，并借助有势力之靠山和强悍之律师的时候，法官的德行就见于能削山填谷把控辩双方摆在平等的地位，从而使自己不偏不倚地作出判决。须知拧鼻子会拧出鲜血，[2]而榨葡萄用力过猛榨出的果汁会有苦涩的核味。故法官务必得当心，解释法律不可穿凿，推理论断不可勉强，因为这世上最要命的曲解就是对法律的曲解。在解释刑法时法官尤须当心，别把旨在以儆效尤的法律变成可滥施的苛刑，别在人民的头顶上铺开《圣经》中说的那张罗网[3]。须知刑法施行过度，就是把法律之网撒向民众。所以对刑法中长期无人援引的条款，或对已不合当今之国情民情的条款，明智的法官应当限制其援用。"既问案情本身，又鞫其背景，此乃一名法官的责任。"[4]故审理人命案时，法官（在法律允许的前提下）应在量刑时想到慈悲为怀，应以严厉的眼光看事，但用仁慈的目光看人。

第二，关于控辩双方律师。耐心而严肃地听取律师陈述，这应是法官的一种基本素质。一名多嘴的法官不啻是一副聒噪的铙钹。对法官而言，凡事先去探询本该到时候才能从律师口中听到的陈述，或过多地中止证人和律师的陈述以显其明察，或用提问（即使是与案情有关的提问）使控方律师不得不提前披露所掌握的情况，都是有失体面的行为。法官开庭审案的职分有四：一是监督律师向证人取证，二是节制冗长、重复或与案情无关的陈述，三是概括、甄选并核实对定案有决定性影响的陈述要点，四是作出裁决或判决。凡超越以上职分的行为都属过度，而过度的原因通常是好夸多言，不耐听讼，或是缺乏与法官之职责相等的记忆力、注意力和沉着稳重。说来也怪，世人每每见到有法官被骄横放肆的律师左右，然而法官本应效法上帝（因他们就坐在上帝的审判席上），而上帝总是"摈斥倨傲者而施恩于谦

---

①《旧约·以赛亚书》第 40 章 4 节云："填平所有沟谷，削平一切山岗，让曲折变笔直，让崎岖变坦平。"

②《旧约·箴言》第 30 章 33 节云："搅牛奶会搅出黄油，拧鼻子会拧出鲜血，动肝火则会动出争端。"

③《旧约·诗篇》第 11 章 6 节有言："他要在恶人的头顶上铺开罗网。"

④引奥维德《哀歌》第 1 卷 1 首 37 行。

恭之人”[①]。但更怪的是，有些法官居然特别喜欢某些知名律师，而这种喜欢只会抬高那些律师的酬金，另外就是使人疑心法院也有后门。当诉讼进展顺利且答辩亦精彩时，法官应用语言或动作对律师表示赞赏，尤其是对败诉的一方，这样既可维护该律师在其委托人心中的声誉，同时亦可使他对其陈述的理由少几分自信。若遇律师在诉讼中施奸耍猾，玩忽职守，举证不实，牵强附会或强词夺理，法官亦应当众给其以适当的斥责。律师不可在法庭上与法官争论，亦不可在法官宣布判决后通过不正当途径使案件重新审理。但另一方面，法官审案不可折中妥协，急于求成，不可让当事人有机会说法庭不听取他的律师和证人之陈述。

第三，关于法庭书记员和执达吏。法院乃神圣之所，因此不仅是法官席不容玷污，而且是法庭的四墙之内都不允许有贪赃舞弊的丑行。因为正如《圣经》所言："从荆棘丛中采不来葡萄。"[②]而若是法院的吏役贪财受贿，法庭也就成了一片荆丛，不可能结出甜美的果实。法院的吏役易受四种恶势力的影响。第一种是专门挑起诉讼以求谋利的讼棍，这种人可使法院逐步增强，但却使国家日渐衰弱。第二种是那些老使法院卷入司法管辖权争论的政客。这种人实际上不是法院的朋友，而是法院的寄生虫。他们鼓吹扩大司法管辖权是为了他们自己的私利。第三种是那些也许可被视为“法庭之左手”[③]的人，这种人刁钻狡猾，满肚子阴谋诡计，并能借此颠倒黑白，误导法庭，从而使审判误入歧途，走进迷宫。第四种是那些敲诈诉讼费的家伙。这些家伙证明了人们把法院比作灌木林并非没有道理，因为来这林中避风雨的羊都得留下一些羊毛。但另一方面，一名熟悉判例、谨言慎行并懂得法庭之使命的资深吏役，则可成为法庭的得力助手，甚至往往能为法官指点迷津。

第四，关于与君王和政府的关系。法官们首先应记住罗马十二铜表法之最后一条：人民之幸福乃最高法律。同时法官们应该懂得，若不以保障人民幸福为目标，法律就只是刁难人的陋规，是未得到神灵启示的神谕[④]。因

①语出《新约·雅各书》第 4 章 6 节或《新约·彼得前书》第 5 章 5节。

②语出《新约·马太福音》第 7 章 16 节。

③喻影响法院公平断案者，因蒙着双眼的正义女神用左手持天平 (右手持剑) 。

④此喻不谬，早在古罗马时期就有人贿赂祭师以求获得满意的神谕。

此国家之一幸事就是君王和政府能经常与司法者协商，而司法者亦能经常向君王和政府商量。前一种协商每每是在司法有碍于政务之时，后一种协商则往往在政府的某种考虑会有碍于法律之实施的时候。须知可引起诉讼的争端也许往往只是归属权问题，但争端的起源及其后果却可能牵涉到国家的核心问题。我说核心问题并非仅仅是指君权，而且指任何有可能导致重大变故、产生危险之先例，或对大部分国民有明显影响的问题。任何人都不可轻率地认为公正的法律和合理的国策会有什么抵牾，因为这两者就像精神和肉体，行动应该协调一致。法官们还应该记住，所罗门王的宝座两边有雄狮护卫。[1]法官也应做雄狮，但仍然是王座下的雄狮，必须时时慎其所为，不可在任何方面约束或妨碍君王行使权力。此外法官们不可对自己的授权缺乏了解，以至于不知要求他们担负的一项主要职责是精到而明智地运用和实施法律。他们恐怕应该记得，圣保罗在言及一部更伟大的法律时说："我们知道这律法天经地义，关键是司法者要依法用之。"[2]

解析

一、法官的职责是：

1. 法律的解释者，而非立法者。

2. 应具有以下品行：

(1) 博古通今；

(2) 受人尊敬；

(3) 谨言慎行；

(4) 刚正不阿。

二、法官的关系——

1. 关于诉讼当事人：

(1) 应努力做到公正及时。

---

①见《旧约·列王纪上》第 10 章 19—20 节。

②语出《新约·提摩太前书》第 1 章 8 节。此引语的后文是："因为这律法并非为好人而制定，而是为……"

（2）压制诉讼当事人的专横跋扈、施技耍奸与强势。

（3）应避免穿凿的解释和勉强的推断。

2. 关于控辩双方的律师：

（1）应该表现出耐心和庄重，记住自己的职责是——

（a）监督取证；

（b）节制陈述；

（c）概括陈述要点；

（d）作出裁决或判决。

（2）不应为律师所左右。

（3）诉讼进展顺利时应对律师表示赞赏，必要的时候也应给予适当的斥责。

3. 对于法庭书记员和执达吏：

（1）应该制止丑闻与丑行。

（2）压制下列人等——

（a）专门挑起诉讼以求谋利的讼棍；

（b）常把法院卷入司法管辖权争论的政客；

（c）玩弄阴谋诡计使审判误入歧途之人；

（d）敲诈诉讼费者。

4. 关于与君王和政府的关系：

（1）应为人民幸福与君王和政府协商；

（2）注意私人问题常常会造成社会后果；

（3）法官应做雄狮，但仍然是王座下的雄狮；

（4）应精到明智地运用和实施法律。

Of Judicature

JUDGES ought to remember, that their office is jus dicere, and not jus dare; to interpret law, and not to make law, or give law. Else will it be like the authority, claimed by the Church of Rome, which under pretext of exposition of Scripture, doth not stick to add and alter; and to pronounce that which they do not find; and by show of antiquity, to introduce novelty. Judges ought to be more learned, than witty, more reverend, than plausible, and more advised, than confident. Above all things, integrity is their portion and proper virtue. Cursed (saith the law) is he that removeth the landmark. The mislayer of a mere-stone is to blame. But it is the unjust judge, that is the capital remover of landmarks, when he defineth amiss, of lands and property. One foul sentence doth more hurt, than many foul examples. For these do but corrupt the stream, the other corrupteth the fountain. So with Solomon, Fons turbatus, et vena corrupta, est justus cadens in causa sua coram adversario.① The office of judges may have reference unto the parties that use, unto the advocates that plead, unto the clerks and ministers of justice underneath them, and to the sovereign or state above them.

First, for the causes or parties that sue. There be (saith the Scripture) that turn judgment, into wormwood; and surely there be also, that turn it into vinegar; for injustice maketh it bitter, and delays make it sour. The principal duty of a judge, is to suppress force and fraud; whereof force is the more pernicious, when it is open, and fraud, when it is close and disguised. Add thereto contentious suits, which ought to be spewed out, as the surfeit of courts. A judge ought to prepare his way to a just sentence, as God useth to prepare his way, by raising valleys and taking down hills: so when there appeareth on either side an high hand, violent prosecution, cunning advantages taken, combination, power, great counsel, then is the virtue of a judge seen, to make inequality equal; that he may plant his judgment as upon an even ground. Qui fortiter emungit, elicit sanguinem;② and where the wine-press is hard wrought, it yields a harsh wine, that tastes of the grape-stone. Judges must beware of hard constructions, and strained inferences; for there is no worse torture, than the torture of laws. Specially in case of laws penal, they ought to have care, that that which was meant for terror, be not turned into rigor; and that they bring not upon the people, that shower whereof the Scripture speaketh, Pluet super eos laqueos;③ for penal laws pressed, are a shower of snares upon the people. Therefore let penal laws, if they have been sleepers of long, or if they be grown unfit for the present time, be by wise judges confined in the execution: Judicis officium est, ut res, ita tempora rerum, etc.④ In causes of life and death, judges ought (as far as the law permitteth) in justice to remember

①A just man, failing in his cause before his adversary is as a troubled fountain and a defiled spring.

②He who wrings the nose violently, draws blood.

③He shall rain snares upon them.

④The duty of a judge is to regard not only facts but their occasions.

mercy; and to cast a severe eye upon the example, but a merciful eye upon the person.

Secondly, for the advocates and counsel that plead. Patience and gravity of hearing, is an essential part of justice; and an overspeaking judge is no well-tuned cymbal. It is no grace to a judge, first to find that, which he might have heard in due time from the bar; or to show quickness of conceit, in cutting off evidence or counsel too short; or to prevent information by questions, though pertinent. The parts of a judge in hearing, are four: to direct the evidence; to moderate length, repetition, or impertinency of speech; to recapitulate, select, and collate the material points, of that which hath been said; and to give the rule or sentence. Whatsoever is above these is too much; and proceedeth either of glory, and willingness to speak, or of impatience to hear, or of shortness of memory, or of want of a staid and equal attention. It is a strange thing to see, that the boldness of advocates should prevail with judges; whereas they should imitate God, in whose seat they sit; who represseth the presumptuous, and giveth grace to the modest. But it is more strange, that judges should have noted favorites; which cannot but cause multiplication of fees, and suspicion of by-ways. There is due from the judge to the advocate, some commendation and gracing, where causes are well handled and fair pleaded; especially towards the side which obtaineth not; for that upholds in the client, the reputation of his counsel, and beats down in him the conceit of his cause. There is likewise due to the public, a civil reprehension of advocates, where there appeareth cunning counsel, gross neglect, slight information, indiscreet pressing, or an overbold defence. And let not the counsel at the bar, chop with the judge, nor wind himself into the handling of the cause anew, after the judge hath declared his sentence; but, on the other side, let not the judge meet the cause half way, nor give occasion to the party, to say his counsel or proofs were not heard.

Thirdly, for that that concerns clerks and ministers. The place of justice is an hallowed place; and therefore not only the bench, but the foot-place; and precincts and purprise thereof, ought to be preserved without scandal and corruption. For certainly grapes (as the Scripture saith) will not be gathered of thorns or thistles; either can justice yield her fruit with sweetness, amongst the briars and brambles of catching and polling clerks, and ministers. The attendance of courts, is subject to four bad instruments. First, certain persons that are sowers of suits; which make the court swell, and the country pine. The second sort is of those, that engage courts in quarrels of jurisdiction, and are not truly amici curiae, but parasiti curiae, ① in puffing a court up beyond

①not “friends of the court”, but “parasites of the court”

her bounds, for their own scraps and advantage. The third sort, is of those that may be accounted the left hands of courts; persons that are full of nimble and sinister tricks and shifts, whereby they pervert the plain and direct courses of courts, and bring justice into oblique lines and labyrinths. And the fourth, is the poller and exacter of fees; which justifies the common resemblance of the courts of justice, to the bush whereunto, while the sheep flies for defence in weather, he is sure to lose part of his fleece. On the other side, an ancient clerk, skilful in precedents, wary in proceeding, and understanding in the business of the court, is an excellent finger of a court; and doth many times point the way to the judge himself.

Fourthly, for that which may concern the sovereign and estate. Judges ought above all to remember the conclusion of the Roman Twelve Tables; Salus populi suprema lex;① and to know that laws, except they be in order to that end, are but things captious, and oracles not well inspired. Therefore it is an happy thing in a state, when kings and states do often consult with judges; and again, when judges do often consult with the king and state: the one, when there is matter of law, intervenient in business of state; the other, when there is some consideration of state, intervenient in the matter of law. For many times the things deduced to judgment may be meum and tuum, when the reason and consequence thereof may trench to point of estate: I call matter of estate, not only the parts of sovereignty, but whatsoever introduceth any great alteration, or dangerous precedent; or concerneth manifestly any great portion of people. And let no man weakly conceive, that just laws and true policy have any antipathy; for they are like the spirits and sinews, that one moves with the other. Let judges also remember, that Solomon's throne was supported by lions on both sides: let them be lions, but yet lions under the throne; being circumspect that they do not check or oppose any points of sovereignty. Let not judges also be ignorant of their own right, as to think there is not left to them, as a principal part of their office, a wise use and application of laws. For they may remember, what the apostle saith of a greater law than theirs; Nos scimus quia lex bona est, modo quis ea utatur legitime.②

---

①The people's safty is the highest law.

②We know that the law is good only if a man use it lawfully.

57.谈愤怒

戢怒霁颜，了无怨愤，这不过是斯多葛派哲学家们的夸夸其谈。世人已有更切合实际的神示："有怒就发，但不可因发怒而犯罪，亦不可待日落西山时还愤愤不平。"[①]愤怒乃人之常情，但必须在程度上有所节制，在时间上有所限制。以下笔者将首先讨论如何克服易怒这种性格倾向和习惯；其次谈谈如何抑制发怒这种特殊行为，或如何使这种行为不造成严重危害；最后再说说怎样使他人动怒或息怒。

要克服动辄发怒的倾向和习惯，唯一的办法就是对发怒的后果进行认真的反思，想想它是怎样搅乱你的生活。反思的时间最好是在一阵怒气完全平息之后。塞内加说得不错："怒气就像倾塌的房屋，它在其倒下的地方留下一片废墟。"[②]《圣经》亦规劝世人"要保持冷静，耐心等待"[③]。谁要失去耐心，谁就会失去理智。而人不可学蜜蜂，"为了那愤怒的一蜇而断送自己的生命"[④]。愤怒无疑是一种可鄙的感情，因为它最常出现在其容易支配的妇孺病残和老人们身上。不过常人须注意，若万一被人激怒，应对冒犯者表示出鄙夷，而不应该表现出畏惧，不然你所受到的伤害就可能显得比实际上更重。这一点不难办到，只要你肯把上述提醒作为自己的规则。

说到如何抑制愤怒，须知发怒主要有三方面的原因。一是对伤害过于敏感。凡动怒者无不觉得自己受到了伤害，所以感情脆弱者必然经常动怒，他们总会遇上那么多令人恼怒的事，而这些事对性格坚强者则无甚影响。第二个原因是受伤害者认为对他施加的伤害及其所处的环境使他蒙受了耻辱，而羞辱和伤害一样可使人怒火中烧，甚至比伤害本身更能使人上火。

①语出《新约·以弗所书》第4章26节。

②语出塞内加《论愤怒》第1章1节。

③语出《新约·路加福音》第21章19节。此乃耶稣向门徒们预言灾难和迫害将临时的告诫。

④引自维吉尔《农事诗》第4章238行。

所以敏于发现自己受轻辱的人常常动怒。第三个原因是舆论侵害了某人的名誉,而这最能使人怒不可遏。抑制这种怒气的办法只有一种,那就是贡萨洛[①]当年常说的“为名誉建造一个更坚固的掩体”。不过在上述情况下,抑制愤怒的最佳办法是为自己赢得时间,使自己相信报仇泄愤的时机尚未成熟,但同时又已预见到了那个时机,这样你便可以使自己平静,从而不致当场发作。

若要使当场发作的愤怒不造成严重危害,有两个要点须特别注意。一是泄愤之言辞不可过于尖刻,尤其是不可指名道姓地恶语伤人,须知泛泛而骂亦可解恨。同时发怒者不可揭人老底,因为那样会使众人都回避与你交往。第二个要点是不可因一时愤怒而断然抛开自己的职责。总之不管你怎样表现愤怒,都不要做出无可挽回的事情。

至于要使他人动怒,这首先是要选择好时机,即要在对方心情最糟、最易发火时激怒他们,另外再用你所能找到的一切手段(如上文间接提及者)来加重对方受辱的感觉。不想让他人动怒的办法正好相反,即如果要向某人讲某件可能会令他生气的事情,开口的时间一定要选在他心情好的时候,因为第一感觉非常重要;另外就是尽可能地使他觉得他所受到的伤害中没有轻辱的成分,你可以把那伤害归因于误会、担心、激动或任何你能想到的理由。

解析

一、愤怒可被控制,但不能被浇灭。

二、要克服易怒的习惯,就该认识到——

1. 它极坏的后果;

2. 它的可鄙性。

三、如何抑制愤怒:

1. 认识发怒的原因:

---

①贡萨洛(1453—1515),西班牙著名将军,一生战功卓著。

(1) 过于敏感;

(2) 认为被人侮辱;

(3) 觉得被舆论侵害了荣誉。

2. 考虑到要为自己赢得从长计议的时间。

四、如何不让愤怒造成严重危害:

1. 言论不可过于尖刻,不能伤人;

2. 不可因一时愤怒抛开自己的职责。

五、怎样使人动怒或息怒:

1. 让人动怒的方法——

(1) 在对方心情最糟、最易发火时激怒他们;

(2) 让他相信自己受到了侮辱。

2. 小心避免这些便能让人息怒。

Of Anger

TO SEEK to extinguish anger utterly, is but a bravery of the Stoics. We have better oracles: Be angry, but sin not. Let not the sun go down upon your anger. Anger must be limited and confined, both in race and in time. We will first speak how the natural inclination and habit to be angry, may be attempted and calmed. Secondly, how the particular motions of anger may be repressed, or at least refrained from doing mischief. Thirdly, how to raise anger, or appease anger in another.

For the first; there is no other way but to meditate, and ruminate well upon the effects of anger, how it troubles man's life. And the best time to do this, is to look back upon anger, when the fit is thoroughly over. Seneca saith well, That anger is like ruin, which breaks itself upon that it falls. The Scripture exhorteth us to possess our souls in patience. Whosoever is out of patience, is out of possession of his soul. Men must not turn bees; ... animasque in vulnere ponunt. [①] Anger is certainly a kind of baseness; as it appears well in the weakness of those subjects in whom it reigns; children, women, old folks, sick folks. Only men must beware, that they carry their anger rather

① ... and they leave their life in the wound.

with scorn, than with fear; so that they may seem rather to be above the injury, than below it; which is a thing easily done, if a man will give law to himself in it.

For the second point; the causes and motives of anger, are chiefly three. First, to be too sensible of hurt; for no man is angry, that feels not himself hurt; and therefore tender and delicate persons must needs be oft angry; they have so many things to trouble them, which more robust natures have little sense of. The next is, the apprehension and construction of the injury offered, to be, in the circumstances thereof, full of contempt: for contempt is that, which putteth an edge upon anger, as much or more than the hurt itself. And therefore, when men are ingenious in picking out circumstances of contempt, they do kindle their anger much. Lastly, opinion of the touch of a man's reputation, doth multiply and sharpen anger. Wherein the remedy is, that a man should have, as Consalvo was wont to say, telam honoris crassiorem[①]. But in all refrainings of anger, it is the best remedy to win time; and to make a man's self believe, that the opportunity of his revenge is not yet come, but that he foresees a time for it; and so to still himself in the meantime, and reserve it.

To contain anger from mischief, though it take hold of a man, there be two things, whereof you must have special caution. The one, of extreme bitterness of words, especially if they be aculeate and proper; for cummunia maledicta[②] are nothing so much; and again, that in anger a man reveal no secrets; for that, makes him not fit for society. The other, that you do not peremptorily break off, in any business, in a fit of anger; but howsoever you show bitterness, do not act anything, that is not revocable.

For raising and appeasing anger in another; it is done chiefly by choosing of times, when men are frowardest and worst disposed, to incense them. Again, by gathering (as was touched before) all that you can find out, to aggravate the contempt. And the two remedies are by the contraries. The former to take good times, when first to relate to a man an angry business; for the first impression is much; and the other is, to sever, as much as may be, the construction of the injury from the point of contempt; imputing it to misunderstanding, fear, passion, or what you will.

---

①a thicker web of honour

②general abuse

58.谈世事之变迁

所罗门说这世间并无新事。[①]甚至像柏拉图以为所有知识都不过是回忆[②]一样，所罗门亦认为任何新事都不过是被人遗忘之往事[③]。由此看来，勒忒河[④]不仅流在冥国，而且也淌在人间。有位深奥的占星学家[⑤]曾说，天地间只有两种东西恒久不变，一种是相互间永远不即不离、保持等距的恒星，一种是永远严守时刻的周日运动[⑥]，除这二者之外，世间万物都转瞬即逝。毋庸置疑，万事万物都一直在不断变化，从未停息。但这世上有两块巨大的裹尸布，它们能把过去的一切都埋入忘川，这两块裹尸布就是洪水和地震。至于大火与大旱，它们虽可造成毁灭，但不会使人类绝种。法厄同驾太阳车不过就跑了一天。[⑦]以利亚时代那场大旱虽延续三年，但却只限于一域，结果

---

①《旧约·传道书》第1章9节云："已有之事，后必再有。已行之事，后必再行。日光之下并无新事。"《传道书》之传道者即大卫王的儿子、耶路撒冷之王所罗门。

②参见柏拉图《对话集·斐多篇》。柏拉图认为灵魂不朽，人降生尘世前在理念世界是自由而有知的，但降生尘世后灵魂被肉体禁锢，人便失去了自由和知识。要想重新获得知识就得回忆，就得闭目塞听，用精神的力量唤起对理念世界的固有记忆。

③《旧约·传道书》第1章11节云："从前之事今世无人记得，将来之事将来的后世亦不会记得。"

④勒忒河乃希腊神话中冥国之忘川，入冥国之鬼魂饮一口忘川水就会忘却人间和世事。

⑤西方学者多认为这位"占星学家"可能指意大利哲学家泰莱西奥（Bernardino Telesio，1509—1588），因其《物性论》第1卷10章中有相似之说。另培根对泰莱西奥推崇备至，称其为"第一个现代人"（"first of the moderns"）。

⑥周日运动乃天体在天球上每一恒星日内绕天轴由东向西旋转一周的运动。这实际上是地球自西向东绕轴自转的反映。

⑦据希腊神话传说，法厄同是太阳神赫利俄斯（后与阿波罗混为一体者）之子，他曾私驾其父的太阳车狂奔，险些使整个世界着火焚烧，幸宙斯见状用雷将其击毙，遂免大难。

人们仍熬过了旱荒。[①]至于在西印度[②]常见的由雷电引起的大火，其燃烧范围也总是有限。这里须进一步指出的是，虽说在毁灭性的洪水和地震中也有人逃生，但幸存者往往都是些无知无识的山民，他们不可能对过去作任何记载，结果就和无人幸存一样，所有往事都被湮没在遗忘之中。若对西印度人详加考察就会发现，与旧大陆的各民族相比较，他们很有可能是一个更新的人种，或者说是一个更年轻的民族。而更有可能的是，虽说埃及的祭师曾告诉梭伦大西岛之沉没是由于一场地震，[③]但曾经发生在西印度的毁灭性灾难却并非是地震，而是一场特大的洪水，因为在那些地区地震很少发生。而且从另一方面看，西印度有许多浩荡的大河，与之相比，欧、亚、非三洲的河流不过是小溪。另外他们的安第斯山也远比我们欧洲的山脉更高。因此可以想象，那里残存的人类正是凭借高山才得以在那场特大洪水中获救。至于马基雅弗利的看法笔者倒不以为然。他认为往事被人类遗忘主要是因为宗教相争，并诬蔑教皇格列高利一世曾倾其全力消灭多神教之古迹古俗。[④]但笔者以为宗教狂热不会有那么大的作用，也不可能延续很长时间，譬如紧随格列高利之后的萨比尼安教皇就曾复兴多神教的风俗习惯[⑤]。

第十重天的变化不宜由本文来讨论。但如果这世界能延续世人所想象的那么久，那柏拉图所说的“大年”[⑥]也许倒真会起什么作用，不过这种作用并非是使每个具体的人死而复生，而是使整个世界周而复始(有人以为天体对世间细小纤微的事也有精确的影响，但这只是想象，并非实情)。彗星对世间大事无疑也具有影响力和作用力，但世人只是对其运行轨道进行注视和观察，而忽略了它们所带来的影响，尤其是各种不同的影响，即忽略了通过观测不同彗星的亮度、颜色、光线变化以及出现在天上的位置或持续

---

①事见《旧约·列王纪上》第17—18章。

②当时世人用“西印度”称新发现的美洲。

③关于梭伦在埃及（以及塞浦路斯和小亚等地）的十年游历，希罗多德和普鲁塔克都有所记载。关于大西岛沉没一说可参阅本书《论预言》末段及其注释。

④参见马基雅弗利《论李维》第2卷5章。

⑤萨比尼安教皇在位时（604—606）曾出现过多神教之复兴。

⑥参见柏拉图《对话集·蒂默亚篇》。古代西人视所有天体在完成其所有公转之后重归世界开始时它们所处的起点那一年为“大年”，并认为世界从这一年又重新开始。

时间，从而得知何种彗星可带来何种影响。

我曾听说过一件有趣的事，而我不想让此事不被人稍加注意就完全丢开。据说有人在低地国家[①]（我不知道在哪个地区）观察到，那里每隔三十五年就会出现一次相同的年景和气候，如严霜、多雨、大旱、暖冬和凉夏等等。他们把这种现象叫做“复初”。我之所以想提及这件事，是因为我回顾过去时亦发现有相似现象。

现在且让笔者抛开自然界之变迁，转而谈谈人世间的变化。人世间最大的变化莫过于宗教派别的更迭，因为宗教对人心的控制就好比轨道对行星的支配。真正的教会建立在那块磐石之上，[②]其余的教会则颠簸于时间的汪洋。所以笔者在此只谈谈新教派产生的原因，并就此提供一点建议，以期人类微弱的识别力能制止如此巨大的变更。

当一个被广泛接受的教会因内部倾轧而四分五裂，当教徒们的神圣感已衰弱殆尽，其行为作风也开始有辱教门，而且这种情形又发生在一个愚昧无知的野蛮时代，那世人便可担心会出现一种新的宗教，尤其是再遇有什么张狂怪异之人自封为新教领袖的时候。但新教派若不具有以下两种特性，世人对其就不必担心，因为它不可能广为传播。这两种特性之一是要取代或反对已确立的权威，须知最得民心的行为莫过于此；其二是允许教徒过一种可花天酒地、寻欢作乐的生活，因为纯理论的异端邪说（如古时的阿里乌派[③]和当今的阿米尼乌斯派[④]）虽然也能极大地蛊惑人心，但却无力造成政局的重大变化，除非他们借助于政治活动。新教派之树立有三种方式：一是借用神迹和奇迹，二是依靠雄辩而明智的布道，三则是凭借武力。至于以身殉教，笔者将其归入奇迹一类，因为殉教之行为似乎超越了人性的力

---

①16 世纪以前指尼德兰地区，后指荷兰、比利时、卢森堡等国。

②“真正的教会”指基督教会，“磐石”之说见《新约·马太福音》第 16 章 18 节。

③阿里乌派是早期基督教一“异端”教派，其领袖阿里乌（Arius，约 250—336）拒不接受“耶稣（圣子）与上帝（圣父）同性（同体）”之正统信条，在公元 325 年的尼西亚宗教会议上被宣布为“异端”。该教派还反对教会拥有大量土地和财产，深得下层人民拥护。

④阿米尼乌斯派是欧洲宗教改革时期一“异端”教派，其领袖阿米尼乌斯（Arminius，1560—1609）为荷兰基督教新教神学家，他坚决反对加尔文的“先定论”（即人在现实生活中的成败和来生是否得救都是在生前由上帝决定的）。

量。而且我还可以把至善至美的圣洁生活也归入奇迹。无可置疑，要防止宗派分裂和新教出现，教会只有革除陈规陋习，调和小的争端，实行温和政策，放弃血腥迫害，对异教发起人运用说服和提升的办法加以争取，而不用暴力和仇恨的手段将其激怒。

战争之变化可谓无穷无尽，不知凡几，但主要的变化在于三个方面：一是发生战争的地域，二是作战使用的武器，三是运用的战略战术。古代的战争似乎多是由东向西，因为充当侵略者的波斯人、亚述人、阿拉伯人和鞑靼人都是东方民族。高卢人当然是西方人，但我们从古籍中得知他们只进行过两次侵略，一次是侵入加拉西亚[①]，另一次是进犯罗马[②]。不过东方和西方在天上并无明确的坐标，[③]故古人对后来的战争不再有自东向西或自西向东的明确记载。但南北两方的方位有明确坐标，所以世人确切地知道少有或不曾有远在南方的民族入侵北方，而相反的情况倒屡见不鲜。由此可见，世界之北部事实上是个更好战的地区，这也许是因为那个地区的星象，也许是因为北方有广阔的陆地(而据世人所知，南方则几乎全是汪洋)，要不然就是因为那个更为明显的原因，即北方地区的寒冷，而那种寒冷使当地居民无需训练便可在身强力壮和勇猛无畏方面无与伦比。[④]

当一个大国或帝国开始分崩离析、风雨飘摇的时候，世人便知肯定会有战争，因为那些庞大的帝国在强盛之时，往往都削弱或取消了它们所征服的各民族国家的武装，整个帝国的防御都依靠统一的帝国军队，所以当帝国衰微时，帝国大家庭的各民族国家也随之没落，成为外族人掠夺的对象。罗马帝国衰亡时的情形就是如此。[⑤]查理大帝之后的查理曼帝国也是这

①加拉西亚乃古时小亚细亚一地区 (在今土耳其境内)，公元前 279 年高卢人入侵该地区并建立加拉西亚王国，该国于公元前 25 年成为罗马帝国的一个行省。

②公元前 390 年，波河流域的高卢人长驱直入，直逼罗马，战败的罗马人不得不退守卡匹托尔山凭借神庙的庇护进行抵抗，后不得不用重金赎城。

③意即东方和西方不像北方那样有北极星作为坐标。

④此段话中所说的南方和北方是以欧洲为中心而言，更准确地说是以西南欧为中心而言。在中世纪前半期，较文明的西南欧人并不把北欧人 (斯堪的纳维亚人) 视为自己的同类。

⑤对风雨飘摇中的罗马帝国进行“掠夺”的外族人有西哥特人 (公元 410 年攻占曾千年不陷的罗马城)、汪达尔人 (先入西班牙和法国，后于 439 年攻占迦太基) 和匈奴人 (443 年进兵君士坦丁堡，东罗马战败求和，向匈奴人交纳岁币) 等。

样，每只鸟都夺得一片羽毛①。而要是西班牙帝国一旦分裂，其结局也不会例外。多个王国之结盟与合并也同样会导致战争，因为当某个国家变得过于强盛时，它就会成为一场必然要泛滥的洪水。这种情形在历史上已见于罗马、土耳其、西班牙和其他帝国。当这个世界的未开化民族占绝对少数，而且当他们多为不知其谋生手段便不愿结婚成家或生儿育女者时(当今除鞑靼地方②外世界各地的蛮族差不多是这种情形)，这个世界并无人口泛滥的危险。但若有人口众多的民族继续繁衍生息而不筹划其国计民生，那他们每隔一两代人就必然要将其人口之一部分迁往他处。而古代北方民族曾用抽签的办法来决定这种迁徙，即根据抽签来决定哪些人可以留下，哪些人应该离乡背井去自谋生路。③当一个尚武的国家日薄西山之时，它也肯定会招来战争，因为这种国家在武力上走下坡路时往往会在经济上变得很富有，所以早已成了别人想啃的肥肉，而它们军事上的衰微必然会鼓励他国对其用兵。

说到武器的使用，这几乎无章可循且不大为世人所注意，然而笔者仍发现，连武器之使用也有其变化与轮回。可以肯定的是，世人已知印度人在奥克斯拉斯城之战中曾使用过火炮，即那种被马其顿人称为雷电或魔火的武器。④而众所周知，中国人使用火炮大约已有两千年历史。武器的性能和使用有以下变化趋势：一是要能攻击远处目标，以减少使用者的危险，这种变化已见于大炮与滑膛枪的出现；二是攻击力要强，在这方面大炮已超越了各种攻城槌和古代的所有发明；三是要使用方便，即要容易携带，容易操纵并在任何气候条件下都能使用等等。

①“夺得一片羽毛的鸟”也许指后来将帝国一分为三的查理大帝的三个孙子，也许指夺得地中海西部控制权的阿拉伯人、夺得多瑙河流域的马扎尔人 (匈牙利人) 和夺得法国西北部滨海地区的诺曼人等。

②这是个较模糊的地理概念，中世纪时指受蒙古人统治的自东欧至亚洲的大片地区。

③相传最初从北方迁徙 (或曰入侵) 不列颠的盎格鲁人和撒克逊人就是用抽签的方法从他们的部落中选出的。

④公元 327 年，亚历山大大帝率领的马其顿大军曾占领过印度西北部。但关于印度人使用火炮一说似乎并无正典记载。据说菲洛斯特拉托斯所著《阿波罗尼乌斯传》言及印度人使用火炮事，但阿波罗尼乌斯在当时 (公元 1 世纪) 就被世人视为术士 (magician)，其言不足为凭。

至于战略战术的变化，起初人们作战很依赖军队的数量，战争主要是靠兵力和士气取胜。那时候他们往往是选定日子对阵厮杀，在公平的战斗中决出胜负。可以说当时他们还不懂排兵布阵。后来他们慢慢懂得了兵不在多而在精的道理，并逐渐学会了抢占有利地形和迂回包抄、声东击西等战术，而且指挥部署的能力也大为提高。

一个国家年轻时往往武事最盛，到壮年时其学术则会繁荣，然后会有一段文武并兴的时期，最后便步入文竭武衰的残年，但此时其工艺技术和商业贸易则最为发达。学术也自有其幼稚的童年期，接着才有风华正茂的青春期，然后是厚积薄发的壮年期，最后便步入每况愈下的暮年晚景。然而这轮回变迁之世事不宜多看，以免那无常的巨轮令我们头晕。至于无常的巨轮是如何旋转，那不过是一整套妄语虚言，故不宜由本文来加以解说。

解析

一、所有的知识都是回忆；相反，所有表面的毁灭都只不过是变化与遗忘。

二、造成遗忘的——

1. 大多是洪水(美洲)、地震；
2. 少数是大火、干旱；
3. 极少是宗教相争(格列高利一世和萨比尼安教皇)。

三、自然界之变迁——

1. 整个世界的周而复始可能造成过去事件的重现；
2. 应仔细观察彗星的影响；
3. 应该注意每三十五年就会出现一次相同气候这一现象。

四、人世间之变迁——

1. 宗教上：

(1) 派别产生的原因——

(a) 内部倾轧；

(b) 教士道德的败坏；

(c) 愚蠢、无知和野蛮的时代。

(2) 派别巩固的原因——

(a) 取代或反对已确立的权威;

(b) 允许教徒过一种花天酒地、寻欢作乐的生活。

(3) 派别树立之方式——

(a) 神迹和奇迹;

(b) 雄辩和明智;

(c) 武力。

(4) 阻止派别分裂的办法——

(a) 革除陈规陋习;

(b) 调和小的争端;

(c) 实行温和政策;

(d) 赢得异教领导人。

2. 战争中:

(1) 发生战争的领域——

(a) 通常由东向西(高卢人侵犯加拉西亚和罗马例外);

(b) 很少由南向北;

(c) 出现在下列情况后——

大国分崩离析,

人口的膨胀,

帝国衰微。

(2) 作战使用的武器——

(a) 大炮胜过攻城槌;

(b) 它的优点在于——

射程远,

攻击力强,

便于携带。

(3) 运用的战略战术——

(a) 起初依赖于军队的数量;

(b) 现依靠兵力和适当的战略;

(c)一个国家年轻时武事最盛,壮年时学术繁荣,衰竭残年时工艺技术和商业贸易最为发达。

Of Vicissitude of Things

SOLOMON saith, There is no new thing upon the earth. So that as Plato had an imagination, That all knowledge was but remembrance; so Solomon giveth his sentence, That all novelty is but oblivion. Whereby you may see, that the river of Lethe runneth as well above ground as below. There is an abstruse astrologer that saith, If it were not for two things that are constant (the one is, that the fixed stars ever stand a like distance one from another, and never come nearer together, nor go further asunder; the other, that the diurnal motion perpetually keepeth time), no individual would last one moment. Certain it is, that the matter is in a perpetual flux, and never at a stay. The great winding-sheets, that bury all things in oblivion, are two; deluges and earthquakes. As for conflagrations and great droughts, they do not merely dispeople and destroy. Phaeton's car went but a day. And the three years' drought in the time of Elias, was but particular, and left people alive. As for the great burnings by lightnings, which are often in the West Indies, they are but narrow. But in the other two destructions, by deluge and earthquake, it is further to be noted, that the remnant of people which hap to be reserved, are commonly ignorant and mountainous people, that can give no account of the time past; so that the oblivion is all one, as if none had been left. If you consider well of the people of the West Indies, it is very probable that they are a newer or a younger people, than the people of the Old World. And it is much more likely, that the destruction that hath heretofore been there, was not by earthquakes (as the Egyptian priest told Solon concerning the island of Atlantis, that it was swallowed by an earthquake), but rather that it was desolated by a particular deluge. For earthquakes are seldom in those parts. But on the other side, they have such pouring rivers, as the rivers of Asia and Africa and Europe, are but brooks to them. Their Andes, likewise, or mountains, are far higher than those with us; whereby it seems, that the remnants of generation of men, were in such a particular deluge saved. As for the observation that Machiavel hath, that the jealousy of sects, doth much extinguish the memory of things; traducing Gregory the Great, that he did what in him lay, to extinguish all heathen antiquities; I do not find that those zeals do any great effects, nor last long; as it appeared in the succession of Sabinian, who did revive the former antiquities.

The vicissitude of mutations in the superior globe, are no fit matter for this present argument. It may be, Plato's great year, if the world should last so long, would have some effect; not in renewing the state of like individuals (for that is the fume of those, that conceive the celestial bodies have more accurate influences upon these things below, than indeed they have), but in gross. Comets, out of question, have likewise power and effect, over the gross and mass of things; but they are rather gazed upon, and waited upon in their journey, than wisely observed in their effects; specially in, their respective effects; that is, what kind of comet, for magnitude, color, version of the beams, placing in the reign of heaven, or lasting, produceth what kind of effects.

There is a toy which I have heard, and I would not have it given over, but waited upon a little. They say it is observed in the Low Countries (I know not in what part) that every five and thirty years, the same kind and suit of years and weathers come about again; as great frosts, great wet, great droughts, warm winters, summers with little heat, and the like; and they call it the Prime. It is a thing I do the rather mention, because, computing backwards, I have found some concurrence.

But to leave these points of nature, and to come to men. The greatest vicissitude of things amongst men, is the vicissitude of sects and religions. For those orbs rule in men's minds most. The true religion is built upon the rock; the rest are tossed, upon the waves of time. To speak, therefore, of the causes of new sects; and to give some counsel concerning them, as far as the weakness of human judgment can give stay, to so great revolutions.

When the religion formerly received, is rent by discords; and when the holiness of the professors of religion, is decayed and full of scandal; and withal the times be stupid, ignorant, and barbarous; you may doubt the springing up of a new sect; if then also, there should arise any extravagant and strange spirit, to make himself author thereof. If a new sect have not two properties, fear it not; for it will not spread. The one is the supplanting, or the opposing, of authority established; for nothing is more popular than that. The other is the giving license to pleasures, and a voluptuous life. For as for speculative heresies (such as were in ancient times the Arians, and now the Arminians), though they work mightily upon men's wits, yet they do not produce any great alterations in states; except it be by the help of civil occasions. There be three manner of plantations of new sects. By the power of signs and miracles; by the eloquence, and wisdom, of speech and persuasion; and by the sword. For martyrdoms, I reckon them amongst miracles; because they seem to exceed the strength of human nature: and I may do the like, of superlative and admirable holiness of life. Surely there is no better way, to stop the rising of new sects and schisms, than to reform abuses; to compound the smaller differences; to proceed mildly, and not with sanguinary persecutions; and rather to take off the principal authors by winning and advancing them, than to enrage them by violence and bitterness.

The changes and vicissitude in wars are many; but chiefly in three things; in the seats or stages of the war; in the weapons; and in the manner of the conduct. Wars, in ancient time, seemed more to move from east to west; for the Persians, Assyrians, Arabians, Tartars (which were the invaders) were all eastern people. It is true, the Gauls were western; but we read but of two incursions of theirs: the one to Gallo-Grecia, the other to Rome. But east and west have no certain points of heaven; and no more have the wars, either from the east or west, any certainty of observation. But north and south are fixed; and it hath seldom or never been seen that the far southern people have invaded the northern, but contrariwise. Whereby it is manifest that the northern tract of the world, is in nature the more martial region: be it in respect of the stars of that hemisphere; or of the great continents that are upon the north, whereas the south part, for aught that is known, is almost all sea; or (which is most apparent) of the cold of the northern parts, which is that which, without aid of discipline, doth make the bodies hardest, and the courages warmest.

Upon the breaking and shivering of a great state and empire, you may be sure to have wars. For great empires, while they stand, do enervate and destroy the forces of the natives which they have subdued, resting upon their own protecting forces; and then when they fail also, all goes to ruin, and they become a prey. So was it in the decay of the Roman empire; and likewise in the empire of Almaigne, after Charles the Great, every bird taking a feather; and were not unlike to befall to Spain, if it should break. The great accessions and unions of kingdoms, do likewise stir up wars; for when a state grows to an over-power, it is like a great flood, that will be sure to overflow. As it hath been seen in the states of Rome, Turkey, Spain, and others. Look when the world hath fewest barbarous peoples, but such as commonly will not marry or generate, except they know means to live (as it is almost everywhere at this day, except Tartary), there is no danger of inundations of people; but when there be great shoals of people, which go on to populate, without foreseeing means of life and sustentation, it is of necessity that once in an age or two, they discharge a portion of their people upon other nations; which the ancient northern people were wont to do by lot; casting lots what part should stay at home, and what should seek their fortunes. When a warlike state grows soft and effeminate, they may be sure of a war. For commonly such states are grown rich in the time of their degenerating; and so the prey inviteth, and their decay in valor, encourageth a war.

As for the weapons, it hardly falleth under rule and observation: yet we see even they, have returns and vicissitudes. For certain it is, that ordnance was known in the city of the Oxidrakes in India; and was that, which the Macedonians called thunder and lightning, and magic. And it is well known that the use of ordnance, hath been in China above two thousand years. The conditions of weapons, and their improvement, are: First, the fetching afar off; for that outruns the danger; as it is seen in ordnance and muskets. Secondly, the strength of the percussion; wherein likewise ordnance do exceed all arietations and ancient inventions. The third is, the commodious use of them; as that they may serve in all weathers; that the carriage may be light and manageable; and the like.

For the conduct of the war: at the first, men rested extremely upon number: they did put the wars likewise upon main force and valor; pointing days for pitched fields, and so trying it out upon an even match and they were more ignorant in ranging and arraying their battles. After, they grew to rest upon number rather competent, than vast; they grew to advantages of place, cunning diversions, and the like: and they grew more skilful in the ordering of their battles.

In the youth of a state, arms do flourish; in the middle age of a state, learning; and then both of them together for a time; in the declining age of a state, mechanical arts and merchandize. Learning hath his infancy, when it is but beginning and almost childish; then his youth, when it is luxuriant and juvenile; then his strength of years, when it is solid and reduced; and lastly, his old age, when it waxeth dry and exhaust. But it is not good to look too long upon these turning wheels of vicissitude, lest we become giddy. As for the philology of them, that is but a circle of tales, and therefore not fit for this writing.

59.论谣言

诗人把谣言视为一种怪鸟，其记述谣言的文字往往既精致优雅，又简练庄重。他们说，瞧呀，谣言有多少羽毛，就有多少只眼睛、多少根舌头、多少种声音，而且她还竖起那么多耳朵。此即谓绚词丽句。其后尚有绝妙的比喻，诸如说谣言总在流传中积聚力量；说谣言在地上行走，却把头藏在云中；说谣言白天藏在瞭望塔，多在夜间飞驰；说谣言总把已行之事和未行之事混为一谈；还说谣言于通都大邑不啻为恐怖之缘由。[①]不过最贴切的一种比喻是：谣言系大地女神该亚（即向天神朱庇特挑战并被其消灭的那些提坦巨神之母亲）[②]因儿子们战败而在一怒之下所生。这种比喻甚妙，因为被喻为叛乱者的提坦神与煽动叛乱的流言蜚语一阳一阴，可谓兄妹。但眼下若有人能驯服这只怪鸟，将其收养，令其听命，并任其去追逐并消灭其他鸷禽，这倒堪称可为之举。不过笔者也难免会沾染一些诗人风气。若以严肃认真的态度来加以谈论，可以说在所有政治话题中，最值得谈论而又最少被谈论的莫过于谣言这个话题。因此笔者将谈论以下几点：何谓假谣言，何谓真谣言，二者该如何辨别？谣言如何散播并扩散，如何煽动并蔓延，又该如何将其抑制并平息？以及其他有关谣言之性质的问题。谣言的影响力极大，几乎在所有重大事件（尤其是战争）中，谣言都起了一种重要作用。穆奇阿努斯使维特里乌斯[③]失去帝位，凭的就是他散布的一则谣言：说维特里乌斯

---

①这些比喻见于维吉尔《埃涅阿斯纪》第4卷第173—188行，诗人在这一节中把谣言的化身描写成一个行动迅捷的鸟形怪物，其眼、耳、口、舌多如其羽毛。

②谣言女神之希腊名为Pheme，拉丁名为Fama，英文名为Fame，中文名译为“法玛”，虽然赫西奥德、维吉尔和奥维德等古代诗人在各自的作品中都对她有所描述，而且雅典城还供有她的一座祭坛，但一般“神祗谱系表”（包括赫西奥德的《神谱》）没有法玛出生的记载。

③维特里乌斯（公元15—69），罗马皇帝（在位期公元69年），暴君尼禄死后三位短命继承人之一。

计划将驻叙利亚的军团调往日耳曼，而将驻日耳曼的军团调往叙利亚，结果驻叙利亚的军团被完全激怒了。[①]恺撒对庞培攻其不备，使其懈怠的原因也是恺撒巧妙放出的一则谣言：说由于疲于征战，又负载从高卢获取的战利品，恺撒的军队对恺撒已不再拥戴，一到意大利就会把他抛弃。莉维亚能安排好一切，使儿子提比略继位，靠的也是不断放风，说她病重的丈夫奥古斯都正在恢复，即将痊愈；[②] 而这也是土耳其那些帕夏[③]的惯用伎俩，他们往往对苏丹驾崩的消息秘而不宣，以免禁卫军和驻外军团依旧习劫掠君士坦丁堡和其他城镇。特米斯托克利[④]令波斯王薛西斯一世[⑤]仓皇撤离希腊，也是凭放出传闻，说希腊人准备摧毁他搭建的那座横跨达达尼尔海峡的舟桥。此类史例数以千计，多得没必要一一枚举，因为世人对此随处可见，随处可闻。鉴于此，所有明智的统治者对谣言均须密切关注，时时警励，就像他们亲自关注其行动计划一样……

[此篇未完]

①这段历史在塔西佗的《历史》第 2 卷第 80 章和苏维托尼乌斯的《罗马十二帝王传》第 8 卷第 4 章均有记载。另参见本书《论虚荣》第 3 段相关注释。

②提比略系莉维亚与其前夫所生，奥古斯都病危时提比略不在罗马，莉维亚一边急信召儿子回京，一边散布丈夫将痊愈的消息。塔西佗《编年史》第 1 卷第 5 章对这段历史有记载。另参见本书《论伪装与掩饰》第 2 段和《论帝王》第 6 段之相关内容及其注释。

③奥斯曼帝国、土耳其和北非一些国家（19 世纪之埃及除外）高级文武官员的一种非世袭称号。

④参见本书《论友谊》第 6 段和《论国家之真正强盛》第 1 段相关注释。

⑤薛西斯一世（又译泽尔士一世，在位期公元前 486—前 465），大流士一世之子，公元前 480 年率海陆大军远征希腊，其陆军破温泉关，入希腊，占雅典，其海军却在萨拉米海战中惨败给由特米斯托克利指挥的雅典海军。其后薛西斯一世唯恐希腊人断其归路，率海军残部仓皇撤退。萨拉米海战是历时半个世纪的希波战争之转折点。

Of Fame

THE poets make Fame a monster. They describe her in part finely and elegantly, and in part gravely and sententiously. They say, look how many feathers she hath, so many eyes she hath underneath; so many tongues; so many voices; she pricks up so many ears. This is a flourish. There follow excellent parables; as that, she gathereth strength in going; that she goeth upon the ground, and yet hideth her head in the clouds; that in the daytime she sitteth in a watch tower, and flieth most by night; that she mingleth things done, with things not done; and that she is a terror to great cities. But that which passeth all the rest is: They do recount that the Earth, mother of the giants that made war against Jupiter, and were destroyed by him, thereupon in an anger brought forth Fame. For certain it is, that rebels, figured by the giants, and seditious fames and libels, are but brothers and sisters, masculine and feminine. But now, if a man can tame this monster, and bring her to feed at the hand, and govern her, and with her fly other ravening fowl and kill them, it is somewhat worth. But we are infected with the style of the poets. To speak now in a sad and serious manner: There is not, in all the politics, a place less handled and more worthy to be handled, than this of fame. We will therefore speak of these points: What are false fames; and what are true fames; and how they may be best discerned; how fames may be sown, and raised; how they may be spread, and multiplied; and how they may be checked, and laid dead. And other things concerning the nature of fame. Fame is of that force, as there is scarcely any great action, wherein it hath not a great part; especially in the war. Mucianus undid Vitellius, by a fame that he scattered, that Vitellius had in purpose to remove the legions of Syria into Germany, and the legions of Germany into Syria; whereupon the legions of Syria were infinitely inflamed. Julius Caesar took Pompey unprovided, and laid asleep his industry and preparations, by a fame that he cunningly gave out: Caesar's own soldiers loved him not, and being wearied with the wars, and laden with the spoils of Gaul, would forsake him, as soon as he came into Italy. Livia settled all things for the succession of her son Tiberius, by continual giving out, that her husband Augustus was upon recovery and amendment, and it is an usual thing with the pashas, to conceal the death of the Great Turk from the janizaries and men of war, to save the sacking of Constantinople and other towns, as their manner is. Themistocles made Xerxes, King of Persia, post apace out of Grecia, by giving out, that the Grecians had a purpose to break his bridge of ships, which he had made athwart

Hellespont. There be a thousand such like examples; and the more they are, the less they need to be repeated; because a man meeteth with them everywhere. Therefore let all wise governors have as great a watch and care over fames, as they have of the actions and designs themselves ...

[This essay was not finished.]

双语文学经典

《麦田里的守望者》
J. D. 塞林格著 孙仲旭译

《爱情故事》
埃里奇·西格尔著 王悦晨、王东风译

《了不起的盖茨比》
弗·司各特·菲茨杰拉德著 巫宁坤译

《伦敦的叫卖声——英国散文精选》
约瑟夫·艾迪生等著 刘炳善译注

《书和画像》
弗吉尼亚·伍尔夫著 刘炳善译注

《季羡林散文精选》
季羡林著 钱炜、林珍珍译

《廊桥遗梦》
罗伯特·詹姆斯·沃勒著 资中筠译

《一杯安慰:给恋爱中的女人》
考琳·塞尔编 徐莉娜译

《一杯安慰:温馨美食》
考琳·塞尔、杰伊·韦恩斯坦编 张莉译

《牛虻》
埃塞尔·丽莲·伏尼契著 李平注释

新课标双语文库

《老人与海》
欧内斯特·海明威著 黄源深译

《呐喊》
鲁迅著 杨宪益、戴乃迭译

《朝花夕拾》
鲁迅著 杨宪益、戴乃迭译

《鲁迅杂文选》
鲁迅著 杨宪益、戴乃迭译

《繁星·春水》
冰心著 约翰·凯利、鲍贵思译

《边城》
沈从文著 杨宪益、戴乃迭译

《湘西散记》
沈从文著 杨宪益、戴乃迭译

《莎士比亚悲剧故事》
查尔斯·兰姆、玛丽·兰姆改写
萧乾译 文洁若注释

《莎士比亚喜剧故事》
查尔斯·兰姆、玛丽·兰姆改写
萧乾译 文洁若注释

《欧·亨利短篇小说精选》
欧·亨利著 王楫、康明强译

《伊索寓言全集》
伊索著
奥莉维亚·坦普尔、罗伯特·坦普尔英译
李汝仪、李怡萱中译

《圣经故事:亚当夏娃日记》
马克·吐温著 曹明伦译

《鲁拜集》
奥玛珈音著 菲茨杰拉德英译
黄克孙中译

《人间词话》
王国维著 李又安英译

《中国历代名人名言》
尹邦彦、尹海波编注

《新月集》
拉宾德拉纳特·泰戈尔著 郑振铎译

《飞鸟集》
拉宾德拉纳特·泰戈尔著 陆晋德译

《论语》
理雅各英译

《瓦尔登湖》
梭罗著 梁栋译

《先知》
纪·哈·纪伯伦著 冰心译

翻译鉴赏

《散文佳作 108 篇(汉英·英汉对照)》
《名家美文精译 50 篇(英汉对照)》
《美国短篇故事 125 篇(英汉对照)》
《英汉名篇名译》
《英汉·汉英美文翻译与鉴赏(新编版)》
(英汉·汉英对照)
《"韩素音青年翻译奖"竞赛作品与评析全集》
《英汉美文小品》

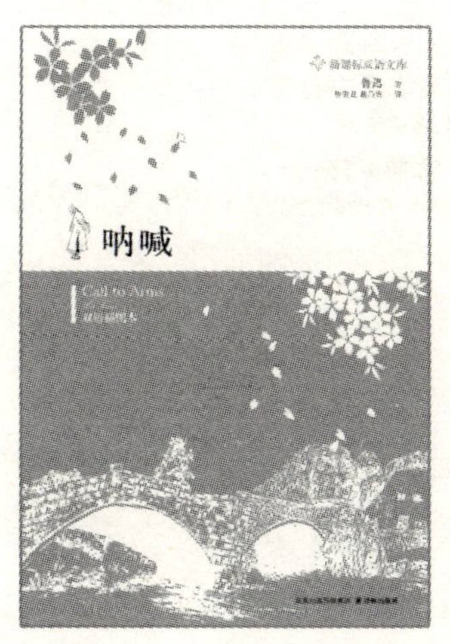

呐喊

《呐喊》是鲁迅 1918 年至 1922 年所作的十四篇短篇小说的结集。作品真实地描绘了从辛亥革命到五四时期的社会面貌，无情地鞭挞了封建制度和封建礼教的种种弊端，对辛亥革命以来的经验和教训做出了深刻的总结，对社会变革时期的个人悲剧进行了全面的剖析，表现出了对国民精神的热切关注和对社会变革的强烈渴望。

鲁迅杂文选

杂文是鲁迅的文学创作中极其重要的部分。透过鲁迅杂文，读者可以了解他对中国文化的理解,也可以管窥鲁迅所生活的年代、身处的中国的社会状况。本书选取了鲁迅约四十篇极具代表性的杂文，其中有他对中国传统文化的深刻批判,也有他对当时社会现象的无情针砭。

莎士比亚悲剧故事

莎士比亚在其作品中展现出的对人性的洞察，几乎可与上帝相媲美。莎翁的创作至今已历四百余年，语言的变迁与时代的隔膜使今人在拜读莎翁原著时往往产生隔靴搔痒之感。本书收入兰姆姐弟根据莎士比亚悲剧改写的故事六篇,根据莎士比亚传奇剧改写的故事三篇,文字通俗易懂,明白晓畅,自问世近两个世纪以来一直是莎剧的启蒙读物。

莎士比亚喜剧故事

本书共收录莎士比亚喜剧故事十一篇，包含脍炙人口的《仲夏夜之梦》、《威尼斯商人》、《第十二夜》等。经兰姆姐弟的改写,莎士比亚喜剧典雅、诙谐的语言特点得以保留,并转化成可读性极强的通俗故事,集中反映了原作浪漫、多姿的风貌。故事围绕爱情与友谊这两大永恒主题展开,轮廓清楚分明,充满诗情画意,蕴含着人文主义者的美好理想。

鲁拜集

《鲁拜集》是波斯诗人奥玛珈音 (Omar Khayyam) 的四行诗集，内容多感慨人生如寄、盛衰无常，以及时行乐、纵酒放歌为宽解。英国的爱德华·菲茨杰拉德(Edward Fitzgerald)把这本诗集译介到英语世界，他的翻译保持了原诗的韵律形式，已成为英国文学的经典。美国麻省理工学院教授黄克孙先生以七言绝句衍译，获钱钟书先生盛赞，黄译已成为英诗翻译的典范之作。

湘西散记

杨宪益、戴乃迭选译的这十一篇作品，是从沈从文的《从文自传》、《湘行散记》、《湘西》及题附在香港重印的《散文选》中的《劫后残稿》四个不同性质的集子中选出的。其中描写了作者从童年到少年的成长与蜕变，介绍了沅水流域和五个地方支流的人事、生产，也记录了凤凰普通人间的恩怨情仇，充满了传奇色彩。

中国历代名人名言

中国历代先圣时贤、名士俊杰的有关著述中广纳着极丰富的隽语箴言，本书即是自先秦至当代中国历代名人名言汉英对照的汇编。书中共收录条目一千一百余则，坚持思想标准和艺术标准相结合，让读者在领略中国传统智慧、体验汉语韵律美感的同时提高英文水平。

圣经故事:亚当夏娃日记

《夏娃日记》和《亚当日记》是马克·吐温根据《圣经》故事改写的两篇小说。马克·吐温用了十余年才完成这两部传世之作。作家以日记形式讲述了亚当和夏娃之间的感情故事，礼赞了自然、生命和两性间的依恋。全篇于朴实中暗藏睿智，于浅显中蕴蓄深沉，于天真中饱含幽默，笔触欢快，感情真挚，行文如歌。本书还配有 Lester Ralph 和 F. Strothmann 所画的插图，均为插图爱好者的典藏版本。